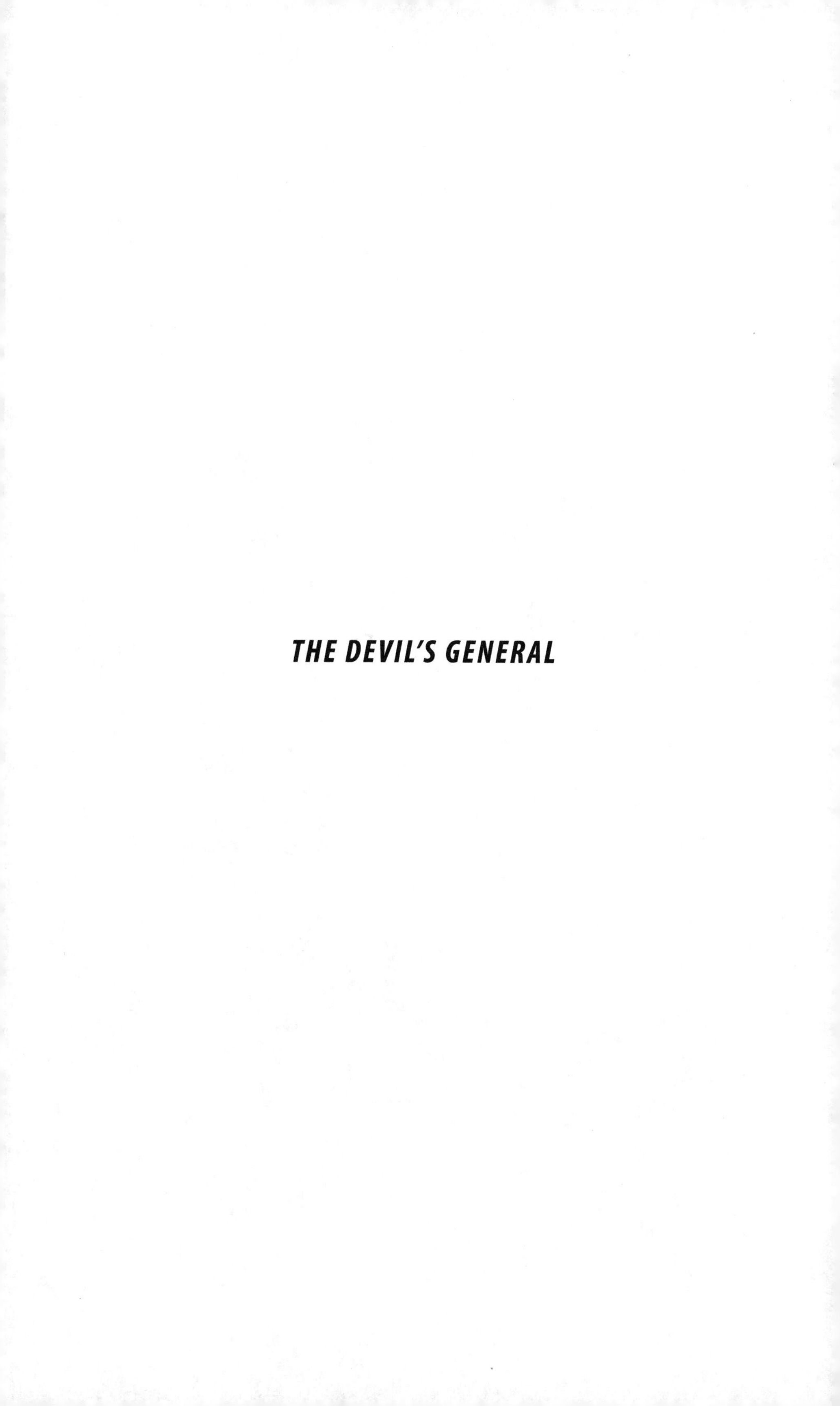

THE DEVIL'S GENERAL

THE DEVIL'S GENERAL

THE LIFE OF HYAZINTH GRAF VON STRACHWITZ, "THE PANZER GRAF"

RAYMOND BAGDONAS

Philadelphia & Oxford

Published in the United States of America and Great Britain in 2013 by
CASEMATE PUBLISHERS
908 Darby Road, Havertown, PA 19083
and
10 Hythe Bridge Street, Oxford, OX1 2EW

ISBN 978-1-61200-222-4
Digital Edition: ISBN 978-1-61200-223-1

Cataloging-in-publication data is available from the Library of Congress and the British Library.

10 9 8 7 6 5 4 3 2 1

Printed and bound in the United States of America.

For a complete list of Casemate titles please contact:

CASEMATE PUBLISHERS (US)
Telephone (610) 853-9131, Fax (610) 853-9146
E-mail: casemate@casematepublishing.com

CASEMATE PUBLISHERS (UK)
Telephone (01865) 241249, Fax (01865) 794449
E-mail: casemate-uk@casematepublishing.co.uk

CONTENTS

DEDICATION

This book is dedicated to my grandchildren, Sofia, Veronique, Trinity, Sterling and Rimas. May their generation be spared the horrors suffered by the generation depicted in this book.

ACKNOWLEDGMENTS

VERY FEW BOOKS ARE WRITTEN WITHOUT SOME ASSISTANCE and I would like to express my thanks to those who helped me. Firstly to Garry Dillon for his typing, encouragement and continuing help. His computer skills were especially helpful, and along with his friendship, much appreciated.

To my typist Liesa Hogg, who had to decipher my scrawled longhand and deal with so many unfamiliar military terms, a big thank you. To my daughter Natalie for her courier service, and my wife Gail for her patience and forbearance in dealing with someone living simultaneously in two worlds, the present and the Russian front in the past. I would also like to thank Jason Mark for his timely help and assistance.

Finally I would like to thank Steven Smith, Casemate's Editorial Director, for his faith in me and the book.

"Be careful, enemy forces are led by that devil's general von Strachwitz.
Avoid if possible until reinforcements arrive."

Intercepted Soviet radio message on the Northern Front, 1944

INTRODUCTION

HYAZINTH GRAF STRACHWITZ VON GROSS-ZAUCHE UND Camminetz was the most decorated regimental commander, and one of the most effective panzer leaders, in the German Army.

He was one of only 27 men in the entire Wehrmacht to be awarded the Knight's Cross with Oak Leaves, Swords and Diamonds. Of these he was the only one to receive grades of the decoration for both bravery and his command abilities, which led to the significant outcomes which merited the award. The other Diamonds recipients received awards for either their bravery and combat accomplishments, such as Erich Hartmann for his 352 aerial victories, or for their skill in command, such as Hans Hube and Walter Model. In the latter cases their men did the actual fighting and the award was as much for the units under their command as for them.

Von Strachwitz's rapid rise during World War II from a lowly captain to a lieutenant general, equivalent to a major general in the UK and US armies, was nothing short of extraordinary, and this in an army not lavish in granting promotions.

He fought in nearly all of the major campaigns—the invasions of Poland, France and Yugoslavia, and the important campaigns and battles in the east including Operation *Barbarossa*, the battles of Kiev, Stalingrad, Kharkov, and Kursk, the Baltic States and finally of Germany and his beloved Silesia—his service being almost a microcosm of World War II in Europe. In the course of these battles, not only did he win renown—becoming a legend among those who fought on the Eastern Front who gave him the title Panzer Graf (Armoured Count)—but was also wounded 14 times, probably was probably unique amongst the ranks of Germany's senior officers and a testament to his leading from the front.

Such an extraordinary record of courage and command would have made him unique in any army of World War II. Yet he is a man of mystery, with very little known about him and nothing of substance yet been written. He is mentioned in countless books, articles and websites, but at most is only given a brief biographical outline, and even this is often inaccurate in parts. Günter Fraschke wrote a German-language biography in 1962, which, if largely factual, was nevertheless discredited for its inaccuracies and sensationalism and rejected by the Panzer Graf himself.

Unfortunately the Panzer Graf himself wrote no memoirs; left no diary, and any notes and papers were lost along with his home in 1945. His records of service in the 16th Panzer Division were destroyed along with the division in the battle of Stalingrad in 1943. After a period of distinguished service with the elite Grossdeutschland Division, he served as commander of several ad-hoc units, some bearing his name, in a period when records, if kept at all, were scanty, or lost. It all makes for a rather threadbare paper trail. His comrades-in-arms have now all passed away, so there are no witnesses to his many battles and exploits.

All of this of course makes writing a full-length book about him enormously difficult. It is only possible with reference to the academies that he attended, the units he served in or alongside, the battles in which he fought and the many outstanding men he met or served with, as well as the events that shaped him and his world. This book must then of necessity deal not only with his life, but the broader topic of the times in which he lived.

The amount of research and effort required to tell his story, taking in a great many major and minor little-known events, was quite daunting, as was of course the scarcity of detailed information about him, yet he is indeed a subject worthy of the effort. Of equal importance was to produce a serious, studied and accurate representation of his life without the sensationalism that his exploits could easily lead to. I hope I have succeeded in this and beg forgiveness if I have lapsed occasionally in some descriptions that add colour and life to some of his actions. I hope also that this book fills the gap that currently exists, and gives him the proper recognition that he deserves, not only as the superlative warrior, war hero and panzer commander that indeed he was, but also as the decent and honourable man of integrity that he remained throughout his life.

Finally, it must be remembered that all too often good men, through no fault of their own, are forced to serve an evil cause. He served his cause without adding to its criminality, and sought to end it honorably if the opportunity arose.

Little more could be asked of any man.

ONE

EARLY YEARS

The armoured force waited impatiently to do battle. The surging horde from the east would soon be upon them, ready to tear the heart out of Christian Europe.

It could be a scene from Upper Silesia in 1945, where Lieutenant General Hyazinth Graf (Count) Strachwitz von Gross Zauche und Camminetz waited with his Panzerjäger (Tank-hunter) Brigade to block the Russians invading his beloved Silesian homeland. But instead it was Liegnitz, 9 April 1241, where the 20,000-strong army of Duke Henry II The Pious was preparing to fight a Mongol force of similar size. In his army were the flower of Silesian chivalry, among whom were several knights and retainers of the von Strachwitz family.

The Mongol horde was a diversionary force, sent to plunder parts of Poland and divide the Christians while the main force invaded Hungary. At Liegnitz the Mongols surrounded and destroyed the Polish and Silesian cavalry, before attacking the infantry from the flanks and routing them. Duke Henry attempted to flee but was caught and beheaded. To count the dead, the Mongols cut off the right ear of the fallen, filling nine large bags with their grisly trophies. The entire von Strachwitz contingent, 14 family members and their retainers, was wiped out. But it was not in vain, for the casualties suffered by the Mongol diversionary force made them loathe to proceed further, and they retreated to join their main force. It was believed by many that Duke Henry's sacrificial battle had forced the Mongol retreat and he was declared a hero.

The von Strachwitz family was proud of their ancestors' heroic stand, which set a precedent for military service and glory which then became part of the family ethos. Over the years the family garnered wealth, titles and position. The brothers Christof and Maximillian were created barons (Freiherr) in 1630. Johann Moritz von Strachwitz (1721–81) was the apostolic vicar and bishop of Breslau, highlighting the family's strong and enduring connection with the Roman Catholic Church.

Moritz Graf von Strachwitz (1822–47) was a renowned lyric poet, indicating that not all in the family were involved in, or famous for power and politics; however Hyazinth Graf von Strachwitz (1835–71) resumed the prior trend by entering the German Reichstag.

The family became wealthier through the time-honoured way of the aristocracy—marriage to wealthy heiresses. It was much easier than having to work for a living, tending to unprofitable estates or through vulgar commerce, which at that time were below the diginity of the aristocracy. This way they added Zauche and Camminetz to their name: the former came from the marriage of Nicholas von Strachwitz to Katherine von Zauche, the daughter of a prominent Breslau family, added to distinguish the line from the Strachwitzs of Gabersdorf; the latter was added by the acquisition of the village and estate of Kaminetz and Dombrowka by Karl von Strachwitz.

The family seat was in Gross-Stein, named for the limestone deposits in the ground. The manor house and estate were purchased in 1808, then steadily built up to comprise an estate of 10,150 acres, of which 2,920 acres were farmland, 6,764 were forest and 41 acres consisted of gardens and parkland. The estate also held a quarry, limekiln and distillery. The family used it as their principal residence until 1944 when it was turned into a hospital.

Silesia had a very chequered history, forming at times part of Greater Moravia, Bohemia, Poland, the Holy Roman Empire, Austria, Prussia and finally the Greater German Reich, first under the Hohenzollern kaisers and then under the Third Reich. The Poles, when their country was not being dismembered and part of another empire, laid claim to it, a claim which would later involve von Strachwitz in fighting to keep it German, as for him it had always been.

Hyacinth was born on 30 July 1893, his parents' second child. His mother was Maria Aloysia Hedwig Frederike Therese Octavia Grafin (Countess) von Matuschka and Freiin (Baroness) von Toppaczan und Spaetden, named after many ancestors, who was just 20 years old when she gave birth to her son. His father was also named Hyacinth (1864–1942), in accordance with the family tradition that dictated the first-born son was always named Hyacinth after St Hyacinth, a Dominican preacher who was canonised in 1594. The saint was connected to the family by marriage in the distant past. Being very proud of the connection, the family had venerated the saint ever since. The Panzer Graf later adopted to spell his Christan name "Hyazinth," particularly during his army career, and his army documentation reflects this. Hyazinth was particularly close to his older sister, Aloysia, born on 28 June 1892. His younger siblings were Celaus, born 1 December 1894, Elisabeth born 20 December 1897, Manfred born 17 April 1899—who also became a panzer commander in World War II—Mariano, born 28 November 1902 and Margarethe, born 12 July 1905.

Hyazinth's upbringing was one of aristocratic privilege and luxury, tempered by strict discipline and devotion to church, family and class. Tradition and responsibility went hand in hand with noble rank and lineage, and these were to be young Hyazinth's guiding principles throughout his life. Even in the less class-conscious army of Nazi Germany he insisted on being addressed as Graf and was singularly conscious of his family history and status. Living on a large agricultural estate, horsemanship and farming were a part of his daily life, and it was especially in riding that he excelled, taking to it with a natural talent. So his young life was sheltered and, for his time, idyllic. Given his rural background and interest in an outdoor life it was only natural that he would be steered towards a military career, the more so as under Kaiser Wilhelm II (r. 1888-1918), Germany became a militarised state with the army, especially the officer corps, enjoying a high prestige within all levels of society. It was expected, almost incumbent upon higher-ranking families to have at least one son enter the military.

For its part, the army looked to the higher classes to supply its officers while the elite guards regiments looked to the aristocracy to provide theirs. When it came to advancement, high social rank was more important than educational achievement, thus, the dull-witted or lazy scions of the aristocracy were treated, initially in their careers, equally to the intelligent and industrious, and well ahead of any diligent or clever members of the middle classes.

There were two main routes to becoming an officer: candidates from rich and upper-class families went through the cadet school system, while the less privileged went straight to a regiment. To do this, an officer aspirant had to be recommended by the colonel of the regiment. Often the aspirants were known to the colonel or another ranking officer, or had some other connection to the regiment. The potential officer then had to spend six months in the ranks as an advantageur or officer candidate, which gave him a few privileges but also saddled him with high expectations and sometimes extra bullying and punishments to test his mettle. He had to either provide evidence of his higher educational qualifications or pass an examination. On completion of his service in the ranks and proof of his leadership abilities and character, he had to be approved in turn by his future company, battalion and regimental commanders. This method of promoting from the ranks was widely used by the 1930s, with front-line soldiers being designated as officer candidates for a lengthy period before being sent to an officer candidate school.

The alternative route saw boys, often as young as ten, enter one of the eight cadet preparatory schools in Germany, and remain there until seeking admission to the central cadet school at Gross Lichterfelde—the German equivalent to the British Sandhurst or American West Point—at the age of 15. Hyazinth von Strachwitz attended Whalstatt Junior Cadet School in Silesia, a popular choice for the Silesian upper classes. Johann von Ravenstein, who would earn a Pour le Merite in the Great War, and achieve fame fighting the British under Erwin Rommel in Africa, was a graduate, as was the fighter ace Manfred von Richthofen, and General Erwin von Witzleben.

The life that von Strachwitz experienced at Wahlstatt was austere and often harsh. Discipline was strict, and bullying rife. The staff was generally second rate, and a great deal of control was left to the older boys, with a head boy called the *aclteuter* in charge of each dormitory. His word was law and most were little dictators lording over their charges with little restraint or supervision from the senior staff. Punishments for the smallest infractions, real or imagined, were routine, and at times bordering on the sadistic. No matter, for it all ostensibly built character.

The young von Strachwitz wore a military uniform, his classes were called companies, with teachers holding nominal military rank. Drill and discipline were the watchwords of the school and every activity was carried out to shouted orders, even praying and sleeping.

The school was deeply unpopular with most, if not all of its students, and Hyazinth von Strachwitz would have been no exception. Manfred von Richthofen disliked it so much that he expressed his poor opinion of it and his contempt for its staff in his memoirs.

From Whalstatt, von Strachwitz went on to the Central Cadet School at Gross Lichterfelde, on the southern outskirts of Berlin, where he would live and study until he received his commission. The Kaserne was a rather ugly red-brick building whose cornerstone was laid on 1 September 1873 in the presence of the Kaiser himself. The original construction included an administration building, residential area for senior officers, and two chapels, Catholic and Protestant. Later additions included a barracks, mess hall, stables, gymnasium, shooting ranges and a hospital. All this was constructed for the princely sum of nine million marks, an enormous amount of money for the time. As befitted Germany's premier cadet school, the staff was highly competent. In 1911 Lichterfelde had a staff of 72 real officers—as opposed to the mostly nominal or low rankers at Wahlstatt—and military instructors, as well as a civilian staff of 41 professors, teachers, chaplains and doctors. Its academic status was equivalent to the German Gymnasium, or senior high school, meaning that basic education subjects were given priority alongside military studies and physical education. Its guiding principles were obedience, comradeship and duty. These were not just hollow words, but concepts for the cadets to live by and follow.

A wide range of subjects were on offer for the 1,000 cadets, and Hyazinth would have studied mathematics, history, drawing, geography and languages, ranging from Latin, English and German to French. Military studies were a compulsory part of the curriculum. The academic subjects were studied in the mornings, with the afternoons reserved for sport, which included football, tennis, hockey, riding and fencing. Hyazinth proved to be an excellent fencer and swordsman and was well above average in athletics, but it was in horsemanship that he excelled, becoming the top in his class.

Three meals a day were provided, with breakfast eaten standing up, a practice which Princess Louise of Prussia—the youngest of whose three sons attended Lichterfelde in 1907—found "strange and bad for their health."[1] She also disapproved of the fact that the boys did not bathe in the evenings, since the military governor of the college at the time, Captain von Gartner, did not regard personal hygiene important. It was all she could do to persuade him to allow the cadets a small jug of water for this purpose. His replacement, Freiherr (Baron) von Schleintz, was a little more amenable, but by this time the princess was thoroughly sick of fighting the system.

The best of the cadets, which would have included von Strachwitz, were often called upon to attend the Kaiser on special occasions at the Emperor's Neues Palais (New Palace) at Potsdam. Here duties included waiting on the tables of the great and mighty—ambassadors, generals, ministers and visiting royalty—with one privileged cadet standing directly behind the Kaiser's chair, often for very long periods of time (causing the future General Ravenstein to almost faint on one occasion). However this was a small price to pay for the privilege of overhearing the Kaiser's tabletalk. Other duties included running errands and messages, as well as any other tasks required by senior courtiers. Notwithstanding the lowly nature of these tasks, to serve was considered an honour, and the cadets would have vied for the opportunity. Just to be in the corridors of power and overhear privileged conversations was considered enough for some. The court marshal, Graf Robert Zedlitz-Triitschler, was a Silesian nobleman and landowner who would have been aware of the young von Strachwitz and may well have kept a paternal eye on him.

Physical fitness was vital, with emphasis on gymnastics, which was practised daily. The best gymnasts were expected to leap from a springboard over two rows of cadets interlocking their rifles with fixed bayonets. Duelling, although forbidden and not commonplace, still happened in secret, as a cadet's honour, like an officer's, was paramount. The scars often inflicted during these encounters were worn with pride.

The regime was demanding, but for von Strachwitz—young, fit, smart enough to handle the academic side, and totally committed to sports and the outdoor life—the experience as a whole was an enjoyable one, and far removed from his time at Wahlstatt. Von Ravenstein, von Richthofen, von Kleist and others had similar appreciation for Lichterfelde, and given the future careers of these men it could be said that the cadet school was hugely successful in its raison d'être—turning out accomplished future officers.

The young Graf von Strachwitz would have enjoyed his time there, mixing with an exclusive group of young men with similar backgrounds, interests and prospects to himself. The physical life and comradeship appealed, and it allowed for free rein and appreciation of his horsemanship, the love of which would stand him in good stead for his career. Prowess with women was equally prized by the testosterone-charged young cadets. The cadets were considered a good catch by most young women, and with his dark good looks von Strachwitz undoubtedly attracted some attention.

As in many exclusively male structured societies, homosexuality almost certainly existed, and although forbidden, was rarely brought to light as exposure would have demeaned the reputation of the cadet school and indeed the whole of the officer corps. There was a major scandal in Germany in 1907 when accusations of homosexuality were made that involved the Kaiser's senior aides-de-camp, including his close friend and confidante Prinz (Prince) Phillip zu Eulenburg, whose friendship with von Moltke, a cavalry officer and military commander of Berlin, raised eyebrows. The scandal was in reality part of a court power play to remove von Eulenburg from the Kaiser's close circle since, apart from jealousy, there were those who considered von Eulenburg's influence on the Kaiser to be far too pacifist. The Kaiser abandoned von Eulenburg and his ADCs, and insisted that von Moltke sue in order to clear his name and prevent any tarnishing of the Kaiser by association. In four trials over two years, a whole lurid tale of perversion and homosexuality came out. The accusation of tawdry orgies in the Garde du Corps, von Strachwitz's regiment of choice, would have particularly concerned him at the time.

Scandals at the top and in the Garde du Corps notwithstanding, Gross Lichterfelde enjoyed a high reputation throughout German society. Among its many graduates were Colonel General Hans Guderian, father of the German Panzer arm (graduated 1907); Manfred von Richthofen; Field Marshal Gerd von Rundstedt, army group commander on both Western and Eastern fronts; Werner von Blomberg, War Minister under Hitler, Erwin von Witzleben, a major conspirator against Hitler; Field Marshal von Hindenburg, president of the Weimar Republic and World War I army commander; Field Marshal Fedor von Bock, army group commander of Army Group North in the invasion of Russia; Field Marshal von Manstein, commander of Army Group South in Russia; Franz von Papen, chancellor of the Weimar Republic; and Reichmarshall Herman Goering, Luftwaffe commander-in-chief. Three thousand Lichterfelde graduates gave their lives for Germany in World War I. So important was it to Germany's military officer corps and ethos that after Germany's defeat in 1918, the Allies insisted on its closure, accurately assessing it as a hotbed of Prussian militarism. It became a state high school and later the barracks for Hitler's bodyguard regiment, the Leibstandarte SS Adolf Hitler.

On graduating from Lichterfelde, Hyazinth von Strachwitz's name was submitted for commissioning to the elite Garde du Corps, the personal bodyguard of the German Emperor. Founded in 1741 by Frederick the Great, it was the premier regiment of the German Army, ranking higher even than the Emperor's Foot Guards. Garrisoned in Potsdam, it formed part of the elite 1st Guards Cavalry Division. The Garde du Corps' officers were almost exclusively aristocrats. In 1890, 98% of the corps' officers were noble, and although members of the middle classes were admitted, they occupied the technical, clerical and quartermaster positions, thus relieving the aristocrats of the boring but very essential service tasks. After 1908 the Kaiser began recruiting more army officers from the middle classes, but by 1914 the process was still incomplete and had barely started to take effect in the elite guards regiments.

The Kaiser's attitude to his guards was summed up in his statement that with them, "I found my family, my friends, my interests, everything I had previously missed." In 1891 he addressed new recruits to his guard:

> You have sworn me allegiance. That, children of my guard, means that you are now my soldiers. You have given yourselves over to me body and soul. There is only one enemy for you and that is my enemy, with the present socialist agitation it may be that I shall order you to shoot down your own families, your brothers, yes your parents without a murmur.[2]

After receiving the Kaiser's approval, von Strachwitz was commissioned; the regiment now owned him body and soul. It was his second, and more immediate family. He was expected to wear his uniform everywhere, civilian clothes or mufti being an inferior form of dress. Being deprived of the right to wear the uniform was a singular dishonour. Captain Hoenig, a crippled veteran of the Franco-Prussian War and a military historian who dared to criticise the General Staff, was deprived of his right to wear the uniform by a kangaroo "Court of Honour" consisting of officers with whom he had served, a judgement which disgraced him in German eyes.[3]

His new uniform gave Hyazinth entrée to the best social circles and restaurant tables, with unquestioned respect from a public conditioned to honour and admire the military. In the street, civilians made way for him, while ladies would have discreetly admired him, seeing first his uniform and then his face.

His life consisted of riding, manoeuvres, watching an NCO supervise his soldiers' drill, and an endless round of visits and dinners where he was expected to drink prodigiously, but always hold his liquor. A move towards temperance in 1910 was only partially successful, and heavy drinking remained a normal part of garrison life. There was also the opera and numerous balls. The polka had waned in popularity, the gavotte was in but fading, while the waltz was perennially popular. Von Strachwitz would have been expected to dance every dance.

Military manoeuvres and war games involving the Garde du Corps were invariably attended by the Guards' commander-in-chief—the Kaiser—meaning that the Guards were always on the winning side. A feature of these war games was that each officer participating acted one rank higher to his own, testing his ability for higher responsibility and command. Foreign observers often attended these manoeuvres, the military correspondent of British newspaper *The Times* being particularly scathing of the manoeuvres he observed in 1911:

> The infantry lack dash, display no knowledge of the ground, are extremely slow in their movements, offer vulnerable targets at medium ranges, ignore the service of security, perform the approach marches in old-time manners, are not trained to understand the connection between fire and movement, and seem totally unaware of the effect of modern fire.

However as to the cavalry he had this to say: "The cavalry drill well and show some beautifully trained horses, while the cavalry of the Guard is handled well."[4]

As a lieutenant von Strachwitz earned less than £60 per year, a salary which would rise over time to £120. It was certainly not enough to maintain the lifestyle expected of a cavalry guards officer, so an allowance from home was a necessity. This ensured that only men from wealthy families would try to join the elite Guards units, let alone the Guard cavalry, especially the Garde du Corps. Equestrian and uniform costs were essential and could be considerable. Officers were proud of their horses, purchasing the very best, along with the best equipment and accessories they could afford. Von Strachwitz was expected to maintain nine different uniforms, for gala, guard, gold society, street, dancing, service, light service, court and party duties. He also had to provide a cuirass, and a gold parade helmet surmounted with the imperial eagle, which was unique to the Garde du Corps.

Von Strachwitz might have perhaps spared a thought for the ordinary soldiers, who earned less than a penny a day; however, it is very unlikely that he would have given them the slightest consideration. The gulf between officers and men in all units, but especially the Guards, was so great as to be unbridgeable. It would take World War I, together with Hitler's military expansion, his dislike for aristocratic officers in general, and increased promotion through the ranks to change all that.

In 1912 von Strachwitz attended the Cavalry School in Hanover, a recognition of his equestrian ability and a clear sign that his talent had been noted, and that he was on the road to eventual senior rank. The cavalry school was renowned throughout Europe for the quality of its horses and instruction. It had a staff of three officers, and took 133 students of whom 91 belonged to the cavalry and 42 to the horse artillery. The course took one year, with the more proficient, like von Strachwitz, being given an extended course of another year. Three years earlier, in 1908/09, Paul von Kleist had attended the Cavalry School. He would rise to command 14 divisions, including the 16th Panzer Division in which von Strachwitz would serve in 1941.

Von Strachwitz's time at Hanover was spent learning advanced horsemanship, dressage, hurdles jumping, cavalry drill and advanced tactics. Sports were again on the agenda and this included hunting with a hound pack personally provided by the Kaiser as a special gift. There being no foxes in the area, the officers had to be content with hunting wild pigs.

While he was at the cavalry school the 1916 Olympics would have been clearly in von Strachwitz's sights. There is no doubt that he would have made the team and quite likely been a medal contender, had not World War I intervened.

During his sojourn at the school von Strachwitz almost certainly studied the book just published by the military theorist General Friedrich von Bernhardi, *Deustchland und der Nächste Krieg* (*Germany and the Next War*). It would have been enough to set his pulse racing, for what young officer does not long to go to war. But of course junior officers' desires are of no consequence. What does matter is what the politicians and generals think, and with barely more restraint they too longed for war. It would not be long in coming.

NOTES

1. Rowland Ryder, *Ravenstein: portrait of a German General* (Hamish Hamilton, London, 1978).
2. Robert K. Massie, *Dreadnought Britain, Germany and the coming of the Great War* (Jonathan Cape, 1991).
3. John Laffin, *Jackboot: The Story of the German Soldier* (Cassell & Co, 1965).
4. Ibid.

TWO

WORLD WAR I AND CAPTIVITY

While Hyazinth von Strachwitz was training for his commission and developing his military skills, Europe was moving inexorably towards conflagration.

In August 1914, over one and a half million Germans with spiked helmets on their heads and glory in their hearts streamed into neutral Belgium and France. A shot in distant Sarajevo, the provincial capital of Bosnia Herzegovina, was the starter's gun, but the powers of Europe had been lining up and sparring well before this. There was a flurry of telegrams, ultimatums, diplomatic threats, overtures and bombast beforehand, but the push to war had by this time developed a momentum of its own. An extremely strong will and fervent desire for peace by all parties would have been needed to stop it, but this was absent in the summer of 1914. The expectation of a short war made it all acceptable, especially when weighed against each country's perceived gains.

"You will be home before the leaves have fallen from the trees" the Kaiser, his withered arm tucked against his side, moustache bristling, extorted his departing troops.[1] The German plans depended heavily on a short six-week campaign to defeat France, after which she would switch her forces to face Russia, which her general staff had accurately calculated would need six weeks to fully mobilise. As for the English, "The lowdown shopkeeping knaves," as the Kaiser had once written, their inconsequential army would be rolled up along with the French.

The fact was that most of the leading statesmen and generals in Europe in 1914 misunderstood the nature of modern warfare. Based on past experience they anticipated conflicts to be short wars of manoeuvre with minimal causalities, even though the American Civil War and the Russo-Japanese war had provided salutary lessons to the contrary. Only a tiny minority—like General Helmuth von Moltke the Elder, who predicted after the Franco-Prussian War that the next war could last seven years, and Lord Kitchener—foresaw a much larger war than their contemporaries.

There was, then, not just an expectation of war by the different nations, but on the part of many generals and politicians, a real, almost palpable desire for war.

Germany, feeling alone and friendless, was desperately seeking greater power, status and respect, and a voice in world affairs. Germany's army was acknowledged by many Euopean military officers to be the best in Europe, and therefore the world—as the armies outside Europe were not given much attention or credit despite Japan's victory over Russia—and its navy was being built up to rival Britain's mighty fleet. The Kaiser himself, although Queen Victoria's favourite grandson, was jealous of Britain's wealth and vast colonial empire. For him the issue was personal, and he went to great pains to snub Edward, Prince of Wales, at every opportunity. Germany certainly felt hemmed in, prevented from realising her true greatness, a feeling summed up by "Little Willie" the Crown Prince when he wrote the introduction to the book *Germany in Arms*: "It is the holy duty of Germany above all other peoples to maintain an army and a fleet ever at the highest point of readiness. Only then, supported by our own good sword, can we preserve the place in the sun which is our due, but which is not willingly granted to us."[2] The Kaiser's comment to an Austrian officer really sums up many leading Germans' attitudes. "I hate the Slavs. I know it is a sin to do so. We ought not to hate anyone. But I can't help hating them."[3] This rather widespread dislike of the Slavs, partially brought about by a fear of Russia's immense empire, was an attitude Hitler would take to the extreme, an extreme of which the Kaiser would not have approved, but which, like anti-Semitism, was nevertheless buried deep in the German psyche.

The French, for their part, wanted a war with Germany in order to take back the provinces of Alsace and Lorraine, lost in the Franco-Prussian War of 1870–71. Russia, as self-styled protector of the Slavs, felt obliged to protect Slavic Serbia from the threats and ultimatums of Austria-Hungary. Besides which, Russia was tied to France by treaty. Of all the nations, Britain had the least reason to go to war. The invasion of Belgium was the excuse, but Britain's treaty obligations to defend Belgium did not apply to a co-signatory of that treaty such as Germany. Britain had other concerns, but not compelling reasons, and the warmongers, which included H.H. Asquith, Sir Edward Grey and Winston Churchill, needed all their skill and persuasive powers to win over the Cabinet and Parliament. Britain also expected a short war in which its main contribution would be from the Royal Navy, meaning that casualties would be kept to an acceptable minimum. Going to war with such a scenario was really all too easy.

The machinations and discussions in the palaces and chanceries of Europe resulted in a chain reaction of events in late July and early August 1914, an all too neat timetable that would have made any railway station-master proud. Russia mobilised on 30 July. On 1 August France and Germany mobilised. Two days later, Germany gave Belgium an ultimatum to allow free passage of her forces through Belgian territory to attack France in a wide-flanking move as set down in the Schlieffen Plan. On 4 August, Britain declared war on Germany following Germany's failure to comply with Britain's ultimatum to respect Belgian neutrality. Germany then invaded Belgium. On 6 August, Austria, the country which had started the whole process after Sarajevo, almost tardily declared war on Russia.

So finally after years of arms build-up, treaty negotiations, diplomatic plots and subterfuges, Europe got the war she wanted, indeed deserved; but it would not be the short war expected. It would last four long, blood-soaked years, causing fifteen million deaths.

For Hyazinth von Strachwitz, it was war at last, and with it dreams of glory. Cavalry charges with the sun gleaming on burnished breastplates, pennants fluttering on lances, thundering horse's hooves trampling down a fleeing enemy. All very normal, and for the time, praiseworthy thoughts for a young cavalry officer seeking to prove himself in his chosen profession. Victory and a hero's return were never in doubt, so the sooner he could get to grips with the French, the better. He would no longer have to cast envious eyes at the grizzled veterans of the victorious Franco-Prussian War.

He rode out to war at the head of his squadron with the shouts and cheers of ecstatic civilians ringing in his ears, a joyous sound filling him with pride. But the euphoria was not to last. On average a corps required just over 6,000 wagons, and all too soon the moving columns all piled up. Dust settled in clouds over parched and thirsty troops, while men and wagons slowly crawled forward, or waited interminably for their turn to move. No gaily uniformed Napoleonic columns these, but a grey purposeful mass. Only the infantry constantly singing the national anthem and popular songs like "Die

Wacht am Rhein" brought any life to the march, but even this began to irritate the quieter cavalry after a while.

The young Garde du Corps officer was still optimistic that this would be a cavalry war, like so many of the wars in the past, and indeed his superiors had similar expectations, although they were going to be more clever in the use of their horsemen compared to the glory-seeking French, for whom the massed charge was de rigueur, epitomising their offensive spirit. The British also hoped to use their cavalry extensively, although some—like General Sir Ian Hamilton, who had been an observer during the Russo-Japanese War—had a more realistic view. Based on his observations he concluded that in a modern war, the only role for the cavalry was to cook rice for the infantry.[4] It was a view that did not go down well with the British War Office.

Despite the feelings of junior officers like Hyazinth von Strachwitz—and indeed many senior officers—and much to their chagrin, the Germans deliberately sought to avoid a major cavalry encounter. However, notwithstanding this reluctance, on 17 August, the 3rd Squadron had its baptism of fire in the region of Dinaut. While on its march to the Marne the regiment fought several engagements, including one at St Quentin and one attacking Givenchy. These clashes, given the size of the German cavalry force available, were not significant.

At the commencement of hostilities the 1st Cavalry Division consisted of the 1st Cavalry Brigade; the Garde du Corps; the Guard Cuirassers; 2nd Cavalry Brigade of Uhlans (Lancers); 3rd Guards Cavalry Brigade of Dragoons, heavy cavalry, essentially mounted infantry; 4th Guard Cavalry Brigade of Hussars (Light Cavalry); and Uhlans (Lancers). This last brigade was shortly broken up, with its squadrons assigned as divisional cavalry to the 1st and 2nd Guards Infantry Divisions. Machine gun, signals, pioneer, and motorised transport units were not up to established strength and were added during mobilisation.

Lieutenant von Strachwitz's first assignment was leading a reconnaissance screening patrol ahead of the main body. His mission was to try to find the enemy and report back. He was under strict orders to avoid large units and only engage smaller ones if unavoidable or if he had the possibility of capturing a prisoner. He was to observe enemy formations or columns to gauge their strength and the direction of their march. If he encountered a larger formation of cavalry, a brisk exchange of fire was all that was expected, followed by a retreat of carefully judged speed, in hopes of luring the French back onto the waiting machine guns and rifles of the Jaeger Light Infantry.

To a headstrong, eager young lieutenant, it was boring work, no matter how necessary or effective it was. For the most part there was no enemy to be seen. Although squadrons of French cavalry in their blue coats and helmets topped with flowing horsehair mane were out scouting, and spoiling for a fight, the Garde du Corps officer could not engage them. This was not what he or his men had envisaged the war to be, or indeed what a cavalry troop was trained to do.

A new opportunity presented itself, and he volunteered to lead long-range reconnaissance and fighting patrols deep behind the enemy lines. It was an extremely dangerous assignment, but it gave him what he craved: an independent command, and above all, action in the finest cavalry tradition. It was heady work. They cut telegraph lines, vital for enemy communications, then ambushed the repair parties. They also attacked small supply columns, captured couriers and slashed through any small rear-area units made indolent by their safe and comfortable billets.

His first patrols were still near the fluid front line. His results in disrupting the enemy rear and the intelligence he gathered were outstanding, so that he was quickly awarded the Iron Cross (2nd Class). He was establishing a reputation for himself as a daredevil, gaining the nickname of the last horseman (cavalryman). He gradually extended his operations further into the enemy's rear where he found vulnerable and less alert foes. These actions led to him being recommended for the Iron Cross (1st Class).

One one extended raid the French sent their cavalry in pursuit, but von Strachwitz never tarried in one spot so the French were always behind him, not knowing where he would strike next. Nevertheless the net was closing in, so von Strachwitz took the more audacious course, and went even deeper behind the French lines. His patrol also disrupted the Limoges–Bordeaux railway, and he blew up the signal box at the Fontainebleau station. His patrol actually reached the outskirts of Paris before wheeling away. Increasingly alarmed, the French increased the number of troops searching for him. Several battalions of infantry and squadrons of cavalry were out searching for him, and the populace was alerted to his presence. A German patrol causing mayhem well in their rear was not just a serious affront to their Gallic pride, but as they were well aware, it was an important intelligence source for the Germans.

Von Strachwitz felt the full weight of the pursuit and knew that if he remained where he was, capture was only a question of time. He attempted a breakthrough to the German lines at the Marne, near Chalons; however, the

French forces were too thick on the ground. Over the next six weeks he was constantly on the move, getting very little respite as French units continued to seek him. A skirmish with one of these left one of his men wounded, slowing them down. His only option now was to make for the Swiss border, where he would not only find safety but also medical treatment for his wounded cavalryman. The weather now turned against him. Heavy, unremitting rain drenched him and his men to the skin. His men's health had now also become a factor. He had no option but to rest his exhausted men near a village.

Whether by luck, or more likely due to information from a French villager, a French patrol came across the bivouacked Germans and surrounded them. The inevitable capture had serious consequences for von Strachwitz. He and his men had been captured wearing civilian clothes. This meant that they would be treated as spies or *francs-tireurs* (partisans), and as such could be tried and shot. Von Strachwitz claimed, and subsequently used as his defence, that he had merely stolen some civilian clothes for his men to wear while they dried out their uniforms.

This rather lame excuse does not sit well with either von Strachwitz's temperament and character, or standing military practice as carried out by all armies, especially the Germans, for whom the uniform was sacrosanct. Throughout both the world wars, armies were frequently exhausted and soaked to the skin from rain, snow and mud, often for weeks at a time. At no point did their commanders, especially in the presence of the enemy, insist that they pillage and wear civilian clothes. It was not only against the strict rules of war, with the death penalty on capture, but against army regulations. Furthermore it was a simple matter of pride to wear the national uniform, no matter how wet, torn or ragged it got. Civilian clothes were used by selected units or for special missions—e.g. the Brandenburg Regiment wore civilian clothes on missions behind enemy lines for sabotage or reconnaissance in World War II. The wearing of such garb was a seriously considered military tactic. Von Strachwitz, aware of the regulations, and of the consequences if he was caught in civilian clothing, would not have ordered his men to wear them simply to keep dry—the death penalty was a high price to pay for comfort. More likely his use of civilian clothing was a deliberate attempt to deceive the enemy, and his best, perhaps only chance of escape. It fits with his imaginative, daring tactics of World War II when he sent his panzers behind Russian lines, often pretending to be a Russian tank column.

The French of course were not having any of his excuses. Von Strachwitz was rightly treated as a spy or a partisan and was almost shot on the spot.

Only a last-minute reprieve to ensure his interrogation and a show trial saved him. But not for him the barbed wire of a prisoner-of-war camp and the company of his fellows. He was tried by a court martial, found guilty and sentenced to death, a harsh blow to a young man in his prime, and a degrading one for a proud aristocratic cavalry officer.

Fortunately for him, on 14 October 1914, his sentence was commuted to life imprisonment in a French penal colony. It was a questionable improvement given the harsh treatment in the French civilian prisons and the hellish conditions of their penal colonies, where brutal treatment and tropical diseases eventually killed off most inmates. He was in the fetid hold of a French prison ship when the decision on his incarceration was reversed and he was sent back to a mainland prison. There is no doubt that had he been sent on to the penal colony, his end would have been completely different.

Little changed since the early to mid-19th century, French prisons at this time provided no stimulation, with no exercise beyond walking around a prison cell, poor and monotonous food, and all too often harsh treatment from the guards. It was a depressing life of drudgery and boredom, that stultified the mind and made the body listless, and for the guards more manageable. For a physically active, mentally alert person like von Strachwitz, it was hell on earth. Escape was permanently on his mind, necessary for his survival in order to escape the rot entering his mind and soul, enfeebling his body. He kept his mind active by endlessly searching for escape possibilities, observing guard and prison routines and the system and physical structure of the prison, looking for weaknesses or lapses. He befriended warders for information. This self-imposed reconnaissance, and his resulting escape attempts kept him sane. His general debilitated condition, however, made his frequent escape attempts futile, though he never gave up. If the attempt was all that he had, then it mattered for its own sake, so he kept at it, despite frequent beatings from his guards. The brutality of the guards and their treatment of him varied, too, depending on French successes or losses at the front.

He spent time in several prisons, often being moved after an unsuccessful escape attempt. He was incarcerated in prisons in Lyon, Montpellier, Île de Re—a citadel on a rather flat island which was one of the largest prisons in France—and Fort Barre, a particularly harsh prison for the worst offenders, where he was starved and routinely beaten. Here he began digging an escape tunnel, but it was detected. As a punishment he was put into solitary confinement, where his only sustenance was a loaf of coarse bread, and a pitcher of water. He was then sent as a punishment to be chained up in the fetid hold of a French cargo ship, plying its way between Toulon and Thessalonika in Greece. Brutalised, starving and left to rot in his own excrement he was very close to death, so was sent back to Fort Barre.

Eventually he was transferred to a camp for German officers at Carcassone. From there he escaped and was on the run for two weeks before being recaptured, after a cut to his heel gave him blood poisoning, rendering him too ill to continue. His health steadily deteriorated until the French authorities became concerned. They were therefore amenable to a Swiss Red Cross request, after one of their routine inspections, to transfer him to a hospital in Switzerland for treatment and convalescence. The intention was that after a period for recovery, he would be returned to the French penal system. It was none too soon, for had his incarceration continued von Strachwitz would have died, or at best suffered permanent physical disability.

He was transferred to a hospital in Geneva where his treatment undoubtedly saved his life. Proper food, medicines and rest slowly restored his health. He was allowed visitors, which included his mother and even the Kaiser's sister, the Queen of Greece. However, the fact remained that he was still a French prisoner, and would have to return. Escape remained a distinct and attractive option, but his past escape attempts had taught him that capture and swift deportation to France was the most realistic outcome. His solution was to feign insanity brought about by his brutal treatment. It was more than plausible to the Swiss who had seen his condition when he entered their hospital, and perhaps it was not too far from the truth for von Strachwitz himself.[5]

He was sent to an insane asylum in Herisau, Switzerland, where if conditions were bad, they were still a vast improvement to a French gaol. It was here that he sat out the rest of the war. He thus avoided the brutal, muddy reality of trench warfare that would otherwise have been his lot, which might have been an experience almost as bad as his imprisonment. A cavalryman to his boot-tips, the static warfare of the Western Front would have horrified him, and perhaps even killed him while carrying out some reckless charge or raid on the enemy trenches. Or perhaps he would have volunteered to fly, an occupation with an equally low life expectancy, but where the possibility of a hero's life and glory, however brief, awaited. The fact that he did not experience the stalemate of the trenches certainly helped to maintain his belief in the cavalry ethos of rapid movement and dashing attack. He would put such conviction to good advantage in the war to come, when he led his panzer formations with the same daring he had led his cavalry patrol in World War I.

NOTES

1. Barbara W. Tuchman, *The Guns of August* (Folio Society, 1997).
2. Ibid., p.67.
3. Barbara W. Tuchman, *The Proud Tower* (Folio Society, 1997), p.323.
4. Tuchman, *The Guns of August*, p.76.
5. Günter Fraschka, *Der Panzer Graf* (Erich Pabel Verlag, 1962); Hans Joachim Roll, *Hyazinth Graf Strachwitz* (Fleschig, Germany, 2011).

THREE

POST-WAR FREIKORPS ACTIONS

After the armistice, Graf von Strachwitz returned to a country that was almost unrecognisable as the one he had left in 1914. Germany was in turmoil. Revolution and the collapse of authority were spreading like a forest fire throughout the nation. The problems were ignited by a mutiny in the High Seas Fleet when the sailors refused to steam out and attack the enemy in a last suicidal mission on 28 October 1918, designed to restore the reputation of the hitherto moribund fleet. The crews raised the red flag of revolution, formed soviets as in Bolshevik Russia to control their ships, and seized the port of Kiel. Three naval officers were killed while preventing the red flags being raised on one vessel. Elsewhere the traumatised officers simply caved in. Dock workers in Hamburg and Lubeck followed the example of the sailors by taking control of their cities, much to the consternation of the authorities.

The army, which had been doing all the fighting while the fleet rotted at anchor, was bled white and close to collapse. Although suffering as much as the French, it had never mutinied as the French army had in May and June 1917, but the German High Command was convinced that if pushed much further, mutiny or at least a complete rout, in the summer of 1918, was a strong possibility. The senior commanders, particularly Field Marshal Paul von Hindenburg, Chief of the General Staff, and his deputy, General Erich Ludendorff, had to admit the war was lost. Ludendorff told the Kaiser the news, on 14 August 1918. So blinded was Wilhelm by his own bombast that he could not believe it. Five weeks later, after the Kaiser had absorbed the unpalatable truth, Germany called for an armistice.

The Imperial Chancellor Graf Georg von Hertwig resigned to make way for the more liberal Prince Max of Baden, the Kaiser's cousin, who by 26 October had transformed Germany into a parliamentary democracy, albeit with the Kaiser still at its head.

On Friday, 8 November, at Compiegne, northeast of Paris, an ashen-faced German delegation was read the 18 points their nation would have to abide by for the armistice to take effect. These included withdrawal from all occupied territories within 14 days, surrender of the submarine and High Seas fleets, and crippling reparations in cash and material. It was not to be a peace with honour. The Germans were to be cast as villains and would pay accordingly. As bad as the 18-point treaty originally drafted by US President Wilson was, the actual peace treaty the Germans had to sign on 28 June 1919 was far worse.

The French, clamouring for revenge, would not countenance any form of conciliation. Fully realising they had not defeated Germany on their own, and fearing—with good reason as it turned out—a resurgent Germany, the French suggested a complete dismemberment of Germany. This the British and Americans flatly rejected; however, they did agree to the harshest terms possible. The provinces of Alsace and Lorraine would be returned to France, which was reasonable and expected, seeing that it was what the French had wanted all along. The German Saar, an industrial region, was ceded to France for fifteen years. Austria, dismembered from Hungary and the rest of its Empire, was expressly forbidden from merging with Germany. The new state of Poland was given a large swathe of German territory including a corridor through East Prussia to give her access to the sea. The Baltic seaport and surrounding territory of Memel was given over to Allied control.[1] Germany was shorn of all her colonies, ostensibly because she was unfit to govern other races, but in reality to prevent her from rivalling Britain and France overseas.

The German Army was to be limited to 100,000 men, a self-defence force only. The German General Staff, by virtue of its supposed unbridled militarism, was to be abolished. The truncated army was forbidden to have tanks or armoured vehicles, while the navy was not permitted to purchase or manufacture submarines, and its existing submarines were turned over to the Allies. Military aircraft were also banned, denying Germany an air force. Allied garrisons were to be deployed on a strip of territory on both sides of the Rhine for a period of fifteen years.

Most intolerable of all, emotionally, was Article 231, which firmly laid the blame and guilt for the war on Germany as the aggressor. This neat piece of chicanery made Germany the unquestioned bogeyman of Europe, if not the world. The reparations were set so high as to beggar Germany for years to come. The initial payment of 20 million marks was the first installment only, with many more to follow. All of these terms were far in excess of what President Wilson had set down when the armistice was first proposed.

In inflicting such severe penalties, but not going as far as France's suggestion of dismembering Germany, they were opening the door to the worst outcome possible, giving Germany the time to recover and good reason to start another war. Perhaps the Allies should have heeded Machiavelli, who advised his prince to totally destroy a defeated enemy, so that they would never rise again or alternatively be so magnanimous so as to preclude any desire for revenge.

The Germans regarded the Treaty of Versailles as an abomination, a betrayal of their original agreement when the armistice had first been signed. Later the USA and Britain, and even some voices in France, tended to agree, but by then it was too late. The French Marshal Foch predicted the result of the treaty when he famously growled, "This is not peace. It is an armistice for twenty years."[2] And so it was to be, with World War II even more cruel and devastating then the prior one, emanating partly from the harsh terms of the first.

However, all this was in the future. For Kaiser Wilhelm II, the reckoning was to come well beforehand. On 8 November, Prince Max of Baden telephoned him, as a friend and relative, urging him to abdicate. The Kaiser refused point blank. He may have lost the war, being let down as he was by his army, but he nevertheless expected to keep his throne. It was thus left to the army to force the issue. On 9 November Field Marshal von Hindenburg and General Wilhelm Groener, Ludendorff's replacement as Quartermaster General, drove to Spa where the Kaiser and the Imperial General Staff were quartered. Wilhelm, still recovering from the sudden, and to him, inexplicable shock of losing the war, was trying to take an optimistic view of things, at least as far as his own position was concerned. He fully expected the Allies, alarmed by the march of communism and its success in already taking over Russia, to intervene on his behalf, quash the communists and socialists currently running rampant through German cities, and thereby enabling him to retain his throne. Certainly, it would be as a monarch of a parliamentary democracy, as in Britain, but a monarch nonetheless.[3]

Ushered in to see the Kaiser, Hindenburg's nerve failed him. Overcome with emotion and unable to speak, Groener had to impart the bad news. He outlined the seriousness of the situation: revolution was rampant, with scarcely any loyal troops to put it down. Some had in fact joined the revolutionaries, while the majority simply wanted to return home. The fate of the government, or more particularly, of the Kaiser, simply meant nothing to them. "Sire, you no longer have an army. It no longer stands behind your majesty," Groener finished gravely.

The Kaiser was shocked. Perhaps most galling of all, his own troops, the 2nd Guard Division, who had taken a personal oath of loyalty to him, had refused to suppress a rebellion in Cologne. Wilhelm was left with no other recourse but to abdicate. His son Wilhelm, Crown Prince of Prussia, was even less popular than the Kaiser so there was no option for him to ascend the throne. It was the end of the monarchy and the Prussian Hohenzollern dynasty.

The following morning the republic was declared with undue haste, perhaps to prevent a monarchist uprising, as many senior and even junior officers still believed in its retention. It would be safe to assume Graf von Strachwitz would have been in this category. He was too much the aristocrat, too proud of his lineage and what the nobility meant in terms of service and continuity, to feel otherwise, and an aristocracy without a monarchy was strictly nominal only. The Kaiser chose to go into exile in Holland, where he remained until his death in 1941.

In Berlin, the socialists under Frederick Ebert took over as the new government as they were the majority party, but they did not have full control of Berlin, let alone the country. The streets were swarming with protesting revolutionaries of the far left, communists—called Spartacists after the slave who rebelled against Rome—and demobilised soldiers searching for employment, action, or just revenge for real or perceived grievances.

Groener pledged the army's support if Ebert was prepared to restore order. This the new Chancellor willingly agreed to do, asserting his bitter enmity towards the revolutionaries, regardless that many of them were socialists and former allies. Thus reassured, Ebert settled back to wait for the army to suppress the rebellion, saving both his government and Germany.

The problem was, however, that the army was fast disintegrating. Only well-liked and popular officers had any control over their troops, and this was solely based upon shared front-line service and mutual respect. The vast bulk of the army could simply not be counted on. The answer was to gather whatever troops remained loyal into special units. So the Freikorps was born. Many of the first soldiers of the Freikorps were former members of the stormtroopers, specialised assault troops used to clear enemy trenches to pave the way for main attacks. They had a freebooting spirit and a singular loyalty to their officers, who shared with them a camaraderie born of great personal danger. Later, less disciplined troops and thugs attracted to violence would also join, giving the whole concept an unsavoury character.

The Freikorps became a collection of unofficial military units varying in size from division to, more often, battalion or company strength, which supported the government temporarily to crush communists and other left-wing malcontents, and restore order. They were commanded by army officers ranging in rank from generals to captains, and it was to these officers that the men gave their first loyalty. Some were merely a collection of thugs and adventurers, although most were staunchly anti-communist, nationalistic, and a few perhaps even idealistic. However no matter what their composition or motivation, most disliked the socialist government but hated communism more. They were very often all the government had to ensure its survival.

Although the revolution had spread to various parts of Germany, Berlin was the first priority of all sides. The Spartacists under Karl Liebknecht and Rosa Luxembourg could bring the masses out on the streets, but thereafter often lost control. Unlike Lenin and his murderous cohorts in Russia, the German communists were badly organised, lacked clear aims, detailed plans and discipline. Nevertheless they remained a real threat to Ebert's stumbling socialist government.

The revolution certainly worried von Strachwitz, and like many of his fellow officers he resolved to personally do something about it. He no doubt saw it as his mission to save Germany from Bolshevism. One of the many Freikorps units then becoming operational at this time was the Garde Kavallerie Schutz Division, a division of the Horse Guards, now converted to an infantry role under General von Hoffman. It was to this Guards Cavalry division that Hyazinth von Strachwitz would have attached himself, it being only natural that he would wish to join a Guard Cavalry unit even in its altered state.

Fighting between the Freikorps and Spartacists was well underway when the Garde Kavallerie Schutz Division, together with the Iron Brigade from Kiel, 2,400 men from General Maercker's unit, and General von Roeder's Scouts, marched into Berlin. The columns passed through the suburb of Lichterfelde, and von Strachwitz must have surely felt a pang as he entered the familiar grounds of his youth.

An enthusiastic crowd greeted the disciplined troops, glad that peace and order were being restored at last, and the troops felt like returning heroes rather than the defeated troops they had been. A Spartacist machine-gun nest was eliminated from the triumphal arch at the Brandenburg gate as the Freikorps men deployed to do battle.

While the Iron Brigade took charge of the Moabit barracks, Maercker's men took over Lichterfelde. The Horse Guards Division marched into the suburb of Zehlendorf taking control there with very little opposition. Another section of the Horse Guards, together with attached units, took control of Berlin's southern suburbs, deploying along a line from Buckow to Zehlendorf.

The next evening, preceded by an artillery bombardment, the Freikorps attacked the revolutionaries' headquarters at the Police Presidium building on the Alexanderplatz, in eastern Berlin. The front of the building was demolished and the Spartacists were driven out only after a furious exchange of gunfire and hand-to-hand fighting, with the communists retreating room by room. Mopping-up operations with the occasional skirmish followed. The Freikorps units then consolidated their positions. The Horse Guards Division occupied part of the government district comprising the Reichstag, the Ringbahn and the Potsdamen Platz. The divisional staff commandeered the luxurious Eden Hotel for its headquarters. The overall Freikorps commander, General Walter von Lüttwitz, set up his headquarters in Dahlem.[4]

After a few weeks at most, with the main part of the fighting over, Graf von Strachwitz called it a day, and returned to his native Silesia, where trouble with the restive Silesian Poles was brewing. It was just as well that he left when he did, for the Horse Guards were soon to gain a notoriety with which von Strachwitz would not have felt comfortable. After he had left, the Freikorps concentrated on hunting down the Spartacist leadership. This task was given to Captain Waldemar Pabst, Chief-of-Staff of the Horse Guards Division.

On 9 December a unit of the Horse Guards raided the offices of the *Rote Fahne* (*Red Banner*), the communist newspaper which Rosa Luxembourg used for her inflammatory editorials. Their mission was to murder Karl Leibknecht, an associate editor of the paper, and who was expected to be hiding there. As an incentive they had been promised a reward of 50,000 marks by the billionaire industrialist Georg Sklars. The once-proud Horse Guards had sunk so low as to become hired assassins. Liebknecht had fled however, joining Rosa Luxembourg in the communist-controlled Neuholm. The Horse Guards undertook house-to-house searches, flushing the pair out of

Neuholm and into the middle-class suburb of Wilmersdorf where they found refuge in an apartment. Here Rosa Luxembourg continued her work, dictating pamphlets and articles while Liebknecht simply gave up, telling stories to their hosts' children.[5]

On 15 January a Horse Guards detachment under Lieutenant Linder, acting on a tip, raided the apartment and captured the pair. The prisoners were roughly manhandled then taken to the Horse Guards Division headquarters at the Hotel Eden where Captain Pabst was waiting. Here, under Pabst's direction, they were interrogated and badly beaten.[6] Karl Liebknecht was then handed over to Naval Lieutenant Horst von Pflug-Hartung from the Iron Brigade, which had been temporarily seconded to the Horse Guards Division. He and some other naval officers drove a short distance then ordered Liebknecht out of the car. The broken man had barely staggered a few steps when von Pflug-Hartung shot him in the back. Not to be outdone, the other officers quickly joined in, firing their pistols into their victim. His body was driven a short distance further, and dumped unceremoniously outside the steps of a nearby morgue. A short while later Rosa Luxembourg was roughly hauled out of the Horse Guards headquarters. On the way out a cavalryman callously clubbed her with his rifle butt, seriously injuring her. Horse Guards officer Lieutenant Kurt Vogel and five of his men threw her into a car and drove off, shooting her soon thereafter. They weighted her body with stones and threw it into the Laudwehr canal. Her badly decomposed body was not found until five months later.[7] Pabst reported that Liebknecht had been shot while attempting to escape, which no one seriously believed, while Horse Guards Lieutenant Linder asserted that a mob had surrounded his car and spirited Rosa Luxembourg away.

To his credit, General von Hoffman ordered an immediate investigation. Lieutenant Vogel and von Pflug-Hartwig were quickly arrested. Waldeman Pabst appointed an equally slippery friend of his, Naval Lieutenant Wilhelm Canaris—who would rise to the rank of admiral and become head of Military Intelligence under Hitler, whom he would then plot against—as an associate judge of the case. Canaris immediately set about perverting the course of justice, even holding a mock trial in Moabit Prision to coach the defendants in a series of lies and false trails. He also organised false passports and an escape plan should the trial not deliver his expected outcome. The General Staff of the Horse Guards, eager to play their part in assisting their brother officers, raised 30,000 marks for an escape fund.

At the trial Canaris went to great lengths to ensure that Captain Pabst was not implicated in any way, that the real events were completely obscured, and the anticipated verdict was delivered. One officer received a six-week gaol sentence for exceeding his authority. The horse guardsman who had clubbed Rosa Luxembourg, the only enlisted man on trial, felt the full brunt of the law and was sentenced to two years' imprisonment. Lieutenant Vogel, thanks to eyewitness reports that could not be refuted, was given two years and four months' imprisonment, and no doubt felt aggrieved being the only officer to be seriously punished. Canaris, not to be outmanoeuvred by justice, subsequently engineered Vogel's escape, with Horse Guards officers simply turning up at the gaol with false papers for the prisoner's transfer. What Graf von Strachwitz would have thought of this saga can easily be imagined. For him, justice was not to be trifled with, as he would subsequently show when plotting to arrest Hitler.

Graf von Strachwitz only enjoyed a few years of peace, where he could recuperate from his prison ordeal and lead the life of a gentleman farmer tending his estate. In 1919 he married Alexandrine (Alda) Grafin (Countess) Saurma-Jeltsch, a slim, striking woman with dark hair, high cheekbones and an angular face. She came from a prominent aristocratic family, so he had done his duty by not marrying below his station. Nevertheless it was, by aristocratic standards, a love match, which produced two sons, the eldest called Hyazinth as tradition demanded, born on 2 May 1920, Hubertus Arthur, born 11 March 1925, and a daughter, Lisalotte. So the line of succession was secured.

Meanwhile Silesia was in turmoil, facing difficult but different problems from the rest of Germany. The region's chequered history meant that over the centuries Silesia had been subject to Polish, Bohemian, Austrian, Prussian and Imperial German rulers, often with a mixture of overlords governing different localities. This was reflected in its demographics with a mixture of German and Slavic ethnic groups. Lower Silesia was German Protestant, while Upper Silesia was strongly Catholic with a large Polish population—comprising 61% of the population of the region in 1829. Forced Germanization reduced the Polish proportion to 58% in 1849. In 1900, in the Austrian part of Upper Silesia, 44% of the population was German, 33.2% was Polish and 22.5% was Czech, with loyalties flowing accordingly to Poland or Austria/Germany in proportion.

The first drafts of the Treaty of Versailles added Upper Silesia to the newly independent state of Poland, but British Prime Minister David Lloyd George rejected this and forced through a clause calling for a plebiscite.[8]

Poland was unhappy with this and two insurrections of the Silesian Poles, under Wojciech Korfanty and Josef Rymer, were organised before the plebiscite took place on 26 March 1921. Given the Weimar Republic's inability to effectively intervene, due largely to Allied pressure, the German Silesians formed their own Freikorps equivalent, the Selbstschutz Oberschleisen, which both Graf von Strachwitz and his younger brother, Manfred, joined. The unit was more in the nature of a local militia, with the men being called upon when needed. Being a lieutenant, Hyazinth did not play a major role in the unit. His lack of front-line experience meant that he was less likely to be given a commanding role, although his two Iron Crosses no doubt impressed his contemporaries and gave him credibility.

The first Polish uprising began in August 1919, but was not supported by the Polish government and was quickly put down by the Weimar government's Grenzschutz division. This unit of 3,000 men was only capable of vigorous police actions, so while they could react to attacks, they were unable to secure Upper Silesia. The Poles were only temporarily subdued, going underground to await their next opportunity. This came on 19 August 1920 with a general strike. The Polish insurrectionists followed this up with an armed uprising, which seized control of several districts. The Allies intervened, and after some negotiations it was agreed that a mixed police force would be established, which satisfied the Poles for the time being. By August 25 the whole affair had fizzled out. Both insurrections were localised and brief, so Graf von Strachwitz would not have been involved in any heavy fighting.

The following year the Allied-sponsored plebiscite was held on 20 March, with 706,000 people representing some 792 communities voting to remain with Germany, and 479,000 people representing 682 communities voting to merge with Poland. It wasn't a huge win for the Germans, and solved nothing as the Poles refused to accept the result, and rose up in revolt under their leader Korfanty.

The Weimar government wanted to send in troops from its truncated Reichwehr, but this was once more blocked by the Allies who feared a direct war between Germany and Poland. Better they fight it out through their surrogates, the Silesian Freikorps against the Silesian Polish Nationalists. This left the German government no choice but to employ the Freikorps. However, mobilising the disparate units and sending them under cover from different locations took over two weeks, with many Freikorps fighters making their own way there thinly disguised as miners or farmers. Several of the

Bavarians arrived trying to look inconspicuous wearing the Bavarian national dress of leather shorts, long socks and alpine hat. They of course fooled no one.

On 3 May the Poles launched their offensive. They quickly pushed the smaller units of the Selbstschutz Oberschleisen back towards the west. Panic began to set in, and the German Silesian calls for help grew ever more strident. Together with other units, Hyazinth's detachment became involved but their numbers were still insufficient to hold back the Polish force which drove them back to the line of the River Oder. The Poles' other objective was capturing the strategic Annaberg hill which they did on 4 May.

The hill, 400 metres in height, overlooked the Oder valley and commanded the east bank of the River Oder. On its peak sat the Catholic Monastery of St. Anna, a place of reverence for both Germans and Poles. Both sides considered control of the hill to be vital to their campaign.

By now the Freikorps had finally gathered in Upper Silesia. They comprised Maecker's Laudes-Jagerkorps, the Stahlhelm (Steel Helmet), the Jungdeutsche Ordern (The Young German Order), von Aulock's Freikorps, and individuals from the Rossbach Freikorps and Peter von Heydebreck's Wehrwolves. The largest unit, 1,650 men strong, was the Bavarian Oberland Freikorps. It was a well-organised, highly effective unit of tough WWI and post-war revolutionary fighters. It had included, at one time or another, such future Nazi luminaries as Heinrich Himmler, the future Reichsfuhrer SS, who wasn't present in Silesia; Sepp Dietrich, who would later command the Leibstandarte SS Adolf Hitler and become an SS field army commander, who was present during the campaign; future Waffen SS Brigadefuhrer Fritz von Scholz, who distinguished himself as an SS general; and Hilmar Wackerle, future commandant of Dachau Concentration Camp. Non-military members included Elenore Bauer, aka Sister Pia, a nursing sister and early Nazi Party member who received the Blood Order for her part in the Beer Hall Putsch; Arnold Runge, the philosopher; and author Bodo Uhse, an early Nazi party member and later communist. Altogether an eclectic mix of thinkers, fighters and thugs. One Oberlander who didn't fit the description was Frederich Gustav Jaeger, future army colonel and early Nazi party member. He reached the rank of Army Colonel, receiving the Knight's Cross in the process (1940). He then turned against Hitler, and was executed by the Nazis in August 1944 for his part in Stauffenberg's failed putsch.

The Oberland's military commander had visited the headquarters of the Selbstschutz Oberschleisen on 7 May and had been visibly unimpressed.

Housed in lavish quarters the place was a shambolic mess of confused orders, lack of direction and disorganised administration. The Freikorps and Selbstschutz were placed under the overall command of General von Hoefer, a World War I veteran. He was ready to launch an immediate counterattack, but was being held back on orders from Berlin, which in turn was waiting for a ruling from the Allied Commission on the situation in Upper Silesia. Von Hoefer made his feelings known to a journalist of the *New York Times* when he angrily declared: "What a rotten humiliating position for a general to be in. For a German general! My men will follow me and I can't lead them to the attack. Because of policy . . . bah! . . . politics has fallen into my anus and blocked me."[9] His deputy, General Lieutenant Bernhard von Hulsen, after some prodding from Major Horadarm, the Oberland commander, decided to override his superior and attack the Annaberg.[10]

The Poles outnumbered the Germans but lacked combat experience, as a large proportion of them were civilians, although some had fought in the war.[11] They had French officers acting as unofficial advisers, as the French actively supported the Poles, while the British and Italians stationed in Upper Silesia supported the Germans, although only morally. The Polish forces were dug in around the approaches to the mountain as well as on the hill itself, and were prepared to make a fight of it. Their main force consisted of a regiment of volunteers from Katowice as well as Polish Silesians from Gross Strehlitz and Tor, and a brigade of regulars, who were located at the edge of the mountain. On the mountain itself were more miners from Katowice and a number of other troops.

The German attack commenced at 2:30 a.m. on 21 May against the Poles' outlying positions. It was spearheaded by the Bavarian Oberlanders and the Selbstschutz Oberschleisen where Graf von Strachwitz was serving as an Oberleutnant (1st Lieutenant). The German force consisted of 900 men divided into two columns for a left and right flanking attack.

The Polish artillery opened up unexpectedly, causing casualties with its first salvoes. The Germans went to ground, but with encouragement from their officers resumed their attack using fire and movement. The Poles fought back valiantly but against the greater skill of the Germans were forced to give ground, losing two artillery pieces in the process. These were turned around and used by the Germans against the Annaberg itself.

The Poles counterattacked with great valour but little effect. The Germans stood their ground and their machine guns cut the attackers down. Polish enthusiasm was no match for sustained machine-gun and rifle fire.

However, the Germans did not escape lightly, losing eight dead and 50 wounded. It was von Strachwitz's first real taste of infantry warfare from fixed positions. The Oberland commander Horadam now prepared for the assault on the Annaberg itself. Taking some of his staff with him to a vantage point to scout the terrain, he found it occupied by some 30 Poles. After a brief firefight he drove the Poles off and later deployed his captured guns on the height.

On 23 May the German attack began. One battalion attacked through the woods in front of Annaberg while another went around to the rear of Annaberg village, thus surrounding the mountain. Supported by their captured artillery, the Germans stormed forward against the dug-in Poles. Using stormtrooper tactics perfected in World War I, they cleared the Polish trenches. Hand grenades, bayonets, rifle butts, knives and fists were used in vicious hand-to-hand combat. After some twenty minutes it was over; the shocked Poles fled in disarray leaving behind 100 men as prisoners. The Germans lost two dead and 20 wounded. The Poles were still not prepared to give up and launched a counterattack, but it was repulsed, causing them heavy casualties.

Hyazinth von Strachwitz fought well at Annaberg, and his efforts there were always a source of pride for him, irrespective of his later, far greater achievements. His brother Manfred also fought with some distinction, being badly wounded in action at Krizova. Sepp Dietrich also distinguished himself at the Annaberg. Von Strachwitz may well have made his acquaintance, but given his aristocratic outlook it was unlikely that he would have considered the rough former NCO as a friend or close comrade in arms.

The Allies stepped in once more to stop the fighting in Silesia. They pressured the German government to initiate peace talks, which they did by insisting that the Selbstschutz commence negotiations with the Poles. This was done on 25 May and succeeded, apart from the odd skirmish, in ending the fighting. Allied troops then moved in, including four battalions of British troops moved from occupation duties in the Ruhr, and the Germans and Poles withdrew to their respective lines as drawn up from the plebiscite.

No recognition was accorded to von Strachwitz and the other fighters in the Silesian campaign by the Weimar Republic. This caused a great deal of resentment as they were defending German soil, which the Weimar could not, or would not, do. However von Strachwitz and others were awarded the Order of the Silesian Eagle, in his case, in the 1st Class, with Wreath and Swords, a private decoration instituted by General Leutnant Friedrich

Friedeburg, commander of the VI Army Corps on 16 June 1919. It was one that was especially dear to him, and the only Freikorps decoration officially permitted to be worn on one's uniform during the Third Reich. Von Strachwitz would always wear his. With peace restored, Graf von Strachwitz could resume acclimatising to civilian life.

NOTES

1. The newly independent state of Lithuania drove the occupying French troops out and annexed the territory in order to obtain a seaport. The League of Nations ratified the annexure, but the Germans were loathe to accept it and Hitler took it back with the threat of force in 1934.
2. D. J. Goodspeed, *The German Wars* (Bonanza Books, NY, 1985), p.274.
3. The Germans held similar views in 1945, hoping the British and Americans would join them in fighting the Russians in order to prevent Eastern Europe and Germany falling to communism.
4. Nigel H. Jones, *Hitler's Heralds. The Story of the Freikorps 1918–1923* (John Murray Publishing, 1987).
5. Jones, *Hitler's Heralds.*
6. Ibid. Pabst always denied the beatings but eyewitnesses contradicted him.
7. Jones, *Hitler's Heralds.*
8. Lloyd George could have saved a good deal of bloodshed and trouble had he left well enough alone, as Upper Silesia ended up becoming part of Poland in 1945.
9. *New York Times* (June 1921), p.13.
10. Charles Messenger, *Sepp Dietrich: Hitler's Gladiator* (Brassey's Defence Publishers, 1988), p.31.
11. During World War I, Poles fought as legions or units for the Allies (Russia) and also for the Germans and Austrians, depending on their domicile and political beliefs, future independence being their main aim.

FOUR

JOINING THE NAZI PARTY AND SS

WITH CALM RESTORED TO SILESIA, HYAZINTH VON Strachwitz could begin to lead a normal family life at Gross-Stein. His castle or manor house with its surrounding lands offered a secure, comfortable lifestyle. It was located 17 kilometres southeast of the regional capital, Oppeln. It consisted of a large rectangular building of four storeys including the attic, which ran along the length of the building. Its dominant feature was a large square tower. There was a large raised terrace along most of the front of the building, which was planted as a formal garden. It wasn't spectacular, but was large and pleasant to the eye. However, due to growing disagreements and estrangement with his father, who was as strong willed and determined as he was, he moved his family to a 583-hectare manor at Alt Seidel. There he lived a comfortable life until 1929 when, after reconciling with his father, he returned to Gross-Stein.

The countryside surrounding Gross-Stein was typical of Upper Silesia, flat with large tracts of forest. The village of Gross-Stein, home to around one thousand people, was a short distance away. The woodlands were an important source of income for the estate, its management requiring a good deal of time and knowledge, so the Graf took up forestry studies in 1929. Dairying was another major source of revenue and Hyazinth became the manager of a dairy co-operative. In addition to this, the estate grew vegetables, potatoes, barley, corn and rye, and had the usual range of farm animals, pigs, chickens, geese and above all, horses. This made the family largely self-sufficient so while they were affected when the Depression hit in the early 1930s, they could cope far more readily than most. Nor was the rampant unemployment an issue, for it provided cheap labour for their estates. So despite some yearning to be active in the military again, life for von Strachwitz was uneventful, staid and pleasant.

Elsewhere, however, conditions were anything but idyllic. Germany, still traumatised by the war, was feeling the burdens of the Treaty of Versailles and was almost crippled by the reparations. The French occupation of the Ruhr in 1923 was a running sore, a constant reminder of defeat and a massive loss of resources, with the occupying French plundering some $106 million worth of goods, further draining the Germany economy.[1]

Inflation was rampant, affecting every facet of life, with one US dollar being worth 5,000,000 Marks. The middle class had their wealth eroded or wiped out, while wealthy industrialists paid off their massive debts with the almost worthless paper money. Large landowners like von Strachwitz could buy up more land, but it was all at the expense of the lower classes, who increasingly resented the powerless Weimar government. These were conditions a demagogue could thrive on. One was in the making.

Adolf Hitler, an Austrian, unsuccessful artist, a former corporal in the German Army—albeit as an Iron Cross winner—and post-war informer for the government, was taking his first steps in politics. In September 1919 he joined the miniscule Nationalist Socialist German Workers Party, which he had been sent to spy on by the army who were wary of any party with socialist in its title. He built up the membership who were enthralled by his oratory and captivated by his zeal. The expansion also applied to the party's Sturm Abteilung (SA) which consisted of brown-shirted street fighters and thugs. Its main purpose was to protect the Nazis' own meetings and disrupt their opponents', namely the communists. It would rise to be a force that would rival, and indeed threaten, the army. With some adroit manoeuvres Hitler took over the party on 28 July 1921. He would never look back. With an almost pathological belief in himself and his destiny, and an iron will, he was determined to win over anyone who could be useful, and crush anyone who stood in his way. In this he was singularly successful. He was a forceful orator, exciting the crowds and whipping them into frenzies of support, and for many, adoration.

Hitler's overconfidence led him into an abortive putsch in Munich in November 1923, which was easily put down by a fusillade of shots from the police. He was arrested, tried and sentenced to five years in Landsberg prison. It was hardly onerous; he had his own quarters and cronies to accompany him. His cell on the second floor was comfortably furnished and filled with wine, beer, fruit, flowers and food brought in by his wealthy supporters. So much so that he put on considerable weight during his incarceration. He was allowed out during the day to visit Landsberg. Prison warden Otto Loybold wrote of him on 18 September 1924, "Hitler was always reasonable, frugal, modest and polite to everyone, especially officials of the facility,"[2] a model prisoner. He only served nine months of his sentence, being released due to political influence and pressure. He used the time to dictate to Rudolf Hess, the party secretary, his political manifesto and memoir, *Mein Kampf* (*My Struggle*). In it he clearly stated his political aims and beliefs, rampant anti-Semitism, anti-communism and the acquisition of *lebensraum* (living space) in the east at the expense of Russia—he would build a large Germanic empire at the expense of Eastern Europe. There was a lot more, but this goal would cause the greatest bloodshed and misery. The book eventually became a best seller and an important source of income, earning Hitler 1,500,000 Reich Marks in 1933. It should have been a source of great concern to any normal, sane-thinking people but, as is often true with the Bible, hundreds of thousands of homes had a copy but very few people actually took the trouble to read it. Anyone but the most fanatical Nazi would have very quickly put it down, due to its turgid prose and nonsensical views. Even Hitler's friend and ally, Benito Mussolini, gave up in disgust, finding it too boring and difficult to read. A great orator Hitler was, a writer he wasn't.

Oddly enough, and contrary to what many believe, Hitler became Chancellor of Germany through the democratic process. In the elections of 5 March 1932 the Nazis received 13.4 million votes (36.8%), disappointing for Hitler, but a solid result nevertheless. Hitler's 1933 election vote was 17.27 million (43.91%), a much better tally, and if not a majority it nevertheless made the Nazis the largest party in the Reichstag (Parliament). This led, after some political manoeuvring, to President von Hindenburg reluctantly offering Hitler the chancellorship of Germany. Hitler was in, and it wouldn't be too long before democracy was out.

Along with the vote, Nazi Party membership was also increasing. In 1931 the party had 400,000 card-carrying members, with the figure rising to 900,000 in 1932. This was before Hitler's accession to power in 1933 when the party received a massive influx of members. These new members were always looked down upon by those who had joined before 1933. Those who had joined earlier, even if only by a year, had committed themselves before the fruits of office and headiness of power had materialised, and considered themselves the true believers, the rest being mere opportunists.

Hitler's acquisition of dictatorial power also used the democratic process. The Enabling Act of 1934, after Hindenburg's death, was passed by the Reichstag with the necessary help of the Catholic Centre Party. This enabled Hitler to rule by decree. In the meantime, democracy or not, Hitler had been busy removing his enemies and cementing his support. On 30 June 1934 he arrested or murdered the leadership of the SA, his two-million-strong party militia which, under its leader Ernst Rohm, was getting too independent and powerful.[3] More ominously it was part of a deal with the army, which regarded the SA a rival. To get army support for his assuming the presidency after the octogenarian Hindenburg's death, Hitler agreed to downgrade the SA and ensure that the army would be the country's main bearer of arms. In its gratitude the army proposed that its members take a personal oath of loyalty to Hitler.[4] All of this would affect Graf von Strachwitz in the future. The time would come when he would have to search his own conscience vis-à-vis his oath to Hitler. This would be an important issue for a man whose decency, integrity and humanity outweighed a personal but artificial sense of honour.

At the same time as bringing the SA to heel, Hitler, Goering and Himmler took the opportunity to settle old scores and eliminate any other opposition through their new paramilitary arm, the Schutzstaffel (SS). Hundreds were murdered, including close associates of Vice-Chancellor Franz von Papen, such as his secretary Hubert von Bose and Erich Klausener, the Catholic Action leader. General Kurt von Schleicher, the former Chancellor, and his wife were murdered in their home, and Gustav Ritter von Kahr, the former Bavarian State Commissioner, who smashed Hitler's putsch attempt in 1923 was also murdered. Goering and Goebbels suppressed details of the murderous events, sending out the message that they had blocked an attempt by Rohm and others to seize the government. Hitler gave a speech in the Reichstag on 13 July justifying his actions, and the Reichstag applauded them. As far as the German public was concerned—and this included von Strachwitz—it was a job well done. For the Graf and indeed for most army officers, the move against the SA was more than welcome. He would have shared the army's concern about the party militia, and the result would only have confirmed his commitment to Hitler and the party.

On Hindenburg's death in August 1934, Hitler assumed the presidency, thus becoming both president and chancellor of Germany, a title which was shortened simply to *Führer* (Leader). The Enabling Act of 1933 gave him dictatorial powers with the ability to rule by decree without recourse to the

Reichstag. The army, happy to have the SA neutralised and anticipating a major rearmament programme, meekly went along. Any voices of dissent were too small to be heard. There was now no turning back.

Like the majority of Germans, Hyazinth Graf von Strachwitz did not oppose Hitler's seizure of power. He had joined the Nazi Party in 1932 (party no. 1405562) before Hitler had become Chancellor so he was a real Nazi, not a mere opportunist nor just a sympathizer or supporter.

So why would a proud aristocratic reserve army officer and devout Catholic join one of the most odiously evil organisations in the history of mankind? He didn't need membership to secure his future, or career, as many certainly did. He seemingly had very little to gain from membership. Wealth, status, security, social acceptance, were all his already.

Moreover he was not a political animal per se. He was however, directly affected by the Polish claims to Silesia, and worried by the spread of communism, having fought communists while in the Guard Cavalry Freikorps. A staunch nationalist, it grieved him to see Germany belittled, shunned and kept deliberately suppressed by the Allies and the Treaty of Versailles. His concerns would most likely have included the economy, unemployment, abrogation of the Versailles Treaty, rearmament, defeating communism, restoration of German pride and national consciousness, securing Germany's borders (Silesia from the Poles) and obliterating the Polish corridor separating East Prussia, to name a few. What happened to Germany in the broader sense mattered greatly to him, hence his interest in politics. These were all matters Hitler was resolved to fix or had already taken measures to fix. It was a strong inducement for von Strachwitz to join and become involved.

The lesser option of just being a supporter also had appeal. There were, after all, aspects of Nazism that gave him great disquiet, such as anti-clericalism and anti-Semitism. He could easily have opted for the role of supporter which would have involved no more than a vote at elections, perhaps a donation to party coffers and optional attendance at some public meetings or private functions. Instead however he chose to become a full member, an open public commitment for the record.

While history has thoroughly examined and judged the Nazi regime to be evil, many people at the time believed in the purity and good intentions of the Führer and the wisdom of his policies. This was, of course, because they wanted to, and because they were manipulated by an unrelenting campaign of propaganda and indoctrination. For them, and for von Strachwitz, Hitler was not all bad. In the 1930s, Hitler did a great deal of good for the

German people, unifying the country, reducing unemployment, abrogating the Treaty of Versailles, ending the French occupation of the Ruhr, restoring the economy and national pride.

Hitler's murderous intent and thirst for war were known only to a few of his acolytes and generals, and while the Nazis' anti-Semitism would eventually result in the horror of the Final Solution, such sentiment was nothing new in Europe. It had risen its ugly head through the centuries, at times inflamed into hatred, resulting in pogroms and often outright murder. Nazi propaganda and indoctrination would do the same in Germany. A classic example of the conditioning that incessant propaganda can achieve is illustrated by an incident Siegfried Knappe describes in his memoir:

> While doing some of my paperwork one evening I was distracted by shouting. I recognised the voice as Hauptwachtmeister Schnabel's and went to investigate. I found him in a school building with a middle-aged Polish civilian. He was not only shouting at the man, he slapped him in the face!
>
> "Schnabel," I shouted.
>
> "Jawohl, Herr Oberleutnant," he responded, coming to attention.
>
> "What do you think you are doing?" I demanded.
>
> "But he is a Jew, Herr Oberleitnant," Schnabel assured me.
>
> "I don't care what he is or who he is, as long as you are under my command you will not mistreat anybody," I ordered.
>
> His actions were obviously the result of incessant anti-Jewish propaganda of the Nazi government. He undoubtedly was doing what he thought was expected of him, but the incident enabled me to establish to my men that I would not tolerate such behaviour, and it never happened again in my unit.[5]

It also shows that not everyone was taken in by the propaganda, and decent standards could be set by those prepared to maintain them.

At the time that Graf von Strachwitz joined the party there was nothing to suggest that the Nazis' bullying, intimidation and denial of civil rights to Jews would turn into industrialised mass murder, something that was so evil as to be totally incomprehensible to him. So if anti-Semitism was of some concern at the time, it was not the major issue; the major issues were Germany's straitened economy, weak military, communist resurgence, the Polish claims on Silesia, and its corridor separating Prussia from Germany. Hitler's aims to fix these problems, and then his actions in carrying most of them out and rebuilding Germany, would have outweighed any doubts von Strachwitz may have had.

Hitler began rearming after he came to power, surreptitiously at first, then more brazenly, building up the armed forces for the war he planned. This gave the economy a boost and helped alleviate unemployment. He also began a major building programme, constructing autobahns, bridges, buildings and other infrastructure, creating even more jobs. This meant a rise in living standards for most Germans and great wealth for some. Unemployment, the blight of the Weimar Republic, was eliminated as economic growth took on a greater pace. Finally compulsory labour service was introduced. The state labour service and the Hitler Youth organisations were quasi-military in nature, and a further extended means of indoctrinating children and young men in Nazi ideology, along with healthy outdoor activities. Given his own youthful military training at the cadet schools, von Strachwitz would have approved of both organisations.

Hitler lauded the greatness of the German people, making them feel special and therefore good about themselves. That this exceptionalism was due to their Aryan race implied that other races, particularly the Slavs, were inferior. As for the Jews they were even worse than inferior, they were considered vermin, as Goebbels' fake documentary *The Eternal Jew* clearly implied. This was part of a sustained, relentless propaganda campaign, which brooked no contrary opinions or opposition.

As for the army, an organisation close to the heart of Captain (Reserve) von Strachwitz, it was once more given an eminent place, second or equal to the party, in German society. Given the quasi-military nature of the Hitler Youth and the Reich Labour Service, together with the expanding armed forces, Hitler effectively militarised German society. This was virtually an extension of the Kaiser's Germany, so the people readily adapted. The Weimer democracy had been a mere interruption, a bump in the road.

The Nazi Party's anti-communism was a big plus for von Strachwitz, who had been personally involved in combating it with the Horse Guard Cavalry Freikorps in Berlin. Communism was a threat to Germany as a nation, and to him personally, given that he was an aristocratic class enemy and devout Catholic.

Upper Silesia was Graf von Strachwitz's great love. It wasn't just his home, but had nurtured his family for generations, being a source of their pride and wealth. The family was rooted in its soil, its traditions and culture. He had fought for it against the Poles, whom he knew still had designs on it. A mere plebiscite was not going to stop them. Here Hitler's militarism and fervent nationalism was Silesia's best defence against any future Polish actions.

Finally, Hitler was charismatic, a demagogue who could sway the masses to a fever pitch of adulation and support for a greater Germany, unified under his leadership. It was no small thing to unify a nation so recently and violently divided on ideological grounds. That force and repression was also used was generally overlooked. On a personal level Hitler could be extremely affable and charming, almost mesmerising.[6] Among others, General Werner von Blomberg, his war minister, was totally enthralled by him and incapable of any realistic and sensible opposition to his expansionist territorial goals.[7] Officers meeting him for the first time in the early war years commented on his warmth, extraordinary presence and his piercing blue eyes. These personal qualities gradually declined with the pressure of defeats, exhaustion, suspicion and the drugs being prescribed by his physician, Dr. Morell.

There remains the question of Graf von Strachwitz's Catholicism, given that a large part of the church, especially the Episcopate, opposed National Socialism as being incompatible with the church's teachings. The parish priest of Kirschhausen informed his parishoners that a Catholic could not be a card-carrying member of the Hitler Party. The Vicar General of Mainz supported his stand, declaring that the Nazi Party policy of racial hatred was "un-Christian and un-Catholic," and that despite seeming to be supportive of the church in his book *Mein Kampf*, Hitler's religious and educational policies "were inconsistent with Christianity."[8]

Indeed, Hitler was conciliatory to Christianity, writing in *Mein Kampf*, "Political parties have nothing to do with religion as long as they are not alien to the nation undermining the morals and ethics of race; just as religions cannot be amalgamated with the scheming of political parties." In 1927 Hitler ordered that statements about religion be prohibited for political reasons. His aim throughout was to avoid confrontation with the Catholic Church. In his speech to the Reichstag in 1933 prior to the Enabling Act, he declared that churches were to be an integral part of German national life, and affirmed his support for Christianity and the Catholic Church. Of course this was just a cynical exercise to win over the Catholic Centre Party whose vote Hitler needed to pass the Enabling Act. Hitler's private attitude to Christianity and the Catholic Church was the exact opposite to his public statements. He fully intended, after dealing with the Jews and subjugating the Slavs, to eliminate

Christianity. He made his views clear, declaring to his cronies, "You are either a Christian or a German. You cannot be both."[9] And again in July 1941: "Christianity is the hardest blow that ever hit humanity. Bolshevism is the bastard son of Christianity, both are the monstrous issue of the Jews."[10] Later in December he remarked ". . .and I shall see my task as cleaning up the church problem. Only then will the German nation be completely safe . . ."[11]

Of course Hyazinth von Strachwitz was not cognisant of Hitler's private views. He was only aware of his supportive public stance. Just as important for Graf von Strachwitz's opinions, the Catholic bishops' opposition was weak, uncoordinated and at times divided. The Bavarian bishops declared in February 1931 that "As guardians of the true teaching of faith and morals, the bishops must warn against National Socialism, so long and so far as it proclaims cultural and political opinions that are incompatible with Catholic teaching." However, after Vatican pressure was applied by the future Pope, Cardinal Pacelli, the Vatican Secretary of State Cardinal Fiellhaber wrote to his bishops' conference: "I must after what I encountered at the highest places in Rome—which I cannot communicate to you now—reserve to myself, in spite of everything, more toleration towards the new government which today is not only in a position of power—which our formulated positions could not reverse—but which achieved this power in a legal fashion."[12]

The signing of the concordat between Germany and the Vatican in 1933 was for von Strachwitz—as it was for most Catholics—convincing evidence of Hitler's positive attitude toward the church. The previous Weimer government had refused to sign a concordat as they could not agree to the Vatican's terms. Hitler of course could, as he had no real intention of abiding by it in the long term. For Hitler, treaties like the Munich Agreement with Chamberlain, the German/Russian Pact and the Concordat were merely pieces of paper. As he declared to Generals Krebs, Westphal and Field Marshal Keitel on 31 August 1944, "I guess I have proved plenty of times during my life that I am capable of achieving political success. I don't have to explain to anybody that I won't pass up an opportunity."[13] A treaty's intent and provisions were only important in as far as they suited either his short- or long-term goals. When they ceased to be helpful, they could be discarded without a moment's hesitation.

The Concordat didn't end Catholic opposition but it certainly muted it. Nor did it stop Hitler from persecuting and harassing Catholic priests, nuns or their institutions. Von Strachwitz would have been aware of this but would have probably put it down to the actions of petty officialdom and overzealous party functionaries, who were acting without the full knowledge or even consent of the Führer, whose attitudes and statements were clearly supportive of the church.

When Cardinal Bertram of Breslau made a statement warning against political extremism and the wickedness of racism, the Graf would have unreservedly agreed with him. Party member though he was, he did not consider himself a racist, and certainly did not support violence and hatred towards the Jews. Nor did he consider the Nazi Party as being at the political extreme, as by this time the party had become, by fair means and foul, mainstream.

So the Nationalist Socialist Party and Hitler in particular were in tune with many of Graf von Strachwitz's ideas and had achieved a great deal that was, in his eyes, good for Germany. That then leaves the question of why he joined Heinrich Himmler's Schutzstaffel (SS)? Party membership should have been sufficient, particularly as he was non-political. At least as far as political activism per se was concerned, there is nothing on record to suggest that von Strachwitz was anything more than a fairly passive member. Nor could he have been under great pressure to get heavily involved. The local party functionaries would have been singularly happy enough just to have someone with his title and local prominence as a member.

Why then did he join the SS? A major reason was his love of horses and the equestrian life. The Allgemeine SS (General SS) had 24 cavalry units (*Standarten*) with attached riding academies, which would certainly have been a big inducement for joining. Here horsemanship was the raison d'être and was highly prized, the military role being secondary. In fact, all the Standarten were disbanded at the beginning of the war,[14] and these units were specifically excluded when the Nuremberg War Crimes Tribunal declared the SS a criminal organisation.

He may also have been persuaded or pressured to join by Heinrich Himmler. In the early years of the SS, Himmler went to great pains to recruit members of the aristocracy in order to add prestige to his nascent SS formations. These aristocrats, like Graf von Strachwitz, would join the reserve Allgemeine SS in an honorary capacity as opposed to the full-time Security (SD) headquarters or guards units, such as the Leibstandarte SS Adolf Hitler Guard Regiment or the Totenkopf (Death's Head) units, some of which guarded the concentration camps.[15] The Allgemeine SS enabled people to join on a part-time or purely honorary basis without any time-consuming or onerous duties to perform. In 1938 it had over 480,000 members, though only 13,800 were full-time. Many industrialists also joined, hoping to curry favour with Heinrich Himmler. Nevertheless, although unconnected to the nefarious activities of the other branches of the SS, and far removed from the murderous activities of the concentration camps and execution squads, the General SS was part of the organisation, and membership in it was still membership of the SS. That said, at the time the General SS was a relatively innocuous organisation to which to belong, being comparable to service in the diplomatic corps or the army, where von Strachwitz held the rank of captain in the reserve. As he was already a party member, joining the General SS was not really a big step to take; moreover, it did confer some advantages such as the Reiter Standarts which gave him access to their riding academies. Von Strachwitz could not have known just how murderous and sinister the SS was to become. At the time that he joined, it was generally considered an elite organisation of the party, and for him involved no onerous duties.

Admitted with the SS no. 82857 he was given the starting rank of Untersturmführer (2nd Lieutenant) on 20 March 1934. He was then progressively promoted to Obersturmführer (1st Lieutenant) on 15 June 1934; Hauptsturmführer (captain) on 13 September 1936; Obersturmbannführer (lieutenant colonel) on 30 January 1943; and Standartenführer (colonel) on 1 September 1943. These were standard promotions given his length of service and his decorations for bravery. The Graf neither actively sought nor desired promotion within the SS. He rapidly gained high army rank, reaching major general (General Leutnant) which was a high achievement, and for him more than sufficient.

In order to consider the Graf's attitude to Hitler as a dictator, it must be remembered that von Strachwitz had little experience of a proper functioning democracy. The Kaiser had been an autocrat, despite having a parliament, while the immediate post-war period had been rent by insurrection, mutiny, revolution and turmoil. The Weimar Republic, Germany's only true democracy, was weak and buffeted by events over which it had little or no control. For many Germans, including the army, the experience was a bad one, and they looked for a strong leader to restore Germany's prominence and prosperity. For von Strachwitz, Hitler's assuming supreme power was not necessarily a matter for concern. He also judged Hitler by the standards set for normal people, not realising that Hitler was anything but normal. Hitler was totally devoid of any conscience, bereft of compassion, with absolutely no moral compass. Deeds that were evil by any normal standard were acceptable to him as either necessary or convenient in order to meet his aims and manifest destiny. If millions had to die, including his own people, then so be it, morality had nothing to do with it. His only true love, if it could be called that, was his belief in himself, his iron will and destiny. The lives and sacrifices of others meant absolutely nothing to him. He made his attitude clear in a meeting on 31 August 1944 with Generals Krebs and Westphal and Field Marshal Keitel, his toadying commander of the OKW:[16]

> I think it's pretty obvious that this war is no pleasure for me, for five years I have been separated from the rest of the world. I haven't been to the theatre. I haven't heard a concert, and haven't seen a film. I live only for the purpose of leading this fight because I know that if there is not an iron will behind it, this battle cannot be won.[17]

With millions dead, wounded, crippled, traumatised, homeless, tortured and suffering from hunger, fear and exhaustion, all Hitler could think of was is his own petty inconveniences. The death and suffering of others, even his own people, just didn't matter.

So ultimately Hyazinth Graf von Strachwitz was duped by Hitler, but he was not alone. Hitler also deceived world leaders, politicians, the army, the church and the German people.

NOTES

1. D. J. Goodspeed, *The German Wars* (Bonanza Books, NY, 1985).
2. Jan Friedmann, *Spiegel Online*, International Article.
3. Rohm, who was a homosexual, which Hitler conveniently overlooked, wanted the SA to become the people's army and the nation's bearer of arms, which the army naturally vehemently opposed. He also opposed Hitler on ideological grounds, believing that the socialism in the party's name actually meant what it said.
4. This oath was used by many German officers as an excuse not to act against Hitler, even after they knew of his grossly criminal actions and incompetence. For some, their personal code of honour far outweighed the greater imperative of morality and decency.
5. Knappe, *Soldat*.
6. Unlike his fellow dictator Joseph Stalin, who evoked fear and dislike not just with his immediate entourage but his family.
7. It didn't do Blomberg much good however, Hitler sacking him after complaints about his second marriage to a former prostitute.
8. John Cornwall, *Hitler's Pope* (Viking), pp.108–109. It is perhaps worth remembering that Hitler was an Austrian Catholic, albeit one who rejected his church.
9. *Hitler's Pope*.

10. *Hitler's Pope*, p.261, citing *Adolf Hitler: Monologue in Führerhauptquartier 1941–1944* (Hamburg, 1980), p.41.
11. *Hitler's Pope*, p.261.
12. *Hitler's Pope*, p.137.
13. Felix Gilbert (trans. and ed.), *Hitler Directs His War* (Award Books, 1950).
14. The Waffen SS, however, established several cavalry divisions during the war which performed effectively as mounted infantry. Hermann Fegelein, Hitler's future brother-in-law, whom he had executed in 1945, commanded a cavalry division in Russia. Two SS cavalry divisions—the 8th and 22nd—were annihilated in the siege of Budapest in 1945. Several other units fought the partisans in the east.
15. The Allgemeine SS consisted of all the branches except the Waffen SS but each branch used its own title, i.e. RSHA, SD, etc., and the Allgemeine SS attended to the part-timers.
16. Oberkommando de Wehrmacht—High Command of the Armed Forces.
17. Gilbert, *Hitler Directs His War*, p.161.

FIVE

THE INTER-WAR YEARS AND THE INVASION OF POLAND

In the mid-1920s, Graf von Strachwitz, bored with farm life, joined the 7th Reiter (Cavalry) Regiment as a reserve army captain, called Rittmeister in cavalry units. It was part of the 2nd Cavalry Division and was based in Breslau, the Silesian capital. His unit followed the traditions of the Imperial Army, which made it all the more attractive. It originally had the rather grandiose title of the "1st Silesian Life Guards Cuirassier Regiment The Great Elector" prior to World War I, when it was renamed with the more prosaic Reiterregiment 7.

Enlisting a little before him in the same regiment was Frederick von Mellenthin, a fellow Silesian who enlisted as a private in 1924. He rose to the rank of Generalmajor in World War II and was decorated with the Knight's Cross.[1] Another notable member was Rudolf Christoph Freiherr von Gersdorff, who also became a Generalmajor and awarded the Knight's Cross. He became a hero of the German resistance and a major plotter against Hitler. Martin Unrein also belonged to the regiment, becoming a GeneralLieutenant and Knight's Cross bearer; he served as the Regimental Adjutant in 1928. Overall it was a very conservative aristocratic unit, that was fully aware of its traditions and which tried to preserve all the old formalities of the Imperial Army. Graf von Strachwitz would have felt right at home in this atmosphere, which was probably strongly reminiscent of his former regiment the Garde du Corps.

The 2nd Cavalry Division itself was a bastion of the old guard and had as its commanders the cream of the aristocratic old school, such as Gerd von Rundstedt who reached the rank of Field Marshal under Hitler, and Ewald von Kleist, who was also created a field marshal and represented the very best and most honourable of the German officer corps. He was to command the panzer group to which the 16th Panzer Division and von Strachwitz were attached during Operation *Barbarossa*. He was also perhaps the only German Army commander who told the Gestapo, SS and SD unit commanders in his operational area to act correctly and treat the civilian population humanely. This they did, and over 800,000 Soviet Asians of various ethnic groups, including Cossacks, volunteered and fought for the Germans.[2]

As determined as some senior officers were to continue with cavalry divisions, events were slowly overtaking them. Colonel Heinz Guderian, later to be promoted to Colonel General, was heavily pushing for the establishment of panzer (armoured) divisions. He met stiff opposition from General Beck, the new chief of General Staff, whose attitude was neatly summed up when he said to Guderian, "No, no, I don't want anything to do with you people [armoured troops]. You move too fast for me."[3]

Despite this opposition, a Motorised Troop Command was established in June 1934 under the command of General Lutz, and on 15 October 1934, three panzer divisions were formed. These were the 1st Panzer Division under General Freiheer von Weichs, a future army group commander; the 2nd Panzer Division under Colonel Guderian, based at Wurzburg; and the 3rd Panzer Division under General Fessmann in Berlin. The armoured force displayed its power during manoeuvres in 1934, which Hyazinth von Strachwitz attended as an observer. It was not an outstanding success, but it was enough for the Graf. In the panzers he saw the future, the new cavalry. Over 300 Panzer Mark Is and a lesser number of Mark IIs, manoeuvring en masse made for an impressive and unforgettable sight. Unstoppable, they rolled forward, crushing obstacles, sweeping all before them, a mass of steel, seemingly invincible. It was heady stuff and von Strachwitz resolved to be part of this new armoured force. He could see that it was a breakthrough weapon par excellence, which could pursue a fleeing enemy, and rampage in its rear like the cavalry of old, and as the cavalry had been expected to perform, but failed to, in the last war.

Impressed as he was, he didn't see the hidden flaw that lay at the heart of the panzer force. The tanks were obsolete. The Panzer Mark I was really a tankette with a crew of two and armed with two 7.9mm machine guns. It was little more than an armoured mobile pillbox. The larger Panzer II wasn't much better with a three-man crew and one 20mm gun. Its success with the German Legion in the Spanish Civil War deluded the Germans into thinking it was suitable for use against other tanks. Both tanks were only effective when used in large numbers for shock effect, and then only if there was no significant opposition from larger enemy tanks or numbers of heavy antitank guns. Fortunately for the Germans their future enemies in the west, the British and French, had better and larger tanks, but used them in small units as infantry support vehicles. As for the Poles they just didn't have sufficient quantities of light or medium tanks. So the German Panzer arm was successful due to the mistakes of its enemies, and the superiority of its tactics, rather than because of the inherent quality of its armoured fighting vehicles. The Germans would have a larger version, the Panzer Mark IV—with a five-man crew and 75mm short-barrelled gun—ready for the French campaign, but not in enough numbers to make any difference. Moreover the short-barrelled gun had a low velocity, meaning that its use as an antitank weapon was limited.

Still, these factors did not concern von Strachwitz at this particular moment, although they certainly would when he came face to face with the vastly superior Russian T-34. That lay in the future. For now all that mattered was joining the new cavalry, the tank arm. On returning to the 7th Cavalry he immediately applied for a transfer. It was a slow process, but to his great joy his application was eventually successful and he was posted to the newly formed 2nd Panzer Regiment of the 1st Panzer Division. Unfortunately the only position available was that of a supply officer, and it says a lot for both his determination and basic humility that he was prepared to accept it. He could work his way into commanding a tank company or operational unit from there. Interestingly, had von Strachwitz remained with the 7th Cavalry Regiment he would have automatically been transferred to the panzer arm when the cavalry regiments were absorbed by the newly formed 2nd, 3rd, 4th and 6th Panzer Regiments, but his experience then may have been totally different.

The 2nd Panzer Regiment was stationed at Eisenach, an industrial and garrison town with a long military history going back to before World War I. In the early to mid-1930s a large new base complex was constructed there, comprising several large three-story barracks, mess halls, a training building, officers' mess, and administration buildings. The overall base commander was Colonel von Prittwitz Zu Gaffron, who would be killed leading the 15th Panzer Division at the battle of Tobruk in North Africa in 1941. The base was large, new and modern, and the Graf would have been more than impressed when he arrived in 1935. The 1st Panzer Division's headquarters, artillery and signals were at Weimar, and the 1st Panzer Regiment was located at Erfurt. The two infantry regiments belonging to the division were quartered at Weimar and Langensalza respectively. An anti-tank battalion joined the division at Eisenach in 1936. It was equipped with the woefully inadequate 37mm anti-tank gun, which earned the nickname the "door knocker" when in Russia due to its failings.

The 1st Panzer Division's tank company strength in 1935 was initially eight tanks, rising to a more acceptable 22 in 1936. However the companies were still equipped with the woefully inadequate Panzer I and II. Gunnery training was conducted at the Putlos gunnery range, company training at their home bases and regimental training at the Staumuchlen training grounds on the Seene. Supply officer though he may have been, the Graf nevertheless got involved in the platoon- and company-level training when he could. This required the good will of battalion and company commanders, but the Graf was determined and likeable enough to get their approval more often than not. His World War I Iron Crosses and aristocratic rank also gave him a certain cachet, which made his unofficial involvement a lot easier. In addition to this invaluable if unofficially sanctioned training, friendly contact in the officers' *casino* (mess) would have enabled the Graf to add to his expanding body of knowledge about his new arm of service.

In 1936, production commenced on the new Panzer Mark III, which was to be the mainstay of the Panzer force for several years to come. It had a five-man crew, a 50mm main gun, and would go through several upgrades—mainly in gun calibre and armour—over the next few years. It was a vast improvement over the Panzer I and II, but was found to be virtually helpless against the Russian KV-1 and KV-2 heavy tanks and T-34 medium tank from 1941 onwards. The Panzer III could not destroy the KV-1 or KV-2 at any range, and had to get almost suicidally close to a T-34 to have any chance of success. Again the quality of the superior leadership, training, discipline and tactics were to make all the difference until larger German medium and heavy tanks came along.

The first major operation undertaken by the 1st Panzer Division was the 1938 occupation of the Sudetenland. This was a strip of territory along the border of the recently created country of Czechoslovakia, of about 31,000 square kilometres containing three million ethnic Germans. Hitler had demanded that the Czechs cede the territory to the German Reich. After a tense conference at Munich, Britain and France had pledged not to intervene, so Hitler marched his troops in, among them Graf von Strachwitz, taking part in his first foreign invasion.

However there was no opposition.[4] On the contrary, the Sudetenlanders were ecstatic at the prospect of returning to the German fold. They had considered themselves second-class citizens in Czechoslovakia, and in many respects they were, so this was a homecoming for them. Graf von Strachwitz's car, as with every other vehicle in the division, was bedecked with flowers on General Guderian's orders,[5] and he was enormously surprised and pleased at the rapturous welcome he received. Girls in national dress offered drinks and threw flowers, while others gaily waved swastika flags. It was clearly a triumph for Hitler, and if von Strachwitz had had any doubts over Hitler's adventurous foreign policies, they would have been quickly, if only temporarily, dispelled by the welcoming crowd.

On his way, crossing the German-Czech border, von Strachwitz could not have failed to notice the extensive, but now redundant Czech frontier fortifications. They were extremely well built, with some considerable depth. Clearly a great deal of planning, expense, and work had gone into their construction. It was obviously designed not just to delay, but halt any German invasion. He might have grimly noted the price in blood that had now been spared. General Guderian also saw the defences and remarked how easily they could have been overcome. A classic difference in outlook between a General who just saw an objective that he knew could be taken and a junior officer who would have to take it, and pay the price in death or wounds in the process.

Later, an exultant Führer made his triumphant entry to the Sudetenland on a cold drizzly October day, and reviewed his troops, including the 1st Panzer Division. Hitler awarded all the participants with the Sudetenland Medal to commemorate the event. Panzerregiment 2 spent a quiet time in occupation duties based at Saatz and Kaaden, until 16 October 1938, when it returned to Eisenach. In the meantime, Poland was in the process of taking a slice of the disputed Texhen region of the now dismembered Czechoslovakia. That same year, 1st Panzer Division received its supply, medical, and repair units, all absolute necessities if the division was to go to war, and certainly an indicator that war could not be far off.

The following year, 1939, was to be momentous, with a long rollercoaster ride to war. With his eyes fixed firmly on Czechoslovakia's industrial capacity, especially its well-developed armaments industry, Hitler marched into the remaining rump of the country. On 15 March he declared it to be the Protectorate of Bohemia and Moravia. Occupied they might have been, but the Czechs did not have to pay the same price as the Sudetenlanders, many thousands of whom were soon to be killed or injured fighting for the Reich they had just joined. Britain and France did nothing, not wishing to go to war over a *fait accompli*, using the Munich Agreement that Chamberlain had signed with Hitler to avoid any military involvement. The Allies claimed that they were not ready for war, needing time to rearm and prepare. Of course, had they refused Hitler the Sudetenland, and stood alongside the large, well-armed Czech army, behind its border fortifications, the outcome might have been very different.

Hitler, his thirst for territory still unquenched, forced Lithuania to hand over Memel—its only port—on 22 March. The excuse was once again that there were ethnic Germans living in the area. Lithuania, being too small to fight, caved in to Hitler's demands. He also visited this city, giving what was for him, a very moderate speech. On 20 April, as part of 1st Panzer division, Graf von Strachwitz, took part in Hitler's birthday parade in Berlin, a grand expression of Germany's military might.

On 23–24 August the Soviet–German non-aggression pact was signed, surprising everyone, including the staunchly anti-communist Graf von Strachwitz. After all, one of the attractions of Hitler, and one reason that the Graf had joined the Nazi Party, was their uncompromising anti-bolshevism. Very few suspected that the pact was only agreed to by Hitler to gain time to defeat Poland without Russian interference. In fact a secret protocol was included for Russia to invade Poland from the east and allow for the eventual annexation of the Baltic states of Lithuania, Latvia and Estonia. The pact also meant that Hitler would only have to fight on the Western Front, giving him time to defeat France and Britain before turning on his real enemy, Russia. For his part Stalin was also playing for time, time that he needed to rearm and reorganise the Red Army before fighting Germany, which he fully expected to do before long. Time was all the more important for the Soviet dictator, for he had purged his officer corps in 1937, liquidating 35,000 of his finest officers. These included three of five marshals of the Soviet Union, 13 of 15 army commanders and over half his generals. At all levels from brigade commander upward, the leadership of the army was in a perilous state.

With Stalin ostensibly on side, Hitler could now turn to Poland. This was a long-term goal of both Hitler and the army. As early as 1920 General

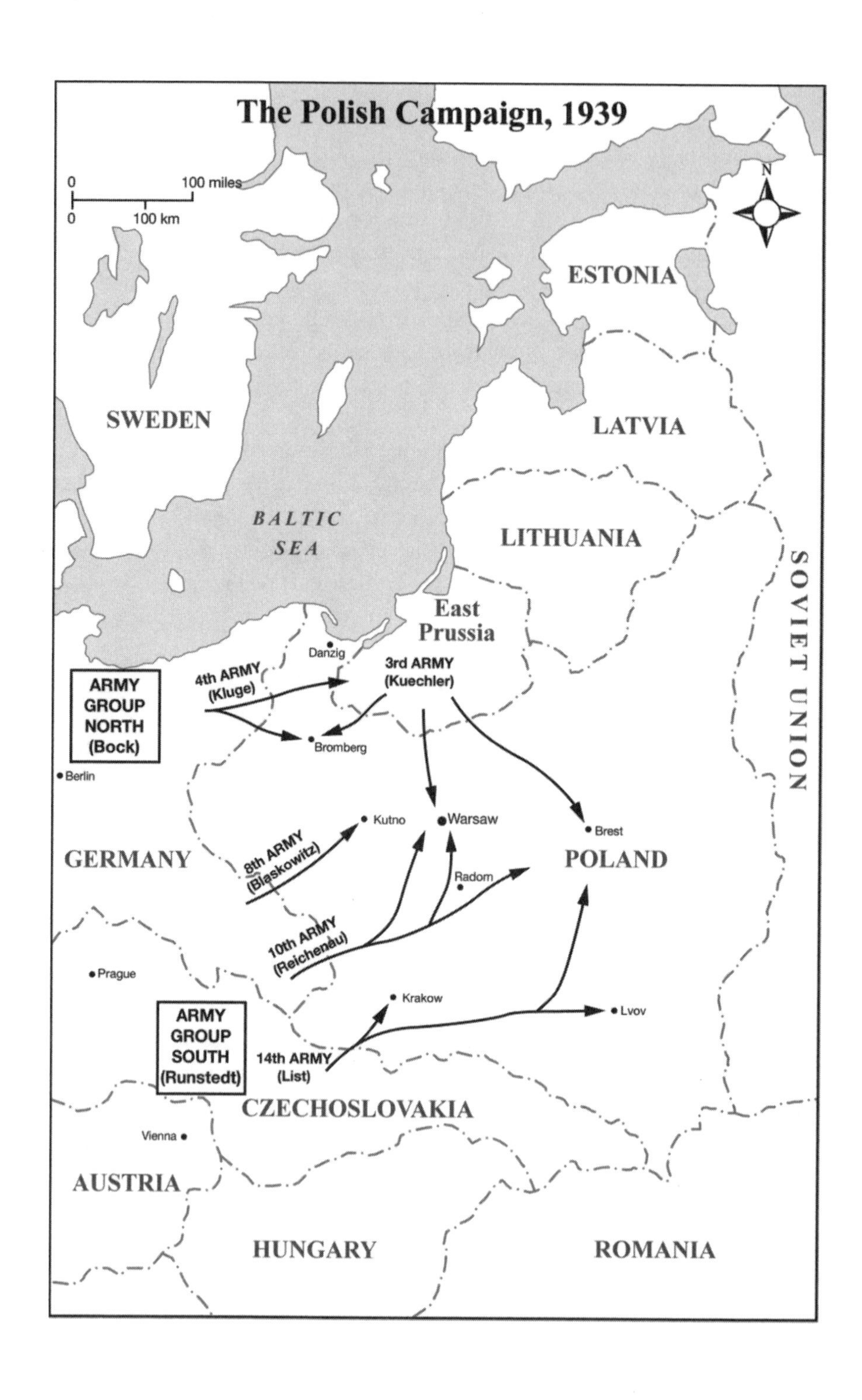

The Polish Campaign, 1939
0
100 miles
0
100 km
N
SWEDEN
ESTONIA
LATVIA
LITHUANIA
BALTIC SEA
East Prussia
SOVIET UNION
Danzig
ARMY GROUP NORTH (Bock)
4th ARMY (Kluge)
3rd ARMY (Kuechler)
Bromberg
Berlin
Kutno
Warsaw
Brest
GERMANY
8th ARMY (Blaskowitz)
POLAND
Radom
10th ARMY (Reichenau)
Prague
Krakow
Lvov
ARMY GROUP SOUTH (Runstedt)
14th ARMY (List)
CZECHOSLOVAKIA
Vienna
AUSTRIA
HUNGARY
ROMANIA

Hans von Seeckt, commander of the Troop Office declared, "Poland must be destroyed" and that Poland was Germany's "mortal enemy." An army document of March 1926 stated, "The return of the Polish Corridor and (eastern) Upper Silesia were principal goals of the German military."[6] Most Germans felt about eliminating the Polish Corridor separating Germany from East Prussia as the French did about recovering Alsace Lorraine. However, not all the military agreed with von Seeckt, as Guderian wrote in his memoirs: "We did not go light headedly to war and there was not one general who would not have advocated peace."[7] However there were very few generals who openly advocated peace, and despite their private reservations, if any, they were more concerned about the possible intervention of the British and French than about Poland or the criminal immorality of their actions. Von Strachwitz, for one, would certainly not have opposed the invasion of Poland. He had fought the Poles once already, and they were still just on the border, with their claims on Upper Silesia very much alive. The elimination of this threat, even if it was not an immediate one, would have been welcome to him.

Hitler did not feel he needed an excuse to invade, but for propaganda purposes the SS staged a fake attack on a German radio station at Gliewitz on 31 August, undertaken by German operatives wearing Polish uniforms. That it fooled no one except the German people was of no consequence.

At 4:45 a.m. on 1 September 1939, the aging German battleship *Schleswig-Holstein* opened fire on the Polish Westerplatte Fort in Danzig, the opening salvoes of what was to become World War II. Simultaneously, 62 German divisions, 1,850,000 men, 3,100 tanks, and 2,085 aircraft stormed across the border. Among them was the 1st Panzer Division, with Graf von Strachwitz serving as a supply officer. The division was in the XVI Panzer Corps which belonged to the Tenth Army under General von Reichenau, a committed Nazi. The Tenth Army was part of Army Group South commanded by General Gerd von Rundstedt, which also incorporated the Eighth Army under General Blaskowitz and the Fourteenth Army under Colonel General List. It also contained the Wehrmacht's strongest armoured force with 2,000 tanks, mostly Panzer Is and IIs, and 800 armoured cars.

The 1st Panzer was particularly well equipped with armoured fighting vehicles, its Panzer Regiment under Colonel Karl Keltsch having 93 Panzer Is, 122 Panzer IIs, 26 Panzer IIIs with the factory paint barely dry, and 59 Panzer IVs. Including command tanks, which carried extra radios but little or no armament, the division had 309 tanks.[8] Its tactics were soon to become familiar—heavy artillery and aircraft bombardment preceding massed tank attacks which were followed up by supporting infantry. The Polish infantry units—with very few anti-tank weapons and no aerial support—had no answer to this kind of assault and soon gave way.

Overall the Poles had seven frontline armies, with one army and miscellaneous units in reserve. They only had 660 tanks, of which 450 were tankettes, which were used in small packs for infantry support. In this way they were quickly overwhelmed. Their aircraft, mostly obsolete bi-planes, were largely destroyed on the ground. Where they did manage to take off, they bravely attacked, despite being outnumbered and outgunned. Many of their pilots took the opportunity to escape, reaching England from where they later took part in the Battle of Britain. The Poles were famed for their cavalry, of which they had 11 brigades, but contrary to popular belief they did not make suicidal attacks, sabres held bravely aloft, against German tanks. The only recorded instance of an attack against armour was when a Polish cavalry unit unexpectedly came up against a German armoured car column when, after a brief exchange of fire they quickly retreated.[9]

The 1st Panzer Division clashed with the Polish 7th Infantry Division, which fought bravely but, having little in the way of anti-tank guns, was overmatched. On 2 September near the village of Biala, 155mm howitzers of the Polish artillery destroyed three tanks, causing casualties among the crews. These were the division's first armour casualties of the war. The division then fought near Czestoehowa and Piotrkov, and by the 7th had reached the vicinity of Jomazow. Air support was provided by the Luftwaffe's VIII Fleigerkorps under General Major Wolfram von Richthofen, a relative of the famous World War I fighter ace, whose aircraft would support Graf von Strachwitz's tanks at the battle of Stalingrad. Aircraft from JG102 stationed at the newly built airfield outside the Graf's estate at Gross-Stein were also involved.

On 3 September Britain and France declared war on Germany. Graf von Strachwitz's worst fears were now realised. He had fought against, and suffered defeat, at the hands of the Allies in World War I, and he now faced the same enemies for the second time. No matter what the confident young German soldiers thought, von Strachwitz knew better—a hard struggle and uncertain future awaited.

The Poles weren't meekly rolling over. Despite being outnumbered and outgunned, they stood and fought. On 6 September two German Army Groups linked up at Lodz in the centre of Poland, trapping most of the Polish forces against the German border and cutting them off from supplies. The panzer divisions then struck, splitting the Polish forces into five separate pockets, in Pomerania, Pozan, Lodz, Krakow and Carpathia. With no hope of resupply or reinforcements, the Poles were forced to surrender. On 8 September the panzers were on the outskirts of Warsaw, having covered 180 kilometres in eight days.

At the battle of Kiennozia, 1st Panzer units attacked Polish screening forces, pushing them back until they reached well-prepared Polish positions. Both of the panzer regiments were dispersed during the attack, cut off from their supporting infantry and surrounded. A large number of German tanks were disabled, some by artillery fire, others through shedding tracks or mechanical failure. The panzer troops moved what tanks and men they could forward to provide cover for the tanks. This included the Graf, with his supply echelon fighting as infantry.

They had a bad and sleepless night as the Poles tried to infiltrate their positions. Firefights took place at close quarters with the Graf firing at the enemy gun flashes that seemed only metres away. Occasionally someone would cry out with pain, hit by random fire, the medics feeling their way around to find the wounded. Flares rained upwards, bursting in an eerie light, showing dark shadows of Polish troops closing in. Sustained fire brought them down, then darkness cloaked the scene once again. This went on repeatedly, with the Poles determined to finish the Germans off before daylight and possible relief. The Germans' night fighting skills were poor, which resulted in unnecessary casualties, a lesson the Graf took on board for the future. Finally the Poles abandoned their infiltration attacks and brought forward their artillery as close as they dared. As dawn slowly crept over the lines, von Strachwitz and the other defenders, red-eyed and exhausted, gripped their weapons, waiting for the attack. Instead the Poles, using their artillery as anti-tank guns, began firing on the disabled tanks, destroying them one by one.

With daylight, German artillery intervened, laying down a curtain of fire, silencing the Polish guns. With their panzers up front, the Germans attacked back toward their own lines. Von Strachwitz found himself in the unfamiliar role of a panzer grenadier, attacking behind the tanks. He led his mixed group of supply clerks, cooks, drivers, and crews from disabled tanks, with a panache born of his old cavalry days, yelling and firing from the hip. The stunned Poles gave way and the Germans broke through safely to their supports. On 10 September Colonel Keltsch recommended Graf von Strachwitz for the Iron Cross (2nd Class), which would be worn as a clasp to the Iron Cross (2nd Class) he had earned in World War I.

Hard fighting followed in the Petrikan area with several Mark Is and Mark IIs and a more valuable Panzer IV destroyed, and several more temporarily disabled. A Polish regiment was routed and its Colonel and many of the men captured. As the Poles retreated they left many scattered units behind, and these soon became a problem for the advancing Germans. Many surrendered when they realized the hopelessness of reaching the safety of their own lines, while others fought on, ambushing couriers and small supply units, and had to be eliminated by a concerted effort.

Polish civilians also occasionally took part in the fighting as Alexander Stahlberg, a panzer division officer, recounts:

> I was on my motorbike on the way to divisional headquarters. A crowd of German soldiers was standing in the middle of a village, gazing silently in one direction. I stopped and asked someone what was going on. "An execution," came the answer. When the village was occupied, shots had been fired from an attic and there had been losses. The house had been stormed and two marksmen had been found in the attic. They had been wearing civilian clothes without insignia or armbands, their weapons and empty cartridge cases had been found: hunting guns, cases of shotgun cartridges. This was a clear infringement of the international rules of the Hague Convention on land warfare. The divisional court martial had met, the two Poles had confessed, and the sentence was now being carried out. I looked over the heads of the curious onlookers. At that moment the salvo from the firing squad cracked out: the first deaths I witnessed in the war.[10]

It is noteworthy that these Germans abided by the Hague Convention and convened a court-martial, which stands in sharp contrast to the actions of SS units in Poland, and both army and SS units in Russia later in the war, where partisans and innocent civilians were summarily executed.

The Polish army launched a major counterattack at Bzura and the 1st Panzer Division was involved in heavy fighting. Once more it suffered armoured losses including Panzer IIIs. The Germans surrounded the Poles at Bzura and closed in, while the Luftwaffe mercilessly battered them from the air.

The Poles withdrew for a last stand in the east of the country, but on 17 September Russia invaded Poland from the east with 1.5 million men and 6,000 tanks, forcing the gallant Poles to fight on two fronts. It was the death knell for their army. On 24 September Warsaw was bombed by massed aircraft, and the bombing continued until the city surrendered. The heart of the Polish capital was ripped apart. On the 27th, after 18 days of aerial and artillery bombardment, Warsaw surrendered. The 1st Panzer went on towards the demarcation line with the advancing Red Army, meeting little resistance as it did so. Isolated pockets continued to hold out, such as Polish Admiral Unrug's garrison on the Hela Peninsula, which capitulated on 1 October, while the remaining Polish forces surrendered near Luch on the 3rd. The war cost the Poles 700,000 surrendered to the Germans and 200,000 to the Soviets, most of whom were sent to Siberia. Their exact number of dead is not known, but would have been close to 60,000. The Germans for their part lost 10,000 dead and, 30,000 wounded.

The Germans and Russians then dismembered Poland's carcass between them. The Russians took a large swathe of mostly agricultural territory, but which included the important fortress city of Brest Litovsk which would cost the Germans much blood to take in 1941. Stalin then proceeded to round up any possible opponents and class enemies of his regime, which included the aristocracy, intelligentsia, businessmen, priests, government officials, politicians and officers—many of whom would be found buried in mass graves by the Germans at Katyn, after they invaded the Soviet Union. He also rounded up anyone who had served in the Polish Army during the Soviet invasion of Poland in 1920, and sent them to Siberia for a lingering death. Stalin had a long and bitter memory.

The Germans had begun engaging in atrocities much earlier. Virtually a few days after the invasion, Jews were rounded up, with some being summarily murdered, as were members of the Polish intelligentsia and ruling classes. The Poles were to be left as leaderless slaves, in the service of the Reich. General Blaskowitz, the commander of the Eighth Army, to his credit, protested, sending a memo of his objections to be forwarded to Hitler. The memorandum expressed his concerns about the shooting and arrests of Jews and Poles without due process. He was concerned about his soldiers' discipline and morale after seeing these incidents (not the inherent criminality of the actions, but perhaps he thought citing these would be a waste of time). His efforts to stop them were unsuccessful, as the SS men involved claimed they were acting under Himmler's orders. When Major Engel, Hitler's army adjutant, handed the memo to Hitler, the Führer promptly launched into a tirade against the army in general, and Blaskowitz in particular, ranting that he would relieve Blaskowitz of his command.[11]

For von Strachwitz, without an operational command, and ostensibly ensconced in the rear area, there was—except in a few instances—very little fighting. However, in his own inimitable way he went off on his own to the front and often beyond, as the front was extremely fluid. He took great personal risks in doing this, often finding himself alone without help of any kind should he get himself into trouble, which on one occasion he did. Alone in his vehicle on a dirt road in a forest, he was fired upon by a sniper. He quickly piled out of his car, but as he was armed with only a pistol, he was not in a position to do much, besides which he couldn't see his assailant. Tense moments passed. He made a move to the rear of the car when another shot rang out. There was still no sign of the enemy as the Graf anxiously looked through the trees. He waited for what seemed an eternity, then made a dash for the nearby trees behind him. Another shot rang out, but he made it safely to cover. He then decided on a flanking movement further along where he could cross the road and take his enemy by surprise in the rear. Movement had to be painfully slow but he eventually crossed, and then silently waited for any sign of movement. Nothing stirred. A half-hour ticked by. He rose to his feet and was about to move when the sound of a vehicle stopped him. A German light armoured car from his division drove up and stopped next to his car. Its commander was carelessly leaning out of the turret but he drew no fire, so von Strachwitz stepped out onto the road. Of the sniper there was no sign. His little adventure was over with his mysterious attacker simply vanishing.

This little episode didn't stop his movements at, or near the front, as his insatiable curiosity and cavalry spirit meant that he couldn't behave in any other way. These unofficial reconnaissance trips did have positive results, however, as he often spotted the enemy, sometimes coming under fire, and just as importantly found out where the enemy wasn't, which proved useful in finding gaps in their lines. He also saw the shambolic agony of war. Smashed Polish supply columns, wrecked smouldering tanks, bloodied carcasses of dead horses, Polish and German dead, and the despairing, dusty columns of Polish prisoners of war, trudging despondently to the rear. Equally sad were the long columns of helpless refugees—old men, women and children, burdened by whatever possessions they could carry – seeking to escape the fighting and the advancing Germans.

His opinion that swift penetrating attacks to the enemy's rear were vital for a panzer division, was now confirmed. This, coupled with surprise, and the shock of armoured attack, was the most effective way of waging war. He would further hone these lessons in France, and apply them with devastating effect in Russia.

NOTES

1. He is noted for his book *Panzer Battles*, first published in 1955, an excellent treatise on the war with Russia.
2. For this von Kleist was sentenced by the Soviets to 25 years' imprisonment. He died in captivity while many generals who were really guilty lived in peaceful retirement.
3. General Heinz Guderian, *Panzer Leader* (Futura Publications, 1952), p.32.
4. Nor was there anyone to actively oppose the move on the German side, except for General Beck, who, honourable man that he was, resigned in protest. If he had hoped other generals would follow his example, he would have been sadly disappointed.
5. Guderian used this same tactic during the annexation of Austria in March 1938, asking for Hitler's permission to do so again.
6. Alexander B. Rossino, *Hitler Strikes Poland.*
7. Heinz Guderian, *Panzer Leader*, p.66.
8. http://www.achtungpanzer.com/, excellent website dedicated to the German armoured force in WWII.
9. Perpetuating the myth of Polish sabres against German Panzers suited both the Poles and the Germans. For the Poles it was an example of raw but hopeless courage, and for the Germans, Polish officers' ineptitude and disregard for their own men's lives.
10. Alexander Stahlberg (trans. Patricia Crampton), *Bounden Duty: The Memories of a German Officer 1932–45* (Brassey UK, 1990).
11. General Blaskowitz was relieved of his command on 29 May 1940 but later reinstated in command posts well below his abilities. He did however receive the Oak Leaves and Swords to the Knight's Cross. He was put on trial at Nuremberg along with the entire German High Command but died, ostensibly by suicide (others assert he was murdered) while in captivity. Field Marshal von Kluge also protested but only verbally to Hitler's adjutant Gerhard Engel. He told Engel, "There had been some very bad goings on in Poland and that he had to intervene personally on several occasions, for example in Modlin and Lublin." Engel reported von Kluge's comments to the Führer. Gerhard Engel, *At the Heart of the Reich* (Greenhill Books, 2005), p.113.

SIX

THE BATTLE OF FRANCE

WHILE THE GERMANS WERE BUSILY BATTERING POLAND into submission the French were largely content to do nothing. Certainly they had to complete their mobilisation, but they nevertheless had sufficient troops and tanks on the ground to make life exceedingly difficult for the Germans, so as to force them to take some divisions from Poland to reinforce the mere 28 divisions they had guarding their frontiers. The French excuse was that they were waiting for the British Expeditionary Force (BEF) to come over and deploy for action. They did manage to make an incursion into Germany, but it was only of short duration, and far too small to have any effect or unduly worry the Germans. The Poles, who had every right to expect some assistance, and planned their strategy on receiving some, were cruelly disappointed. It was all the more disappointing as France had, to quote General Heinz Guderian:

> The strongest land army in Western Europe, France, possessed the numerically strongest tank force in Western Europe. The combined Anglo–French forces in the West in May 1940 disposed some 4,000 armoured vehicles: the German Army at that time had 2,800, including armoured reconnaissance cars; and when the attack was launched only 2,200 of these were available for the operation.[1]

He went on to say that the "French tanks were superior to the German ones both in armour and gun calibre, though admittedly inferior in control facilities and speed."[2]

With better leadership and tactics the French could and should have smashed the German panzer arm but, still traumatised by memories of World War I, they lacked the motivation for a hard-fought war. They were more than happy to sit behind their heavily fortified Maginot Line and hold the Germans off. They applied World War I tactics to their armoured force, using it in separated, small amounts as infantry support, rather than en masse as a hard-hitting break-through or annihilation force. Used in this way, even their superior tanks could not match the massed might of the German panzers. Nevertheless as reluctant to fight as their men may have been, the French High Command was still supremely confident it could halt the German offensive when it came.

The British for their part were only slightly more motivated, and the will to tear out the heart of the Hun was sorely lacking. As for their tank force, it was used in the same manner as the French and was therefore no match for the Germans. All this would change, but only after the Battle of France was over.

Hitler moved his divisions from Poland to the West and waited. The winter of 1939/40 was bitterly cold and all sides seemed content to try and keep warm by staying indoors and avoid the inconvenience of fighting. The Allies called it the Phoney War, and the Germans the Sitzkreig.

The Allies considered several options. One was to move their forces along Belgium's main line of defence running from Antwerp to the Meuse, provided the Belgians invited them in before the Germans invaded. The second option was to advance on the left to the line of the Scheldt as far as Walcheren and level up with the Belgians at Antwerp while advancing along the Meuse from Grivet to Namur. The Belgians were understandably less than enthusiastic with this plan, as it meant abandoning most of their country to the Germans. The third option, and the one adopted as a compromise, was to advance to the River Dyle with a defence line from Antwerp through Wause to Namier. The Belgians assured the French commander, Marshal Maurice Gamelin, that they would construct defences along the Dyle. This plan shortened the line by 70+ kilometres leaving 20 divisions for a strategic reserve.[3]

All these options were defensive in nature. A war of manoeuvre, to encircle and destroy the German invaders was never envisaged. France's credo in WWI had been the offensive and attack, but it had had that concept knocked out of it by the bloody battles, mutiny and near-defeat in the war.

Not to be outdone in lacking imagination, the Germans came up with a variation of the old Schlieffen Plan that had been used in a modified version in the previous war. The changes were not as bold as had been planned for World War I. The Germans would still invade poor little Belgium, and this time Holland as well, scythe around into France, capture whatever territory they could, and finally destroy the Allied armies coming to meet them. If it all sounded very simple and obvious, it was. It was not intended to end the war as quickly as von Schlieffen's original plan had been.[4]

So the scene was set for a long drawn-out slugging match, until German General Erich von Manstein came along with his own variation, which was to use the Schlieffen-like offensive as a feint, but launch the real attack behind the Allied armies once they had moved toward Belgium. His thrust, dubbed "Sichelschnitt" (sickle stroke) would be launched through the Ardennes Forest region, which the French considered impassable for tanks. Von Manstein's criticisms of the German High Command's plan, and persistence in advocating his own, annoyed the German planners, so they relegated him out of the way by giving him command of an Infantry Corps and hoped he would finally keep silent. Not to be undone, while on a courtesy visit to Hitler as a new corps commander, von Manstein outlined his plan to the Führer, who liked it. Hitler then passed it on for adoption, much to the chagrin of his planners. He may have been given some extra incentive to adopt it after some Luftwaffe staff officers whose aircraft crashed with details of the original plans, fell into Allied hands. Either way, it turned out to be one of Adolf Hitler's better decisions.

While the phony war was ebbing slowly away, Hyazinth von Strachwitz and the 1st Panzer Division concerned themselves with repair and maintenance of equipment after the rigours of the Polish campaign. Sorting out their supplies, which involved von Strachwitz directly, and above all in training exercises at all levels. Decorations were also given out, with Graf von Strachwitz being given his Iron Cross (2nd Class), which had been awarded for his actions in Poland. His award consisted of the Third Reich's German eagle clasp to be appended to the buttonhole ribbon of his Iron Cross (2nd Class) from World War I.

He was preparing to meet his old foe, the French, and this time was more confident of victory. The German Army was bloodied, and had gained valuable experience fighting the Poles. They had learned from their mistakes and there had been many, including the use of tanks in urban combat. The 4th Panzer Division had lost 60 tanks fighting in Warsaw's outer suburbs, so standard practice was now to use infantry in street fighting, and tanks only if absolutely necessary. It was a valuable dictum but one that would be continually abused by infantry commanders, unaware of a tank's limitations in built-up areas. They also learnt the limitations of their weapons and had a greater appreciation of what could or could not be achieved, and how to use them to their best advantage.

Von Strachwitz's eldest son, also called Hyazinth, would also be joining his father in the French campaign. He too had joined the Panzer arm and was commissioned as a 2nd Lieutenant in the 16th Panzer Regiment as a platoon commander. This was a source of both pride and concern for von Strachwitz as his son was now following in his father's footsteps, by joining not only the army but a panzer division. He was not only following in the cavalry tradition, but being in a tank also increased his survivability over leading from the front in the infantry, where the ultimate casualty rate was around 96%.

On 1 March 1940, the 54-year-old Generalmajor Freidrich Kirchner took over command of the division. Born in 1893 he was only eight years older than von Strachwitz, but had made a career in the military, serving in the Reichswehr between the wars when the Graf had returned to his estates. He was a very capable, if not flamboyant, commander of armour, and would rise to the rank of General of Panzer Troops, as corps commander, and be awarded the Knight's Cross with Oak Leaves and Swords. He would also be injured in the French campaign when a German vehicle ran over one of his legs.[5] Von Strachwitz did not get to meet his new commander at the time, as he was in hospital suffering from meningitis. The Pomeranian Colonel Johannes Nedtwig, a future 5th Panzer Division commander, commanded the 1st Panzer Regiment. Lt. Colonel Hero Breusing commanded the 2nd Panzer Regiment. He would go on to command the 122nd Infantry Division as a Generalmajor. Graf von Strachwitz was in this regiment's 1st Battalion. The infantry battalions had one or two companies equipped with half-tracked armoured personnel carriers (APCs), known as *Schutzenspahwagons* (SPWs), which were a major innovation. The quantity was increased to equip a full battalion later in the war but there were never enough to go around to equip a regiment, so panzer divisions still had to rely on trucks as the main means of transport for their infantry. Increasingly, the infantry would ride on the tanks themselves.

The division was then transferred to the Mosel and southern Eifel where it was attached to the XIX Motorised Corps commanded by General Heinz Guderian.

On 9 May Adolf Hitler arrived at his forward HQ, dubbed the Eagle's Nest, to direct Operation *Case Gelb* (yellow), the attack in the west. On the same day Graf von Strachwitz returned from another sojourn in hospital, where he had been since 28 April for a foot injury. All along the frontier, German forces moved up to their assembly positions for the invasion. The French had timely warning provided by their military attaché in Switzerland, as well as by aerial reconnaissance. In any case, the massive amount of activity on the German side of the border could not be missed. For instance, the buildup for the thrust through the Ardennes created an almost stationary line up of vehicles from Koblenz to the border. The noise alone, if nothing else, should have woken French General Maurice Gamelin up to the fact that something was afoot.

At 4:00 a.m. on 10 May, the 75 German divisions of the invasion force attacked across a 280-kilometre front into Holland, Belgium, Luxembourg and France, with air strikes, infantry assaults, armoured thrusts and paratroop landings. The last included a particularly daring drop on top of the supposedly impenetrable Belgium fortress of Eben Emael. On the same day, Great Britain replaced its pacifist Prime Minister, Neville Chamberlain, with the pugnacious Winston Churchill.

The thrust through the Ardennes was a risky gamble involving five armoured and three motorised divisions, comprising 1,500 armoured vehicles and 130,000 men with thousands of trucks, cars and motorcycles, clogging up the roads in a long winding traffic jam that invited aerial attack. But none came, because Gamelin regarded the Ardennes as "Europe's best tank obstacle."[6]

The spearhead of the Ardennes thrust was General Guderian's XIX Corps, which included the 1st Panzer Division with Graf von Strachwitz still serving as a supply officer. It crossed the Luxembourg frontier at 5:30 a.m. near Wallendorf and headed for Martelange. With its tanks leading the way it attacked the fortifications on either side of Neufchâteau where it engaged the Belgian Chasseurs Ardennais and units of French cavalry, which quickly withdrew after a brief firefight. The division then took Bertix but was halted at Bouillon by strong French resistance, which lasted throughout the night.

The following morning at 7:45 a.m., 1st Panzers' 1st Infantry regiment, led by Lieutenant Colonel Balck, mounted a strong attack, supported by heavy artillery fire, which breached the French defences and took the town. Hermann Balck was a Prussian who would rapidly rise to become a General of Panzer troops and an army commander. He was one of the elite few to be awarded the Knight's Cross with Oak Leaves, Swords and Diamonds.

The bridge over the Samois had been destroyed, so the engineers began constructing a new one. Later in the day, General Guderian paid a visit and experienced his first air attack as French aircraft attempted to destroy 1st Panzer's bridge.[7] The 1st Panzer Regiment set up its HQ at a small hotel north of Bouillon, and Guderian paid another visit only to be bombed again, this time by Belgian planes attacking the panzer regiments' encampment.

By 13 May, Guderian's XIX Corps had crossed the Meuse at Sedan. They were supported by twelve squadrons of Junkers 87 Stuka dive-bombers that attacked from 8:00 a.m. to 4:00 p.m. in continuous waves. These unceasing attacks had a devastating effect on French morale, far in excess of the actual damage inflicted. The Stukas were equipped with sirens that wailed like a banshee as they dived. This frayed the nerves, especially with the knowledge that at the end would be an explosion that could tear someone apart. The artillery crews dived for cover and refused to fire their guns, which were left exposed in the open. The infantry cowered trembling in their trenches, and offered very little resistance. So the Germans crossed the river virtually unopposed. Their penetration into the French rear sowed panic among the second-line troops who simply fled. The French guns, which should have caused fearful execution at the German crossing points, were simply abandoned. Thousands of French soldiers were captured, having surrendered or simply been overtaken by the advancing Germans.

On 14 May, the 1st Panzer took Chehery, while in Holland the Luftwaffe bombed an almost defenceless Rotterdam, killing 30,000 innocent civilians. The French sent in General Charles de Gaulle to lead a counterattack against the growing panzer bulge in their midst. De Gaulle, who considered himself an armoured commander par excellence, was easily repulsed.

At Chehery, 1st Panzer destroyed 50 French tanks, so a pleased Guderian paid them another visit. Soon after he had left, German Stukas dive-bombed 1st Panzer positions by mistake, causing heavy casualties. Guderian was still bringing the bombers with him.

Together with the 2nd Panzer Division, 1st Panzer then headed for the Ardennes canal, crossing and capturing Snigly and Vendresse in quick succession despite ferocious French opposition, which caused infantry casualties and tank losses.

On 16 May, Guderian drove to 1st Panzer's HQ to ascertain the current position. He was told the situation was still unclear but heavy fighting had

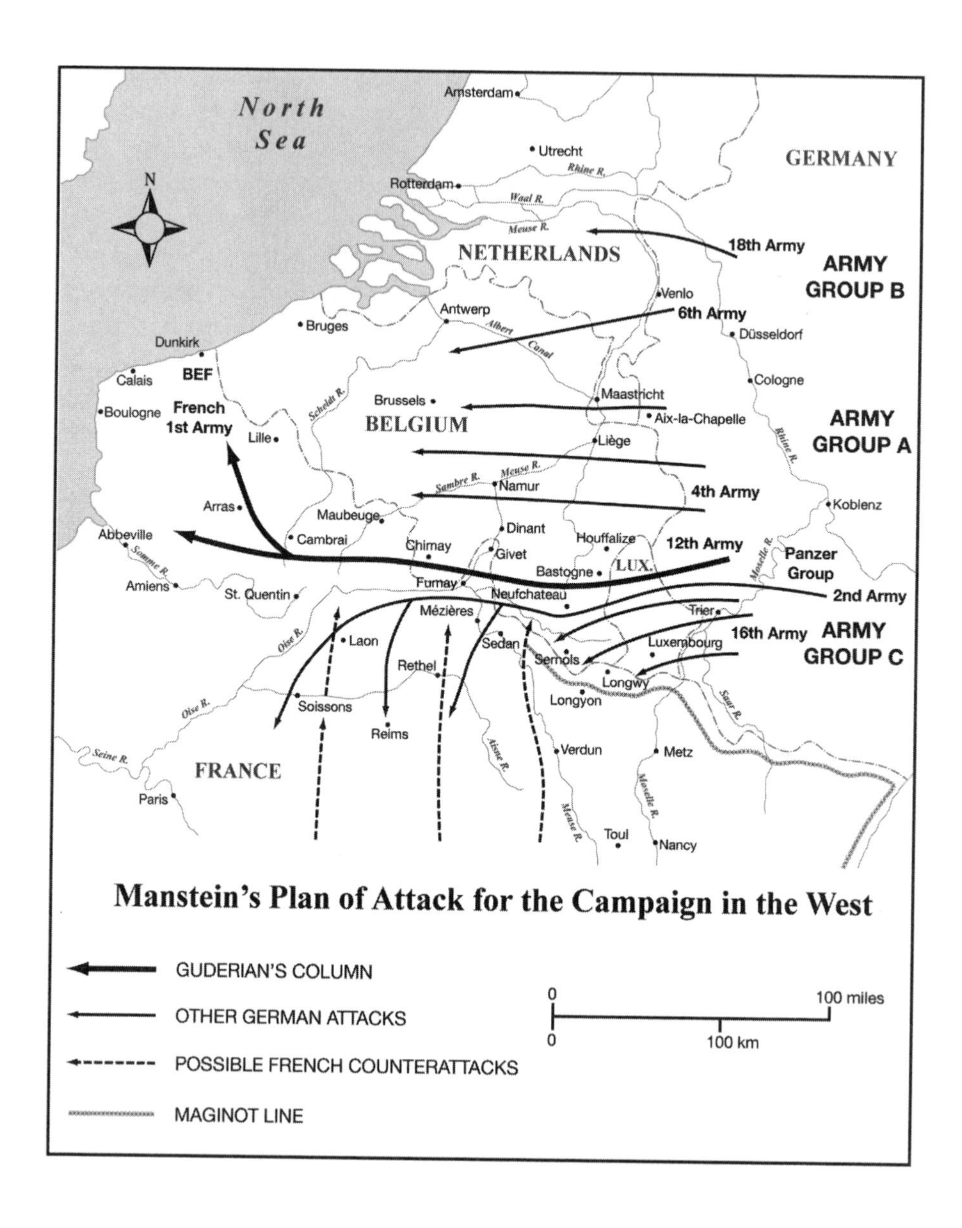

Manstein's Plan of Attack for the Campaign in the West

been reported at Bouvellemont. He dashed there, and in his memoirs described the situation he found:

> In the main street of the burning village I found the regimental commander, Lieutenant Colonel Balck, and let him describe the events of the previous night to me. The troops were over-tired, having had no real rest since the 9th of May. Ammunition was running low. The men in the front line were falling asleep in their slit trenches, Balck himself, in wind jacket and with a knotty stick in his hand, told me that the capture of the village had only succeeded because when his officers complained against the continuation of the attack, he had replied: "In that case I'll take the place on my own!" and had moved off. His men had therefore followed him. His dirty face and his red-rimmed eyes showed that he had spent a hard day and a sleepless night. For his doings on that day he was to receive the Knight's Cross.[8]

On 17 May, French Prime Minister Paul Reynaud[9] replaced General Gamelin with General Maxime Weygand, who was a much better soldier than Gamelin, albeit more aged. He tried manfully to restore the situation, even dismissing 15 French generals to try and instill some fighting spirit into the remainder, but it was to no avail. On the same day, General Guderian met with his superior, General von Kleist, which developed into a blazing row.

> I was personally to report to General von Kleist who would come to see me at my airstrip at 07:00 hours. He was there punctually and without even wishing me a good morning, began in very violent terms to berate me for having disobeyed orders. He did not see fit to waste a word of praise on the performance of the troops. When the first storm was passed, and he had stopped to draw breath, I asked that I might be relieved of my command. General von Kleist was momentarily taken aback, but then nodded and ordered me to hand over my command to the most senior general in my corps. And that was the end of our conversation.[10]

Reading his account one would believe that Guderian was serenely calm and polite throughout. He not only had a fiery temper—he even had screaming matches with Hitler later in the war—but was also extremely argumentative and demanding, as he showed during the opening months of Operation *Barbarossa*. He was in addition a prickly, stubborn and difficult subordinate, so it is inconceivable that he did not fly back at von Kleist and give as good as he got. His offer of resignation was probably angrily shouted out, rather than given calmly as his memoir recounts. In the event Colonel-General von Rundstedt, the army group commander, sent Colonel-General List to calm the situation and stop Guderian's resignation from going ahead.

The altercation between von Kleist and Guderian would poison future relations between the two men. This became noticeable during the invasion of Russia when each general commanded his own panzer group, with von Strachwitz then serving in von Kleist's group. It made for poor cooperation between the two, when cooperation, given the stretched resources of the Germans, was paramount.

While the generals were dealing with their differences, the war went on, and 1st Panzer kept up its advance to capture Ribemont and Crécy, the site of the famous battle between the French and the English. It then crossed the Oise and established a bridgehead across the Somme near Perrone, an advance so rapid that several French staff officers were captured while venturing towards Perrone to ascertain what was going on.[11] The 1st Panzer attacked Amiens on 20 May, capturing it by midday, then continued to advance another 8 kilometres. Its progress was continuously stalled by long columns of refugees filling the roads, who were too slow to escape the Germans. These civilians didn't know which way to flee and were often overtaken by the fighting, being strafed and bombed by mistake. They became a familiar sight for von Strachwitz as he often moved along with the spearheads. He just couldn't keep himself back and became a familiar sight to the front-line troops, particularly as his decorations had not yet become commonplace, and he wore a thin black moustache which was unusual among German officers.

The next objectives were the French channel ports, with 1st Panzer given the objective of taking Calais. To assist it, Guderian gave it the Infantry Regiment Grossdeutschland which—after it became a panzergrenadier division—would later become Graf von Strachwitz's parent unit. Fierce fighting took place at Desvres south of Boulogne where some British units were encountered. The Royal Air Force made its presence known with several strafing and bombing attacks. While still on its approach march to Calais, Guderian diverted the division to Dunkirk, then Gravelines. Meanwhile the Leibstandarte-SS Adolf Hitler (Adolf Hitler's SS Bodyguard) was attached to Guderian's Panzer Corps, a unit von Strachwitz would fight alongside in the battles around Kharkov in the Ukraine.

Kirchner's division reached the Aa Canal on 25 May and was abruptly ordered to halt. This puzzled von Strachwitz and the other officers of the division, for there seemed no reason for it. Certainly the men were tired and the vehicles needed maintenance, but not urgently so, and not enough to halt the division in mid-march. In fact all the panzer divisions had been halted, on Hitler's personal orders. Debate still goes on as to the reason for the halt. One possibility was that he wished to show good will to the British before his peace offer in the Reichstag, but if that was the case then why did he give in to Goering's boasting that the Luftwaffe would destroy the British Expeditionary Force from the air. One reason Hitler put forward was that the ground was not suitable for tanks, but his commanders would have told him otherwise. It may have been nervousness about letting his panzers become involved in a slugging match in built-up areas, on soft ground, against a desperate BEF. He would have envisaged that the casualties to his precious panzers would have been enormous. This was important, as already he was planning a massive expansion of the panzer force and would need every tank available to create viable new divisions. If the Luftwaffe could carry out the destruction of the British with no casualties on the ground, then so much the better. Goering boasted that it could be done, and Hitler wanted to believe him. In some ways this made sense. Bombing helpless troops into submission was an easy option. Sinking large evacuation ships would cause enormous casualties, as in fact happened when the *Lancastria* was sunk on 16 June, during the final evacuations from France, with a loss of 3,000 men. However it was also the riskier option with a far greater chance of allowing the BEF to escape, which is what happened. The RAF was not prepared to let bombers attack unopposed, and swarmed in with the courage of desperation. The Luftwaffe spent more time defending itself than attacking the troops. Just as importantly the British used some 800 small craft, as well as large ones, in the evacuation. These small boats were hard to strafe and almost impossible to bomb, and when they were sunk, it only resulted in the loss of a small number of lives. In all, the amazing total of 338,000 troops—mainly British but also French and Poles—were evacuated. Britain had managed, through Hitler's blunder, and its own astounding resourcefulness, to save its army to fight another day.

Graf von Strachwitz and the men of the 1st Panzer division watched as the Luftwaffe bombers and fighters went in, weaving, diving, attacking and strafing, but also engaging in endless dogfights with the defending British aircraft. The air battles raged across the sky, with planes trailing long plumes of smoke and flame and smashing into the earth nearby. It was an impressive sight, but he could only wonder how effective the bombing was, given the stiff opposition the Luftwaffe had encountered. Later he saw the devastating effects of the Stuka attacks in Russia, but these were mostly without Russian fighter opposition, so the Germans had free rein to bomb accurately and often. When Adolf Hitler finally gave his panzers the order to advance on 26 May the evacuation was all but over. Only the debris, abandoned vehicles, and equipment of the defeated British remained. Mostly, only French prisoners were taken. They had defended the perimeter in heroic self-sacrifice to allow the British rearguard under Sir Harold Alexander to finally get away. When well led and motivated, the French could, and did, fight extremely well. Calais fell to the 10th Panzer Division on 26 May with 20,000 prisoners taken, of whom 4,000 were British, while 1st Panzer went on to attack Gravelines, taking it on 29 May.

Guderian was given his own Panzer Group on 28 May in recognition for his superlative results and command abilities. 1st Panzer was then transferred to the XXXIV Army Corps of the Panzer Group. The Corps also had the 2nd Panzer Division and the 29th (Motorised) Infantry Division. The term "motorised" was used to denote one of the new divisions that used trucks for all its transport needs. The other infantry divisions, the majority, relied on horses and wagons with only a small number of trucks, cars and motorcycles. So much for the Germans being a mechanised army. The situation did not improve as the war dragged on. It only got worse. The need got greater, but trucks got scarcer, due to attrition through enemy action, overuse, breakdowns, neglect and the stress of unsuitable roads and terrain. The Germans did capture thousands of French vehicles, but even these proved to be insufficient, and finding spare parts caused problems. The motorised divisions were eventually, later in the war, given a battalion of tanks, or more usually assault guns, and designated panzergrenadier divisions.

With its new corps posting, 1st Panzer had to move to its new assembly area, which with detours for blown bridges, meant a road march of over 300 kilometres. By this time the troops and vehicles were exhausted and run down. Little or no maintenance had been possible, and supplies had trouble keeping up with the fast-moving spearheads, a portent of what would become a crisis in Russia. The Graf was not immune to the supply problems, with which he was directly involved, nor the physical exhaustion. He was older than most in the division, and not being involved directly in the fighting, did not have the effects of adrenaline and sheer determination to keep him going. A few days of rest were finally ordered. The Graf didn't take advantage of these as he was too restless a spirit to sit still for long, and took himself off with his driver to conduct his own forward reconnaissance.

Approaching a small town, along a narrow road bordered by a stone wall on either side, he unexpectedly came up against a barrier with a guardpost. Von Strachwitz realised that the road led directly to a French army camp. He ordered his driver to halt, then considered his options while the sentry watched them curiously. If they turned the car quickly it would alarm the sentry; if they did it slowly, the sentry could not help but see the German Balkan cross painted on the car door. Either way he would probably fire, at close range. Boldness was von Strachwitz's best option, and characteristically he took it, ordering his driver to drive forward slowly. The driver stopped at the barrier, and the Graf got out of the car, slowly approached the sentry and asked to see the commandant in flawless French --his years in French prisons were at last proving useful.

After staring for a moment, the sentry lifted the barrier, and led von Strachwitz through to the orderly room, where he introduced himself to the lieutenant: "I am Captain Comte von Strachwitz of the German 1st Panzer Division" (using the French "Comte" for Count, to emphasise his title). He always used his title and insisted his troops used it in preference to, or with, his military rank. It was a practice he continued throughout the war, even after he attained the rank of general.

Von Strachwitz continued before the lieutenant could reply, demanding to see the commandant. Shocked, the lieutenant complied, while the Graf waited, seeming quite relaxed. When the lieutenant returned with the commandant, von Strachwitz explained that he had come to call for the camp's surrender, adding that there was an entire German armoured division just a short distance down the road. He said that his divisional commander had ordered him to arrange for the camp's capitulation, wishing to avoid unnecessary bloodshed. He added that the French could of course choose to fight, but had no chance against an entire armoured division. The commandant, who knew that his signals battalion had no chance against an armoured division, left to consult his officers while von Strachwitz again relaxed, smoking a cigarette.

Von Strachwitz's plan was very clever: even if the French rejected the demand, they would have to let von Strachwitz go, as he was ostensibly an emissary and would be required to report back. Thus he could simply walk back to his car and go. This was the main point of the whole charade, to allow him and his driver to escape unscathed. He then would return with units of his division and his prediction to the commandant would prove true. If the enemy by some chance did decide to accept his surrender demand then that was an unexpected bonus.

The commandant, clearly upset, returned and accepted von Strachwitz' offer, asking for the terms of surrender. Hiding his shock, von Strachwitz made some up, then watched out the window as men scurried around the camp, gathering their possessions, with their NCOs barking orders.

When they were finished, von Strachwitz saluted the commandant and got back in his car, still expecting the French to realise the ruse and take him prisoner. But it didn't happen. Instead, in orderly formation, the French battalion marched out, almost happily it seemed, and followed von Strachwitz toward their captivity. Singlehandedly he had captured a battalion of some 600 officers and men.

The surrender of the French solidified his reputation as a daredevil and an officer of exceptional bravery. It assured his promotion to major, which he received at the end of the campaign, and helped earn him the Iron Cross (1st Class), 1939 Eagle Clasp which he wore above his Iron Cross (1st Class) from World War I.

The episode showed clearly von Strachwitz's ability to think quickly and clearly in a crisis situation. This was absolutely vital for a successful armoured commander who has to deal with fast-moving and changing battle conditions. It showed boldness and unorthodoxy—two of his personal characteristics—and above all an ability to read his enemy. He knew his surrender demand was a wild gamble but not an outrageous one. He had observed the poor fighting spirit and morale of the French. Many of their units—but by no means all—had been quick to surrender, often without putting up a fight. So the possibility of the French accepting his demand was a real one.

This ability to read a situation was not uncanny; he was simply good at closely observing his enemy, his tactics, motivation, fighting skills, morale, training and national characteristics, then apply the knowledge intelligently. To do this he had to see through the turmoil, noise, confusion, chaos and fear of death, which formed a pall over a battle, preventing the clarity needed for focused observation. Once this was done it was a matter of applying the knowledge and information acquired. It sounds simple enough, but in reality is difficult to do, especially on an ongoing basis. Distractions, exhaustion, demanding duties, personal needs and fears all get in the way. It needs conscious effort to acquire the knowledge and persist with it, as times and conditions change. Finally it requires the ability to arrive at the right conclusions and to apply them correctly, for knowledge on its own is not sufficient. This is where he did have a gift. He had a combination of intelligence, clarity of thought, courage and above all boldness. These were his personal characteristics which put together made him a formidable adversary, and which he would use to such deadly effect in the east.

On the other side of the ledger, von Strachwitz was inordinately proud, sometimes to the point of arrogance. He could be haughty, which came from his aristocratic upbringing, and was a prickly and difficult subordinate, not suffering fools gladly even when they were his superiors. He was stubborn and determined to get his way, especially when he thought he was right, which was most of the time. He was a strong personality with a determined character, who drove himself and others hard. Being very focused, he could appear to be aloof, but in fact he wasn't. However, he was urbane, could be very charming and exceedingly polite if he had to be. He had a sardonic sense of humour and was considerate. He cared for his troops, and if his actions seemed rash, foolish even, it was because he considered it the best course of action to not only succeed but to keep his men alive. He was in every sense a true cavalier, and one of the last cavalrymen.

Having returned to the bosom of his division with his booty—which included the equipment and vehicles of the signals battalion—von Strachwitz continued with his division's advance. On 9 June the 1st Panzer was located just north of the small town of Chateau-Porcien, ready to move to the bridgehead there. From the bridgehead the division made some rapid advances as the French changed their tactics, choosing to abandon the open ground and only defend the woods and villages where the German tanks were at a disadvantage.

The 1st Panzer then attacked along both banks of the Retourne with the tanks on the south bank and the infantrymen on the north. The division reached Juniville in the afternoon and while still in march formation was attacked by a French armoured force. A tank battle quickly developed. The French pressed their attack, their heavier guns smashing apart the more lightly armoured Mark IIs and IIIs of the Germans, whose only hope was to get in close, or manoeuvre to the rear or flanks of the larger French tanks, where their amour was thinnest. The French were outnumbered and in the end outmanoeuvred, but gamely fought on. Smoke and dust shrouded the battlefield and explosions rent the air as tanks were hit and their fuel and ammunition ignited. Tank crews from disabled tanks scattered in all directions, seeking safety from the inferno only to be cut down by machine-gun fire or crushed to a bloody pulp under the treads of an enemy tank.

The Germans threw everything into the fight, even their half-tracked light anti-aircraft guns, one of which was blown up with the loss of seven killed or wounded, but they managed to destroy at least one British Mark IIA light tank. Even Guderian got involved: "I attempted in vain to destroy a chap with a captured 47mm anti-tank gun; all the shells I fired at it simply bounced harmlessly off its thick armour. Our 27mm and 20mm guns were equally ineffective against this adversary. As a result we inevitably suffered, sadly, heavy causalities."[12]

The battle lasted for two murderously gruelling hours before the French finally gave up and retreated. They left a battlefield strewn with burnt-out and disabled tanks, and dead and wounded spread over a wide area. The Germans would recover their disabled tanks, the French had to abandon theirs.

The 1st Panzer Division then put in a classic attack with artillery, tanks and infantry capturing a village and advancing towards Bétheniville, when the French counterattacked with 50 tanks. They didn't press their attack and were repulsed. The Germans then captured the villages of Beine-Nauroy and St Hilaire le Petit in quick succession.[13]

On 14 June the Germans entered Paris, which had been declared an open city. It was a sad day for France. At the same time 1st Panzer reached Saint-Dizier taking numerous prisoners from the French 3rd Armoured Division, 6th Colonial Infantry Division and 3rd North African Division. These and other French colonial troops from Algeria and Morocco formed a significant part of the French Army, and while some fought extremely well, most were keen to surrender.[14]

After Saint-Dizier was taken, Guderian ordered 1st Panzer to capture Langres, which it did on 15 June, taking 10,000 prisoners. However it was still not allowed to rest on its laurels, being ordered to take Gray-sur-Saone and Besancon.

French Prime Minister Reynaud resigned on 16 June and Marshal Petain, the hero of World War I, took over. He immediately requested an armistice. The Germans tarried however, and it would be another nine days before they finally agreed. On the 15th the French High Command ordered their now totally redundant troops on the Maginot Line to fight their way out. On the 17th and 18th the British evacuated 136,000 of their remaining troops, together with 20,000 Poles who had been fighting the Germans, and who would form the basis of the Free Polish Army. They were taken off from the French ports on the Cherbourg peninsula.[15]

In the meantime, the 1st Panzer took part in the capture of Besançon on 17 June, capturing 30,000 prisoners.[16] From there it advanced to Montbéliard. On reaching that town Major Walther Wenck, the division's operations officer, advised that he had sufficient fuel to keep going on to the fortress town of Belfort. Guderian approved and they advanced, taking the surrender of numerous columns of dispirited French troops along the way. The town itself was quickly taken but not the forts, which refused to surrender.

General Guderian caught up with the division and paid a visit to General Kirchener at the hotel where he had made his headquarters. On his arrival he was informed that General Kirchener was taking a much-needed bath. Rather than enquire why Kirchener was taking a bath rather than a fort, Guderian contented himself with eating a hearty breakfast which had been prepared for the French staff officers who had been the hotel's previous occupants.[17] He then stayed to observe the division's attack on the forts. Waiting with him, but not part of his entourage, was Hyazinth von Strachwitz.

While the forts were being taken, other units of the division under Colonel Nedtwig reached Giromagny, north of Belfort, and took 10,000 prisoners, 40 mortars and seven aircraft. From Belfort, the division took the heights of Belchen, Ballon de Servance and Le Tillot. The French were now in a state of complete collapse, and all that remained for the division to do was gather prisoners and secure French equipment. The campaign was all but over.

In six weeks, France, along with Belgium and Holland had fallen. Allied casualties were 360,000 dead or wounded 1,900,000 captured and 2,233 aircraft destroyed. The Germans had 153,276 casualties of which 1st Panzer's losses were 45 officers and 448 other ranks.[18] The Germans also lost 1,365 aircraft and 795 tanks—relatively light losses for the gains achieved. The French had fought badly, the English gamely and the Germans superbly. It gave the Germans confidence to take on new conquests, and while they would continue to fight exceedingly well, in the end it would not be enough.

NOTES

1. General Heinz Guderian, *Panzer Leader* (Futura Publications 1952), p.94.

2. Ibid.
3. D.J. Goodspeed, *The German Wars* (Bonanza Books, NY, 1977), p.350.
4. Ibid., p.352.
5. Kirchner was a solid, capable commander and perhaps deserves a better reputation than he got.
6. Dennis Showalter, *Hitler's Panzers* (Berkley Publishing, NY, 2009), p.104.
7. Guderian, *Panzer Leader*, p.100.
8. Ibid., pp.107–108.
9. Reynaud would go on to become a leading collaborator with the Nazis.
10. Ibid., p.109.
11. Ibid., p.111.
12. Ibid., p.125.
13. Ibid., p.26.
14. They fought harder in the Allied invasion of Italy, and later Germany, as part of the Free French forces.
15. Goodspeed, *The German Wars*, p.369.
16. Horst Riebenstahl, *The 1st Panzer Division 1935–1945* (Schiffer Publishing Ltd, 1990).
17. *Panzer Leader*, p.133.
18. R.L. Dinardo, *Germany's Panzer Arm in WWII* (Stackpole Military History Series), p.109.

SEVEN

ROMANIA AND YUGOSLAVIA

After the French campaign, 1st Panzer Division remained in France to regroup, refurbish and repair equipment, and undertake further training. Home leave was given out, a practice the German Army continued throughout the war even until early 1945 when defeat loomed. It was a major factor in maintaining morale in an increasingly long and brutal war. So Graf von Strachwitz returned to Gross-Stein for a short period to be reunited with his family. His father was particularly proud of him; he had another Iron Cross to wear on his uniform, but more importantly he had returned from France, this time unscathed. The Panzer Graf's son Hyazinth also returned safe and sound, wearing his own Iron Cross.

It was a time of euphoria and contentment as Major General von Mellenthin recounts:

> For the German Army the summer of 1940 was the happiest of the war. We had gained a series of victories unprecedented since the days of Napoleon; Versailles had been avenged, and we could look forward to the prospect of a secure and glorious peace. Our occupation forces in France and the Netherlands settled down to the calm routine of peacetime soldiering. Riding parties and hunting parties were arranged, and there was talk that our families might be allowed to join us.[1]

So it was at Gross-Stein—parties and family reunions were held, all with hopes of a brighter and peaceful future. Hyazinth brought back champagne, cognac, perfumes, cheeses and chocolate from France and could enjoy the pleasures of his homecoming.

Those still with the division in France went on leave locally, enjoying excursions and French food in abundance. Even Hitler relaxed a while to enjoy his triumph, visiting Paris in the early hours of 23 June where he took in the sights of that great city. Then it was back to planning more campaigns, such as Operation *Sea Lion*, the invasion of Great Britain, which was abandoned after the Luftwaffe lost their superiority over the skies of England in the Battle of Britain. But that was just an interruption. Britain could wither on the vine while he planned his biggest campaign of all, Operation *Barbarossa*, the invasion of Russia. The preliminaries for this began as early as 21 July 1940 at a conference when Hitler told his generals they must prepare for an attack on the Soviet Union.

On 5 September, 1st Panzer Division boarded trains for transfer to East Prussia, where its units were divided between Zintern, Sensburg, Allenstein and Rostenburg. The 1st Panzer Regiment was based at Zintern, which had the best facilities to house and repair its tanks and equipment. In October the division was visited by Gauleiter Saukel, the Nazi party's top administrative official for Thuringia and later chief administrator for labour deployment, which involved organising slave labour for German industry. He was hanged in 1946 as a war criminal; at the time of his visit, however he was just another high-ranking Nazi official who liked to be seen with the troops.

New and improved weapons were provided for the division as it underwent a major reorganisation. This was brought about by Adolf Hitler's desire for more panzer divisions after they had proved so successful in the Polish and French campaigns. The simplest way to achieve this was to remove a panzer regiment from an existing panzer division and attach it to a motorised or infantry division, while at the same time removing an infantry regiment from the recipient division. This reduced the firepower of the panzer division but made it less unwieldy to handle. Divisions with two panzer regiments required almost double the number of rear-echelon troops and support vehicles which could, and in France did, create major traffic jams and logistic difficulties.[2] Firepower could be partially restored by providing better tanks with larger calibre guns and thicker armour, i.e. Panzer Is and IIs could be replaced by Panzer IIIs and IVs. In fact the obsolete Mark Is were replaced, but many divisions still retained Mark IIs and the equally ineffective Czech 38(t) at the beginning of Operation *Barbarossa*.

This expansion of the panzer arm required 1st Panzer to give up its 2nd

Panzer Regiment with its two tank battalions, where Graf von Strachwitz was serving, to the 16th Infantry Division. There is no doubt that 1st Panzer offloaded its worn-out equipment to the 2nd Panzer Regiment, exchanging it with the best that 2nd Panzer Regiment had to offer. On receiving the panzer regiment, the 16th Infantry Division, in turn surrendered one of its infantry regiments since the order of battle for a panzer division only required two infantry regiments.

This meant that Hyazinth Graf von Strachwitz became a member of the 16th Panzer Division. More importantly he had been promoted to the rank of major in the reserve[3] and was made the battalion commander of the 1st Tank Battalion. This promotion and appointment was in recognition of the command and fighting abilities he had displayed in both the Polish and French campaigns. It was also the operational command he had been craving all along. Major Sauvant was the commander of 2nd Battalion.

The 16th Panzer Division consisted mainly of Westphalians and a few Prussians. It was a veteran division, having served with distinction in the Battle of France, particularly in the battle to take Mont Damion, which was mentioned in the Official War Bulletin and became part of the text at the War Academy. In all the division lost 690 men in the campaign. Its home base was in Wuppertal, where it completed its reorganisation.

The Panzer Graf was extremely fortunate in having General Hans Valentin Hube as his divisional commander. Hube was possibly the most capable armoured force tactician in the German Army. (The distinction of most capable strategist belonged to von Manstein.) Hube commanded the 16th Infantry Division from 17 May 1940 when he took over from General Major Krampf who had fallen ill, until 15 September 1942, overseeing its transition to a panzer division and leading it in Operation *Barbarossa*, the Battles of Dubno, Kiev, Uman and Stalingrad. Hube left the division to take over command of the XIV Panzer Corps, which he led until September 1943. He then commanded the 1st Panzer Army as a colonel general until 21 April 1944. Due to his superlative leadership abilities, three German armies escaped almost certain annihilation: in Sicily 1943, Cherkassy 1944 and Kamenetz-Podolsk in 1944.[4] He found renown at Cherkassy when, with his army completely surrounded, he moved it as a wandering pocket in a fighting withdrawal to the German lines. It took superior fighting and leadership skills to achieve, and is still studied in war colleges. For this achievement he was one of the very few to be awarded the Diamonds (the 13th recipient) to the Knight's Cross with Oak Leaves and Swords. Tragically he was killed in an air crash on 21 April 1944 after his award of the Diamonds. He was accorded a full state funeral, for apart from being a war hero, he was one of the few generals Hitler not only respected and trusted but actually liked, even though Hube was not a member of the Nazi party.

Like von Strachwitz, Hube was a World War I veteran, losing his left arm fighting at Fontenoy on 20 September 1914. Too tough to be held back he returned to the front where he earned the Iron Cross (1st Class) in 1917 and the House Order of Hohenzollern. He was also recommended for the Pour le Mérite, Imperial Germany's highest bravery award, but the war ended before the award was processed.

After the war he was one of the select few officers retained in the 100,000-man Reichswehr, despite his amputated left arm. He recounted that he managed to do this by jumping into a water obstacle from a ten-metre tower wearing full uniform with pack and rifle while telling the assembled officers there, "If you won't select me, then I will demand that each officer who is taken ahead of me must first make this jump"[5]

Hans Hube was a plainspoken man, a born soldier without false airs or graces. For him the military was a genuine vocation. He was adored by his troops who nicknamed him *Der Mensch* ("The Man") and he certainly looked the part: burly, tough, with a round honest and open face. They knew he would go anywhere they would, and not ask them to do anything he wasn't prepared to do himself. He led from the front, seemingly ignorant of danger. He had genuine warmth and understood people, knowing how to get the best from them. Graf von Strachwitz benefitted from this understanding enormously. It was Hube who let him have his head in charging forward with his battalion even if it was reduced to a mere handful of tanks, disregarding his extended flanks and distant supply points. Other commanders—concerned about the enemy's superior strength, exposed flanks, and ammunition or fuel shortages—would have tried to rein him in. Hube didn't. He knew what the Panzer Graf was capable of, trusting his judgement completely. Von Strachwitz didn't let him down.

Von Strachwitz was equally lucky with his new regimental commander, Colonel Rudolf Sieckenius, a fellow Silesian. Sieckenius served as an infantry officer in World War I, a police officer after the war, and a cavalry officer from 1934. He then transferred to the panzer arm where he served as a company then later battalion commander. During the Battle of France he served under General Rommel in the famed 7th Panzer Division, being the only battalion commander able to keep up with his fast-moving division commander. He was appointed to command the 2nd Panzer Regiment in April 1941, replacing Colonel Hero Breusing, who had led the regiment ably throughout the French campaign. This caused a great deal of resentment among the regiment's officers, particularly as there appeared to be no valid reason for Breusing's removal. The fact that Breusing had written a memorandum criticising the removal of a panzer regiment from the existing panzer divisions was probably known to some or even all of them, but what they didn't know was that it had reached Adolf Hitler, who ordered Breusing's removal from command of his regiment.[6] Undoubtedly Graf von Strachwitz was one of those who shared in the disquiet at Breusing's removal, though perhaps he was a little too urbane to show it. Fortunately General Hube was more understanding and stepped in, telling his officers to give Sieckenius a chance, and work with him. The respect felt for Hube meant that his intervention settled the matter there and then.[7]

This was fortuitous for all concerned, for Sieckenius was an extremely effective armoured commander and more than capable of filling Breusing's shoes. He was awarded the Knight's Cross for his personal bravery and his regiment's success in the Dubno tank battles, a success for which von Strachwitz contributed the major part. Still, it was to Sieckenius' credit that he worked solidly alongside von Strachwitz, enabling them both to achieve the success they did. He went on to lead the regiment during the battles of Kiev, Uman and Stalingrad, from where he was evacuated. He went on to become 16th Panzer's commander when it served in Italy and came close to pushing the Allies back into the sea at Salerno. It wasn't close enough for Hitler, however, and he made Sieckenius the scapegoat for the failure, dismissing him from his command. The Führer progressively downgraded Sieckenius to command an infantry division and finally a security division, both of which he led effectively. He was killed in the final battles in Germany in April 1945. He certainly deserved, and was capable of, a lot better. Graf von Strachwitz and Sieckenius understood one another and got along as true comrades-in-arms, forming an extremely effective fighting team.

In mid-December the division was moved by rail to Romania, crossing the Hungarian–Romanian border near Arpad. The German Army moved its panzer divisions by rail whenever possible to spare wear and tear on the vehicles, to increase speed of movement and later in the war because there were insufficient trucks. The division's mission was to provide tank training to the Romanian Army and bolster security for the oilfields at Ploesti, which were essential to keep the German war machine running. The division was located in the Banat, and Siebenburgen district, which had large Swabian ethnic German populations. The language, culture, dress and customs were all German and had been maintained this way for centuries. The Banat Germans provided many soldiers for the Third Reich, including manning an entire German SS Mountain Division the SS-Gebirgs-Division Prinz Eugen, which served in Yugoslavia against Tito's partisans.

The troops were billeted in halls and houses, being made very welcome by their Swabian hosts. Romances quickly blossomed between the Banat girls and German soldiers, the most notable being General Hube, who married a lady from the area. The soldiers lived and ate well, their rations being more than supplemented by the local fare. As most houses had well-stocked wine cellars with local vintages, they also drank well. Their peaceful existence was interrupted by a minor civil war. In January 1941 the Romanian Fascist Legion of St Michael, also known as the Iron Guard, under the leadership of the Deputy Premier Horia Sima, rebelled against Romania's dictator, Ion Antonescu.

Three days of savage fighting took place across the country before the rebellion was quashed. In the Banat, the 16th Panzer was rapidly deployed to restore order. Troops and armoured vehicles quickly moved to place themselves between the warring parties and secure important buildings and locations. Captain Murray, commanding officer of the 3rd Company of the Engineer Battalion, negotiated a peaceful end to the affair in Temesvar, where the Legion looked like creating the most trouble. The local population was so grateful for the German intervention in preventing bloodshed that they presented General Hube with an old Turkish scimitar, a relic of some medieval Balkans battle. It was a gift he valued highly as it was given from the heart.[8] The division then returned once more to its pleasant lifestyle, contentedly unaware that their Führer was planning other campaigns for them.

Caught between the two belligerent dictatorships of Germany and Russia, Hungary, Romania and Bulgaria had all signed alliances with Germany for territorial gains or simply out of self-preservation. Yugoslavia, with its pro-German regent, Prince Paul, joined the Axis on 25 March. In the meantime Mussolini, tired of watching Hitler making his conquests, decided to invade Greece. The Greeks were having none of it and gave the Italians a thoroughly sound thrashing. Hitler, concerned about British involvement and his vulnerable southern flank, planned Operation *Marita*, the invasion of Greece. On 27 March, before he was ready to attack, a pro-British Yugoslav general, Dusan Simovic, organised a military coup against Prince Paul. Hitler was livid at the effrontery of the Yugoslav army and ordered planning for an invasion of Yugoslavia. The invasion would take place simultaneously with the attack on Greece.

In March, the 16th Panzer was allocated to the Twelfth Army as a reserve division, and at the end of the month moved to Bulgaria in preparation. It was quartered between Bargaz and Plovdiv-Pazardshik. The younger soldiers were craving for action, but only the 1st Panzer Battalion commanded by Hyazinth von Strachwitz was chosen to take part in the invasion. It was chosen possibly because Hube wanted to give Graf von Strachwitz experience commanding an armoured formation in battle, as hitherto he had served only in a logistics capacity, even though he had personally exceeded that role. The campaign was not expected to be demanding but would be invaluable to a novice battalion commander. The battalion was to be deployed alongside the Grossdeutschland Infantry Regiment, providing it with armoured support. Graf von Strachwitz was familiar with this unit, having fought alongside it while serving with the 1st Panzer Division in the French campaign. It was a reliable, hard-fighting unit.

The Yugoslavs were doomed from the start. They only had 28 divisions, three cavalry brigades, and no armour to speak of. Their equipment was outdated, while their air force had only 300 aircraft, although some of these were Hurricanes they had acquired form the British.[9] To add to their woes, their army was torn by internal dissent because of its ethnic composition, which brought about severe morale problems and drastically affected its fighting spirit. The Croats had no love for the majority Serbs, with many actually welcoming the invading Germans as liberators. They could not surrender quickly enough, with some actually turning their weapons against the Serbs. The Slovenes disliked both the Croats and the Serbs, and none of them had any love for the Muslim Bosnians. The Bosnians reciprocated the hatred and didn't want to fight at all.[10] To make matters worse, if that was possible, only two-thirds of the army was mobilised, not that this made a real difference to the end result.

The German plan was for its Second Army to advance on Zagreb, the Croatian capital, and then on to the Bosnian capital of Sarajevo. The Twelfth Army was to attack from Bulgaria and capture the Yugoslav capital, Belgrade.[11] The attack commenced on 6 April with the Twelfth Army meeting very little resistance, taking Skopje on 10 April. Its left wing then swept into Greece to bail out the beleaguered Italians. General von Kleist's push into Yugoslavia crushed all resistance, such as there was, and his troops entered

The Yugoslavian Campaign, 1941
0
100 miles
0
100 km
N
GERMANY
2nd Army
HUNGARY
SOVIET
UNION
LII Corps
LI Corps
XLIX Mtn
Corps
3rd Hungarian
Army
XLVI Pz
Corps
2nd
Italian
Army
Zagreb
XLI Pz
ROMANIA
Sava R.
Belgrade
YUGOSLAVIA
Danube R.
1st
Panzer
Group
BULGARIA
Adriatic Sea
12th Army
XL Pz Corps
11th Italian
Army
XVIII Mtn
Corps
XXX
Corps
ITALY
ALBANIA
Salonika
GREECE
Aegean
Sea
Ionian Sea

Vis on 9 April. They then thrust towards Belgrade. The Yugoslav Army fell back rapidly, abandoning even the mountainous areas and the easily defended mountain passes. Flight or surrender were the only two things that occupied the Yugoslav soldiers' minds. The German XLVI Panzer Corps, opposed by mainly Croatian troops who fled before the Germans even drew close, had a leisurely road march into Belgrade, entering it on 17 April. There was no resistance in the capital as its defenders were already in the process of surrendering their weapons to a young SS Haupsturmführer, Fritz Klingenberg, who had seized the city with a few of his motorcycle troops in a *coup de main*.[12] Helmut Günther, a motorcyclist in Klingenberg's 2nd Company, Motorcycle Battalion of the Das Reich Division described his part in the affair:

> A last shock and shudder ran through our barge. We were on shore. The combat engineers of the 5th Company quickly fashioned a debarkation ramp from boards nailed together. The first motorcycles rolled onto the bank. There was no firing. We were considerably relieved. Not a soul was to be seen. The road on which we assembled was empty and abandoned. Everything went pretty fast, and soon we had the trusty mutter of our machines in our ears. Slowly, ready for action, we rolled into the city.
>
> The city was dead, the shutters rolled down on the shops; it was a gloomy picture. Where were the Serbian soldiers? We did not yet know that Klingenberg had worked it out with the officers in charge during the night so that all the soldiers were to immediately report to the citadel and lay down their weapons there.
>
> We later found out that a single *Rottenführer* with his submachine gun was standing guard at the door of the fortress, allowing the soldiers in but not out again. While this was happening, a *Sturmmann* inside had to make sure that the Serbians really tossed their weapons on a heap. How the knees of those two must have shaken! But he who dares, wins—that was uniquely shown by this whole action.
>
> We were then in the midst of the city. A man in a comical costume stood at a street corner. Gray pants, gray tunic without any rank insignia, collar turned up, both hands in his pants pockets. When the commander pulled even with this vagabond, he threw his right arm high. It was *Hauptsturmführer* Klingenberg! The column halted. Klingenberg crossed the street and walked over to the com-

> mander's staff car. He reported the surrender of the city of Belgrade to him. A propaganda man who had accompanied us on our "sea journey" dashed up with his camera and shot one photo after another. Then he stood on the staff car and panned his camera around to get us in the picture, too. The tension that had still gripped all of us was released.[13]

Two days later Yugoslavia capitulated. The brief campaign was a huge disappointment to Graf von Strachwitz. There had been no enemy armour for him to fight. What infantry he saw was mainly surrendering in long columns, while the artillery, what there was of it, was usually seen at the side of the road abandoned. In the end 345,000 Yugoslav soldiers marched into captivity while German casualties were 558. It was, as General von Mellenthin stated, "virtually a military parade."[14]

Still, for the Graf there were some lessons to be learnt, but these were merely of movement control, logistics and—perhaps more importantly given the conditions to come in Russia—vehicle maintenance and damage from the dust and poor-quality roads. What little resistance he encountered was easily disposed of, being mainly light infantry rearguard actions, and sporadic, poorly controlled artillery fire.

At Pancevo troops of the Grossdeutschland, to whom the Graf's battalion was attached, were involved in an atrocity. A sniper, possibly a civilian, killed a German soldier. The SS who were present in the area rounded up 100 civilians at random, taken off the streets or from their homes. A drumhead court martial was quickly set up and found 36 of the hostages guilty and sentenced them to death. An execution squad from Grossdeutschland then shot 14 of the condemned hostages. There was apparently no protest or even serious inquiry from Grossdeutschland officers as to the shootings, or why 14 people were killed when there was only a single sniper. This incident was a harbinger of worse to come in Russia where even the charade of a court martial was dispensed with and whole villages were slaughtered in reprisal for a shooting or partisan attack. It is almost certain that von Strachwitz had no direct knowledge of this affair, although it is possible he may have heard a rumour or passing reference to a trial and execution taking place. At Pancevo the Graf met up with his eldest son, who was serving with the 11th Panzer Division.

The campaign in Yugoslavia over, the Graf returned with his battalion to his parent unit. Once there he was involved in hard training in basic tactics at platoon, company and finally battalion level. For most of his men it was refresher training, while for von Strachwitz it was invaluable hands-on practical training which would stand him in good stead in the next campaign. He was also able to draw on the experience of men like Rudolf Sieckenius and his company commanders, who had fought so splendidly in France. The division was then moved once more by rail to its new concentration around Neisse and Breslau in his native Silesia. It would be an all too brief homecoming.

NOTES

1. Major General F. W. von Mellenthin, *Panzer Battles* (Futura Publications, 1977), p.31.
2. Dennis Showalter, *Hitler's Panzers* (Berkley Publishing, NY, 2009).
3. Graf von Strachwitz was officially in the army reserve and his rank showed his reserve status. For simplicity I have omitted the "reserve" normally placed after his rank in the text.
4. Günter Schmitz, *Die 16 Panzer Division Bewaffnung. Einsatz. Manner 1938–1945* (Dörfler im Nebel Verlag Gmbh, 2004).
5. Günter Fraschka, *Knights of the Reich* (Schiffer Publishing Ltd, 1989), pp.162–163.
6. The dark stain of Hitler's hand stayed with Breusing throughout his career. He went on to command other panzer regiments but never commanded a panzer division. He finished the war as a general major commanding the 122nd Infantry Division. His World War II decorations didn't go beyond the Iron Cross (1st Class).
7. Samuel W. Mitcham, *The Generals Who Served Under Rommel* (Stackpole Books).
8. Schmitz, *Die 16 Panzer Division 1938–1945*.
9. Mellenthin, *Panzer Battles*, p. 34.
10. During the German occupation they were intent on slaughtering each other. The Croats murdered Serbs and Muslim Bosnians. The Serbs were divided between communist partisans and monarchist Chetniks fighting each other as much as the Germans. The Bosnian Muslims who were formed into an SS Division by Himmler mainly concerned themselves with massacring Christian civilians.
11. Mellenthin, *Panzer Battles*, p. 35.
12. He received the Knight's Cross for this action and went on to a distinguished career in the Waffen SS, becoming the commander of the 17th SS Panzergrenadier Division Götz von Berchlingen. He was killed on 22 March 1945.
13. Helmut Günther (trans. by Fred Steinhardt), *Hot Motors, Cold Feet* (J. J. Fedorowcz Publishing Canada, 2004), p. 45.
14. Mellenthin, *Panzer Battles*.

EIGHT

OPERATION BARBAROSSA

HITLER AND HIS HIGH COMMAND—FIELD MARSHAL Walter von Brauchitsch, Commander-in-Chief of the German Army, Field Marshal Wilhelm Keitel Chief of Staff of the Armed Forces High Command (Oberkommando der Wehrmacht or OKW), Colonel General Alfred Jodl, Chief of Operations of OKW and Colonel General Franz Halder, Chief of the General Staff—were very optimistic about the decision to invade Russia. They had every reason to be, with any doubts dispelled by the dramatic lightning victories in France and the Low Countries. No force had thus far defeated the German Army. Germany had conquered most of Western Europe in short campaigns, and they could expect to do the same in Russia. Only Great Britain remained undefeated, but she had been driven out of France, Norway and Greece. So hubris reigned supreme, and the few generals who felt disquiet or opposed the plan remained silent. However, they had all underestimated the strength of the Soviet colossus. They were helped in their optimism by the gross miscalculations of Foreign Armies East, a branch of Army Intelligence headed by Colonel Eberhard Kinsel.[1] His department estimated the Russians had no more than 200 effective divisions when in reality they had more than 360.[2]

The plan presented to Hitler was to invade Russia with three army groups. Army Group North, under Ritter von Leeb, would strike from East Prussia through Lithuania and the Baltic States to advance on Leningrad. Army Group Centre, under Fedor von Bock, would thrust through Byelorussia and on to Moscow. Army Group South, headed by Gerd von Rundstedt, would capture the resource-rich Ukraine. For Adolf Hitler, resources were a vital part of his plans for a rich and sustainable Reich. He was acutely aware that in the last war, German society and parts of its military disintegrated through privation, lack of resources and hunger brought about by Germany's insufficient agricultural and industrial strength, along with the inability for replenishment due to the British naval blockade. The grain, coal and industrial might of the Ukraine would prevent a repetition. For this reason, Hitler placed great emphasis on Army Group South. Many of his generals, however, including Guderian, Halder, von Bock and others were fixated on Moscow. This was the political, commercial, transport, and communications hub of the Soviet Union and was their primary target. The difference in emphasis between Hitler and his commanders was to create a great deal of discord in the months to come.

To make matters worse, Operation *Barbarossa* did not have clearly defined objectives, beyond drawing a halt line that stretched from Archangel to the Caspian Sea. This would be where the German forces would halt to consolidate and absorb the conquered territory that would provide the living space for German colonists and resources for the Reich. The occupied peoples were to provide slave labour for their German masters.

To reach this stop line, the Red Army would have to be destroyed, and this was *Barbarossa*'s general objective. It was anticipated, going on past experience in France and elsewhere, that this would not take long; or as Hitler told von Rundstedt, "You have only to kick in the door and the whole rotten structure will come crashing down."

The chief instrument of this destruction was to be the German armoured force. Its tanks were to be concentrated into four separate panzer groups. The 4th Panzer Group under General Hoepner would be attached to Army Group North. The 2nd and 3rd Panzer Groups under Generals Guderian and Hoth were part of Army Group Centre, with nearly 1,500 tanks between them. Army Group South's 1st Panzer Group under von Kleist had five Panzer and three motorised divisions with 600 tanks, mostly Panzer IIIs. It was to this Panzer Group that Graf von Strachwitz and the 16th Panzer Division were attached as part of the XIV Panzer Corps under General Gustav von Wietersheim.

Von Kleist's Panzer Group faced the Soviet South-Western Front. This was the strongest of the Soviet Groups, as the Russian dictator also valued the riches of the Ukraine, which he had plundered at the expense of the native Ukrainians, and was fully cognisant of Hitler's need of it to fuel his war machine and feed his Reich. The war would develop into an economic one, based on manpower, fuel, food, mineral and industrial strength, all of which Germany lacked in sufficient quantities to sustain her war effort over a long period of time. The Soviet Union and the West dwarfed Germany's available resources, although the full extent of this factor was not fully appreciated by Adolf Hitler or his planners. Had he been fully aware, the Führer would still have invaded Russia on ideological grounds and belief in his own unconquerable will. He may however have hesitated, or refrained, from declaring war on the United States of America, although this was done partly in the hope that Japan would reciprocate by declaring war on Russia.

For Germany to achieve victory, it had to wage a "total war." Adolf Hitler made this very clear to his generals in Mach 1941 when he told them it would be a "clash of civilisations" and the Wehrmacht would have to be part of "a war of extermination." He could not have made it any clearer, so his generals should not have been under any illusion as to what was expected of them. To give practical meaning for his words and to translate them into a workable policy Hitler issued an order to be given to all army, corps and divisional commanders concerning the treatment of the civilian population and prisoners of war in Russia. It stated, that in the event of any excesses committed against civilians or prisoners, the soldiers responsible for these excesses were not to be automatically punished according to military law. Disciplinary action was to be at the discretion of the soldiers' immediate commander. Field Marshal von Brauchitsch and Colonel General Guderian, among others, were concerned about the effect the order would have on preserving discipline. To this end von Brauchitsch appended an addendum stating that the order would only apply if there was no danger of discipline suffering because of it.[3] The sheer criminality and immorality of the order was not remarked upon, nor was it challenged on those grounds. Discipline was the generals' only concern. Along with this order was another specifying that all political commissars who were captured were to be summarily executed. This was more overtly criminal and was objected to more vociferously by a greater number of officers. Then again, this could have been because it was disseminated more widely. Some corps and divisional commanders didn't pass these orders on, while others briefly mentioned them with the implication being that they were not to be rigorously enforced, if at all. Alexander Stahlberg, in his memoir, gives one example of how the order was transmitted and received. The order was passed on by the divisional commanders to the battalion commanders, who then announced it to their officers:

> He announced the Commissar order. When he had finished there was deathly silence in our circle, until one of the company commanders asked how would one recognise a Commissar. Lieutenant Colonel Becker seemed to have been expecting the question and said cuttingly that he had no idea, nor did he wish to know. He and all the other commanders had been ordered by the divisional commander to pass this order on to all officers—but only to officers. The order came from the highest level. He, Becker, had now carried out his orders.
>
> After another pause he said: "Gentlemen, the officers briefing is not yet over. There is reason to remind you of The Hague Convention on Land Warfare. I am now speaking of the treatment of prisoners and wounded. Anyone who abuses prisoners and wounded I shall have court-martialed. Do you understand me, gentlemen?[4]

Nevertheless many commanders did enforce the order. General Hube ensured that the order would not apply to the 16th Panzer Division. Even if he had tried to implement it, there would have been no chance for it to be carried out by men like von Strachwitz and Sieckenius. Their code of honour and inherent decency would not have allowed it. Field Marshal Kluge also had his concerns about the order and the SS activities behind the lines. It should be noted these concerns were not about the Waffen SS (military wing of the SS) but of the Security police. He sought to have the order rescinded, albeit not personally, as Major Gerhard Engel recorded in his dairy for 23 May 1941:

> Visited Field Marshal v Kluge. Kluge more or less confirmed scenario. Russians were marching up and massing near border. Numerous grass airstrips in immediate proximity to frontier. Kluge pleaded with me to get F. to change the dangerous Commissar Order, and especially to put the SD Kommandos more under military control. There had been some very bad goings on in Poland, and he had to intervene personally on several occasions, for example in Modlin and Lublin. Considered political tactics in Poland as very unfortunate.
>
> The worst was the uncertainty about police and SS measures. In the evening I reported this in same terms to F.[5]

One could well imagine the Führer's reaction and it was another reservation Hitler had about von Kluge.

By 22 June when Operation *Barbarossa* was launched, the Germans had amassed 136 divisions including 19 Panzer divisions along the frontier with the Soviet Union. The Romanians and Finns also joined in from their borders, while the Slovaks, Croats, Italians and Hungarians were to contribute smaller contingents. The Germans left 46 divisions to guard the West, far too large a number considering there was no real threat of an invasion by Britain. Half that number would have been more than sufficient while the remainder would have made a welcome addition to the invasion force. The total number of tanks fielded by the Germans was 3,550. Opposing them the Soviet had 193 equivalent divisions near the frontier and a staggering 12,000 tanks, most of which were the BT-series light tanks, but there were sufficient T-34 medium tanks and KV heavy tanks to make a significant difference.[6]

At dawn a massive artillery barrage blazed across the entire frontier, pulverising Soviet defensive positions in a storm of fire and hot metal. Werner Adamczyk, an artilleryman, described the barrage in his memoir:

> 0500: The inferno broke loose. North and south of us our artillery began firing at a rapid pace. I could not see anything of the action, except clouds of smoke rising in the air not too far away. The dense forest obstructed our view. The artillery fire increased steadily. I learned quickly to distinguish between the muffled sound of the guns firing and the sharp crackling sound of the shells landing. But soon the firing was so fast that the sounds mingled into one incomprehensible wall of noise. I could feel vibrations shaking the earth and the air.[7]

The shocked and dazed survivors staggered around while their equally stunned commanders—those who still had some communications intact—called for instructions and assistance. They had very little time to grasp the reality of the situation and organise a defence, for as soon as the barrage lifted hundreds of thousands of men in field-grey uniforms stormed into the Soviet defence line. They cut down with machine pistol and rifle fire anyone who dared to resist while the German tanks clattered through the lines, spitting death and destruction as they thrust towards the Soviet interior lines.

The Russians were taken completely by surprise, despite many warnings that the invasion was coming. The Lucy Spy Ring passed on full details, while aerial reconnaissance revealed the massive buildup on the border. The night before the attack three German deserters crossed the lines to warn the Russians. When he was told about them Stalin raged that it was disinformation, that they had been planted by the Germans to provoke him into action. He ordered that at least one—Alfred Liskow, a young communist from Berlin—be summarily executed, so convinced was he that the German invasion was a sheer impossibility. Stalin simply refused to believe that Hitler would attack. Just as importantly he did not want to believe it. After all he was not ready to face Hitler just yet. His plan was to let Hitler and Britain fight themselves to exhaustion, and then he would simply move in and mop up. At the very least, he wanted time to build up his strength and take on Hitler at the time and place of his own choosing, or defeat Hitler with a massive counter-blow should the German dictator invade first. Because of his unpreparedness, Stalin would go to any lengths to avoid provoking the Nazis, so he refrained from any action at all. His generals, being acutely aware of their master's wishes, were equally prepared to do nothing as the episode between General Ivan Boldin, deputy commander of the Western Military District and defence commissioner Semyon Timoshenko shows:

> "Comrade Boldin, remember no action is to be taken against the Germans without our knowledge." Timoshenko told him, "Will you please tell [General Dimitry] Pavlov that Comrade Stalin has forbidden to open artillery fire against the Germans."
>
> "But how is that possible?" Boldin yelled. "Our troops are in full retreat. Whole towns are in flames, people are being killed all over the place."[8]

Timoshenko would not relent, not while Stalin was determined to refuse to face reality. Even when Stalin's chief of General Staff, Geogy Zhukov, informed him of heavy German shelling and bombing raids all across the western frontier he ordered him to avoid retaliating. He later told him, "Hitler surely doesn't know about it," speculating that the German military was acting on its own. He sent Molotov, his foreign minister, to see the German ambassador Graf von Schulenburg, for clarification; from him he got the official declaration of war.

Crucial to the Germans' continuing success was the destruction of the Soviet Air Force. Most Soviet airfields were close to the frontier, and every one was bombed and strafed comprehensively. By 23 June the Soviets had lost 1,811 aircraft, of which 1,489 were destroyed on the ground. After 90

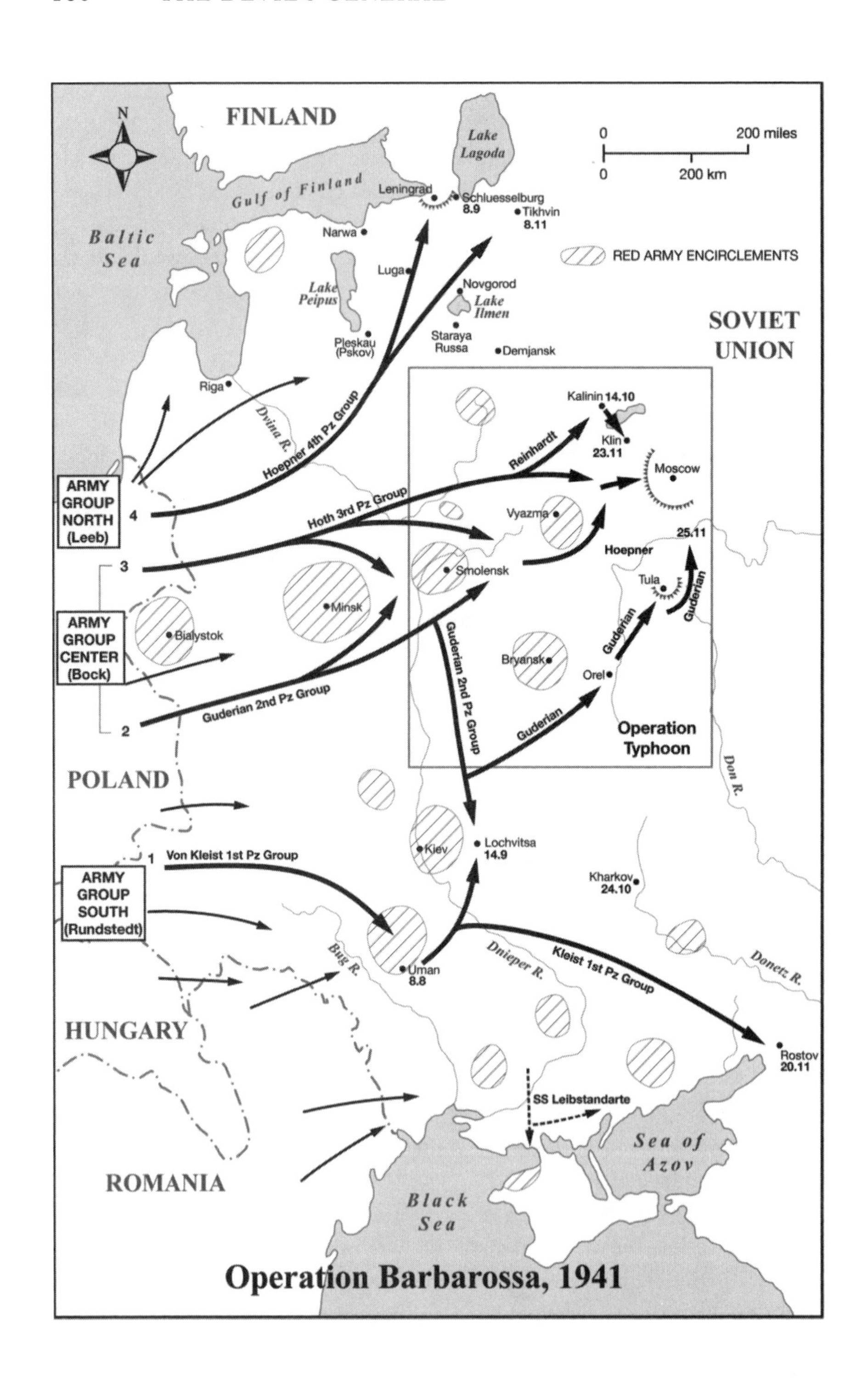

Operation Barbarossa, 1941

days their losses totalled 4,800 with 3,176 being destroyed on the ground. The pilots of those planes destroyed on the ground were of course still available to fly other and better aircraft later, so it was a temporary victory only. The Germans for their part lost a mere 330 aircraft.[9] Most importantly they had achieved total air supremacy in a very quick time. This was essential if the blitzkrieg and swift destruction of the Russian army was to be achieved.

An excellent representative summary of how the campaign was actually conducted in the early stages is given by Siegfried Knappe, an officer of the 87th Infantry Division, in his memoir:

> Our forward scouts—usually motorcycle troops [in Panzer divisions it could also be armoured cars, light tanks or troops in armoured personnel carriers] although we had some cavalry—went ahead of us, reconnoitring. When they drew fire, the point battalion would immediately spread out. The troops behind the point battalion would also spread out from the road on which we were marching. Once we knew how strong the resistance was we would prepare an attack. We would have an idea how strong the resistance was from the type of fire we received. The first fire would always be rifle fire and sometimes machine-gun fire, but the type of fire that followed—mortar, tank, artillery—would tell us a lot about how strong the resistance was. We would then make decisions based on that information.
>
> Interestingly the forward scouts were rarely killed, and far more often they were not even hit. The Russian soldiers firing at them were usually not there to fight, but only to stop us momentarily, and then very quickly get back to report to their superiors what they had seen.[10]

Overall resistance was patchy. Some Russian units fought ferociously to the last man, while others were quick to flee or to surrender. Some even cooperated with the Germans. In one instance a Soviet artillery officer actually gave his captors the coordinates to his guns as the Germans were firing short. This was more evident on the southern front where Ukrainians in the Red Army had scores to settle with the Soviet regime. It is estimated that some 20,000,000 Ukrainians died from starvation brought about by the forced collectivisation of peasant farms. Well-to-do peasants, known as kulaks, as well as the intelligentsia, and any objectors were shipped off to Siberian slave labour camps from which very few returned. There was thus a large reservoir of hatred for the communists in the Ukraine and indeed all over the Soviet Union, which the Germans squandered by their bestial behaviour towards the conquered peoples. Overall, apart from committed Communists there was no great love for the Soviet Union, but there was for Mother Russia and it was to this patriotism that Stalin was forced to appeal. Many of his soldiers wanted to surrender simply to fight against Communism, and entire units would surrender upon the approach of the Germans. In other instances the troops shot their commissars or any officers who objected to their surrendering. They were also more than willing to point out any commissars taken prisoner, who were pretending to be common soldiers. All this would change when the brutality of the Germans in the rear areas became evident and the criminal neglect of the prisoners of war became known.

On the southern front where Graf von Strachwitz was located with the 16th Panzer Division, the Germans assembled 34 divisions and 809,000 men. Of these, five panzer divisions including 16th Panzer and eight motorised divisions were combined into the 1st Panzer Group under von Kleist. In all, they had 923 armoured fighting vehicles, of which 425 were Panzer IIIs and short-barrelled Panzer IVs, none of which were a match for the Russian T-34 medium or KV heavy tank.

Facing the Germans was the Russian South-West Front under Marshal S.M. Budenny, a civil war crony of Stalin's and completely out of touch with modern warfare, and General Kirponos, a far more competent armoured force commander. Their force consisted of 58 divisions and 907,000 men, of which 16 were tank, and eight were mechanised divisions. Their tanks totalled 5,465 including 496 T-34s with their deadly 76mm long-barrelled guns and sloped armour, and 278 heavy KV-1s and KV-2s. These last two were slow but heavily armoured, with 90mm and maximum 110mm frontal armour, and gunned with a 76mm or 152mm gun. Despite their armour superiority the Soviet tanks had a major weakness. Unlike the Germans, the Russians did not carry radios, so communication was by flags waved from the command tanks, rarely visible in the heat of battle. Changes in tactics or movement were not easily communicated, so the individual tanks generally followed the original plan, or the movement of the command tank if it could be seen or was still mobile. Some command tanks carried radios, but could only contact higher headquarters and were unable to communicate with other tanks.

The Soviet crews also lacked training in modern up-to-date tactics, which the Germans had acquired through their recent campaigns. Just as importantly they lacked vital battle experience, which the veteran German tank crews had in abundance. These factors went a long way in negating Soviet armoured superiority. Graf von Strachwitz made full use of these Soviet disadvantages to destroy superior Russian forces time and again. It was a question of knowing one's own strengths and the enemy's weaknesses. It might sound obvious but few commanders exploited these to the same effect as did Graf von Strachwitz.

However, these weaknesses were not clearly apparent to the Soviets and did not diminish their capacity to do battle. They were more than willing to fight, and General Kirponos was not prepared to remain on the defensive. He attacked at every opportunity. His actions made a lie of the German propaganda, which showed an all-conquering German Army steamrolling everything before it. Certainly the Russian Army was in headlong retreat with long columns of dejected prisoners trudging into a captivity that would result in most of them dying from disease, starvation, deprivation and execution—but it was nowhere near the easy battle the propaganda portrayed.[11]

For Hyazinth von Strachwitz and 16th Panzer, the campaign started a little late as they were kept in reserve. His brother Manfred, a panzer battalion commander in the 18th Panzer Division, had already crossed the River Bug with 80 submersible tanks, seeing action well before his older sibling. On 24 June the advance guard of 16th Panzer crossed the River Bug near Sokol-Krystinopol, leaving Russian-occupied Poland and entering Soviet territory for the first time. Marching in the wake of the 11th Panzer Division, where Graf von Strachwitz's eldest son was serving, Hube's division began its odyssey into Russia. The amount of combat Hyazinth von Strachwitz and his men saw in the first few days was negligible, consisting of gunning down pockets of resistance from hold-outs and taking some sporadic artillery fire. Nevertheless these hold-out actions were both numerous and often fanatical as Dr Heinrich Haape, a doctor with the 18th Infantry Regiment, recounts:

> Suddenly shots rang out not more than fifty feet ahead of us from a field of rye. Neuhoff pulled his horse back onto its hind legs. We dismounted and in the confusion a volley of bullets went over our heads as Hillemanns, the adjutant and a number of our men dashed into the cornfield firing their rifles and automatics as they went. There was a melée in the tall corn, a confusion of revolver shots, upraised rifle butts and screams.
>
> A tall infantryman from the HQ company brushed his way back

> through the rye. With his hands still gripping the barrel of his rifle he shrugged and said "Finished!" I noticed the butt of his rifle was splashed with blood.
>
> Neuhoff and I strode into the corn. A commissar and four Russian soldiers were lying on the trampled earth, their skulls battered into the soil, which had been freshly dug and thrown up into a mound for their suicidal ambush. The commissar's hands were still grasping uprooted cornstalks. Our casualties were negligible—one man with a bayonet wound in the arm, another man with a grazed calf. A little iodine, gauze and a couple of strips of adhesive plaster and they were ready to march on with the rest of us. Neuhoff, Hillemanns and I rode on together at the head of the column.
>
> "I didn't expect that," Neuhoff said shakily. "Sheer suicide, to attack a battalion at close quarters with five men."[12]

The Panzer Graf had a similar experience with a Soviet rearguard when his tank broke down. He waved the rest on, knowing the repairs would not take long and he would quickly catch up. A major repair requiring separation from his unit would have necessitated his transferring to another tank. The sight of the lone disabled tank was noted by a squad of Russian infantry hiding in a maize field, who rushed at the rear of the tank, away from its gun and hull machine gun. Von Strachwitz saw the danger and reacted instantly. He grabbed a machine pistol, quickly clambered out of the tank and, firing from the hip, he charged the enemy. The surprised Russians were stunned and halted momentarily. It was enough: they were stationery targets. The Graf calmly fired short, aimed bursts, as he had been trained to, bringing three Russians down before they could react. A fourth raised his rifle but was too slow, the Graf's bullets hitting him square in the chest. The remaining two turned and ran in panic-stricken flight. Two short bursts from von Strachwitz's machine pistol brought them down to the ground in a heap. His quick reactions had saved his life and that of his crew.

That sort of exposure to enemy action was typical of von Strachwitz. He personally led from the front and his battalion was usually in the van. He invariably pushed his unit forward in what amounted to a reconnaissance in force. Hube didn't interfere. He had the option of using his reconnaissance battalion, which was lightly armed with armoured cars and motorcycle troops, or his tanks. The reconnaissance battalion could only overcome light resistance, having to wait for reinforcements if engaging a superior force.

Von Strachwitz's tanks on the other hand could smash their way through most opposition, thereby maintaining the momentum of the advance.

As a battalion commander, von Strachwitz had to assess what type of engagements and resistance he was likely to encounter. This was vital for the appropriate logistics required by his unit and for its overall effectiveness. If strong resistance was anticipated, his forward supply echelon would have to carry a greater amount of ammunition than fuel. In this event he had to also decide whether to alter the standard ratio of armour-piercing to high-explosive rounds, depending on whether he expected to be engaging enemy tanks or soft-skinned vehicles, infantry anti-tank guns, or artillery. If his assessment was wrong he would be carrying an excess of the wrong type of ammunition with possible fatal results. The Russian armoured brigades at this time were almost exclusively carrying high-explosive rounds as their envisaged role was that of infantry support. They were changing over to more armour-piercing ammunition when the German panzer force struck. Their mistake would cost them dearly.

If very little resistance was expected, then von Strachwitz's support vehicles would carry more fuel than ammunition. An error here could also prove costly. Insufficient ammunition meant a greater risk of casualties and allowing Soviet tanks to escape destruction. A lack of fuel meant his tanks becoming immobilized and sitting targets at worst, or at best the enemy escaping while his tanks were waiting to be refuelled. Either way the momentum of the advance was lost allowing the enemy to regroup and counterattack. Towards the end of the war when fuel was drastically short, tanks would often have to be abandoned when they ran out of fuel. A grave situation made worse when every single tank was needed to halt the swarms of T-34s surging forward through the German lines. However the Graf's excellent tactical awareness played a vital role and he very rarely made the wrong logistical choice.

Ideally a tank battalion commander led from the front, often along with, or immediately behind the lead company. That way he could quickly assess the tactical situation and react to the changing circumstances as they arose. Not so the Panzer Graf. More often than not he was with the lead platoon, and if his armoured force was small, due to casualties or maintenance requirements, he was in the lead tank. This exposed him to frequent danger, as his 14 wounds testified. For greater observation he spent most of his time with his upper body exposed above the turret. It was the only way to get a good view of the battlefield. For this reason tank commanders suffered heavily from head wounds, often fatal ones, from either rifle or sniper fire and shrapnel from artillery, bombs or high-explosive tank rounds. It wasn't considered unusual for a tank commander to be decapitated.

Von Strachwitz quickly learnt to use only one earpiece from his radio headset. With both ears covered, his hearing was too restricted, and he couldn't track sounds outside the tank. The sound of tank engines or the clatter of their tracks frequently betrayed the presence of the enemy well before they could be seen. It was a practice eventually adopted by the most aware tank commanders along the front.

For all the planning the Graf conducted, nothing prepared him for the sheer brutality of the enemy. The Hague Convention did not exist for the Red Army, and Russia was not a signatory, so as a consequence the Red Cross and respect for the wounded meant absolutely nothing. The 16th Panzer Division's field ambulance unit belonging to the 64th Regiment was overrun by the Soviets during one of their frequent counterattacks. The Russians cruelly massacred the entire unit including the wounded. Their bodies were found mutilated, with most having been subjected to torture and an agonizing death. Dr Heinrich Haape describes an example of the Bolsheviks' disregard for the Red Cross flag in his memoir of the advance into Russia:

> The hollow pointed out by the stretcher-bearer lay a hundred yards from the house. We made a dash for the ditch and plunged into it as sniper's bullets bit into the earth on either bank and showered us with dust. The machine gun from the farmhouse chattered and I seized the opportunity to dash across the remaining twenty yards to the hollow.
>
> Six bodies lay sprawled in the hollow. A stretcher-bearer lay on his back, arms flung wide, and four other soldiers lay close by just as they had fallen. And there was the doctor, lying face downwards, Red Cross band on his sleeve, a bold red cross on the flag by his side. The contents of his medical pack were strewn around him.
>
> As if afraid of being overheard, the Pfarrer whispered: "A hundred yards from here—see, there, behind those gorse bushes, the Russians were lying. The doctor had brought the wounded men into the hollow and was attending to them when the Russians started firing. I was watching from the farmhouse but could do nothing. The doctor stood up and waved his red cross flag, but they kept firing at him. He fell, and they fired and fired until nothing moved in the

hollow. It was horrible . . . cold-blooded murder." His voice broke and tears were in his eyes.[13]

The Russians frequently mounted local counterattacks as their reserve and second-line forces were still largely intact despite being badly mauled by Stuka dive-bombers. In the Huka sector a large Soviet infantry unit attacked the 16th Panzer spearhead. At its very tip was Graf von Strachwitz with a small force of Panzer IIIs. The Soviet infantry surged forward shoulder to shoulder, a mass of brown uniforms, their bayonets gleaming in the sun. They swarmed literally from their hiding places, where they had been waiting concealed for the first German unit to come along. An attack against tanks was suicidal but they were helped along by large doses of vodka. To ensure there would be no shirkers or stragglers, the commissars ran behind them brandishing their nickel-plated pistols ready to shoot anyone who wavered. It was to become a common combination ensuring blind obedience in the face of certain death. Very quickly the Graf's force was surrounded by the horde, and while it looked to be an easy task to wipe out the field infantrymen, in reality it was far from simple. They mounted the tanks, placing grenades in vulnerable spots to disable them, and molotov cocktails to start fires in engine bays, while firing guns fire into the driver's observation slit.

The Graf quickly ordered a defensive circle with each tank covering the one to its front. His orders were clear and calm. To panic now could break their defence and leave them vulnerable. Their machine guns sent long chattering bursts into the enemy masses while their main guns, depressed as low as possible, fired high-explosive rounds into the troops swarming at the tank to their front.

Bodies and body parts flew through the air as Russians fell in groups and rows, yet still they came, trampling over their own dead, seemingly oblivious to the awful carnage around them. The wounded who staggered to the rear were shot by their haranguing commissars, either out of mercy or sheer bloodlust. Many Russians, fuelled more by hatred than alcohol, made almost superhuman efforts to climb on to the German vehicles. The hull machine guns of the tanks blew them away. But nothing seemed to stop the red horde. Not death, wounds or fear. Finally, with almost the last machine gun rounds expended, the attack ebbed away. Even the commissars realized the attack had failed, and ran back with the surviving troops.

When it was over, even the normally imperturbable Graf was shaken. Such fanatical disregard for death was new to him. He climbed out of his tank to survey the damage and remove the bodies sprawled over it. A single shot rang out. Von Strachwitz staggered a step, then collapsed. The bullet had ricocheted off his tank and hit him. The tank commander of the nearest tank scrambled out of his turret and, disregarding his own safety, ran over to assist. No other shots were fired, so presumably it had been the last desperate effort from a wounded or dying Russian.

After a field dressing was put on his wound von Strachwitz was helped into his tank and he returned to the German lines for treatment. Ignoring the doctor's advice, he refused evacuation, opting to stay with his troops. As long as he was capable of leading he would lead. His wound was simply something he had to accept as part of his job, and fortunately it was a ricochet with only shallow penetration. It was the first of many wounds for the Graf.

His shooting was typical of that received by a tank commander, as most deaths and wounds occurred while the crewmen were outside their tanks, or partially exposed in the turret. Commanders frequently had to leave their tanks to reconnoitre, attend orders groups, give verbal instructions to other commanders, liaise with the officers of their supporting infantry, change tanks or undertake a myriad of other duties required of them. Because of their command responsibilities they were at greater risk of death or injury than ordinary tank crewmen. Very often casualties were caused by sudden salvoes of artillery, and snipers were also a constant danger.

The inexorable advance of 16th Panzer continued with the tanks at the front and long trailing columns of motorized infantry, artillery and supply troops bringing up the rear. Soviet aircraft, flying from airfields in the hinterland, tried to hinder the Germans progress. They bombed 16th Panzer's columns in a sustained attack, but the bombs fortunately fell alongside, causing only minimal casualties and damage. The Russian Air Force had a habit of bombing across a column instead of along it, consequently causing nowhere near the damage they would have otherwise. It was certainly less dangerous for the Soviet aircrews, as it reduced their exposure to ground fire because the German self-propelled anti-aircraft guns had very little time to fire. However as a bombing run it often proved ineffectual and the Russian Air Force never achieved the massive impact of the Western air forces, despite having total supremacy for most of the war.

The impetus of the division's advance was slowed by exceedingly heavy rain, which quickly turned the dirt roads into a morass. Soft-skinned vehicles got bogged down to their axles, and only tracked vehicles could move. However there were insufficient tracked prime movers available, so von Strachwitz's tanks had to be employed as towing vehicles, much to his chagrin. Tanks were fighting vehicles not tow trucks. Every hour lost pulling trucks out of the mud delayed the advance by an hour, giving the enemy time to regroup and prepare defences. But there was nothing to be done. To make matters worse, the heavy pulling used up precious fuel, and if that wasn't enough, the fuel trucks were not getting through quickly enough. He partially solved the problem by having his tanks carry fuel cans on their hulls, but this created another problem should they be caught in a surprise attack, with the flammable liquid making an excellent funeral pyre.

Fortunately the rain didn't last but it was a foretaste of what was to come during autumn and the following spring, when whole armies would be immobilised. Hube reported "slow but steady progress" to headquarters, who were greatly unimpressed, wanting lightning advances, smashing into the enemy's rear and capturing large tracts of enemy territory. Little did anyone know, that they were heading into the biggest tank battle of the war so far. Graf von Strachwitz was to have the opportunity to demonstrate his superb tank-fighting abilities.

NOTES

1. Kinsel would be replaced by Colonel Reinhardt Gehlen who proved more realistic in his estimates and raised the ire of his Führer who refused to believe them. He survived Hitler's wrath to become head of West Germany's intelligence service after the war.
2. Alan Clark, *Barbarossa* (Macmillan, 1985), pp. 42–43.
3. General Heinz Guderian, *Panzer Leader* (Futura Publications, 1977), p. 152.
4. Stahlberg, *Bounden Duty*.
5. Major Gerhard Engel, *At the Heat of the Reich* (Greenhill Books, 2005), pp. 113–114.
6. F.J. Goodspeed, *The German Wars* (Bonanza Books NY, 1977).
7. Werner Adamczyk, *Feuer! An Artilleryman's Life on the Eastern Front*.
8. Andrew Nagorski, *The Greatest Battle: The Fight for Moscow 1941–1942* (Simon and Schuster NY, 2007).
9. German Research Institute for Military History Volume IV.
10. Siegfried Knappe, *Soldat*, p. 181.
11. Close to 3,000,000 Soviet POWs died from disease, starvation, overwork and neglect in German captivity. Admittedly in the early stages of the war the Germans were overwhelmed by the number of captives they took, but equally they made very little and often, no effort to care for them so that it amounted to mass murder. The sad irony was that those that did survive captivity were nearly all sent to Siberian slave labour camps for having surrendered, and for being exposed to the West and its ways. It must be added that German POWs fared little better and died in their hundreds of thousands, for the same reasons. Soviet sources admit to 580,589 German deaths, but the

actual number is well in excess of one million.

12. Dr Heinrich Haape with Dennis Henshaw, *Moscow Tram Stop* (Collins Publishing, London, 1957). Dr. Happe was one of only few doctors to be awarded the German Cross in Gold for bravery in recovering the wounded under fire and maintaining his aid post close to the frontlines.
13. Ibid.

NINE

THE BATTLES OF DUBNO AND UMAN

FROM 27 JUNE TO MID-OCTOBER, 16TH PANZER DIVISION was involved in a series of major battles with the Red Army's South-West Front. Because of the short breaks between them they tend to merge into one long campaign of Operation *Barbarossa*, but they can be broken up into fairly distinct stages or battles. The first was the Battle of Dubno-Werba from 27 June to 1 July. This was followed by the Battle of Uman from 15 July to 8 August and then the larger Battle of Kiev, which went to the end of September. From 29 September through to mid-October there were the battles of Rostov and the Azov Sea.

The Soviet South-West Front was commanded by Marshal Budenny. A mediocre general at best, he nevertheless had an able subordinate in General Kirponos who had gained renown while commanding the 70th Rifle Division during the 1939 invasion of Finland. To defend the South-West Front, Kirponos had six mechanised corps—the IV, VIII, IX, XV, XIX, and XII—which were among the best in the Red Army at that stage of the war. On 25 June he launched them against the 11th, 13th, 14th and 16th Panzer Divisions in a bold attempt, not just to halt their advance, but to encircle and destroy them. His VIII and XV Mechanised Corps attacked from Brody while the IX and XIX Corps thrust into von Kleist's Panzer Group's northern flank, with the intention of meeting at Dubno. The Russians had a powerful force of 717 T-34 medium and KV heavy tanks which were half the total available to the entire Russian Army, and was more than sufficient to ensure victory given their superiority to the lighter undergunned German tanks. They eventually took Dubno, badly mauling the 11th Panzer Division, which lost 20 tanks.

The Germans were, however, slowly coming to terms with dealing with the T-34s and KVs. The 50mm guns of the Panzer IIIs could only destroy them at very close range and only then by hitting the Russian tanks' more lightly armoured flanks and rear. At longer ranges their only option was to disable the Russians by hitting their tracks, which of course, still allowed the Russians to keep firing so it was only a partial—and very risky—solution. The majority of the German anti-tank guns were 37mm calibre and absolutely useless, while the heavier 50mm guns were, like the Panzer III, only effective at suicidally close ranges. One can then appreciate the sheer terror and feeling of helplessness the Germans experienced when they encountered these Soviet tanks. Their phrase for it, *Panzerschreck*, meant "tank terror," and they spent a great deal of time, effort, training and weaponry to overcome it. The only effective weapon the Germans had at this stage of the war was the 88mm anti-aircraft gun, a superlative weapon against both aircraft and tanks. General Erhard Raus describes the effort it took to destroy a KV-1 tank at Rossienie, Lithuania, which had broken through and blocked a main supply road:

> The first shot flashed forth from the anti-tank gun. The traced trajectory pointed like a silver ray directly into the target. . . . A glare of fire appeared followed by a violent impact. The tank received a direct hit. A second and third shot followed . . .
>
> The tank did not move. It did not discover the firing battery until it received the eighth hit. Now it took aim and silenced the battery with a few 80mm [actually 76mm] shells. Two anti-tank guns were shot to pieces and the remainder damaged. The battery suffered dead and wounded and had to withdraw the balance of the personnel into safe cover in order to avoid further losses. Only after night had fallen could the guns be recovered.[1]
>
> An 88mm anti-aircraft gun was brought up but the KV-1 destroyed it before it could fire a shot. Volunteers from the engineers placed explosives on the tank that night but even these failed to destroy it. Another 88mm gun was brought in but this time German tanks attacked the Russian tank with fire and manoeuvre to distract it while the 88mm gun got into a favourable firing position. The anti-aircraft gun fired seven rounds into the Russian tank. Only two penetrated, but they succeeded in putting the heavily armoured giant out of action.

When 16th Panzer encountered its first T-34, the anti-tank battalion sent in its 37mm guns, which fired from a range of 120 metres. Two hits were scored in quick succession without result. More guns opened fire, scoring 23 hits in all, with every round bouncing off harmlessly. At a range of 30 metres they finally managed to hit the T-34's turret ring, immobilising its turret and rendering the tank harmless. This all boded ill for von Strachwitz and his tanks with their 50mm guns and relatively thin amour. He would have to rely on guile and superior training as well as the experience garnered by his troops in the French campaign.

Near Dubno, Hube's 16th Panzer Division was attacked on both its flanks as well as frontally. The major threat came from Lieutenant General D.I. Riabyshev's VIII Mechanised Corps, which had the 12th and 34th Tank Divisions and an armoured brigade under Brigade Commissar N. K. Popel. Their objective was to destroy Hube's division from the rear and retake Dubno. The corps was well provided with deadly T-34s but their crews were poorly trained, especially the drivers, who were not yet familiar with their new tanks. The Soviet divisions had also suffered heavy casualties in men and equipment from relentless Stuka dive-bombing attacks while receiving little or no support from the Russian Air Force. Overall the Russian Army in the area lost over 200 tanks to the Luftwaffe attacks, sufficient to considerably weaken it.

Luftwaffe reconnaissance planes warned Hube of the advancing menace and Graf von Strachwitz was sent forward by Rudolf Sieckenius as a reconnaissance in force. Almost instantly von Strachwitz and his battalion were involved in repeated small-scale actions with Russian armoured forces. Excellent command and control, combined with accurate gunnery saw the Russian units engaged and destroyed. All too often the Reds fired while on the move making their gunfire extremely inaccurate. The Germans, on the other hand, always halted to fire. The Graf's personal command tank destroyed many of the Soviets, beginning a tally that would place him among the top German tank aces of the war. Contrary to the practice of most regimental and battalion commanders, he invariably used a command tank carrying a main gun rather than the purpose-built command tanks which carried extra radio equipment in lieu of the main gun, and a dummy gun, which didn't suit von Strachwitz's active fighting command style at all.

General Hube redeployed his division in order to attack Werba. On the way he captured Ort very quickly but was then halted by heavy tank and anti-tank gunfire from positions on the hills north of Plaszowa. The German tanks were engaged in continuous running battles with Soviet armour, requiring individual tanks to retreat to the rear in order to take on more ammunition before returning to the fray. The fighting continued until dusk, with no relief in sight. It was a nightmare of thundering guns, exploding tanks, near misses, smoke, fire, noise and death. Crews of abandoned tanks struggled to make their way back to safety as still mobile tanks had little opportunity to see or collect them.

Russian infantry now surged forward to cut the road where the main divisional battle group was echeloned. Russian tanks smashed onto the road crushing soft-skinned vehicles while firing wildly at the armoured personnel carriers and light flak assembled there. Panic set in as the dreaded tank terror took hold, and German troops ran frantically in all directions to escape the firing steel monsters and roaring Russian infantry. A mad scrambling withdrawal began, covered by the few German tanks and guns available, which just managed to hold the Russians back. Mercifully nightfall prevented a major Russian breakthrough.[2]

Hube called for help from the Graf's 1st Battalion, which had streaked ahead of the main body. On their return the Panzer Graf's battalion came under heavy fire from Russian gun batteries set up on the high ground, which disabled several of his tanks with track damage. This type of damage could be repaired, but not under constant gunfire. As night fell the Germans sought to regroup and repair their damaged tanks. As they did so the Russians launched a massive attack at last light, with tanks and infantry hoping to catch the Germans in the open and off-guard. A wild melée developed as the Graf's men desperately fought to repulse the vastly superior Bolshevik force. Flares and flames lit up the night sky, with light and dark alternating as fleeting shadows of men and tanks criss-crossed between them. Every so often a sharp flash indicated an exploding tank. Tracers streaked in long seemingly endless streams of deadly light, seeking out the soft targets of the advancing Russian infantry.

Von Strachwitz quickly realised that retreat was his only option. To stand and fight would mean the destruction of his vastly outnumbered force, despite killing more than four times his number in enemy infantry and tanks. He remained calm, rallying his force with clear, concise instructions for their withdrawal. He personally led the rearguard as the majority of his force sought to escape into the dark. Howling with rage the Russians infantry pursued, but losing direction soon gave up. The Russian tanks however pushed on.

As one by one his beleaguered tanks disengaged, the Panzer Graf fought on, knocking out or disabling Russian armour at every opportunity. Gradually his men abandoned the battlefield, leaving it strewn with burnt-out and blown-up Russian hulks, along with mounds of corpses from their supporting infantry.

There was very little time for von Strachwitz's battalion to regroup, repair any damage, and take care of the wounded. Any of the wounded who could, stayed with their crews to keep on fighting. Speedily his men reorganised for the counterattack that von Strachwitz was eager to launch.

The Russian tanks had withdrawn, happy with their result, despite suffering horrendous losses. Thinking that the Germans were badly mauled they were not expecting the riposte when it came. The Graf's battalion infiltrated the Russian lines stealthily, slipping in just before dawn. As the first streaks of light lit up the sky, the German panzers stuck. Their prime targets were the T-34s bivouacked for the night. The noise of their engines and clatter of tracks didn't alarm the sleepy Soviet sentries, who merely assumed that it was a Russian tank column moving up. The German tanks moved slowly forward and halted. The Graf took in the scene before him and issued his orders. Every Russian tank was targeted. "Fire!" came his order and the German guns blazed. Immediately hits were registered all along the line. T-34s flamed and exploded in one continuous roar of fire and destruction. The German radio operators who manned the hull machine guns fired frantically into the Russian tank crews seeking to board their tanks or to escape. Very few escaped alive.

The Germans roared on to other targets. The Russian supply vehicles parked nearby were blown to pieces by high-explosive rounds. The Graf then called a quick halt to take stock. Behind him over 30 Russian tanks lay burning and destroyed, some with their turrets blown clear off.

Von Strachwitz's next objective was the nearby Russian artillery positions. He ordered his battalion to follow his lead. The Russian gunners had heard the firing and were alert, but were not aware of the true situation or from which direction the attack would come. As it was, it took them from the rear. Tank fire, red-hot shrapnel and machine-gun bullets smashed through their exposed positions, wiping them out and destroying their guns. Massive explosions rent the air as the ammunition blew up. The gun crews didn't even have time to send out a call for help.

This was still insufficient destruction for the Panzer Graf. His rampaging tanks roared through the Russian rear destroying all before them. Soviet supply columns were easy targets, succumbing to gunfire or simply being crushed by tank tracks. Headquarters units were also caught by surprise and blasted into oblivion as were food and ammunition dumps. Nearby he found a fuel depot, carrying mainly diesel for the T-34s, but enough petrol to refuel his thirsty tanks. At one combined fuel-ammunition depot he found a Russian tank column in the process of replenishing. The Russians didn't stand a chance. Their shock was so great that the crews simply abandoned their tanks and fled on foot. Fourteen Russian tanks were set ablaze without a single shot being fired in return. Straggling Russian tanks were added to the tally as they returned to their rear for repairs or fuel, and a marching column of infantry was nearly annihilated with machine-gun fire before they could flee.

The rampage continued with von Strachwitz roving around the enemy's rear. Rapid movement meant the Reds had no idea where he was, or what his strength was. Their greatest fear was that he represented a major German breakthrough. Fatigue was now his greatest enemy, as his men had had no sleep for two days and nights and were staying awake through adrenalin and sheer willpower. Still their battalion commander drove them on. All that mattered was to keep moving and keep destroying the enemy. His drive and determination kept his men going. If their older battalion commander could do it, then so could they.

The mayhem and uncertainty he caused was a major factor in the Russians' calling off the attack on the beleaguered 16th Panzer Division. The Russians, unaware of von Strachwitz's real strength, or the focus of his attack, sought to regroup in order to counter the threat that he represented. Hube's division was saved. Kirponos had not only been repulsed but he had been forced to withdraw. No doubt the rescue of his division and the Russian withdrawal were major factors in General Hube's later recommendation for von Strachwitz to be awarded the coveted Knight's Cross.

Not all the Russians were happy with Kirponos' withdrawal order. Political Commissar N.N. Vashugin countermanded the retreat order as being gross defeatism. He personally took command of the battered 8th Mechanised Corps and launched his own attack. Unfortunately he led his armoured force into a swamp where his tanks got bogged down, and for want of recovery tractors had to be abandoned. In utter despair at this pointless failure he drew his pistol and shot himself.

The battle of Dubno was the largest tank battle of the war to date, with the Germans fielding 250 tanks combined in the 11th and 16th Panzer Divisions. The Soviets had available 717 tanks, which they concentrated on 16th

Panzer and the 57th and 75th Infantry Divisions. They lost 293 tanks, many of them to Graf von Strachwitz's 1st Battalion. His own personal score would easily have been over 30 enemy tanks. Overall it was a considerable defensive success for the Germans.

General Hube's 16th Panzer then continued its advance. Constant rain, however, slowed its progress, as mud caught vehicles in its glutinous remorseless grip. Von Strachwitz stood at the side of the river of mud that passed for a road and fumed, as his tanks were called in to tow the trapped vehicles through the morass. Never a patient man, he would have been sorely tested as he watched his fighting vehicles being used as beasts of burden, and using up precious fuel in the process. To make matters worse, Russian Rata fighters made several attacks on the almost stranded German vehicles, while at night obsolete Russian bi-planes dropped light bombs to disturb everyone's sleep.

The Russians put up stiff resistance to the German advance at Kremeniece, Gamipol and Starokonstantinov. These were taken by German infantry supported by both battalions of the division's panzer regiment. The division then went on to capture the bridges over the Horin River, and penetrated the Stalin Line near Ryuban with the help of 210mm guns of the heavy artillery.

Along with his regimental commander, von Strachwitz was getting concerned about his supply problems. Food was no problem, as the division had captured over a million eggs from a Soviet supply dump, so they were eating copious amounts of eggs cooked in every way imaginable. Resupply priorities were ammunition, fuel and food in that order, leaving little capacity for much-needed spare parts. The Graf's tanks were in desperate need of repair and maintenance. The dusty dirt roads had scoured his tank engines, degrading their pistons and other parts, while the cloying mud, over a metre deep in places, had strained the tracks and engines. Very often the parts he requested just didn't arrive, or they were the wrong ones, and if they were by chance the right ones they never arrived in the quantity necessary. He didn't know it, but the supply officers back at army headquarters did not believe that his usage figures were genuine. They concluded that the division was simply hoarding in order to build up a spare parts reserve. With no real appreciation of the actual conditions at the front, they sent along only the amount they considered to be realistic and genuine. Von Strachwitz and 16th Panzer were not alone in their problems obtaining spare parts. Every division on the Eastern Front suffered from this difficulty. The situation was exacerbated by the diversity of vehicles in use, which included many captured and requisitioned civil and military vehicles from the occupied countries. For instance 18th Panzer Division had over 100 different types of trucks, 37 motorcycle types and 96 different troop carriers, while the cars were a motley mixture of German, French and Belgian vehicles. The whole front was a maintenance nightmare.

The Germans now planned to cut off parts of Marshal Budenny's Army Group around the city of Uman. Von Kleist's panzers were sent southeast to complete the encirclement. The 16th Panzer moved across the vast fertile fields of the Ukraine with sunflowers as far as the eye could see, all nodding in veneration to the sun. Yet all too often these fields concealed Russian units who were prepared to sell their lives dearly to delay the German advance. Brisk bloody battles took place within the golden fields. No quarter was given or asked, with each taking a small toll of lives from the advancing German infantry, so that their numbers were slowly eroded. Most battalions and companies were at half-strength or less with replacements only trickling in. Most of these replacements were inexperienced, quickly becoming casualties themselves. Here at least Graf's tank men had an advantage, for while their tank numbers were getting lower, the crews themselves had a far higher survivability rate than the infantry.

The Panzer Graf as usual placed himself at the front of the advance, scanning the horizon for the tell-tale signs of enemy armour. In the vast emptiness of the steppes, large forces could pass each other without knowing of each other's existence. It was becoming impossible for the Luftwaffe to provide reconnaissance over the vast distances being covered, a situation that would only worsen. A thin trail of smoke or some distant faint signs of movement were often the only signs to betray the presence of the enemy. Nevertheless the noose was slowly, inexorably tightening around the Russians.

Von Kleist's three panzer corps drove the Russians away from the vital Berdichev–Katazatin railway, capturing both towns in the process on 15–16 July. This severed Budenny's north–south communications, forcing a gap into his armies. Budenny was too slow to order a withdrawal and even pushed some reserves into Uman, which was about to be surrounded.

Pushed back though they were, the Russians were far from being defeated, and had plenty of fight left in them. On 20 July they vigorously counterattacked Kleist's panzers with six infantry and two cavalry divisions. Their infantry attacked in human waves, arms linked in a brotherly embrace of death. Large helpings of vodka fortified them against the knowledge that certain death awaited most, while the lucky few would escape with wounds.

T-34s packed with infantry stormed towards the German lines until stopped by a direct hit, which smashed the tanks and mangled the troops on board. The attack was repulsed with great difficulty, leaving long rows of dead Russians and burning tanks.

The ring around the Soviets closed on 2 August when troops of von Kleist's Panzer Group reached elements of General Stülpnagel's Seventeenth Army. The next day they were reinforced by Hube's 16th Panzer Division which met up with the Hungarian Mechanised Corps. His division formed the eastward crest of the pocket at Monasteryschtsche.[3] Trapped inside the Uman pocket were the Russian Sixth Army under General Muzyrchenko and the Twelfth Army under Major General Ponedelin with the remnants of 20 divisions.

The Reds made desperate attempts to break out of the cauldron, sometimes successfully. The 16th Panzer Reconnaissance Battalion found itself surrounded by escaping Red Army troops in the Oratov forest. A desperate battle for survival followed with Russians hacking, stabbing and killing in frantic efforts to break through the ring, or at least kill as many invaders as possible. The majority of the Germans escaped, but just barely, being forced to abandon all their guns and heavy equipment, which were bogged down in the swampy terrain. There followed a week of heavy fighting as the Germans strived to keep the noose closed tight. The Soviets fought savagely in their attempts to break out, attacking in large and small formations with whatever weapons they had available against the German lines.

Von Strachwitz and his panzers moved around the perimeter, blasting the Reds with high-explosive rounds and scything machine-gun fire. In one instance, trucks crammed full of Soviets charged directly at his tanks, the soldiers firing wildly as they rushed forward. Tank shells blasted the trucks and men to pieces, while machine-gun fire cut down the survivors as they staggered from the wrecks, but not a single one surrendered. For these Russian troops, surrender was out of the question. As long as they held some hope of escape they fought tenaciously, not expecting any quarter nor giving any; it was a fight to the death. Some did escape through gaps in the line, as the Germans lacked the manpower to seal the pocket off completely; however, most ended up as corpses in the fields or as totally exhausted prisoners. Eventually 103,000 would be taken captive, while 100,000 would be either killed or wounded. Some 317 burnt-out or disabled Russian tanks would litter the battlefield. Budenny's headquarters was overrun, with Budenny himself barely making his escape in a light aircraft. He left behind two army commanders, four corps commanders and eleven divisional commanders to march into captivity.[4]

During the battle von Strachwitz's tanks captured Monasteryschtsche railway station, thus preventing any Russian escape by rail. Realising the importance of this escape route the Soviets repeatedly tried to retake it. The Graf's men were exhausted by the continuous combat, as the enemy rarely let up, and constant vigilance was needed to spot infiltrators trying to sneak through the German lines, yet von Strachwitz kept pushing them on, leading by example, never resting and always where the fighting was thickest. He was always calm, almost coldly so, and completely in control no matter what the situation. Every so often, his sardonic humour would come to the surface and genuine warmth flashed in his eyes, giving a very human dimension to a highly disciplined and accomplished warrior.

The Reds, knowing the railway line was their best means of escape, kept up the pressure. They attacked in successive waves yelling their war cry, "Urra! Urra!" as they surged forward, often supported by tanks and armoured cars, or trucks bearing machine guns. However the Germans were equally determined to hold and they turned the railway station into a Russian graveyard. The enemy swarmed around and through their tanks. Frantic messages for infantry support went unanswered, and von Strachwitz soon faced a crisis. Ammunition was dangerously low, a number of his tanks were disabled, and his men were at the very end of their reserves of strength and courage. He was facing the option of abandoning his position or being annihilated. There came a welcome lull in the fighting, but all the old hands knew that it was just the enemy regrouping. At the very last minute a column of relieving infantry arrived to save the day. Even though the attacks still came in, they were stopped far more quickly and effectively. It had been a near-run thing. Slowly and with a great deal of relief, von Strachwitz led his battered battalion back to base and a well-deserved rest.

Any rest was short-lived as Pervomaisk, a large town on the River Bug, had to be taken. Hube tasked von Strachwitz with advancing swiftly to take the bridges over the river, ignoring any Russian units found on the way. In a swiftly moving column von Strachwitz's battalion raced towards their objective. They brushed past light front-line opposition and once behind enemy lines they simply pretended to be a Russian tank column, waving to marching Russian infantry, and ignoring any Soviet mechanised units. It was a risky manoeuvre, which depended on the Russians mistaking the German armor for Russian tanks, but it worked. Only after the Germans had crossed the bridge were the gun emplacements and guard posts taken out in a hail of high-explosive and machine-gun fire. The German tanks, with von Strachwitz in the lead, quickly pushed on into Pervomaisk itself. Russian troops alerted by the gunfire were just rushing out of their billets when the Germans smashed into them, cutting them down with machine-gun fire. Here and there some firm resistance was encountered but the Soviets were too surprised to do much more than surrender or flee.

The capture of the town represented quite a coup for von Strachwitz and his battalion, but he wasn't content just to wait there for his relief. Tanks were meant to keep moving; holding ground was for the infantry. Leaving a reinforced company to secure the town with its vital bridge, his force sped further behind the Russian lines. He came across a long, straggling column of Russian vehicles—trucks of all types, tractors pulling artillery pieces, cars, carts, anti-tank guns and staff officer vehicles—all crowded together, barely moving on a heavily congested road. It was a tank commander's dream.

The Russians paid no attention as the Panzer Graf wheeled his formation around to move in parallel with the column. After all, the front was many kilometres away so the tanks had to be Russian. When his panzers were in position, the Graf gave his order to fire. A ripple of flame flashed along the German line followed quickly by a string of explosions smashing into the Russian column. Explosions rent the air as ammunition trucks exploded, destroying everything near them, fuel trucks went up in huge fireballs, and debris and bodies were flung skywards. Machine-gun fire added to the carnage as the Graf moved along the road like an angel of death. Russians abandoning their vehicles ran aimlessly in all directions, often straight into the gunfire and explosions they were trying desperately to avoid. Those who tried to escape by heading away from the road only got a brief respite until von Strachwitz crossed the road, knocking aside burning trucks, to commence the mayhem on the other side. Russians were crushed beneath the grinding tank tracks while the relentless fire of the Germans continued, spraying the whole column with the hot metal of shrapnel and machine-gun rounds. Not a single vehicle escaped the inferno. Some 300 trucks remained only as twisted, burning piles of debris on the road along with numerous guns, cars and carts. Here and there ammunition was exploding with sharp crackles while grey black smoke smelling of fuel and burning rubber permeated the air. The Russian dead lay strewn all along the road, singly and in clusters. Some bodies were still convulsing in their death throes, while here and there, like spectres through the smoke, shattered survivors staggered about in shock.

For both the Russian column, and the troops waiting for their supplies and reinforcements, it was an utter disaster.

There was grim satisfaction in the scene for it was a serious blow to the Soviets, but the Graf couldn't tarry, as the smoke and noise were bound to bring the unwelcome attention of Russian reinforcements. He had to move quickly before he was taken by surprise. Cleverly he moved his small force some distance away into cover, to await the arrival of the Russian rescue units. He didn't have long to wait. A column of T-34s was soon swiftly making its way along the road towards the plumes of smoke.

Von Strachwitz calmly gave brief firing instructions, allocating his tanks individual targets. When the leading T-34 was comfortably in range for a kill shot he gave the order to fire. His round streaked across, smashing into the Russians' vulnerable side armour. It burst into flame almost immediately. The other German tanks then commenced firing at short range, scoring hits with every shot, disabling or destroying each T-34 in their sights. Black smoke rings spiralled up, indicating a turret blown off or displaced. In a matter of minutes it was all over. More than 20 Russian tanks were blown up and burning, and the crewmen fortunate enough to survive were scattered in all directions, pursued by angry machine-gun fire.

It was a good day's work, but with his tanks almost out of ammunition and low on fuel it was time to go back. Von Strachwitz ordered a withdrawal back to Pervomaisk, where the 16th Panzer had fought its way through to meet him.

NOTES

1. P. Tsouras (ed.), *Panzers on the Eastern Front. General Erhard Raus and His Panzer Divisions in Russia 1941–1945* (Greenhill Books 2002), pp. 39–44.
2. Paul Carrell, *Hitler's War on Russia Vol. 1 Hitler Moves East* (Corgi Books, 1971), pp. 30–31.
3. Günter Schmitz, *Die 16 Panzer Division 1938–1944* (Dörfler im Nebel Verlag Gmbh, 2004).
4. Carrell, *Hitler's War on Russia, Vol 1: Hitler Moves East.*

TEN

THE BATTLE OF NIKOLAYEV

WHILE GUDERIAN, VON BOCK AND HALDER WERE largely fixated on taking Moscow with Army Group Centre, Hitler was still worried about his southern flank and obsessing over the Ukraine. He could see the possibility of a major encirclement of the Soviets there and suggested moving General Guderian's Panzer Group 2 from Army Group Centre to the South, catching the Russians in a large pincer movement. The Army High Command (Oberkommando das Heers, or OKH) wanted to take Moscow and argued against any weakening of Army Group Centre. This left Hitler wracked with indecision—politically (and indeed, strategically) Moscow and Leningrad "had to be got rid of," but economically the Ukraine had to be the objective.[1] These competing political and economic aspects dogged Hitler throughout the war, leading him into decisions that were not militarily sound, although from Hitler's economic and political viewpoint were perfectly justified. His generals, including Guderian and von Manstein among others, could never appreciate this viewpoint and blamed Hitler, sometimes unfairly, for every defeat and setback. In the end, in this instance, Hitler opted to have both Moscow and the Ukraine. As for Leningrad, the former Tsarist capital could be starved into submission, as he had doubts about using tanks to demolish cities. He ordered Guderian southwards but only temporarily, to help linquidate the Soviet concentration around Kiev, after which his panzer group would move back to take Moscow. This delay and shift in resources was fatal, even though it did result in a massive Soviet defeat in the Ukraine.

Stalin expected Hitler to attack Moscow so he concentrated his strength there, although he did send Field Marshal Budenny some reinforcements. Realising that he was going to be surrounded in a pincer move, Budenny requested permission to withdraw. Stalin would have none of it, instead sending him more men to be eventually caught in the cauldron. Sanguine as he was about possible encirclement, Stalin was, however, alarmed at the hasty retreat of many Russian units in the face of what he considered very little pressure. His solution was draconian—the NKVD (internal security troops) formed halt lines behind the front. Their task was simple, to shoot any retreating troops, without question, and they did just that, machine-gunning entire companies as well as summarily executing any individuals found wandering behind the immediate front. There was no trial, perhaps one or two questions if the NKVD officer felt inclined, followed by a bullet to the back of the head. The Soviets admitted to "court-martialling," if that term could validly be used, some one million men during the war but this figure is far too low. If found guilty, which nearly all were, the men were either executed or sent to penal battalions where death came a little later, during suicidal attacks or mine clearance. The figure also does not include summary executions without a trial, or mass shootings of retreating troops by the NKVD. The Germans resorted to similar measures late in the war, with drumhead courts-martial and summary executions for troops found behind the lines without a valid reason and relevant paperwork, however the numbers executed were small compared to the Soviet tally.

If the Russians were in dire straits, the Germans were having major problems of their own. Apart from fuel, food and transport shortages, there was the question of rapidly diminishing manpower. By 2 August the Germans had suffered 180,000 casualties along the Eastern Front, of which 63,000 were sustained by Army Group South, with only 10,000 replacements arriving to fill the gaps.[2] Death was the German soldier's constant companion, often coming very violently with consequential morale problems, as Gunter Koschorrek, a machine gunner with the 24th Panzer Division, described:

> Those who lie here are not just dead bodies with one wound in them, or possibly one part missing. Here are individual lumps of flesh, from arms, legs and buttocks and in one instance a head; onto which part of a damaged helmet still clings. These are the remains of the men of the 88mm A.A. gun and the quad machine gun, both of which received direct hits from the T-34 and were blown apart, blasted into the air. I feel so miserable as we stumble forward.[3]

For tank crews, burns were a serious and common injury while bodies could be horribly mangled by the hot metal hurtling around inside the turret. Nevertheless the steel armour provided protection and therefore increased survivability especially, in the heavier tanks. A crew of the later Tiger tanks had far better chances of surviving than the crew of a Panzer III or IV. Another advantage for tank crews was that they didn't have to walk, marching for hours in all weather. The German infantry marched hundreds of kilometres, and if an infantryman survived the war he would have walked for several thousand kilometres in choking dust, blazing sun, cloying mud, and freezing rain or snow. He was always covered in dirt, hungry, often thirsty and exhausted. For the Panzer Graf and his men, life was better but nevertheless had its hardships. Being confined in a greasy, smelly, dirty steel box wasn't pleasant. In summer it was an oven, in winter a freezer. One tank crewman, Walter Thomaschek of the Grossdeutschland Division, described his life in a tank:

> I never felt comfortable inside the tank. The noise was almost unbearable although we wore earplugs or were wearing headphones. Trapped inside this tin can I quickly lose my sense of orientation and often didn't know in which direction we were heading. Our commander [von Strachwitz] received orders via the radio but didn't give us detailed instructions or information about our whereabouts. ... Only the commander and the driver were able to see the outside world, through small slits covered with bullet-proof glass [hence why most commanders had their heads and/or torsos outside the turret whenever circumstances permitted]. The rest of the crew was not able to see anything. It was a terrible feeling to see nothing during a fight. One could hear bullets ricocheting off the armour and everybody praying that no AT shell would hit us ...
>
> Inside the tank was a terrible mess. Dirt got carried inside our boots. The smell of unwashed bodies was everywhere. Quite often we had to wait in the tank for hours, be it extremely hot or terribly cold. The body hurt from sitting endlessly in the cramped space. Officially we weren't allowed to sleep. Usually we agreed upon one crewmember staying awake to be on guard (rarely the driver as he had the more strenuous job on a continuous basis) while the others slept, but sometimes it happened that the whole crew fell asleep. In cases we couldn't leave the tank we had to urinate and shit through

> the bottom hatch. When this was impossible the Commander told us to "Shit in your pants." An alternative was to use an empty shell casing or tin.

Von Strachwitz himself was not confined as often, having to attend to various command functions, engage in reconnaissance, check out the ground or look for the enemy. Waiting periods were also shorter, but otherwise he shared the privations of his crew and had the added weight of responsibility. After actions the tank crew still had no rest, as Thomaschek explained:

> After the fighting had stopped, or at the end of the day, it was impossible to rest at once. We left the tank with black faces from the gunpowder and everybody would have preferred just to sleep. Impossible. At first we had to tally our equipment. Report how much ammo we had expended, refuel the tank with a manual pump, load ammo and take back the empty cartridges which were collected and sent back to factories. Furthermore, we had to check the damage to the tracks, the gun, etc. This required our attention because these parts of the equipment were prone to damage. The tank needed to get camouflaged (far more necessary on the Western Front) to avoid spotting through enemy air recon. We also had to clean the gun, which required the strength of the whole crew. Then we had to dig the tank in (not all that often). It was incredibly hard work. . . . After the tank we had to clean our rifles. Only after these were clean we could have time for ourselves. Sometimes we didn't have any time for this because new orders had arrived and we had to start moving again. Perennial roll calls and training kept us busy, that way we shouldn't have to think about the war. We were meant to eat, drink, sleep and die. Nothing else. We were completely exhausted and weakened by lack of sleep. . . . We were unshaven and dirty and during the night fleas, bugs and rats made our lives miserable. . . . The encounter with the Ukrainian steppe was quite an experience for everybody. The endless horizon in every direction, brownish vegetation and dust, dust . . . dust.[4]

Over and above all of this the crew had to prepare meals and take care of their personal needs. As a battalion commander Graf von Strachwitz was spared all the cleaning and maintenance duties but was burdened with preparing reports, future operations, logistics, orders groups, correspondence, recommendations for awards and promotions, disciplinary action and training. He had also to oversee his officers, particularly the company commanders, and see to their development. All of this was before and after action, when he had the responsibility of leading his tanks into battle. It gave him no time to brood, or to relax, and usually meant even less sleep than the chronically sleep-deprived tank crews.

Logistical problems continued to bedevil the Germans. Poland, Belgium and France were not only much smaller than the Soviet Union, but had paved roads and advanced infrastructure that was familiar and could be used effectively. The vast spaces of Russia were poorly serviced by rail and roads, with many "roads" just dirt tracks which turned into a morass during autumn, and were deeply rutted and iced over during winter. Even tracked vehicles slid over them. Fuel was becoming increasingly precious as supplies dwindled due to poor roads, congested supply routes, both road and rail, bad weather, and above all lack of suitable transport. Wheeled vehicles were next to useless in the mud and even panzer divisions had to use horses and carts. Later the Germans would develop tracked trucks which could negotiate the bad road conditions or travel cross-country, but their numbers were also well below requirements.

Von Strachwitz fretted and fumed as he struggled to keep his tanks supplied and mobile. On good roads, his Panzer IIIs and IVs consumed 300 litres of fuel for every 100km travelled. Consumption could double in muddy conditions or when travelling cross-country. It would treble when the tanks were employed to tow a string of vehicles through the mud. He tried to conserve fuel where he could, but he couldn't do anything about the Germans' badly depleted motor pool. As the Germans thrust ever deeper into the Russian heartland the wear and tear on vehicles, and on the men, increased. So much so that Field Marshal Gerd von Rundstedt mentioned this in a statement to the men of his army group:

> I know that a great many divisions have been in combat every day since the start of the campaign. I also know that the tanks seem unobtainable and that difficult combat, inclement weather and road obstacles require the greatest efforts of the troops. . . . It is only natural that such great effort would result in fatigue, the combat strength of the troops has weakened and in many places there is a desire for rest.[5]

That was certainly an understatement, and the troops no doubt thought he was stating the obvious, but at least they could appreciate that the field marshal cared enough to acknowledge the immense difficulties the troops were facing.

Von Strachwitz's precious tanks were of course also affected by their sustained use in a challenging environment. Engines in desperate need of major overhaul were kept running with only minimal maintenance. This, together with enemy action, meant that at any one time up to 50% of his tanks would be in for repair with the maintenance company for a day or two, or in the army workshops for several weeks, with tanks shuttling back and forth from repair workshops on a regular basis. This was a problem common to all the armoured divisions. For instance on 17 August, 16th Panzers' neighbour 11th Panzer (where von Strachwitz's son was serving) reported "heavy material and personnel losses rendered the division no longer fully operational." General Halder noted in his war diary that Kleist's First Panzer Group retained only half its original strength, with the quartermaster of the panzer group classifying the supply situation as critical.[6] The 16th Panzer and Graf von Strachwitz's battalion were only marginally better off, yet they had to make do, as very little in the way of replacement parts, men, and machines was expected or indeed available. The division's nearest railhead was some 350 kilometres of bad, congested roads away. In fact, the once-proud motorized division increasingly had to rely on horse transport, like the common infantry divisions.

But despite the shortages, the attack had to continue. Field Marshal von Rundstedt diverted 16th Panzer, along with the Leibstandarte SS Adolf Hitler (LSSAH), commanded by Sepp Dietrich, further south to take the Black Sea post and Soviet naval base of Nikolayev. The two units were combined into a battle group along with the Hungarian Mobile Corps. This last unit consisted of horsed light cavalry, Toldi light tanks, some tankettes, Czaba armoured cars, bicycle-riding infantry and light artillery together with support units. The LSSAH had a nominal strength of 10,000 men plus supporting arms and a few operational tanks. Altogether it was not a large force to take an objective defended by the major portion of the Soviet Ninth Army and the 55th infantry Regiment of the Eighteenth Army. The German battle group would, in the event, prove to be insufficient to completely seal off the town.

With the Hungarians attacking in the south, the Germans struck east, crossing the Ingul River on 12 August. While the Hungarians were held up by strong Russian resistance, the Germans advanced along the east side of the river and were attacked by strong Russian forces. Kurt Meyer, LSSAH battalion commander and future divisional commander of the Hitlerjugend Division, described some of the fighting that occurred there:

> Exact but cautiously the Russians advance. . . . I do not want merely to fend off the attack but to destroy the Russian unit! The moment arrives around 11.00 hours. Fire strikes the Russians from all weapons and tears horrible gaps in their lines. Mortars and infantry guns try to eliminate the enemy guns with precision fire. The attack waves are mown to the ground. They jump up and run forward to their deaths. Commissars and officers attempt to get the attack going again, but I only see individual Russian soldiers running forward, the majority lie nailed fast to the floor.
>
> Now the moment has come for the motorcycles and armoured cars waiting on the flanks. They advance east and then turn in and push the Russians toward our position. By midday 650 prisoners are taken and more than 200 dead counted. According to prisoners' statements, the commander of the 962nd Rifle Regiment shot himself after shooting some of the officers. That regiment is said to have comprised only 900 rifles, it is completely annihilated as a result of these losses.[7]

After a Russian artillery barrage Meyer's unit was attacked again, this time by an armoured force:

> Some amphibious tanks and armoured cars form the spearhead. A direct hit strikes our battery position and one ammunition truck explodes. Once more we let the Russians get close and run into our fire.
>
> The amphibious tanks are the first victims to fly into the air. The familiar smoke clouds cover the battlefield while our armoured cars and fast Panzerjägers [self-propelled anti-tank guns, literally tank hunters] set off and shoot up the widely and chaotically scattering columns. One Panzerjäger comes to a smoking halt. Red flames shoot out of its interior before the driver can save himself. The survivors jump into the glow—they pull their comrade out of the burning hell and smother the flames on his body. My ears are

> ringing with the screams of the badly burned driver. I break away from the group and point my binoculars to the southwest. Thick clouds of dust announce the arrival of more columns which are trying to force a way through to the east. Like panthers, our armoured cars and Panzerjägers pounce on the columns and shoot up the vehicles into flaming wrecks. They try to scatter in all directions but only a few manage to flee. The bulk of the attackers have to trudge down the road to captivity.[8]

16th Panzer found it easy going, with the flat terrain ideal for von Strachwitz's tanks and little opposition initially encountered. His panzers' task was to blast a way through for the German infantry, which he did with dash and vigour. As well as launching counterattacks against 16th Panzer and the Leibstandarte, the enemy also carried out frequent ambushes, one of which killed Major von der Marck—a friend of von Strachwitz and a popular 16th Panzer Division officer—when a Russian tank round destroyed his vehicle.

The Reds massed for a breakout, and as the German containment lines were thinly manned, they were reinforced by the Hungarian 1st Cavalry Brigade. Nevertheless a large part of the Russians managed to break out, crossing the river at Nova Dantzig. They overran 16th Panzer's 6th Company of the 79th Regiment, a large number of whom were taken prisoner. The prisoners were then brutally murdered by their captors. This was a fairly common occurrence and a major reason why the Germans fought so desperately even when the odds were heavily weighted against them. When discovered, many of the bodies showed signs of having been tortured and nearly all were mutilated.[9]

During the next two days, after fierce resistance from Russian marines, the town itself was captured. Here the Germans found the 36,000-ton partially built battleship *Soviet Ukraine* still on the slips. The Hungarian cavalry, led by Major Kalman Mikeeoz, mounted a charge with two squadrons of Hussars (light cavalry). The Russians were so shocked by the sight of massed mounted horsemen bearing down on them with sabres drawn that they abandoned their positions in panic-stricken flight. The use of cavalry was not unusual on the Eastern Front. The Russians used cavalry extensively throughout the war, while the Italians had a cavalry regiment in their expeditionary force. The Hungarians and Romanians were also well provided with cavalry while the Germans had the 1st Cavalry Division, which at one point during Operation *Barbarossa* was the only fully mobile division on the central front. It was later converted to become the 24th Panzer Division and was subsequently destroyed at Stalingrad. The Waffen SS, on the other hand, maintained cavalry units throughout the war, the most notable being the Florian Geyer Division, which was commanded by Hermann Fegelein, Eva Braun's brother-in-law. These units were generally employed in anti-partisan operations.

Heavy fighting then continued for the towns of Ongulka and Peresdavka, which the Germans captured with the help of von Strachwitz's tanks, which had to blast the Russians out house by house. German tank doctrine warned against street fighting, and it was not a form of fighting that von Strachwitz wanted his tanks to engage in, with narrow streets and houses hiding Russians armed with grenades and petrol bombs. There was no room to manoeuvre, rendering the tanks large, slow-moving, targets. He preferred open country, so he pulled them out as soon as it was practical, providing close fire support only when urgently needed.

The division was given a much-needed rest at Kirovograd. This enabled the men to carry out urgent maintenance on the tanks, but this meant that they got no physical rest. Still, the break from the strain of combat was invaluable and the men managed to write some letters home, mend their clothes and eat hot food at their leisure. The Graf could finally catch up with his accumulating paperwork. Most of it was mundane, parade states, checking supplies, chasing up parts, writing reports, authorising leaves and so on. Among the more pleasant tasks were the recommendations for promotion, awards and decorations. Most of his men had earned their tank assault badge while others were awarded the Iron Cross First or Second class. It was around this time that he was informed that his eldest son Hyazinth had been awarded the Iron Cross (1st Class) on 6 August for bravery while serving with his Panzer Regiment. On 25 August, Graf von Strachwitz was awarded the coveted Knight's Cross of the Iron Cross for his personal bravery and leadership in numerous actions, especially Dubno, Uman and Pervomaisk. Unlike many officers who in order to preserve their Knight's Cross, wore the smaller Iron Cross (2nd Class) around their neck, Graf von Strachwitz always wore a full-size decoration, although it may have been a privately purchased jeweller's copy. His regimental commander, Rudolf Sieckenius, had also been presented with this high award as a testimonial to his bravery and leadership, and for the achievements of his regiment to which Graf von Strachwitz contributed so much. The two men had in the heat of battle become firm friends and worked exceedingly well together. Like General Hube, Sieckenius trusted von Strachwitz implicitly, giving him *carte blanche* to undertake his many forays behind enemy lines and dogged pursuits, which took his tanks well ahead of the division spearheads and away from any available support. This trust was repaid by the Panzer Graf's impressive results.

NOTES

1. Major Gerhard Engel, *At the Heart of the Reich* (Greenhill Books, London, 2005).
2. David Stahel, *Kiev 1941: Hitler's Battle for Supremacy in the East* (Cambridge University Press, 2012).
3. Gunter K. Koschorrek, *Blood Red Snow: The Memoirs of a German Soldier on the Eastern Front* (Greenhill Books, 2002).
4. Misoslav Herold (trans. Matthias Noll), *Gefreiter Walter Thomaschek* (http://members.shaw.ca/grossdeutschland/thomas.htm), accessed 24 August 2013.
5. Stahel, *Kiev 1941*, p. 94.
6. Ibid.
7. Kurt Meyer, *Grenadiers* (J. J. Fedorowicz Publishing, Canada, 1994), p. 54.
8. Ibid.
9. Günter Schmitz, *Die 16 Panzer Division Bewaffnung–Einsatz–Manner 1938–1945* (Nebel Verlag GmbH, 2004).

ELEVEN

THE BATTLE OF KIEV

THE REST AT KIROVOGROD WAS ALL TOO BRIEF, AS THE division was called back into action. A forced march—always a strain on tanks and soft-skinned vehicles—took 16th Panzer to the bridgehead at Krementshug to take part in the major encirclement battle of Kiev. Once again Graf von Strachwitz's battalion led the advance. Supported by Stukas, his tanks fought through ever-increasing Russian resistance. General Hube accompanied the lead tanks in his armoured personnel carrier (APC) as they rolled along the flat featureless countryside. Any opposition was quickly put down and the tanks pushed on while the infantry mopped up. Several tanks and APCs were destroyed in skirmishes with the retreating Russians as von Strachwitz pursued them closely. His battalion caught a Russian column as it marched towards them, with raking high-explosive and machine-gun fire destroying Russian guns, towing tractors, trucks and carts. A KV-2 heavy tank was at the rear of the column. The Germans' rounds failed to penetrate the Russian tank's armour. Luckily the Russian tank's retaliatory rounds missed the Panzer Graf's tank, though it did damage a Panzer III. Von Strachwitz knew they needed an 88mm gun, but none were in the vicinity. There were however combat engineers, roaring forward in their APC. Without hesitation they leapt out, clutching explosive charges and mines. The Russian fired his main gun in their direction but missed, then the engineers were on him, placing their charges with deft movements. With a flash of flame and smoke the Russian tank blew up, and everyone heaved a sigh of relief.

Von Strachwitz then pushed his battalion towards Lubny, often overtaking Russian convoys and destroying them on the move, leaving behind a long trail of smashed trucks, cars, artillery pieces and anti-tank guns. The German infantry then retrieved any prisoners and usable booty from the smoking, blackened remains when they passed. The road was muddy from recent rains, which slowed but did not stop the tanks. Soviet anti-tank guns were a constant menace. The Soviet tanks with their high profiles were usually seen early enough, but the anti-tank guns, low to the ground and carefully concealed, were far more difficult to spot, usually only seen after they had fired. The Graf constantly searched for them, looking not just for the guns but for possible ambush sites where a gun was likely to be. Often something that looked out of place or not just quite right would reveal a lurking gun. His ability in spotting these dangerous opponents meant that it could be taken out with a high-explosive round before it could fire, saving his battalion from many casualties.

During its advance on Lubny, 16th Panzer blazed a trail of destruction extending over 80 kilometres. Its tanks, artillery and infantry destroyed or captured 600 trucks, 70 guns, 20 tractors, three aircraft, and took over 1,500 prisoners.[1] A large part of the mayhem was due to von Strachwitz and his panzers as they pushed their way forward.

Hube's division hit Lubny on 13 September, not long after Stalin had replaced the hapless Marshal Budenny with Marshal Timoshenko. The town was heavily defended by fanatical NKVD troops, workers' militia and anti-aircraft units. It was also continuously receiving reinforcements, mainly supply service troops seeking to escape the encirclement of Kiev.

The 3rd Company of Engineers captured the bridge over the Sula in a surprise attack, while Nebelwerfer rocket projectors sent salvo after salvo of screaming smoke-trailing rockets, into the town. The divisional artillery added their weight of fire into the town as the engineers stormed on to take the outlying suburbs. Behind them came the infantry of the 2nd Battalion, 64th Regiment. Savage street fighting quickly developed as the NKVD troops preferred to die than yield any ground. Supported by the civilian militia, who were often forced to fight at gunpoint, the Russians opened fire from the roofs and windows of houses, and barricades in the streets. The division's panzer regiment was then sent in to provide close fire support for the hard-pressed infantry.[2] The panzer battalions attacked from different directions. Von Strachwitz's panzers blasted the houses with high-explosive shells while their machine guns fired into the windows to suppress the opposition. Whole buildings collapsed in smoke, dirt and flying rubble as the Russians were ferreted out of their strongpoints. They scurried from one building to another, firing as they went. The German tanks crashed through the barricades firing their machine guns and crushing the defenders with their tracks. Petrol bombs and grenades were hurled at the tanks but caused only minimal damage. The German combat engineers went into the houses to clear the enemy from the cellars using flamethrowers. Yet the Soviets held grimly on, yielding nothing, dying where they stood.

On 14 September Hube had to send in the 79th Infantry Regiment, a final reinforcement, which proved too much for the Russians. The city finally fell to the Germans that afternoon. The dead and dying, many horribly burnt, littered the streets. Brown Russian uniforms tangled together with grey-green German uniforms. Fires fed on the timbers of burning houses, while smoke rose into the sky in long grey plumes, as von Strachwitz pulled his tanks out of the rubble-strewn streets to rearm and refuel.

General Hube sent his reconnaissance battalion to meet General Model's 3rd Panzer Division from General Guderian's Panzer Group 2, which was coming south from Army Group Centre to close the ring around Kiev. But the Russians, realising their predicament, launched several formations to hold back Guderian's and von Kleist's closing spearheads. Model, with a single regiment flung forward, was struggling to reach Pokhvitsa but had managed to narrow the gap between the two approaching pincers to some 70 kilometres. He sent forward a detachment under Lieutenant Wartmann, which fought its way through to finally reach Lubny, meeting the 2nd Company of 16th Panzer's engineer battalion to effect the link up and formally close the ring, 260 kilometres east of Kiev. Within the German encirclement were five Soviet armies with 50 divisions.[3]

Stalin had ordered Kirponos to stand his ground. Stavka (the Soviet High Command) could not send any relief force as all available reserves were needed to defend Moscow. Supplies were also not getting through, making the Russian position untenable. Stalin's decision doomed over 600,000 men to death or captivity.

The Germans now proceeded to compress the ring and wipe out the trapped Russians. Initially the resistance was fierce, with the Russians storming the German lines on foot, or on whatever vehicles they had, often resulting in their wholesale slaughter. Nevertheless at times they managed to break through, albeit with heavy casualties on both sides. Other times the Russians made their escape singly or in small groups, most staying in the area to form the partisan bands which would cause the Germans so much trouble later

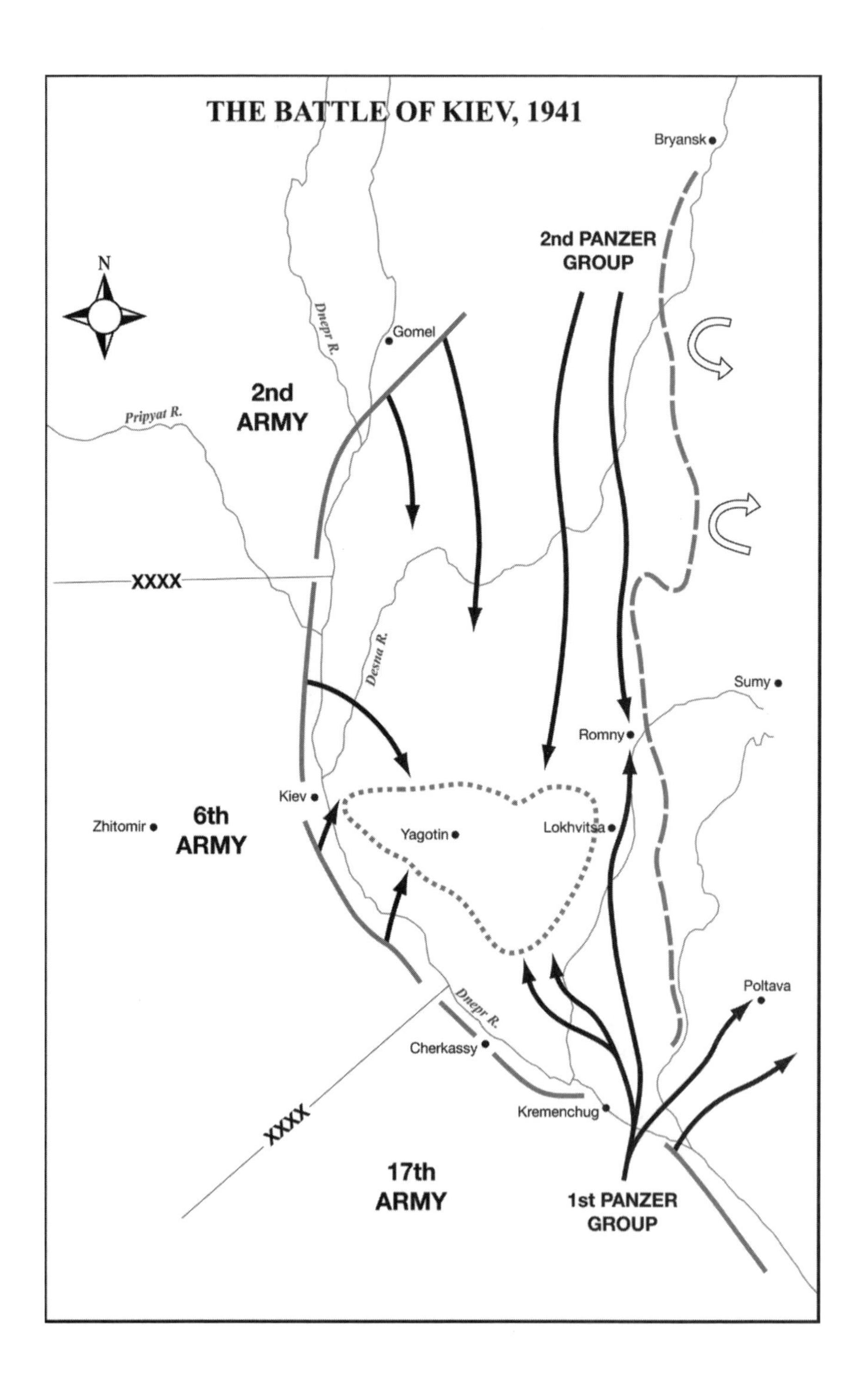
THE BATTLE OF KIEV, 1941
N
Bryansk
2nd PANZER GROUP
Dnepr R.
Gomel
2nd ARMY
Pripyat R.
XXXX
Desna R.
Sumy
Romny
Kiev
Zhitomir
6th ARMY
Yagotin
Lokhvitsa
Poltava
Dnepr R.
Cherkassy
Kremenchug
XXXX
17th ARMY
1st PANZER GROUP

on. They would find succour from the Ukrainian villagers, who, brutalised by the German occupation forces, were only too glad to help them. Conversely, there were many Red units—exhausted, hungry, short of ammunition and angry at being abandoned—who surrendered, and the numbers of those surrendering increased as the ring slowly contracted.

The fighting before and during encirclement took a steady toll on the German forces with many infantry companies reduced from a peak strength of some 160 to 16–30 men. Guderian's Panzer Group 2 was particularly hard hit, suffering 32,000 casualties in three months. Overall the German Army had lost 460,169 men up to September.[4] Officer casualties were particularly high, with sergeants now commanding platoons and sometimes companies, and lieutenants commanding battalions. Even field marshals and generals were not spared combat as Field Marshal von Reichenau wrote to General Paulus: "I led the assault for three kilometres, quite literally, not only with the first wave, but as the leading man in it."[5] He led the assault because there were no officers left alive and the attack was faltering, but this took nothing away from his courage, panache and motivation. Von Strachwitz could take comfort in the fact that he was not alone at the sharp end when field marshals were leading assaults.

The Panzer Graf's main problem was a shortage of operational tanks. His tanks were all too often undergoing repair, and the major workshops were a long distance from the front. This involved long transport delays in shipping tanks by rail or special trailers, and on occasion his tanks would be stuck in sidings to make way for trains carrying urgently needed ammunition and fuel. This meant that very often his battalion could be reduced to fewer than 20 tanks, sometimes to below a dozen. Later in the war the repair and maintenance facilities were moved well forward, with the divisional repair companies being located near the regimental headquarters, and company repair facilities were greatly improved. It meant a much quicker turn around in tank repair, with repairs often being carried out at some risk near to, or at the front.

Overall the final tally of the Kiev encirclement resulted in 665,000 Russian prisoners, 3,718 guns destroyed or captured and 884 armoured fighting vehicles destroyed.[6] This would be the largest number of prisoners taken during the war. It was a major defeat for the Russians, and certainly justified Hitler's decision to send Guderian south. Hitler's sycophantic generals—Keitel, Jodl, and up to a point, Halder—were now even further convinced as to Hitler's intuition and that it should not be opposed. All this would have fateful consequences for Hitler's hubris and future decisions. With the great victory of Kiev accomplished, Hitler now gave the approval for Operation *Typhoon*, the seizure of Moscow.

While the mopping up around Kiev continued,[7] General Hube was ordered to take his 16th Panzer Division south to cut off Russian forces still defending the southern sector of the Dnieper River. Once more Graf von Strachwitz pursued the retreating Russians, often overtaking them to circle around and attack them more effectively from the rear. The Soviets never knew when and from where he would strike next. The Russians were engaged at Novo-Moskovsk on 29 September, Kamenovatka on 1 October Seminovka on 3 October, Verchne Yokmak on 5 October and Pologi on the 6th.[8] On the same day von Kleist's Panzer Group 1 was renamed the 1st Panzer Army.

By the end of September von Kleist had completed the destruction of the Red forces in the Kiev cauldron, and with the Russian Dnieper defences overwhelmed he turned south towards the Sea of Azov. He then struck at the rear of two Russian armies who were in the process of attacking the German Eleventh Army under its new commander, von Manstein.[9]

The 16th Panzer was heavily engaged fighting the trapped Russian Eighteenth Army around Andreyebka. Here the Panzer Graf pushed himself and his men remorselessly. Once again he rampaged across the front and rear of the enemy. He penetrated as far as their artillery positions, surprising the Russians at dawn before they could man their guns. High-explosive shells blew the guns apart while the panzers' machine guns chattered their deadly crescendo amongst the panic-stricken gun crews. Supply trucks flamed, ammunition exploded, tracers streaked over the ground, targeting the fleeing Russians. In a short while it was all over, and his tanks moved back to refuel, rearm and then repeat the process all over again. During one of these actions, his own tank was disabled and he had to transfer to another, to continue leading his battalion in the attack.

In this wild melée spread along the Nogay steppe, the Russian Eighteenth Army was smashed. By 10 October over 65,000 Russians were marching dejectedly into captivity. They left behind 672 guns and numerous burnt-out and disabled tanks. The Soviet commander Lieutenant General Smirnov was killed in the fighting, and General Hube had him buried with full military honours, saluting him personally at the graveside. Two days later 16th Panzer Division was ordered to advance to Rostov on the River Don.

The terrain would have been unfavourable in any situation, but now

An athletics demonstration at Lichterfelde Cadet School, 1912. Athletic ability as well as equestrian and sports prowess was highly prized at the academy.

Pre-WWI German cavalry. The two on the left are from von Strachwitz's regiment, the Garde du Corps. Note the eagle on their helmets, only worn by the elite unit.

Parade of the Kaiser's Garde de Corps regiment at his Potsdam palace in 1914. As this involved the entire regiment, Lt. Graf von Strachwitz would have been present.

Pre-WWII German cavalry on parade. Graf von Strachwitz served with these units prior to joining the Panzer arm.

Annaberg Hill and monastery. Hyazinth von Strachwitz fought to take this hill near his home from Polish opposition in May 1921.

Men of the Oberland Freikorps who fought alongside von Strachwitz's Silesians at the Battle of Annaberg.

Hyazinth von Strachwitz in black Panzer uniform, wearing his Knights Cross with Oak Leaves. This photo appeared in the German press.

Bottom left: A pensive General Hans Guderian. He was the Panzer Graf's corps commander during the Battle of France.

Bottom right: Otto Carius, after his promotion to lieutenant in 1942.

Günther von Kluge

Erich von Manstein

On this page are four Field Marshals under whom von Strachwitz served in the East.

Friedrich Paulus

Gerd von Rundstedt

SS General Sepp Dietrich. Von Strachwitz fought alongside Dietrich at Annaberg, and later with Dietrich's SS Liebstandarte in Russia.

Otto Remer. A committed Nazi, he was instrumental in putting down the attempted coup in July 1944. Nevertheless, he was a brave and capable battalion-level Grenadier commander who fought alongside von Strachwitz at Kharkov and Kursk.

General Walter Hornlein (center) with his officers. Note that he has his epaulettes covered, a precaution against snipers who targeted officers. The man on the right is wearing the black panzer uniform.

1st Panzer Division commander Friedrich Kirchner during the Battle of France, June 1940.

Colonel Graf von Strachwitz decorating his 1st Battalion commander, Major Pössl, with the Knights Cross, April 20, 1943.

Colonel Graf von Strachwitz (right) with Major Pössl reviewing the men of Grossdeutschland's Panzer Regiment after Pössl's award of the Knights Cross.

Top left: A soldier from a Panzer division shows the strain of battle. A veteran, he is wearing the wound badge and Panzer assault badge in silver.

Top right: General Hans Hube bidding farewell to Colonel Rudolf Sieckenius, his Panzer Regiment commander. Hube had been promoted to command the XIV Panzer Corps.

Left: General Hube in his APC outside Stalingrad. Below him is Luftwaffe general Wolfram von Richthofen. The Airfleet commander provided 16th Panzer Division with close support during the campaign.

Hans Ulrich Rudel and his gunner, Oberfeldwebel Hentschel, being feted after returning from their respective 1,300 and 1,000th missions south of Kharkov, 1943.

Below: The Panzer Graf's eldest son, also named Hyazinth, in the turret of his short-barreled Panzer IV. Note 11th Panzer's divisional symbol next to the Balkan Cross. The photo was taken as part of an article in the German wartime magazine *Signal*.

Exercises with a Panzer IV carrying supplies. Graf von Strachwitz and other commanders were often forced to use their Panzers to carry ammunition, fuel and other supplies during the muddy periods when roads were not passable by wheeled vehicles.

Tigers being transported by rail. They required special narrow tracks to fit onto flat railcars.

German troops manning an MG34 in Stalingrad.

Grenadiers in their APC's advancing. A very useful weapon, there were never enough to equip all Panzergrenadier battalions.

Von Strachwitz, the 'Panzer Graf," as he appeared in spring 1943 while commanding Grossdeutschland's Panzer Regiment. The following summer he would take part in history's largest tank battle, at Kursk.

The Mark II "King" Tiger. It was cumbersome and heavy, but was still a deadly weapon and extremely difficult to destroy.

Panzer IV with a short barrel in the ruins of Stalingrad. The city's rubble made tank movement difficult.

A brewed up T-34. Unusually, it has been destroyed from a hit to the front where its armor is thickest, possibly by an 88mm gun.

Otto Carius in his early-model Tiger with the raised cupola.

The Panther tank. This is a later model than the ones commanded by von Strachwitz at Kursk where the Panther made its debut. Despite its faulty start, it turned out to be arguably the best tank of the war.

Grenadiers in their trench awaiting the next attack. Note the stick grenade held by the foremost soldier, which indicates he expects close-quarters work.

Stug III assault guns in convoy. Grossdeutschland's assault guns greatly assisted the Panzer Graf's regiment at Kharkov and Kursk.

Long-barreled Panzer IV's with mounted Grenadiers. Despite the late production of Tigers and Panthers, the Mark IV remained the mainstay of the German Panzer force.

SS Troops with a Mark IV during the 1943 assault on Kharkov. Note the anti-tank mine held by the nearest soldier.

Tiger tanks moving up. The Tiger was the most feared tank of the war. Von Strachwitz commanded these at Kharkov, Kursk, and in the Baltics.

winter set in early. It was to be one of the coldest winters for decades and the German Army was unprepared. The men's uniforms were threadbare and their standard overcoats were totally inadequate for the Russian winter, let alone for a severe one. The cold caused more casualties than combat that winter with 250,000 frostbite cases of which thousands required amputation,[10] and caused untold suffering. Even when winter clothing became available, temperatures of -20°C were difficult to manage and fight in. During periods of retreat the Germans didn't have warm bunkers or shelter and spent a great deal of time living and fighting out in the open. Soldiers wore as many layers of clothing as they could and scarcely removed them, creating ideal conditions for lice, which added to their discomfort.

Vehicles were difficult to keep mobile and fires had to be lit underneath them as their oil froze, or their engines had to be kept running using precious fuel. Weapons wouldn't fire as breech blocks froze, with light guns having to be kept indoors when possible, fires lit under barrels, and rifle bolts kept in pockets. Often soldiers would strip their weapons free of any oil or grease in order to use them. Von Strachwitz's panzers all had narrow tracks of 36–40cm which meant they often sank into the snow, and got stuck because of their limited ground clearance. The narrow tracks also made travelling through the mud more difficult. (Later German tanks, the Tiger and Panther, had wider tracks of 52/72cm and 66cm respectively.) Meantime, the division's mobility ebbed away. Fuel, food and ammunition were only trickling through and had to be severely rationed. It was a new situation for the German Army and for von Strachwitz it was a disaster. Food he could do without, at least for a while, but without fuel he was helpless. The advance ground down to a crawl, then stalled completely. The Graf moved among his troops, cajoling, encouraging, urging his men on, making light of the cold with wry humour and barely felt optimism. It cheered his men but didn't much improve the overall situation.

Hube's division was fighting alongside the Waffen SS Panzergrenadier Division "Viking." Viking was unusual, as it contained a mixture of German, Danes, Norwegians, Finns and later Estonians, and was a hard-fighting elite division.[11] While Hube's men were struggling with the mud, cold and lack of supplies, they were hit by ten Russian divisions.[12] They called for help from SS "Viking" but Viking had its hands full fighting near Rostov, and was also out of fuel.[13] So 16th Panzer was on its own. A ferocious battle for its very survival now took place, with Russians and Germans engaged in hand-to-hand combat for villages and farm buildings that could provide shelter from the bitter cold. The lack of fuel, exacerbated by the muddy conditions, curtailed von Strachwitz's battalion's movements.[14] Ammunition also being scarce, he couldn't deliver the Russians his normally swift and powerful blows. It was now a matter of fighting them off in order to just stay alive. The German MG-34 light machine guns came into their own against the Soviets' now-familiar massed infantry attacks. Firing at 900 rounds per minute they ripped the Russian ranks to shreds, with the machine guns of von Strachwitz's tanks adding to the weight of fire. But as soon one assault collapsed, the Russians launched another. With seemingly endless manpower, the Russians were literally climbing over the bodies of their comrades. The initial attackers were often from the penal battalions. They were expected to die, but in so doing would expose where the German machine and infantry guns were located and any weak points. It was a near-run thing but Hube's men broke every attack. Their valiant efforts defeated, the Russians were forced to withdraw, having suffered enormous casualties.

Not all Soviet formations fought with such grim, almost suicidal determination. In what was still a characteristic of the campaign so far, many units gave up without a fight, killing their commissars and officers to ensure that their surrender would not be opposed, as Graf Engelhardt-Ranzow, serving with SS Viking, related in his diary during the fighting around Rostov: "The Russian officers and Commissars have fled or been shot by their men. The soldiers surrender by the company. We don't have enough men to watch over them or interrogate them, so we tell them to keep moving west."[15]

The 16th Panzer took Golodajewka on the Mius against only slight resistance. The Russians in the meantime regrouped on the high ground east of the Mius. Von Kleist ordered 16th Panzer to attack from its bridgehead at Golodajewka towards Agrafenowka. Behind them SS Viking would cross the Mius then turn north to guard the northern flank. The 1st Panzer Army commenced its attack on 5 November with Hube's 16th Panzer Division making good progress. The Russians gave way before its tanks, but then closed ranks against the following German infantry. Savage mopping-up operations took place. On their flank SS Viking was attacked by a formation of 600 Cossack cavalry by mistake. The commander thought Viking was a Russian unit and got too close to withdraw, so had to order an attack. The mistake cost him 300 dead.[16]

On 11 November 16th Panzer linked up with units of Viking, after defeating strong enemy formations between Darjewka and Astachowo. Meanwhile Viking itself was under extreme pressure from Russian attacks. The

XIV Panzer Corps—to which 16th Panzer belonged—ordered Lieutenant Colonel Sieckenius' panzer regiment to be attached to SS Viking's operational control. Knowing Viking to be a superb fighting formation with excellent esprit-de-corps, neither Sieckenius nor von Strachwitz had any real objection to this, beyond the fact that they would have preferred to stay with their parent unit. Besides, von Strachwitz was himself a member of the SS. At this stage of the war, army formations were always glad to have Waffen SS units as neighbours, as they were not only well equipped but were less likely to give way under pressure, and so expose their neighbour's flanks. A reliable neighbouring unit was a necessity for continued survival.

To assist Viking, Sieckenius ordered his two battalions into an immediate counterattack against Lilienthal where Red infantry had succeeded in making a penetration. The German panzers swiftly drove the Russian infantry back, but then came up against a large force of T-34s. The Germans were heavily outnumbered, as Sieckenius' regiment was one in name only. Grouping his two battalions together he could only muster one woefully under-strength battalion.[17] Von Strachwitz in effect commanded a reinforced company. The strongest tank they had was a Panzer IV with a short-barrelled 75mm gun, not really a match for a T-34.

The Russians, well aware of their superiority in numbers and weaponry, were eager to give battle. A tank engagement followed, with the Germans trying to rapidly close the range to where their inferior guns would be effective, and the Russians trying to prevent them from closing, engaging them at long ranges, blowing up one German tank after another as they moved forward. As von Strachwitz's panzers closed in, the Russians withdrew a short distance to engage at long range again. Finding it impossible to effect a breakthrough, the Panzer Graf called off his attack.

The Russians attacked the flank of 1st Panzer Army at Zimitanka, leaving it in a precarious position. It had no option but to withdraw to the Rusloff River. During the night of 22 November, 16th Panzer began its own withdrawal. Lack of fuel meant every prime mover had to tow several other vehicles. The divisional engineers left behind minefields and booby traps to delay the pursuing Russians. A rearguard provided by SS Viking and a corps anti-tank gun battalion with Marder III self-propelled anti-tank guns held up the Russians sufficiently long enough for the German corps to withdraw behind the Tusloff and occupy the west bank. However this left von Strachwitz and the 16th Panzer Regiment, which had been attached to Viking, still east of the Tusloff.

General von Wietersheim, the corps commander, visited Sieckenius at his regimental command post, and together the two men discussed a counterattack. After weighing up the odds, von Wietersheim decided against it. Attacking the enemy entrenched on the high ground would have resulted in too many casualties, while the forces available were too weak to ensure success. Instead, the Germans beat off several more Soviet assaults, after which Sieckenius' regiment was finally allowed to return to its parent division.

The west bank of the Tusloff was not a viable long-term defensive position as its winding course required far too many troops to defend it, while at some places it was no obstacle at all. Von Kleist therefore decided on a withdrawal to the Mius River, which had a high west bank offering better defensive possibilities. This withdrawal, made without Hitler's permission, so enraged Hitler that he ordered Field Marshal von Rundstedt, the commander of Army Group South, to be sacked. This was the beginning of a pattern that would last the remainder of the war.

Hube's division took up its defensive positions on the Mius near Matayev where it set up a strong defence line covered by extensive minefields. His men had barely dug themselves in when the Russians commenced their massed attacks. The minefields caused enormous casualties in the first waves, but this was of no consequence to the Russians, who had sent out the expendable penal battalions first in order to clear a path through the minefields.[18] The failure of these attacks brought about a lull in the fighting as the Russians regrouped to consider their options.

The 16th Panzer's tank battalions were now sent for much need refitting and reorganisation to Stalino-Makeyvka where the rear supply base was located. The move could not come soon enough for the Graf's battalion. His men were exhausted to the point of numbness and the few tanks they had left were in a sorry state: it was a battalion in name only. The regiment's second battalion was in no better shape, so there was very little of the regiment for Rudolf Sieckenius to command. During the move to Makeyevka, numerous trucks got stuck in deep snowdrifts and had to be towed out by tractors, meaning that the occupants often had to spend the night exposed to the cold until help could arrive. The fighting against the Russians may have waned, but the fight continued against the biting winter cold, snow and ice.

At Makeyvka there was some rest at last for the tank crews, but for their commanders like von Strachwitz and Sieckenius there was none. Sieckenius left to organise new replacement tanks for his almost non-existent regiment. Von Strachwitz remained at the rear base to oversee repairs and organise resupply of necessary items from spare parts to uniforms, especially winter clothing. He was not very successful in acquiring the latter, as very little was available, a great deal of it being stuck in warehouses and rail sidings in Poland and Germany. His men had to freeze in their basic, threadbare standard uniforms. He carried out the usual administrative tasks and what training could be carried out indoors. In many ways it was a grim time for him. It was his first major retreat of the war and he found it a galling experience. His training and whole cavalry ethos was for mobility and attack, so he chafed at the inaction, and the retreat was a harsh, unwanted lesson. He could not know at the time, but this was only the first of many.

NOTES

1. Ibid. p. 127.
2. Paul Carrell, *Hitler's War on Russia Vol. 1 Hitler Moves East* (Ballantine Books, 1963), p. 125.
3. David Stahel, *Kiev 1941: Hitler's Battle for Supremacy in the East* (Cambridge University Press, 2012), p. 221.
4. Ibid., p. 233.
5. Ibid., p. 235.
6. Carrell, *Hitler's War on Russia Vol. 1 Hitler Moves East*, p.129. These figures are from German sources and the ones most often quoted. The Soviets admit to a lower figure of some 400,000 total casualties and prisoners. The truth probably lies in between, with some 500,000 prisoners over and above the dead and wounded.
7. Not long after Kiev was occupied the Einsatzgruppen moved in to round up the Jews. Some 65,000 innocent men, women and children were marched to the ravine at Babi Yar and murdered by SS, SD and policemen who made up the murder squads.
8. Günter Schmitz, *Die 16 Panzer Division 1938–1945* (Dörfler im Nebel Verlag Gmbh, 2004).
9. Von Manstein was given command of Eleventh Army after its commander Ritter von Schobert was blown up when his Fieseler Storch courier plane inadvertently landed on a Russian minefield.
10. Timothy Wray, *Standing Fast: German Defensive Doctrine on the Russian Front during World War II* (United States Government Printing, 1987), p. 195.
11. A report of 18 August 1941 listed a Finnish battalion and contingents of 621 Dutch, 194 Norwegian, 216 Danes, and even a few Swedes. The Finns lost 255 killed while serving with Viking. Source Peter Strassner, *The 5 SS Panzer Division "Viking"* (J. J. Fedorowicz Publishing, Canada, 2006).
12. Russian divisions had less manpower than the equivalent German divisions. For instance a Russian infantry division had 10,000–12,000 men while a German infantry division had 11,000–20,000. A Russian mechanised brigade was roughly equivalent to one German Panzer division.

13. Strassner, *The 5 SS Panzer Division "Viking,"* p. 69.
14. For example, Panzergrenadier Division Viking, which had a contingent of tanks on strength, normally used 136 cubic metres of fuel daily but required 350 cubic metres in heavy mud. And like 16th Panzer, it was a long distance from its depots using 700 cubic metres of fuel to get the fuel it required from its depot at Dnjepropetrowsk. Ibid., p. 69.
15. Ibid. p. 69.
16. Ibid. p. 75.
17. A German panzer regiment at this time should have had 150–200 tanks, and a battalion 75–100 tanks, however the regiments generally had far less than half that number, sometimes being reduced to 30 tanks or fewer, although numbers constantly fluctuated as damaged tanks were repaired.
18. The Soviet penal battalions held very few criminals. Many in them were "political prisoners," others were there because they had retreated in battle. Minor infractions of military discipline could also be a reason depending on the whim of the unit commander. The majority of the men of these units were killed so membership was tantamount to a death sentence. Only serious wounds offered a chance of escape, being regarded as atonement by blood.

TWELVE

THE BATTLE OF KALACH

THE BITTERLY COLD WINTER CONTINUED INTO EARLY 1942. There was cheering news, however: on 16 January General Hube was awarded the Oak Leaves to his Knight's Cross for the superlative performance of 16th Panzer Division during the previous year and the capture of Nikolayev. The award reflected on the entire division and was well received by the men. Hube had been at the forefront of every battle, his bulky figure with his worn greatcoat and black-gloved artificial hand a familiar and welcome sight to his battle-weary, soldiers on the front line. His earthy soldier's humour and words of encouragement were greatly appreciated, almost as much as the comforts like cigarettes and chocolates that he distributed during his visits. He shared a fondness for these treats and liked his food, making sure that he ate regularly irrespective of the tactical situation. Not a good nighttime sleeper, Hube would often take brief naps at quiet times during the day which even the odd air raid could not disturb.

Graf von Strachwitz, just recently returned from convalescent leave in Germany, also received good news. His promotion to lieutenant colonel of the reserve had come through, so he could add a pip to the silver braid of his major's epaulettes. This now made him the second-ranking officer of the panzer regiment after Rudolf Sieckenius, and eligible for a regimental command when a suitable one became available.

Equally welcome was the new equipment the division received, with Rudolf Sieckenius returning with brand new tanks, including a few examples of the new Mark IV variant with long-barrelled 75mm gun. Eventually the short-barrelled Panzer IV would be replaced. It was intended as an infantry-

Eastern Front
22 June–15 November, 1941
N
0
200 miles
0
200 km
GERMAN LINE OF 22 JUNE
GERMAN LINE OF 10 JULY
GERMAN LINE OF 15 NOVEMBER
FINLAND
Lake Lagoda
Gulf of Finland
Leningrad
Schluesselburg
Tikhvin
Tallinn
Baltic Sea
18th ARMY
Luga
Lake Peipus
Lake Ilmen
Staraya Russa
Pleskau (Pskov)
16th ARMY
ARMY GROUP NORTH
Riga
Dvina R.
Kalinin
XXXXX
9th ARMY
3rd Pz Group
4th Pz Group
Moscow
Koenigsberg
Vitebsk
Vyazma
POLAND
Smolensk
Orsha
4th ARMY
Grodno
Minsk
Mogliev
Tula
Bialystok
2nd Pz ARMY
Bryansk
Orel
SOVIET UNION
Warsaw
Brest-Litovsk
ARMY GROUP CENTER
PRIPYAT MARSHES
Lublin
2nd ARMY
Don R.
XXXXX
Rovno
6th ARMY
Irvov
Kiev
Kharkov
CARPATHIAN MOUNTAINS
17th ARMY
Dnieper R.
Bug R.
Kremenchug
Uman
Donetz R.
1st Pz ARMY
Pervomayask
ARMY GROUP SOUTH
Stalino
HUNGARY
Rostov
Taganrog
Melitopol
Odessa
Perkop
Sea of Azov
ROMANIA
Black Sea
11th CRIMEA ARMY
Bucharest
Sevastapol

support tank, as generally a short barrel meant the high-explosive rounds were more effective than with a longer barrel.[1] The reverse was true for anti-tank rounds. Unfortunately there were only 133 of these long-barrelled tanks available to be divided among the 10 panzer and five motorised divisions taking part in the planned southern offensive.[2] But the regiment now had some tanks that were a match for the dreaded T-34s, at least in gunnery if not in thickness of armour and width of the tracks.

Adolf Hitler in the meantime was busy planning his summer offensive, a series of blows aiming one part of Army Group South toward the Volga at Stalingrad while another thrust into the Caucasus to seize the oilfields. The Caucasus operation was only revealed by Hitler to his generals at a later date; the original plan was to just block this area off. Further, just reaching the Volga and blocking that vital river traffic to Moscow was considered of far more importance than taking Stalingrad itself. Hitler only became obsessed with its capture later. Hitler's optimism was shared by his High Command, leading him to believe that achieving both objectives was possible despite the diminishment of his own resources. Hitler had become convinced that the Red Army was about finished, as no army or regime to date had survived the magnitude of losses it had sustained. These amounted to around 5,000,000 killed or wounded with 3,000,000 taken prisoner. In addition, some 21,000 tanks, 32,000 guns and 5,000 aircraft had been destroyed. What Hitler didn't know was that the Soviets still fielded close to 5,000,000 men in front-line units, together with 3,412 tanks, with more of both coming on line. Not only was the Red Army far from beaten, but it was still growing in strength. For instance up to April 1944 the USA sent Russia 3,734 tanks, mostly Shermans, and the British 4,292, with total tanks supplied at war's end being 13,000, all in addition to the vast number of tanks produced in Russia.[3]

While Hitler had some valid grounds for believing the Red Army was beaten, it is more difficult to understand his overlooking the diminution in his own strength. The war in the east had cost the Germans 743,112 dead or wounded since the invasion, plus countless thousands suffering illnesses ranging from dysentery to typhus and frostbite. This represented about a quarter of the original force involved in Operation *Barbarossa*, a force which had struggled with manpower problems throughout the campaign, and was more than 70% more than all casualties sustained in the previous campaigns in Poland and the West. The 136 divisions on the Eastern Front were bled white and now only equated to the manpower of 83 full-strength divisions, not even considering the massive reduction in operational vehicles and equipment, the chronic shortage of fuel, and the increasingly vast distances that the worn-out vehicles were traversing.[4] The Germans did have superiority in tactical skill, but the Russians were learning fast. It would not be long before the Russians were turning the German tactics back onto them. Hitler however wasn't completely blind to his lack of strength and attempted to fix this for the coming offensive by the simple expedient of stripping men, tanks and equipment from Army Groups North and Centre. He ordered the removal of one tank battalion from most of the panzer divisions in these army groups, leaving them with only one tank battalion. This made them weaker than a motorized division (soon to be called Panzergrenadier), which had only one tank or assault gun battalion but had an extra infantry regiment. These panzer divisions, given current losses, were now only equivalent to a reinforced armoured brigade, reducing the offensive capacity of both army groups. By this method 16th Panzer was reinforced with an additional tank battalion on 28 May, giving it a total of around 140 operational tanks, although these included some almost useless Panzer IIs.

Thus Operation *Blue* came into being, which Hitler fervently hoped would finally end the war in the east. The 16th Panzer was attached to Sixth Army, which would make the central thrust. The army's commander was 52-year-old General Frederick Paulus, a tall, immaculately groomed man who changed his uniform twice a day. He was an efficient, indeed meticulous staff officer. Unfortunately he had no operational or combat command experience and absolutely none with commanding tank forces of any size. He was good with statistics, figures and logistics, a useful man to have around a quartermaster's headquarters or assisting an operational combat commander at a map table. He was, however, a firm believer in his Führer and a protégé of his predecessor, Field Marshal Reicheneau, which was enough to secure him the coveted Sixth Army command ahead of more experienced and senior corps commanders, who justifiably resented his elevation. His personality, lack of experience and adherence to Hitler would all contribute to the coming catastrophe.

Meanwhile, Stalin was planning an offensive of his own. Believing the Germans to be severely weakened after their winter withdrawals, and that any renewed drive to the east would occur in the Moscow sector, he resolved to retake Kharkov with a surprise thrust at their southern flank. He failed to realize that the south was precisely where the Germans were in the midst of their own buildup. On May 12, 1942, some 46 Soviet infantry divisions and 19 motorised brigades launched the two-pronged attack.[5] The Soviet northern attack was contained, but their southern thrust achieved a significant breakthrough, advancing over 90 kilometres westward between 12 and 15 May. The Germans kept their heads however, and launched a counterattack against the Russian flanks which stopped them dead in their tracks. A worried Nikita Khrushchev, the army commissar, was told of the gravity of the situation by his army commanders, who urged him to request Stalin for permission to withdraw. Khrushchev flew to Moscow to urge Stalin to order the withdrawal but Stalin was having none of it, angrily telling Khrushchev "Don't put your nose into military matters you know nothing about." Khrushchev, glad to escape the poisonous atmosphere of Stalin's headquarters, flew back to the front. He was grateful to get away with his life, as men had been shot for less, so he was more than happy to take his chances with the Germans.[6] Now Khrushchev and his military commanders had to watch helplessly as the Germans commenced their counterattack. Codenamed Operation *Fredericus*, it thrust against the Soviets' exposed flanks, breaking through to surround 28,000 men. Sieckenius' battle group was heavily involved in the clashes, fighting alongside the 14th Panzer Division.

Battle Group Hube had assembled at Slavyansk while Sieckenius and von Strachwitz were heavily engaged at Barvenkovo. At Barvenkovo, a small armoured force led by von Strachwitz became isolated from the main body in the confused melée that had developed. Surrounded by superior forces in enemy territory, von Strachwitz formed a hedgehog position at dusk to wait out the night. Just before dawn he went on a short reconnaissance outside his perimeter. Taking one of his company commanders, Captain Freiherr von Freytag-Loringhoven, and two artillery observers with him, he climbed a nearby hill. While searching for the enemy through their field glasses the Graf heard the whoosh of incoming shellfire. Yelling out a warning, he dived for cover, dragging von Freytag-Loringhoven down with him. The shells landed nearby, killing the two artillery observers.[7] Von Strachwitz' acute awareness and perhaps a little luck had saved both his life and that of the company commander.

The German victory involved hard fighting by von Strachwitz's battalion against the Soviet Sixth Army around the Izyum–Barvenkovo salient. In one instance he destroyed a Russian tank force by flanking it and attacking from the rear, leaving 24 destroyed tanks, nearly all light battle tanks. Again, and again, he assaulted Russian artillery positions, scattering the crews and destroying their guns. Truck parks and supply dumps went up in flames as his tanks cut a swathe through the enemy rear lines in true cavalry style. The rather confused nature of the fighting made his task a lot easier; however, continued rapid movement and combat took a gradual toll of his tanks and his force was slowly whittled away by enemy action and mechanical problems. Fortunately it was around this time that the third tank battalion arrived, though it was really a much-needed reinforcement for the under-strength existing battalions rather than the extra-strength battalion it was intended to be. Characteristically von Strachwitz continued his actions, even with only a few operational tanks, employing surprise, superior tactics and gunnery to give him the edge. He added considerably to his own tally of destroyed enemy tanks, although unlike most panzer commanders he did not record his kills or have his gun barrel marked with kill rings. Despite this he was by now a leading tank ace of the Wehrmacht.

In all, 1,250 Russian tanks were destroyed with 239,000 Red Army men dejectedly limping off into captivity where most would die from neglect, disease and starvation.[8] The Germans claimed then, as ever, that they had insufficient supplies to feed them. This was partially true; however, they made little or no effort to do so. In contrast, Russians captured by the Italian Eighth Army were fed exactly the same rations as the Italian soldiers, and the Italian supply situation was far worse than that of the Germans.[9] General Paulus was awarded the Knight's Cross for the achievements of his Sixth Army at Kharkov by a grateful Führer.

On 10 June, 16th Panzer, acting as the spearhead once again, captured an intact bridge at Mostovaya, an action that earned them a heartfelt commendation from their corps commander. Hube's division, followed by the 22nd and 14th Panzer Divisions, penetrated deep into the Russian lines along the Burluk River. In so doing it crossed extensive Russian minefields, which took their toll of the Graf's panzers. As these involved track damage they were all easily repaired and the disabled tanks were soon back in action.

It was here in the Oskol River area that von Strachwitz's tankers came across Russian mine dogs. It all seemed innocent enough at first. A large German Shepherd came running towards their advancing tanks. The men were curious where this dog had come from, out in the middle of the steppe where there was not a house in sight. As it drew nearer they noticed a package strapped to its back, which was odd but they thought nothing of it. The dog ran up to the lead tank then dived beneath it. Immediately a blast stopped the tank dead in its tracks with smoke billowing out from beneath it. No sooner had the men gotten over the shock when two more dogs appeared. Suddenly they realised what the dogs were carrying. From their turret hatches the tank commanders blazed away at the dogs with their sub-machine guns, killing both dogs in short order. Knowing their handlers had to be nearby, the Graf sent a platoon of Panzer IIIs to sort them out, which they did, with a high-explosive rounds and machine-gun fire. He and his men then examined the dogs. Both had a mine strapped to their backs with a long detonation wire protruding vertically from the explosives. When the wire connected with the underside of the tank the mine was detonated. The Russians had always fed the dogs beneath tanks, training them to go there to find food. Von Strachwitz and his men, animal lovers all, were horrified at this misuse of man's best friend.

On 24 June, engineers bridged a deep anti-tank ditch so the division could cross. It then swiftly moved on to take the vital railway junction at Kupjansk. The defenders were routed by a swiftly moving attack by von Strachwitz's tanks supported by the infantry in armoured personnel carriers. This helped close the ring around Kharkov, sealing the fate of the Red Army troops who were trapped there.[10]

Concentric attacks destroyed the best part of six Soviet armies numbering some 500,000 men, but many Russians escaped through the numerous gaps in the German blocking lines. Nevertheless heavy fighting took place as the Russians desperately fought to break through or were caught later infiltrating between the German positions.

The division returned to Mareyevka and Stalino for a much-needed refit and replenishment. It also had to prepare for the principal summer offensive, Operation *Blue*. The refit took place from 27 June to 7 July, and it was around this time that the rifle regiments were designated as grenadier and subsequently panzergrenadier regiments, recollecting the famous grenadiers of Frederick the Great.

At his headquarters Hitler, now in direct personal command of the Eastern Front, vacillated whether to capture Stalingrad and cut the Volga supply artery, or maintain focus on seizing the oilfields of the Caucasus which he desperately needed to fuel his armies. In the end, still governed by unrealistic optimism, he decided to do both. He ordered Operation *Blue* to commence on 28 June with an attack force of 68 divisions, consisting of close to 1,500,000 men, and 1,495 armoured fighting vehicles including tanks, assault guns and self-propelled tank destroyers. The assault was supported by Luftwaffe General Wolfram von Richthofen's Fourth Air Fleet with 1,550 front-line aircraft.[11] Richthofen, a distant cousin of the the Red Baron of Great War fame, had served with the Condor Legion in the Spanish Civil

War, and was an early exponent of ground-support squadrons especially with the Stuka dive-bomber.

On 9 July Hitler split his offensive armies in two. Army Group A under Field Marshal von List and Army Group B under Field Marshal von Bock. Army Group A would drive into the Caucasus while Army Group B would capture the Don Basin and Stalingrad. General Paulus' Sixth Army, which included 16th Panzer Division, was in von Bock's Army Group B.

Lieutenant Colonel von Strachwitz's tanks crossed the Donets River along with the division on 12 July, on a captured Russian bridge near Lissitschansk, which was cleverly constructed to lie just below the water so as to evade detection, especially from the air.

Stalin was thoroughly alarmed at the Germans' progress. On 28 July he issued order number 227, commanding "Not one step back." To ensure that it was carried out, the NKVD and army blocking units were out in force. In all they arrested 25,000 Red Army soldiers, summarily shot 10,000, and machine-gunned countless thousands of fleeing troops, the equivalent of several rifle divisions. Others were sent to the dreaded penal battalions. Stalin threw everything he had in the area to halt the Germans. This is contrary to what communist propaganda later asserted, that the Russian retreat was merely a clever trap to suck the Germans into being encircled at Stalingrad. Soviet officer cadets, future NCOs and officers were sent in as whole units and—being without heavy weaponry—were simply slaughtered by the German panzers. A Russian armour training school hastily thrown into battle with British-supplied Matilda tanks were just target practice for von Strachwitz's veterans, who turned their tanks into blazing funeral pyres. The Russians often sarcastically referred to the British and American tanks as coffins for five comrades. Not all the Soviet armour was British-made, however, as Stalin deployed his 5th Tank Army, equipped with T-34s, northwest of Voronezh and, along with other units, it delayed Paulus' Sixth Army's progress in numerous hard-fought confrontations which cost the Germans 10,000 casualties they could ill afford to lose.

Dust and heat debilitated both the tanks and men of the Panzer Graf's battalion, so they often travelled at night, as long as the Russians were in full retreat and not likely to ambush them. Frequently the reverse was true, as they came across scattered Russian units bivouaced for the night.

The Soviets continued their withdrawal. On occasion the withdrawal became a panic-stricken rout, but some units defended their ground to the death. The behaviour of the Russian soldiers depended on where the blocking units were stationed and the strength and influence of individual officers and commissars. The Russians were accustomed to "hold fast" orders and were not trained or organised for orderly withdrawals. This made their situtation more perilous, with officers often deserting their troops, and equipment being abandoned for a lack of orders or system. To von Strachwitz and his men it seemed that the Soviets were on the point of collapse. It was a heady time. On the open steppes the German tanks roamed at will, blasting the fleeing Russian columns, decimating entire regiments, smashing tanks, guns and supply vehicles in an orgy of destruction for which the Soviets seemed to have no answer. "Panzers Vor! Keep moving!" were the panzer troops' watch-words.

Stalin, however, was determined to halt the retreat before the city which bore his name, declaring "The city will be defended by the Second Army to the last man." At Kalach on the Don River the Russians managed to regroup. Their rearguards waited for the German tanks, determined to sell their lives dearly, but the steppe was empty and von Strachwitz's panzers were nowhere to be seen. The 16th Panzer Division wasn't coming because by 28 July it had run out of fuel. This was a result of poor roads, insufficient railway lines, clogged railheads, long supply lines under attack from Russian aircraft and artillery, and insufficient trucks. In addition, many of the trucks in the theatre were non-operational, or were operational but had no tyres due to a massive shortage of spares. The Russians also had their problems, but their situation was constantly improving as they fell back toward their own supply lines and its steadily increasing production, along with the arrival of Anglo-American aid. Foreign transport vehicles alone eventually totalled over 400,000 which meant that not only were the major Soviet transport needs being met, but they could concentrate on tank production, allowing them to eventually swamp the Germans with waves of T-34s. For the Germans the situation would just continue to deteriorate.

All this of course was of little moment for von Strachwitz. His only concern at that time was for fuel. Without it his panzers were going nowhere, reduced to stationery gun emplacements. He pleaded with his regimental commander Rudolf Sieckenius, who in turn pleaded with division headquarters, all to no avail. There was no fuel to be had. All the Panzer Graf could do was carry out routine maintenance of tracks and worn-out engines, clean gun barrels, fill machine-gun belts and conduct static training. All very necessary, but no substitute for combat operations. Days not in operation gave the Russians time to escape, regroup and prepare their defences. This they did, building up their bridgehead at Kalach. Eventually the fuel arrived and 16th Panzer and XIV Panzer Corps could finally continue their advance. The 16th Panzer was part of a pincer movement to trap the remnants of Russian General K.S. Moskalenko's 1st Tank Army in the Kalach bridgehead. The 24th Panzer Division spearheaded the southern arm of the pincer while Graf von Strachwitz's battalion was the very tip of the northern arm.

Approaching the Liska River he noticed an intact bridge at Ostrov. He realized that with a quick assault he could seize the bridge and rushed his battalion forward. His tanks surged into the Soviet positions. Russian infantry, along with their supporting anti-tank guns, were overrun before they could offer much resistance. High-explosive rounds smashed the anti-tank guns while machine-gun fire scattered the infantry. An intense and often confused firefight developed as his tanks smashed anti-tank guns and infantry positions. Without bothering to consolidate or wipe out all the Russian outposts on his flanks von Strachwitz pushed forward to take the bridge. Behind him an armoured panzer grenadier battalion mopped up the remaining Russians. General von Wietersheim, commander of the XIV Panzer Corps to which 16th Panzer belonged, sent von Strachwitz a message of congratulatons.

Von Strachwitz then turned south, overrunning the nearby Soviet defences before pushing on with his advance. The open steppe became a borderless battleground where armoured groups operated independently, like battleships at sea. It was the type of combat in which the Panzer Graf excelled. It was a war of manoeuvre and ambush with each side trying to outflank or surround the other. Here superior German communications, training and tactics all played their part. Frequently von Strachwitz surprised Russian tank concentrations at dawn as they were preparing to move, with the crews often not even reaching their tanks before it was all over. The pall of smoke of the burning Russian tanks and vehicles would attract other Soviet units who were then caught in an ambush. It was a chain of destruction which Russians couldn't seem to break. On seizing a village occupied by Russian supply troops, the Graf would scatter the Russians and destroy their vehicles, then move off quickly to take up ambush positions for any relief force. He employed his standard tactic of taking out the Russian command tank first with the remaining leaderless tanks being brewed up with coordinated fire and flank attacks.

Undaunted, with no time to waste, in order to concentrate his force he set off on his attacking mission. Following his usual tactic he drove deep behind enemy lines, which wasn't difficult at this time as the whole rear area was in flux. As was his custom, he paused frequently to survey the ground ahead with his binoculars, which proved fortuitous on one occasion when he spotted a long column of Russian tanks on the horizon. A close look at the topography alerted him to an excellent ambush position behind a fold in the ground from where he could engage the Russians in an almost hull down position. Without hesitation he ordered his tanks forward to take up their new positions.

The Russian column approached along his front, exposing their flanks as if on a shooting range. The range was close, so any hits would be certain to disable, if not destroy the Russian tanks. However to his increasing dismay, the column seemed endless, and what had seemed a unit of battalion strength was rapidly appearing to be a regiment or brigade. Taking a quick count he arrived at over 100 enemy tanks. The odds seemed suicidal but with surprise, an excellent firing position, and superior gunnery he was quietly confident he could reduce the odds before the Soviets realised what was happening. He didn't hesitate, coolly giving his tanks their instructions. What the commanders of his three under-strength tank companies must have thought can well be imagined.

Calmly, with precision, the German tanks began firing in ragged salvoes. Four, eight, 12, 16 Russian tanks were ignited in quick succession. The Russians were completely non-plussed. They couldn't see where the fire was coming from, and certainly were not expecting a German armoured force anywhere in their area. Their best guess was that they were being subjected to a German aerial attack which meant basically riding out the storm in a zig-zag pattern with hatches closed. Not all the tanks took this approach, with some staying motionless, trying not to attract attention by any movement. These made easy targets and were quickly brewed up one by one.

The smoke from the blazing tanks obscured the battlefield making observation difficult. Most of the Russians hadn't spotted the German tanks, but some did discern where the deadly fire was coming from and turned to confront it. These von Strachwitz and his panzers despatched before they could do any damage. Not having radios, these Russians could not enlighten their comrades as to where the danger lay, so they remained easy targets.

The German gunfire never slackened as smoke, fire, explosions, scrambling crewmen, weaving tanks, all added to the confusion in the Russian column. Several tanks crashed into each other while some crews simply abandoned their tanks, preferring to hide in the open. Many crewmen were crushed by tanks which could not see them in the smoke and confusion.

The Panzer Graf's gunner and loader worked feverishly, responding to his firing instructions, or firing on sight, loading shell after shell. The tanks reeked of gunpowder and sweat. As all the Russian tanks in his immediate vicinity were burning or destroyed the Graf ordered his tank out of concealment. He moved to the rear of the column and began taking out one Russian tank after another. In all of the chaos he was easily mistaken for a Russian and so had no trouble attacking tanks at very close range with deadly effect. A number of Russians were firing, but aimlessly, more from panic than at any identifiable threat. After half an hour of murderous mayhem the surviving Russians fled, leaving close to 50 burning or disabled tanks littering the battlefield. Not content with this victory von Strachwitz pressed on, pursuing the fleeing Russians relentlessly. Over the next three days his battalion brought their total of Russian tanks destroyed to 105, with his 1st Company alone destroying 39. Overall it was a superlative result which few panzer commanders would even come close to equalling, and formed the basis for his recommendation of the Oak Leaves to his Knight's Cross.

Fuel remained a perennial problem, which he only solved by capturing enemy supplies. The Russian tanks used diesel fuel, which von Strachwitz destroyed when found. The gasoline the Russians required for their trucks provided the lifeline for von Strachwitz's tanks. Soviet supply dumps were usually found in the various isolated villages or farms and the numerous *balkas* (ravines) in the steppe. Some *balkas* were large enough to hide trucks and other vehicles. The German Feisler Storch, a slow-moving light plane used for reconnaissance and liaison, proved extremely useful at spotting these supply dumps and Russian armoured forces, then landing or dropping messages for von Strachwitz. Not having an equivalent, the Russians were at a serious disadvantage, and their air force was not yet dominating the sky, allowing Luftwaffe aircraft and German Army Storchs to operate freely. The Red Air Force still challenged the Germans, and battles raged overhead, but the experienced Luftwaffe pilots asserted their dominance with better tactical skill, flying ability and aggression. Many amassed large scores, so that eventually a tally of 100 Red aircraft destroyed became necessary to win a Knight's Cross. Some pilots, like Erich Hartmann, the world's leading fighter ace, and Gerhard Barkhorn, shot down 300 or more Soviet aircraft, with 13 aces downing over 200. It became not unusual to achieve a score of 100. Still, Russian aircraft carried out strafing attacks on the Panzer Graf's tanks, and remained a force to be reckoned with.

Dust clouds signified the movement of vehicles, which could only be identified as distances closed. Superior German optics helped with early identification, giving them an advantage. Here again the Fieseler Storchs, also attracted by the dust, provided vital early warning. Quite often von Strachwitz pretended to be a Soviet column waving to the Russians or showing a captured signal flag. He then closed in from the rear to attack. The first the Russians knew of hostile presence was their tanks exploding and burning around them, with their force often being decimated before they could properly react.

During the fighting Hyazinth was lightly wounded, but he was treated by Dr. Ernst Paal and remained with his troops. Being out of action for a period of days, he was back by the time Soviet General Lopatin launched a counterattack, desperate to forestall the German advance. They were no match for the Panzer Graf's panzers and were repulsed with heavy casualties. Leaving the panzer grenadiers to mop up, von Strachwitz drove his men on to link up with 24th Panzer Division on 11 August and so close the trap on the Russians at Kalach. The now all-too-familiar containment battle ensued. Once again the shortage of German infantry had to be compensated for by the panzers in a role to which they were not suited. With little or no infantry support, von Strachwitz roamed the perimeter of the cauldron, blasting and machine-gunning the frantic Soviets. The battles raged across the steppe once again.

When it was over the Germans had captured 1,000 vehicles of all types and took some 57,000 Russian prisoners, of whom 8,300 were taken by 16th Panzer alone. The division had destroyed 298 Russian guns and 257 tanks, the largest number of which were destroyed by Graf von Strachwitz's battalion. This tank tally brought the total number of Russian tanks destroyed by the division over the previous nine months to 1,000, of which 750 were destroyed by the panzer regiment and 250 by the anti-tank battalion and infantry. This was a kill ratio of four Russian tanks to one of the division's—a much higher ratio than that achieved by the German panzer arm throughout the war on the Eastern Front, which was 3.26:1. This Eastern Front total included the Tiger tank kill ratio—which was 5.412:1—making 16th Panzer's score even more impressive. This kill rate should end any argument against the Tiger tank being the most effective of the war, especially as most of their kills were T-34s. The Russians of course could afford these losses and more, which at the strategic level made the kill ratios meaningless.[12]

With the battle of Kalach successfully concluded, there followed two weeks of mopping-up operations. Russian units, including mechanized forces, were still wandering around seeking to escape and link up with friendly forces. Often Russian and German units would accidentally bump into each other causing a brief firefight before the Russians withdrew or surrendered. Each skirmish, however, took its toll on the Germans, slowly ebbing their strength. Replacements were urgently needed but when they did come they were never enough to replace losses.

Bridges needed to be taken and bridgeheads established across the Don. On 16 August Lieutenant Kleinjohann of the 3rd Company Engineer Battalion captured a major bridge across the Don in a surprise coup. The bridge was already burning when Kleinjohann and his men arrived, and they had to put out the flames while under fire from Russian sentries.[13]

NOTES

1. Dennis Showalter, *Hitler's Panzers* (Berkley Publishing, USA, 2009).
2. Matthew Cooper and James Lucas, *Panzer: The Armoured Force of the Third Reich* (McDonalds Illustrated War Study, 1976).
3. Werner Haupt, *A History of the Panzer Troops 1916–1945* (Schiffer Publishing, USA, 1990).
4. V. E. Tarrant, *Stalingrad* (Leo Cooper, London, 1992).
5. Tim Ripley, *Wehrmacht* (Brown Reference Group, 2003).
6. Interview with Nikita Khrushchev's son Sergi (Military History Channel).
7. Antony Beevor, *Stalingrad* (Penguin Books 1999), pp.66–67.
8. Tim Ripley, *Wehrmacht* (Brown Reference Group 1992).
9. Hope Hamilton, *Sacrifice on the Steppe* (Casemate PS, 2011).
10. Günter Schmitz, *Die 16 Panzer Division* (Dörfler im Nebel Verlag Gmbh Eggolsheim).
11. Paul Carrell, *Hitler's War on Russia Vol 1 Hitler Moves East* (Ballantine Books, 1963).
12. Christopher W. Wilbeck, *Sledgehammers: Strengths & Flaws of Tiger Tank Battalions in World War II* (The Aberjona Press, Bedford PA, 2004).
13. Carrell, *Hitler's War on Russia, Vol. 1: Hitler Moves East.*

THIRTEEN

THE ROAD TO STALINGRAD

STALINGRAD, A CITY OF 400,000 AND AN IMPORTANT industrial centre on the Volga River was to become the site of a vicious, merciless battle of attrition. The city itself became a huge funeral pyre, a smashed pile of rubble, strewn with corpses. Well over a million men would be killed or wounded in an inferno of hatred amidst a stubborn will to conquer or die. It was, during the height of battle, never still. Explosions shook the ground, artillery shells, mortars and bombs continuously rained down, fires blazed, and smoke bellowed high into the sky. The gloom beneath the smoke was illuminated only by tracer rounds, while small-arms fire crackled all around. Positions changed by the hour in attacks and counterattacks, men clawing, clubbing and fighting for every metre of rubble. If they lost ground, then they attacked to retake it, no matter the cost in lives. Stalingrad was one of the most horrendous, savage clashes of arms of World War II. Men died from the combined effects of constant fear, total exhaustion, nervous tension, unremitting traumatic stress, hunger, thirst, malnutrition, hatred, anger, depression and despair.[1]

Not knowing what lay ahead, von Strachwitz and 16th Panzer cheerfully marched towards Stalingrad, with the 3rd and 60th Motorised Divisions, all still part of XIV Panzer Corps under von Wietersheim. A Silesian and ex-guardsman, like von Strachwitz, he was no Nazi or great believer in Hitler. He got on very well with Hube and his divisional commanders who respected both his integrity and ability. Hube, it must be said, got along with most people, as did von Strachwitz, although the latter could not tolerate fools and slaggards and on occasion could not hide his feelings.

XIV Panzer was the only panzer corps in Sixth Army, with the majority of panzer divisions being attached to von Kleist on his march to the Caucasus. This would later change when Hitler and the High Command saw the need for armoured reinforcements for Sixth Army and sent 4th Panzer Army to support the drive on Stalingrad.

On 22 August the battle groups of the division moved along the dusty roads down into the river valley to assemble near Lutichenski on the south bank of the Don. Here they were supported by the very effective HS129 ground-attack aircraft, which were armoured and specialised in destroying Russian tanks. These aircraft often destroyed the Russian tanks well before von Strachwitz and his men got to them. Stukas also flew support missions, their gull-wing shapes plummeting down onto Russian positions a welcome sight to the advancing tanks and grenadiers. On completing their missions the Stukas frequently flew low over the panzer columns, their sirens screaming in a comradely greeting.

Lieutenant Radu, the assistant ordnance officer of the division's 64th Panzergrenadier Regiment, was travelling by motorcycle carrying a despatch when he suddenly came up against a Russian light tank. Refusing to accept that this was an unequal struggle, he swiftly threw a hand grenade into the tank's open hatch, forcing the concussed and slightly wounded crew to surrender.

Von Strachwitz's battalion, supported by the truckborne 2nd Battalion, 64th Panzergrenadier Regiment, crossed the Don at dawn of what promised to be another hot and dusty day. As per Hube's instructions he ordered his panzers to move at all speed, ignoring any enemy at the flanks and engaging only those to their front or who challenged their progress. The cavalryman in him exulted at the rapid thrust deep into enemy lines, the very tip of the spearhead of his division and the entire Sixth Army. It was heady stuff and what he was bred to do. His only fear was an aerial attack for which he had no riposte. Of particular concern was being attacked by German Stukas, who would not be expecting a German formation to be this far forward and might not see the recognition flag on his tank. Fortunately both German and Russian aircraft had more urgent business elsewhere. He pushed his men relentlessly. Any tank that fell out due to mechanical problems had to wait alone on the open steppe until repairs could be effected or until the division caught up.

Resistance was light. Some of the Russians they came across were already on the run; they simply scattered or surrendered, to be waved westwards. Others were elements heading for the front, which were quickly disposed of if they were prepared to resist, or given a friendly wave and ignored if they mistook the German tanks for their own.

On 23 August the Panzer Graf's advance took him to Gumrak airfield where Soviet aircraft were still taking off and landing, as the Germans were considered to still be several days away. Von Strachwitz coolly and methodically deployed his panzers, then gave the order to fire. Tracer streaked towards parked planes, while high-explosive rounds crashed into hangers, vehicles, buildings, gun emplacements and aircraft. Chaos erupted, fuel and ammunition exploded, aircraft burned then exploded as the flames ignited their fuel and munitions. Flying debris and shrapnel did fearful execution to men and machines alike, as the airfield was consumed in flame, smoke, and flying rubble.

The anti-aircraft gun crews frantically turned their guns onto their land-based antagonists but they were too slow to adjust their sights for the correction. They also had trouble spotting their ground targets, for which they were completely untrained. They became easy targets for the German panzers. Blast after blast demolished the gun emplacements sending body and gun parts hurtling through the air. German machine guns cut a swathe through the Soviet positions shooting down those who had survived the high-explosive rounds.

A German Stuka squadron joined the fray, plummeting in steep dives to release their bombs on the mayhem below. Some of the Soviet anti-aircraft guns diverted their fire to the more familiar threat from above. Despite the hurricane of fire engulfing them, none of the gunners abandoned their post. Whenever the anti-aircraft rounds managed to hit a panzer they invariably bounced off, streaking off into the sky.

The Panzer Graf ordered his tanks to close in. Firing their machine guns the panzers smashed onto the airfield, shooting or grinding down with their tracks anyone who stood in their way. When opposition was finally silenced, the Graf halted his panzers. An entire aerial regiment had been destroyed along with the anti-aircraft regiment providing it with protection. It was a grim but exceedingly satisfactory result. Von Strachwitz's men began joking that instead of painting tank kill rings on their barrels they would have to paint red stars or aircraft on their turrets. Some of them joked they were now *experten* to rival the Luftwaffe pilots.[2] However when the Graf and his men dismounted and moved among the carnage they recoiled in horror. Many of the gun crews were women, some looked like mere schoolgirls. The Germans were aghast that the Russians would employ young girls to operate their guns, feeling anger that they had been forced to kill them. The women had been poorly trained and lacked experience, but they didn't lack courage. Vasily Grossman, the Soviet journalist, who was present at Stalingrad was told about the action by the anti-aircraft regiment's commanding officer, Lieutenant Colonel German:

> On the night of the 23rd, eighty German tanks advanced on the Traktorny in two columns, and there were a lot of vehicles with infantry. There are many girls in German's regiment, instrument operators, direction finders, intelligence and so on [including anti-aircraft gun crews actually manning the guns]. There was a massive air raid at the same time as the tanks came. Some of the batteries were firing at the tanks, others at the aircraft. When the tanks had advanced right to the battery of Senior Lieutenant Skakun, he opened fire at the tanks. His battery was then attacked by aircraft. He ordered two guns to fire at the tanks and the other two at the aircraft. There was no communication with the battery. "Well, they must have been knocked out," [the regimental commander] thought. Then he heard the thunder of fire. Then silence again. "Well, they are finished now!" he thought again. Firing broke out again. It was only on the night of 24 August that four soldiers [from this battery] came back. They had carried Skakun on a groundsheet. He had been heavily wounded. The girls had died by their guns.[3]

Coming close behind von Strachwitz's battalion was Hube at the head of his panzergrenadiers in their APCs. They had some sporadic fighting but the resistance was disorganised. Overhead, Stukas and Heinkel bombers shepherded by their fighter escorts flew in waves towards Stalingrad. Signals flashed backwards and forwards as corps and army commanders feverishly sought information about progress while maintaining contact with the various combat formations including von Strachwitz's battalion on point. In Hube's APC, his signallers Schmidt, Queteux and Luckner handled over 456 coded signals on just the first day of battle.[4]

Von Strachwitz kept up his momentum, and in what amounted to a *coup de main* his panzers pushed through the industrial suburb of Rynok at the northern edge of Stalingrad to finally reach the mighty Volga. His was the first German tank to reach the west bank, halting while he and his crew silently gazed across. The west bank was exceedingly high, towering more than 500 metres above the Soviet-occupied eastern bank. The river at this point was over two kilometres wide. While the Graf and his crew were staring across to the other bank the rest of his men were rejoicing. They had reached the mighty Volga. Stalingrad would now quickly fall, and they could enjoy their victory with a much-needed respite. It was a happy day, full of satisfaction and relief.

Essentially however 16th Panzer was on its own. It had covered some 80 kilometres in a day, leaving the 3rd and 60th Motorised Divisions of the corps well behind in its wake. Fortunately the Soviets had been taken by surprise and did not immediately close in the gap behind the panzers.

On 24 August a battle group was sent to attack the industrial suburb of Spartakovka. Stukas of von Richhofen's air fleet streamed overhead, bombing the Russian positions ahead of the German advance, but it wasn't enough to stifle the fierce opposition the grenadiers encountered. Machine-gun nests, pill boxes, dug-in tanks, trench lines and bunkers were all heavily manned and stoutly defended by the determined Soviets. Not content with just merely defending, the Russians launched a counterattack with strong tank forces against Hube's northern flank, forcing him onto the defensive. T-34s stormed towards the German lines, some of the tanks manned by workers from the Dzerzhinsky Tractor Works where the tanks had just come off the assembly lines. A few tanks actually broke through to reach the regimental headquarters of the division's 64th Panzer Grenadier Regiment and had to be knocked out by the headquarters troops with hand-held explosive charges.

However, the German assault was not entirely without result. Battle Group Strehlke—consisting of combat engineers, anti-tank troops and artillery men—managed to capture the landing stage of the railway ferry on the Volga, cutting off the Volga connection from south Russia to Moscow.[5] In the process they seized a vast quantity of heavy equipment and weapons.

Elsewhere along the Volga's banks, Hube's gunners played havoc with the river traffic, sinking several barges and ferries. Unknown to the men, one was carrying civilians, a large number of whom were killed or wounded. Civilians were also killed in large numbers on land, some 40,000 by aerial bombing during the battle. Stalin had categorically refused to allow their evacuation on the basis that his troops would fight that much harder to protect them. NKVD and other troops were stationed at the ferry to turn back any civilians who tried to cross to safety.

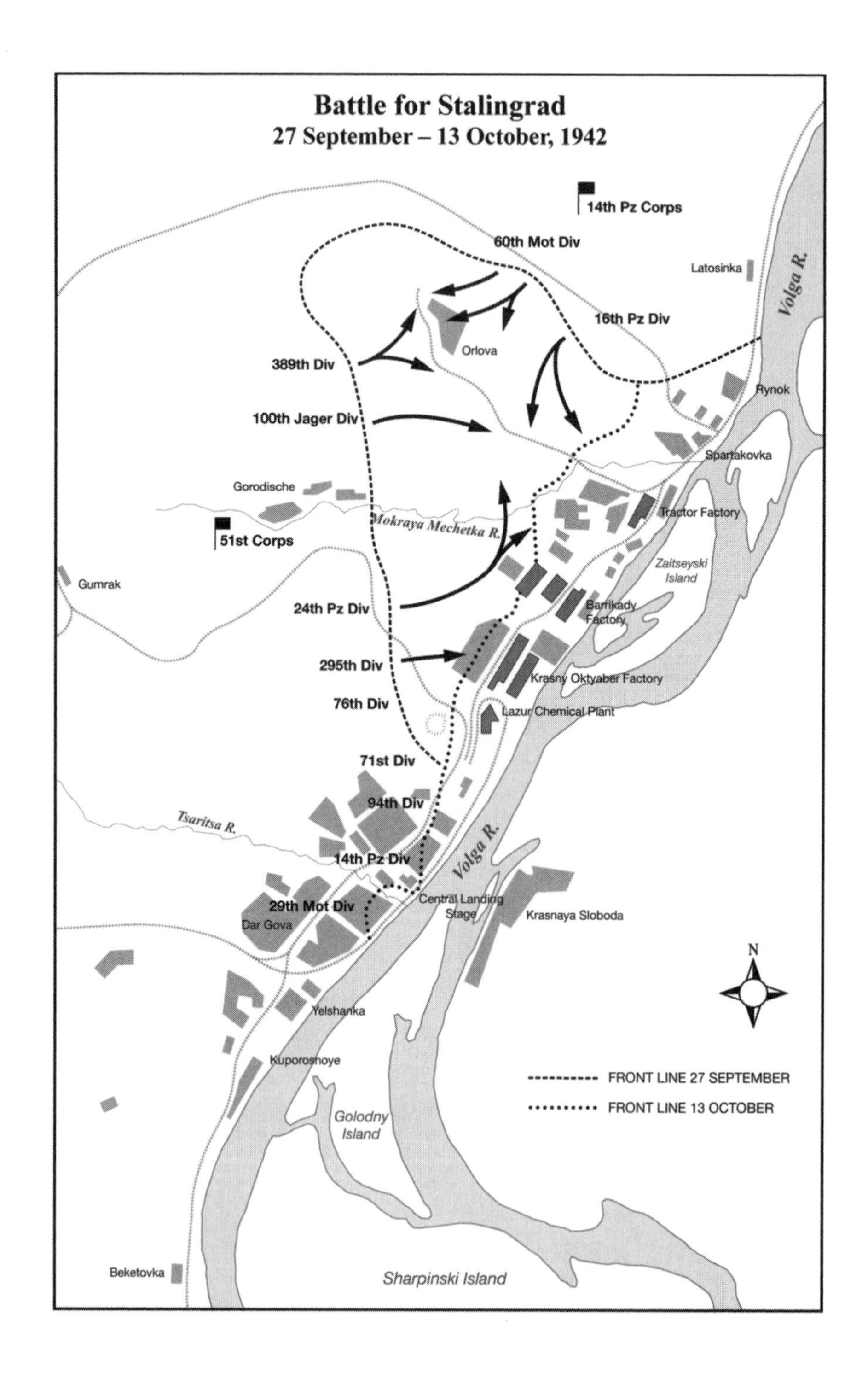
Battle for Stalingrad
27 September – 13 October, 1942
14th Pz Corps
60th Mot Div
Latosinka
Volga R.
16th Pz Div
Orlova
389th Div
Rynok
100th Jager Div
Spartakovka
Gorodische
Tractor Factory
Mokraya Mechetka R.
51st Corps
Zaitseyski Island
Gumrak
24th Pz Div
Barrikady Factory
295th Div
Krasny Oktyaber Factory
76th Div
Lazur Chemical Plant
71st Div
94th Div
Tsaritsa R.
14th Pz Div
Volga R.
29th Mot Div
Central Landing Stage
Dar Gova
Krasnaya Sloboda
N
Yelshanka
Kuporosnoye
FRONT LINE 27 SEPTEMBER
FRONT LINE 13 OCTOBER
Golodny Island
Beketovka
Sharpinski Island

The Russians rushed in reinforcements, sending in the 35th Infantry Division augmented with T-34 and light tanks to seal off the German bridgeheads over the Don and hold the area open for more troops to smash the Don bridgeheads as well as 16th Panzer on the Volga. This move now succeeded in isolating 16th Panzer from Sixth Army, which was still fighting around the Don.

The isolated German division formed a hedgehog defensive position to stave off the Soviet attacks. The shortage of trained infantry forced the Russians to send in raw, cobbled together militia battalions consisting of factory workers, including women. Without training or proper weapons they were slaughtered en masse, their courage no substitute for skill, weapons and sound tactics. Despite the horrendous casualties, their commissars sent the labour battalions into the attack again and again. The 16th Panzer machine guns did fearful execution to their ranks, but still they came on, urged on by their commissars waving their nickel-plated pistols behind them.

Successful as his defence was, Hube was worried. Ammunition, fuel and food were all rapidly running out. Fuel and food could be evenly rationed, but ammunition was essential if his division was to survive. Ju-52 transport planes, the three-engined workhorses of the Wehrmacht, flew in to drop supplies but these were totally inadequate to meet the division's needs. At the rate the Germans were expending ammunition against the militia's suicide attacks, 16th Panzer would be overrun.

To the north of the German hedgehog, the Russians continued to send in their tank brigades. Here von Strachwitz once more came into his own. He led his panzers with his now practised flanking manoeuvres against the Russian tanks, in this way hitting the Russians in their more vulnerable side and rear armour, making nearly every hit lethal. Von Strachwitz manoeuvred as well as the scarcity of fuel allowed. Any of his tanks that were beyond repair were drained of their last drop of fuel as were any knocked-out trucks or cars. Some of his men had to be stopped from trying to clandestinely siphon petrol out of Hube's staff car. The German armour acted as a fire brigade for the hard-pressed panzer grenadiers, who often had no answer to the Soviet tank attacks. Combined Russian infantry and armour attacks blazed all along the division's northern perimeter with von Strachwitz's panzers moving rapidly from one hot spot to another.

Air drops often had to be fought over. On one occasion a German supply drop landed between the lines, resulting in a race between von Strachwitz with four Panzer IIIs and 17 Russian tanks. Knowing that if he got there first he would have to take the Russians frontally and might well be surrounded, he halted his panzers; then turning north he circled round, approaching from the south behind the Russians. The Soviets had stopped at the airdrop point with some crew, probably one from each tank, dismounting to collect the spoils. Thinking the German tanks had retreated, the Russians were relaxed, their guns pointing towards the German lines. Absorbed in collecting their booty they didn't notice the Germans coming up behind them. The German tanks halted and von Strachwitz calmly gave the order to fire.

Four barrels flashed, sending their armour-piercing rounds at close range into four Russian tanks, setting them immediately alight. A fifth tank saw them and began turning its turret around. Von Strachwitz gave his gunner new fire directions and the fifth tank exploded. Not having a radio the Russian had not been able to warn his comrades of the threat to their rear. Another four Russians were quickly brewed up before they realised where the danger was coming from. They frantically turned their turrets to face the Germans but were too slow and four more tanks were destroyed. One Russian got off a round but missed while the others accelerated away, just avoiding another German salvo. The Russian who fired was promptly despatched, with hits from two panzers smashing him completely. Von Strachwitz then collected the supplies and several tank crews as prisoners, leaving behind 14 burning Soviet tanks.

Even with the air drops, Hube knew his situation was rapidly becoming untenable. He called all his regimental and battalion commanders together, including von Strachwitz, and told them of his decision:

> The shortage of ammunition and fuel is such that our only chance is to break through to the west. I absolutely refuse to fight a pointless battle that must end in annihilation of my troops and I therefore order a breakout to the west. I shall personally take responsibility for this order; and will know how to justify it in the proper quarters. I absolve you gentlemen, from your oath of loyalty [to the Führer], and I leave you the choice of either leading your men in this action or of handing over your commands to other officers who are prepared to do so. It is impossible to hold our positions without ammunition. I am acting contrary to the Führer's orders.[6]

Hube knew that by ordering this withdrawal he was ending his career, and facing a court martial and possible imprisonment; Hitler would not countenance a withdrawal from such an important bridgehead as this, no matter how decorated or highly regarded the commander. His deliberate absolution of his subordinate commanders is a unique action and the sheer measure of the man. His moral courage equalled his physical, while his unfettered concern for his men and plain common sense was a reflection of his superb leadership ability. If General Paulus or even von Manstein had shown anything near to Hube's moral courage, the disaster at Stalingrad would have been greatly mitigated with tens of thousands of men retaining their lives as a result of an ordered breakout.

In the event, Hube did not have to carry out the fateful order. The 3rd Motorised Division arrived, like the cavalry of old, in the nick of time to link up with Hube's division. It brought with it a supply column of 250 trucks loaded with desperately needed supplies of fuel, food, weapons and ammunition. 16th Panzer was saved. Not that this largesse was provided by the Sixth Army quartermasters; it was simply fortuitous that 3rd Motorised's tank battalion had captured an entire Soviet freight train being unloaded near Kuzsuichi. It was loaded with US-made Ford motor vehicles, food, fuel, ammunition, weapons and other materials, a great deal of which came courtesy of the US and UK governments.

However, as much as the vitally needed supplies and reinforcements of the 3rd Motorised Division improved the situation, the Germans remained isolated by a 50-kilometre gap from the bulk of Paulus' Sixth Army. As if to emphasise this vulnerability, the Russians attacked the western flank of 3rd Motorised, tearing a huge gap in their lines. The very concerned corps commander, General von Wietersheim, radioed Paulus to inform him that they could not stay on the Volga and hold communications to the rear, and asked for a decision. Knowing Soviet resistance was collapsing and that von Wietersheim's divisions would soon be reinforced, he simply replied, "Do not retreat."

Two days later 60th Motorised joined the orphan divisions while another five divisions fanned out behind it to open up a supply corridor between the Don and Volga.[7] By this time the Panzer Graf's tanks were almost running on empty again, facing the prospect of being dug in as static defences, so he was highly relieved to see more supplies rolling in so his precious panzers could move again.

Elsewhere, events were moving favourably for the Germans. General von Seydlitz-Kurzbach, a descendant of Frederick the Great's famous cavalry commander, had launched the two divisions of his corps on a frontal attack at the centre of Stalingrad. After heavy fighting they breached the Soviet defences to come to within 10 kilometres of the city outskirts.

By 31 August General Kempf's Panzer Corps had cut a swathe in the enemy's rear, cutting the railway line south of Pitomik airfield. The Russians, in desperate straits, pulled back, and on 3 September all German units west of Stalingrad finally formed up to create a broad front less than 10 kilometres from the city. The major assault on Stalingrad and one of the greatest battles of the war could now begin.

NOTES

1. The Germans were so concerned by these sudden inexplicable deaths with no recognisable symptoms that they sent a medical specialist to try and ascertain the cause.
2. The Germans did not use the term "ace" to recognise pilots with numerous kills but called them *experten* (experts) a term which implied not only the accumulation of kills, but also flying skill and experience.
3. Vasily Grossman (ed. and trans. Antony Beevor and Luba Vinogradova), *A Writer at War With the Red Army 1941–1945* (The Harvell Press, London 2005), p. 128.
4. Paul Carrell, *Hitler's War on Russia, Vol 1: Hitler Moves East* (Ballantine Books, 1963).
5. Ibid.
6. V. E. Tarrant, *Stalingrad* (Leo Cooper, London, 1992), p. 60, citing AOK6la Kreigstagebuch.
7. Ibid.

FOURTEEN

INSIDE THE CAULDRON

The advance of Sixth Army didn't provide a great deal of relief to the 16th Panzer Division. On 30 October, Russian forces landed at Lukashenka and attacked the division with a mixed force of workers, militia and regular infantry. With some difficulty, the division repulsed all the Russian human wave attacks. Hube ordered a counterattack, which captured the northern strongpoints after vicious hand-to-hand fighting. The Russians counterattacked in turn and recovered their lost positions with both sides suffering heavy casualties, the Red Siberian assault troops proving to be particularly formidable. The Germans launched another attack, dislodging the Siberians, who in their turn drove out the Germans again. Each savage seesaw battle took its toll on the 16th Panzer's shock troops.

On 12 September General Vasily Chuikov was appointed commander of the Russian 62nd Army, which with 54,000 men, 900 guns and mortars and 110 tanks, was defending Stalingrad. He also had 100,000 untrained but fanatical militia to augment his forces.[1] Chuikov was an even bigger thug than Zhukov, and even more profligate with his men's lives, but he was what Stalingrad needed to hold out against the German onslaught at the time.

On this day too, Hitler summoned Paulus and von Weichs, commander of Army Group B, to his headquarters at Vinnitsa in the Ukraine to discuss the final assault. Paulus, already showing the strain of command with a nervous tic affecting his drawn face, told of his concerns over his long exposed northern flank. He also mentioned his mounting casualties which had reached 7,700 dead and 31,000 wounded since 23 August, when his army had broken out of the Don bridgehead.[2] Hitler ignored these figures, and optimistically assured his generals that the Russians were no longer capable of launching a major offensive. He told Paulus that his exposed flanks would be covered by the Romanian Third and Fourth Armies and that he should concentrate on the assault on Stalingrad. Paulus returned to Sixth Army, his faith in the Führer reinforced.

Graf von Strachwitz was still defending the northern flank of the division with countless engagements against Soviet tanks and infantry. Slowly the number of operational tanks available to him was being reduced, although fortunately most of the tanks knocked out of action were repairable. This was mainly because Strachwitz's panzers were able to dominate or hold the battlefield, which meant that his disabled tanks could be repaired on the spot or towed to the rear by recovery vehicles. Still, on occasion, his battalion often had no more than six runners, and sometimes fewer.

In the central and southern area of Stalingrad, the Germans marshalled their troops for the main onslaught on the 400-kilometre front of the Stalingrad axis. The Germans and Russians were equal in manpower in the sector with 590,000 men, but the Germans had more tanks and initially more aircraft.[3]

The onslaught was preceded by a bombardment from 3,000 guns and mortars, while the Luftwaffe launched successive waves of bombers and Stukas which pulverised the Soviet positions in and around the city. The Russians replied with their own artillery, and their defences held firm until 14 September when the Germans gained a narrow corridor to the banks of the Volga. However, they failed to widen this salient and the fighting degenerated into relentless street fighting, where progress was measured in metres.

Paulus made a tactical mistake in not concentrating all possible resources to stop traffic on the Volga. Chuikov was totally reliant on the river crossings for reinforcements and resupply of ammunition and food. The Luftwaffe compounded the error by dispersing its bombing attacks over a wide tactical area instead of concentrating almost exclusively on the river crossings and Soviet concentrations on the east bank. Without men and supplies the Russians at Stalingrad could not have held out.

Some writers and historians are given to repeating Soviet propaganda that Chuikov exercised supreme cunning and tactical skill by feeding just sufficient men and supplies into Stalingrad to hold a bridgehead and keep the Germans fighting so they could be sucked into a trap. But in fact Chuikov had no other choice. He was constrained by both the availability of resources, and what he could get across the river without it being destroyed. He was also initially limited by what he could assemble in a narrow bridgehead without creating a bottleneck that would be an easy target for the German bombers. It wasn't cunning or tactical skill that Chuikov relied upon, but the determination, skill, and courage of his troops. That said, Chuikov conducted an excellent defence, with the use of small units in defence and assault, with specially created kill and defensive zones. The Germans on the other hand were using larger forces that often hampered each other and created larger targets. They had to learn the hard way. Fighting then degenerated into numerous and constant small-unit actions with often just a few men deciding the issue in a small area of intense combat. A lieutenant of the 24th Panzer Division gives a very graphic description of the type of fighting that became the norm:

> We have fought during fifteen days for a single house; with mortars, grenades, machine guns and bayonets. Already on the third day 54 German corpses are strewn in the cellars, on the landings and the staircases. The front is a corridor between burnt-out rooms; it is the ceiling between two floors. Help comes from neighbouring houses by fire escapes and chimneys. There is a ceaseless struggle from noon to night. From storey to storey, faces black with sweat we bombard each other with grenades in the middle of explosions, clouds of dust and smoke, heaps of mortar, floods of blood, fragments of furniture and human beings. Ask any soldier what half an hour of hand-to-hand struggle means in such a fight, and imagine Stalingrad; eighty days and eighty nights of hand-to-hand struggles. The street is no longer measured by metres but by corpses ...[4]

At the northern outskirts von Wietersheim, the XIV Panzer Corps commander, was gravely concerned at the losses being sustained by 16th Panzer. He requested that Paulus replace his troops with infantry divisions better suited to close-quarter fighting. Paulus, stressed, exhausted, racked with dysentery, got uncharacteristically angry at what was a reasonable request. The more so as he had been tolerating General von Seydlitz-Kiesbach who was a far more difficult, arrogant and ill-disciplined commander. He arbitrarily dismissed the brave and capable von Wietersheim from his command on the grounds of defeatism. Hitler took this further by dismissing him from the army. Von Wietersheim ended the war as a private soldier in the Volksturm, Germany's last-ditch home guard militia. Von Seydlitz, however, continued to enjoy Paulus' confidence, eventually turning traitor after his capture and actively assisting the Russians. Paulus' judgement of men, like his military judgement, was seriously flawed.

Von Strachwitz was livid at the sheer travesty of the dismissal. He liked and respected von Wietersheim, an excellent panzer leader and Knight's Cross bearer whom he felt privileged to serve—which for someone of von Strachwitz's ego was a considerable concession. Not one to keep his feelings buried he went to General Hube to vent his feelings, which would have embarrassed Hube who had been promoted to take von Wietersheim's place. No doubt however, the good-natured Hube commiserated with von Strachwitz, probably agreeing with the unfairness of the dismissal.

Whatever his feelings about his promotion, Hube would have felt a pang of regret at leaving the division with which he had shared so many hardships and battles. He certainly felt as much affection for his men as they did for him. So it was with genuine sorrow that he made his farewells. He visited every unit in turn, saying goodbye individually to every regimental and battalion commander, while saying farewell to the troops who had served him so well in many grim battles in the past.

His replacement was Major General Günter Angern, a veteran combat officer who had been awarded the Knight's Cross in 1940. He was a meticulously correct officer, who had genuine warmth and concern for the welfare of his troops. Not as popular as Hube, he was nevertheless a good replacement. Graf von Strachwitz had no trouble working with him, perhaps particularly because Angern had a cavalry background.

On 27 September 16th Panzer, along with 60th Motorised and 39th Infantry Division, was committed to a major attack in the direction of the tractor works. Ferocious street fighting ensued. Concealed Soviet snipers picked men off in all directions. The stubbornly defending Russians had to be dislodged from buildings with sub-machine guns, hand grenades, bayonets and fists. Men fought hand to hand with whatever weapons they could grasp, sharpened entrenching tools being a favourite, but anything that could gouge, club or kill was used. No sooner had the Germans cleared one sector than they were taking fire from the rear as the Russians skilfully infiltrated behind them. There was no let up. The enemy was always close, with unseen snipers taking advantage of the slightest exposure. The men were dirty, unshaven, hollow-eyed and exhausted, their faces etched with stress. Their eyes burned feverishly or were glazed over with mind-numbing exhaustion from the torment of close-quarter combat.

On 29 September two Russian infantry divisions and three brigades attacked the 16th Panzer and 60th Motorised Divisions. The Germans fought back grimly, destroying 72 Russian tanks. So desperate was the situation that Russian soldiers continued to desert to the Germans. Eventually the number of Russians working for 16th Panzer almost equalled the number of Germans fighting.

By early October nearly all of southern Stalingrad was in German hands but at the cost of 40,000 casualties, while the Russians had lost over 80,000 men. The munitions expended were enormous with around 20,000,000 rounds of small-arms ammunition, 750,000 artillery rounds and 500,000 anti-tank shells.[5] The casualties and expenditure of resources began to seriously worry Paulus, who expressed his concerns to General Rudolf Schmidt, head of the Army Personnel Office, when he was visiting Paulus's headquarters. He brightened up considerably when Schmidt told him that Hitler was considering replacing General Jodl, with whom he had just had a fiery argument, with Paulus.

When told of the heavy losses being sustained in the street fighting at Stalingrad, Hitler brushed them aside, emphasising for the first time that the capture of Stalingrad was an urgent necessity, not only for operational but also psychological reasons. As Stalin felt the same way, both dictators were now committed to a fight to the death.

On 14 October Paulus launched his third and final attack to take the city. The 16th Panzer attacked the tractor factory with everything in its arsenal. The ferocity of the assault destroyed the elite Russian 37th Guards Division, splitting the 62nd Army, and advancing 400 metres to take the heavily contested tractor factory and reach the Barrikady factory. By the end of October the Germans took the Red October factory and part of the Barrikady factory where the fighting continued at close quarters without result.

On 13 November Lieutenant Colonel Hyazinth Graf von Strachwitz was awarded the Oak Leaves to his Knight's Cross, being the award's 144th recipient. He had little time to enjoy his award however, for on 17 November 16th Panzer advanced on Rynock in two battle groups, attacking from the north and the west. They made some early gains, but heavy Russian defensive fire caused casualties, as the tanks had little room to manoeuvre. The Russians counterattacked with four tanks and infantry, forcing the Germans back. Casualties for the day were heavy, with four officers and 15 men killed and eight officers and 95 men wounded.[6]

After this intense fighting, 16th Panzer was pulled out of the line to go into reserve for a very necessary refit. All that remained of its fighting strength were 4,000 combat-weary men, which equated to a reinforced battle group or understrength brigade. After it was relieved by the 94th Infantry Division it took up winter quarters near Poteminskaya. During the withdrawal, events overtook it as the Red Army launched a major counteroffensive towards the Don bend.

This strategic offensive, dubbed Operation *Uranus*, had as its objective the encirclement of Sixth Army by first smashing the Romanian Third and Fourth Armies holding its flanks. Later it destroyed the Italian and Hungarian armies deployed further along the Don toward the northwest. The use of these weak Axis armies on such a large scale in vital roles was symptomatic of Germany's shortage of manpower and the overreaching of its goals.

The Russians employed a staggering 1,100,000 troops supported by 1,327 aircraft, 1,560 tanks, 4,215 guns, 11,564 mortars and 440 Katyusha rocket launchers for the offensive.[7] Most of this force crashed down on the hapless Romanians, which consisted of the Romanian Third Army of 150,000 men under General Dumitrescu, with eight infantry and two cavalry divisions, all of which were below established strength. The troops were under-supplied, under-trained, and underwhelmed about their service in Russia. They were mostly equipped with 37mm guns which were next to useless, and only had a paltry seven 75mm anti-tank guns per division, which were supplied by the Germans after much pleading by General Dumitrescu. The Fourth Romanian Army, under General Constantinescu, was even worse off with only 75,000 men in five infantry and two cavalry divisions, whose fighting spirit and morale equalled Third Army's, which was close to zero. The sole Romanian armoured division was in reserve, but was only equipped with Czech 38(t) light tanks carrying a measly 37mm gun, which was just capable of making a noise and scaring off some Soviet infantry. The Romanians then, were a debacle waiting to happen.

Under the Russian onslaught the Romanians quickly and understandably collapsed. The Russians struck them on 19 November, and on 23 November their pincers met on the Don to the west of Stalingrad at Kalach. Some 60 Soviet divisions had now encircled 290,000 Germans, Romanians and Russian Hiwis (ancillaries or helpers to the Axis).[8]

Hans Ulrich Rudel, the ace German Stuka pilot, gave a rather embittered account of the Romanian rout:

> The weather is bad, low lying clouds, a light fall of snow, the tem-

> perature probably 20 degrees below zero; we fly low. What troops are those coming towards us? We have not gone halfway. Masses in brown uniforms. Are they Russians? No. Romanians. Some of them are even throwing away their rifles in order to be able to run the faster: a shocking sight, we are prepared for the worst. We fly the length of the column heading north, we have now reached our artillery emplacements. The guns are abandoned, not destroyed. Their ammunition lies beside them. We have passed some distance beyond them before we sight the first Soviet troops.
>
> We find all the Romanian positions in front of them deserted. We attack with bombs and gun-fire but how much we use is that when there is no resistance on the ground? . . . On the return flight we again observe the fleeing Romanians; it is a good thing for them I have run out of ammunition to stop this cowardly rout. They have abandoned everything; their easily defended positions, their heavy artillery, their ammunition dumps; their cowardice is certain to cause a debacle along the whole front.[9]

The Italian Eighth Army and Hungarian Second Army, both equally bereft of armour and adequate anti-tank weapons, suffered a similar fate. Not that this result was unexpected, as Hitler's generals had repeatedly warned him of the dangers of having Germany's Axis allies guarding the front's extended flanks. Paulus' response was to order the 14th, 16th and 24th Panzer Divisions to move west toward the Don to try and block the Russians' drive across the German rear. This move took place on the night of 19/20 November and was a chaotic shambles. The supporting infantry could not be extricated from the fighting in Stalingrad where the Russians had launched an attack to tie them down. All General Angern had to send was a motley collection of rear-echelon troops. In addition there was no fuel available to make the dash west. Von Strachwitz had to beg, even steal the fuel necessary to make the move. Moreover, the panzers were scattered over a wide area and so could only make the move in a piecemeal fashion. The Panzer Graf only had four operational tanks in his immediate vicinity when ordered to deploy.

When the pincers of the Russian Operation *Uranus* met, they sliced through 16th Panzer, which had been in the process of withdrawing. Trapped inside the encirclement were the divisional headquarters including General Angern, the 79th and the bulk of the 64th Panzer Grenadier Regiments, the artillery regiment and the anti-aircraft battalion. Outside the cauldron were the 16th Tank Destroyer Battalion, 2nd Panzer Regiment, 16th Armoured Engineer Battalion and the 1st Battalion, 64th Panzer Grenadier Regiment. These units were all placed under the command of Colonel Rudolf Sieckenius as a separate battle group. Graf von Strachwitz commanded the armour element.

Rudolf Sieckenius had also been heavily engaged in combat while von Strachwitz was engaging a Soviet tank unit that was attempting a breakthrough. In one instance his force was attacked by a strong infantry force armed with anti-tank rifles, which normally didn't have a major impact on medium tanks, but posed a real threat in large numbers at close range. Vasily Grossman relates the account of Gromov, a Red anti-tank rifleman at Stalingrad:

> When you've hit it you see a bright flash on the armour. The shot deafens one terribly, one has to open one's mouth. I was lying there, I heard shouts: "They're coming!" My second shot hit the tank. The Germans started screaming terribly. We could hear them clearly. I wasn't scared, even a little. My spirits soared. At first, there was some smoke then crackling and flames. Evtikpov had hit one vehicle. He hit the hull, and how the Fritzes screamed![10]

In late November or possibly early December, von Strachwitz was seriously wounded. At first he refused to be evacuated, preferring to stay with his troops, until firmly ordered to fly out by General Hans Hube, who had been kept apprised by the chief medical officer. His participation in the epic battle of Stalingrad was over. This event saved him from death or imprisonment, although it is possible he may have been evacuated anyway as a specialist in tank warfare, as Hube and others were, in order to save key personnel. Due to serious tank losses there was a forced amalgamation of the 1st and 2nd Panzer Battalions. The 3rd Battalion, also seriously under strength, was placed under the command of Captain Freiheer Freytag von Loringhoven. Between 29 November and 2 December it served as a ready reaction force in the Dimireseke, Nowo and Alexandrovski areas, principally assisting the hard-pressed 44th Infantry Division. Freytag von Loringhoven was later flown out to carry important despatches.[11]

Meanwhile, at Sixth Army headquarters, General Hube and the other corps commanders were urging Paulus to break out of the encirclement. Paulus, however, still had faith in the Führer, and believed that the relief effort being organised by von Manstein would rescue him. He also fondly believed that the Luftwaffe, despite their generals' strong assertions to the contrary, would keep his army supplied.

Von Strachwitz and Siechkenius may have been out of the cauldron but the agony for 16th Panzer had still to run its course. On 6 December Lieutenant Mutius, who had supported von Strachwitz's battalion at the Don with his panzer grenadiers, led an attack on some high ground at Babarkin. His men had no sooner taken it when Russian tanks counterattacked in force. Mutius was severely wounded and his men scattered in all directions.

On 10 December von Manstein launched the much-awaited relief attempt. Hitler was keeping his promise to Paulus, but could not provide the forces strong enough to save Sixth Army. All that was available was the full-strength 6th Panzer Division, the grossly understrength 17th Panzer Division, the 23rd Panzergrenadier Division with its one battalion of tanks, and some next to useless Luftwaffe field divisions. This force just didn't have the strength to reach Stalingrad, despite almost superhuman efforts to do so. On 23 December von Manstein abandoned the attempt with a heavy heart. The Sixth Army was now doomed. Von Manstein did urge Paulus to break out, but did not categorically order him to. Paulus refused to follow von Manstein's advice. He would not disobey his Führer. He also knew that he had very few vehicles and very little fuel, but a large number of wounded, all of whom would certainly perish if they fell into the hands of the Reds. He was no Hube, Hausser or even von Reichenau,[12] and would have to face the consequences for his blind obedience.

Meanwhile the agony at Stalingrad continued. On 21 December General Hube was awarded the Swords to his Knight's Cross with Oak Leaves, becoming the 22nd recipient. He was flown to Hitler's headquarters so that a grateful Führer could personally present him with the award. Here Hube urged his leader to allow a breakout, but Hitler assuaged his anxieties with confident talk of relief, supplies and ultimate salvation. Hube was not the only veteran officer to be reassured in this manner by Hitler, who had a knack of often convincing his generals, at least while in his presence, against their better judgement. Hitler often quoted impressive-sounding facts and figures, made promises that couldn't be kept, gave assurances and on occasion, just plain lied. Many generals were convinced that Hitler had a broader, more accurate picture and believed his promises, so Hube's reaction was far from unusual. Major Gerhard Engel, Hitler's army ADC, relates in his memoirs how Field Marshal von Kluge went to see Hitler to resign his command if he could not persuade the Führer to alter the Army High Command to create a new Commander-in-Chief for the Eastern Front and remove Keitel. After four hours alone with Hitler he returned depressed and thoughtful. He told Engel, who was with him, "that he had laid all his cards on the table and the Führer had heard him out in silence. He was in agreement with him about Keitel but then had spoken convincingly about situation possibilities, requirements, and appealed to his conscience to the extent that he had not been able to go through with the final move." Engel finished his memoir note with "It was devastating, but it was always like that"[13]

Relief or not, 16th Panzer continued to carry out its duty. It had shrunk to a ration strength of 7,000 men, of which only 2,000 were combat troops. On 1 December these were augmented by all non-essential rear-area personnel. The gunners from the heavy battalion were also converted to infantry as their guns no longer had ammunition. The light artillery pieces (75–105mm) were limited to just 16 rounds per day.[14] Rations were cut to 200g per day, together with 50g of fat and some horsemeat when available, both of which were put into a watery soup. Despite prodigious efforts the Luftwaffe could not provide the minimum 600 tons that Sixth Army required each day just to function. The maximum it ever supplied was 362 tons, which was just above the 300-ton survival limit, with the average being 120 tons.[15] The troops had difficulty surviving on these rations, let alone continuing to fight. They got progressively weaker and apathetic from hunger, and their morale plummeted when it became clear that the hoped for relief force would never arrive.

On Christmas day, the Russians launched a major attack on 16th Panzer's positions. An 88mm gun located in the front lines destroyed 13 Russian tanks before being blown up by its crew with their last round. The Russians penetrated the division's front lines taking some high ground at hill 139.7. The Germans quickly counterattacked but were repulsed. Soviet tanks posed a major threat at this time as the anti-tank battalion had only one 50mm gun remaining, its surplus troops acting as infantry.

At the end of December the 94th Infantry Division was disbanded, with its remnants being sent to 16th Panzer as much-needed reinforcements. Along with them, the last levy of supply and headquarters troops, many of whom were NCOs, were turned into an ersatz infantry company of 100 men. Even the severely wounded stayed in the front line, such as Lieutenant Lobbecke, who had lost an arm but continued fighting while his wound slowly putrefied.[16]

On 9 January the Soviets issued a surrender ultimatum, promising good treatment in exchange for capitulation. Their emissaries used the issuing of the ultimatum to collect information on conditions and defences. When the ultimatum was rejected, the Russians launched a massive assault with five divisions, with 16th Panzer once again being selected for special treatment. On the 11th, with the Reds infiltrating through the thinly held German lines, General Angern ordered a withdrawal to specially prepared positions in the rear. However the Russians, having suffered horrendous losses during their attacks, couldn't pursue their advantage.

Angern now positioned his artillery directly in the front lines where they could provide direct support by line of sight fire and provide a morale booster for the hard-pressed infantry, who were exhausted and barely hanging on. First Lieutenant Adalbert Holl, who had become a member of 16th Panzer after the disbanding of 94th Infantry Division, recounted how his men were feeling at the time:

> There was nothing left of the spirit that inspired us in the past weeks and the élan with which we wanted to conquer this city of Stalin. We performed our duty like virtual machines. We felt somewhat threatened because something unknown was befalling us and we could not quite admit to it. When pressed hard, we fired and fought back like a fatally wounded animal that had been pushed into a corner and defended itself with all its strength.[17]

General Paulus gave a telling description of conditions to Major Thiel of the Luftwaffe who had been sent to report back on conditions at Gumrak Airfield. Thiel had told Paulus about the major difficulties the Luftwaffe was facing in trying to supply Sixth Army. Paulus' reply was embittered and reproachful:

> If your aircraft cannot land then my army is doomed. Every machine that does so can save the lives of 1,000 men. An air drop is no use at all. Many of the canisters are never found because the men are too weak from hunger and exhaustion to look for them, and we have no fuel to send the transport to collect them. I cannot even withdraw my line a few kilometres because the men would fall out from exhaustion. It is four days since they have had anything to eat. Heavy weapons cannot be withdrawn for lack of petrol and are therefore lost to

> us. The last horses have been eaten. Can you imagine what it is like to see soldiers fall on an old horse carcass, beat open the head and swallow the brains raw? What should I, as commander-in-chief of an army, say when a simple soldier comes up to me and begs "Herr Generaloberst, can you spare me one piece of bread? Why on earth did the Luftwaffe ever promise to keep us supplied? Who is the man responsible for declaring that it was possible? Had someone told me that it was not possible, I would not hold it against the Luftwaffe. I could have broken out when I was strong enough to do so. Now it is too late.[18]

Paulus had conveniently forgotten that the Luftwaffe generals had all warned him that supplying his army by air was an impossibility. The sheer scale of the operation with the number of planes and actual flying days available due to the weather meant that the Luftwaffe had little or no chance of meeting Paulus' daily requirements.

On 18 January General Hans Valentin Hube was wounded. Tough old soldier that he was, he categorically refused to be evacuated. He would stand and die with his men. Hitler, loathe to lose such a capable officer, personally ordered his evacuation but Hube still refused to go. An exasperated Hitler finally sent two security officers to force him onto a plane at gunpoint if necessary. Hube was flown out on a Focke Wulf 200 flown by the *experten* pilot Lieutenant Hans Gilbot. Soon after this, Hitler promoted Hube to the rank of Colonel General of Panzer Troops, one step below Field Marshal.

For 16th Panzer the situation had grown worse. On 21 January the pocket was split in two, with 16th Panzer trapped in the northern part, and Paulus' headquarters in the south. All could now see that the struggle was hopeless, yet pride, discipline, and fear of captivity kept them doggedly fighting. The feelings of the men are described by an anti-tank gunner in a letter written to his loved ones at home:

> On Tuesday I knocked out two T-34s with my mobile anti-tank gun. Curiosity had lured them behind our lines. It was grand and impressive. Afterwards I drove past the smoking remains. From a hatch there hung a body, head down his feet caught, and his legs burning up to his knees. The body was alive, his mouth moaning. He must have suffered terrible pain, he would have died after a few hours of torture. I shot him, and as I did it, the tears ran down my cheeks.

> Now I have been crying for three nights about a dead Russian tank driver whose murderer I am. The crosses of Gumrak shake me and so do many other things which my comrades close their eyes to and set their jaws against. I am afraid I'll never be able to sleep quietly, assuming that I shall ever come back to you, dear ones. My life is a terrible contradiction, a psychological monstrosity.[19]

The Germans finally withdrew to the western outskirts of Stalingrad, in many cases abandoning their seriously wounded, as the troops lacked the strength to carry them, having barely the energy to struggle through the snow themselves. Moreover there were no field hospitals that could take them. Food came in nightly airdrops, but ammunition was no longer being supplied. The troops had to scavenge what they could, or use captured weapons taken from dead Russians as newly promoted 116th Panzer Division Captain Adalbert Holl recounted, regarding a repulsed Russian attack on 26 January:

> Pawellek, Nemetz and two men tried to ascertain how many attackers lay in front and behind us. They also had the task of bringing in all weapons and ammunition from the dead enemy soldiers. When they returned, Pawellek reported: "Eight Russians are lying in the brook area. We brought back four sub-machine-guns with ammunition, four rifles and six hand grenades . . ."
>
> Nemetz returned shortly after: "Five dead on the slope above us, about 20 to 30 metres from here. We brought in three sub-machine-guns, two rifles, ammunition and four hand grenades, as well as a couple of pieces of bread and a little tobacco."[20]

On 31 January the newly promoted Field Marshal Paulus surrendered the southern pocket.[21] He refused the Russians' demand to call for the surrender of the northern pocket or any units still resisting, so the fighting in the north continued. Out of sheer frustration, the Russians launched a massive assault against the hold-outs which was repulsed with heavy losses. However 16th Panzer's neighbour to the left, the 60th Motorised Division, was overrun with only a lucky few able to surrender. The Russians also effected a deep penetration into 16th Panzer's right flank, finally reducing the northern pocket to a few hundred metres in depth. The Soviets then infiltrated through the thinly held lines to the rear, where the divisional headquarters staff became directly involved in the fighting. Major Dormann launched a local counterattack but only encountered groups of Germans already surrendering and being marched away. He barely managed to escape, returning alone.

On 2 February the Russians assaulted the divisional command post, overwhelming the last resistance being put up by the division. General Angern managed to slip away, trying to make his way to the tractor works where resistance was still continuing. However there were too many Russians between him and his objective so, accompanied only by his orderly, he disappeared into the icy wastes. The Russians discovered his body a few days later; he had either been shot or had committed suicide.

The agony of the survivors began anew as they were marched off to collection points and prisoner of war camps. The starved, exhausted, emaciated men were marched for some 50 kilometres. Anyone who dropped out was shot. Rear-echelon Russian troops pillaged and robbed the pathetic belongings of those straggling at the rear of the long winding column, shooting anyone who resisted. Typhus broke out at the initial collection camps, decimating the prisoners who now died in their tens of thousands. The survivors were despatched to various slave-labour camps throughout the Soviet Union. Of the 94,000 who marched into captivity only 5,000 returned home, some as late as 1955.

Paulus, disillusioned with Hitler, co-operated with the Russians, actively so after the failure of the 20 July 1944 bomb plot. He had a relatively comfortable captivity, compared to his men, and eventually settled in East Germany. He never saw his wife again. General Seydlitz-Kurzbach went beyond co-operation, turning traitor, broadcasting propaganda and supporting the setting-up of German prisoners of war to undertake missions against their former comrades. These turncoats were given the nickname Seydlitz troops.

Stalingrad was a major but not strategically decisive German defeat. They lost an entire army which—unlike the Russians—they could not afford to have removed from their order of battle. Nevertheless, they had inflicted at least equivalent casualties on the Soviets, and despite their loss of manpower, the Germans could, and did, launch major offensives in the east after Stalingrad, such as at Kharkov, Kursk and in Hungary. Their capacity to wage war offensively and for an extended time was not critically diminished. Nevertheless it was a major psychological turning point in the war. It showed the Russians and the world that the Germans could be badly beaten, that their high commander was not infallible, or their armies invincible. The defeat haunted the consciousness of general and soldier alike. The spectre of Stalingrad hovered over them all throughout the war, influencing their tactics and actions. The loss of men threw the entire nation into genuine mourning, which affected the morale of both soldier and civilian alike. Three days of official mourning was announced on 4 February. The loss of manpower could not be made up, especially as it involved the loss of many seasoned veterans. The failure of the airlift destroyed what was left of Hermann Goering's reputation.

For the Russians it was a major boost to their morale and confidence, yet the strategic turning point it was not. The turning point had already occurred with the failure of Operation *Barbarossa* the previous year when the Germans' gamble on a short war clearly failed. The Red Army had buckled, then held, and struck back. Since then it had continuously grown stronger as the Germans grew proportionally weaker. New reserves from deep in the Soviet interior were drawn upon, filling out the decimated ranks of the front-line units. Equipment, food and clothing began pouring in from the Western Allies while Russia's own production capacity from factories in the Urals beyond the reach of German bombers increased enormously. Moreover, due to the enormous number of trucks being supplied by the USA, the Soviets could concentrate more on their tank production, which made a decisive difference.

For the Germans it was a case of diminishing returns and insufficient resources to defeat the Soviet Union. Germany was simply not geared to fight a protracted war of attrition, in manpower, fuel, equipment or production capacity. Germany was already stretched in 1941. Its massive victories in 1941 were a testament to its troops' fighting ability, discipline, courage, superior tactics and combat experience, as well as the ability of its front-line commanders. The Russians made mistakes, but given time they adapted and learnt from them. Yet for all the attributes of the German troops, they could not make up in the long run for the lack of resources. Only by stripping the northern and central Fronts of men and tanks were the Germans able to mount the major offensive in the south, and even then this proved to be insufficient for the expanded goal of taking both Stalingrad and the Caucasus.

The Germans had already shot their bolt during Operation *Barbarossa*. From 1942 onwards they had only sufficient forces to continue fighting, albeit with some success, but not to win the war.

Despite the grave German defeat at Stalingrad it must be remembered that Sixth Army's sacrifice on the steppe had averted a more serious one. Had Stalingrad not held out as long as it did after its encirclement, Army Group

A in the Caucasus—comprising three German and one Romanian army—would have been cut off and ultimately destroyed, resulting in a much bigger disaster than the loss of Sixth Army at Stalingrad.

Had Paulus surrendered, or Sixth Army been overrun soon after the encirclement, the Soviet besieging forces would have been free to move against von Kleist's Army Group, seize Rostov and bottle him up in the Caucasus. As it was, von Kleist's men just managed to escape, albeit leaving behind Seventeenth Army on Hitler's orders to hold the Crimea, where it would later be destroyed. Von Kleist's masterly withdrawal was only made possible by the courage of Sixth Army's men in Stalingrad. Writers, and historians like to point to a major battle and label it strategically decisive. It is more glamorous and interesting than a protracted series of battles, events, or logistical and manpower failures such as Operation *Barbarossa*. An epic battle like Stalingrad with all its drama, pathos, heroism and losses certainly stirred the imagination and attracted every label that could be placed upon it. *Barbarossa* on the other hand was too vast in scope, encompassing numerous battles, events and personalities to be truly evocative. Yet its failure decided the war.

NOTES

1. V. E. Tarrant, *Stalingrad* (Leo Cooper, UK).
2. Ibid.
3. Alan Clark, *Barbarossa* (Macmillan, UK, 1985), p. 238.
4. Adalbert Holl (trans. Jason D. Mark and Neil Page), *An Infantryman in Stalingrad* (Leaping Horseman Books, Sydney, Australia, 2005).
5. Tarrant, *Stalingrad.*
6. Holl, *An Infantryman in Stalingrad.*
7. Tarrant, *Stalingrad.*
8. Antony Beevor, *Stalingrad* (Penguin Books, UK, 1999).
9. Hans Ulrich Rudel (trans. Lynton Hudson), *Stuka Pilot* (Euphorion, Dublin, 1952), pp.63–64.
10. Vasily Grossman (ed. & trans. Antony Beevor and Luba Vinogradova), *A Writer at War With the Red Army 1941–1945* (The Harvill Press, UK, 2005).
11. Beevor, *Stalingrad.*
12. During the following February, SS General Paul Hausser deliberately disobeyed Hitler's orders and abandoned Kharkov in order to save his SS Panzer Corps from destruction.
13. Major General Gerhard Engel, *At the Heart of the Reich* (Greenhill Books, UK) p.149.
14. Hans Schaufler, *Panzer Warfare in the East* (Stackpole Books, USA).
15. *An Infantryman in Stalingrad*
16. Beevor, *Stalingrad.*

17. Holl, *An Infantryman in Stalingrad.*
18. Tarrant, *Stalingrad*, p.206.
19. Tarrant, *Stalingrad*, pp.201–202.
20. Holl, *An Infantryman in Stalingrad*, pp.224–225.
21. Hitler promoted Paulus on the premise that a German field marshal never surrenders, and as a reward for Paulus' anticipated suicide. He was very upset when Paulus decided to live and went into captivity instead.

FIFTEEN

THE GROSSDEUTSCHLAND DIVISION

THE YEAR HAD BEGUN WELL FOR HYAZINTH GRAF VON Strachwitz. He had recovered sufficiently from his wound and had been given a generous amount of convalescent leave which allowed him to spend time with his wife and family, although not his sons who were both serving officers. He also used the time to catch up with some old friends who had staff positions in Germany or were on leave from the front. Perhaps just as importantly, he had been promoted to full colonel—a regimental officer's rank—and could add another pip to his silver braided epaulettes.

Around this time, he was also promoted to SS Standartenführer (the equivalent of colonel in the SS). The SS administration had been keeping track of his progress and had been promoting him in parallel to his rise in the regular army. Himmler was particularly pleased that he had an army colonel and Oak Leaves-wearer in his Allgemeine SS and had kept a benevolent eye on his activities. An aristocratic war hero added to the organization's prestige. One can only speculate as to whether Himmler made overtures to von Strachwitz to officially transfer to the Waffen SS. It was not unusual for army officers to make the move on the promise of greater advancement or to be offered inducements. For example, Himmler offered a transfer to tank ace Otto Carius when presenting him with his Oak Leaves, and Freiheer Adrian von Foelkersham, the Baltic Baron, who served with the Brandenburg Commando Special Operations regiment, transferred to Otto Skorzeny's SS commando unit after Brandenburg took on a conventional fighting role. Field Marshal von Manstein's aide Alexander Stahlberg remarked in his memoirs on the number of army officers seeking transfer to the Waffen SS. So it is distinctly possible that Himmler made some type of similar offer to von Strachwitz, as the Panzer Graf would have been a decided asset to one of his elite SS Panzergrenadier divisions, which were now making a name for themselves.

The Graf had also been given a new assignment commensurate with his new rank and battle experience: that of regimental commander of the new panzer regiment being formed with the elite Grossdeutschland Division, which had just been upgraded from regimental to divisional status. As reluctant as he may have been to leave 16th Panzer Division, the stump of which was being reformed, the new posting offered him greater opportunities and command responsibility. It was also more challenging to establish and wield together a new regiment, upon which he could leave his own indelible mark.

The Grossdeutschland (Greater Germany) Division had its genesis as a headquarters guard troop set up in Berlin in 1921 for ceremonial guard and parade purposes. In 1934 its name was changed to Berlin Guard Troop and it gradually increased its strength to seven rifle companies and a headquarters company. Its troops served for six months on detachment from seven infantry divisions. In 1937 its name was changed again, to The Berlin Guard Regiment.[1] A special detachment called the Führer Begleit (Führer's Escort) was set up to provide security for Hitler during his travels.[2] This unit gradually evolved into a brigade and finally as a panzergrenadier division fighting on the Eastern Front. While still a brigade its battalions rotated between frontline and escort duty so its troops were not merely security and ceremonial soldiers. It was considered a sister regiment of Grossdeutschland.

In April 1939 Hitler ordered the regiment's reorganisation and gave it the new name of Infantry Regiment Grossdeutschland. It no longer relied on the rotation of selected infantry division troops but recruited directly, calling for volunteers throughout the Reich without recourse to the military district (*Wehrkreis*) recruiting system which mobilised recruits from set regions in Germany and Austria. As evidence of its elite status its troops wore a GD monogram on their epaulettes, and its regimental insignia was the outline of the German steel helmet. However its guard and ceremonial duties remained the same.

It did not take part in the invasion of Poland but first saw action in the Battle of France where it served as part of Guderian's corps where von Strachwitz was also serving as a member of the 1st Panzer Division. During the campaign 1st Lieutenant Helmut Beck-Brovchsitter's anti-tank company destroyed 83 tanks belonging to the French 3rd Mechanised Division, a feat for which he was awarded the Knight's Cross. Sergeant Hans Hindelane from the same company also earned the Knight's Cross for his platoon's destruction of 57 French tanks. The regiment went to war with three infantry battalions and a fourth battalion which included anti-tank guns and heavy infantry gun companies. This made it the strongest infantry regiment in the German Army.[3] It fought in Luxembourg, Belgium and France where it acquitted itself well.

In August 1940 it was granted a green and white, later black and white-edged cuff title, showing the division's name, worn 14cm from the right cuff. This was in the nature of an honorific as few cuff titles were awarded to army units, although it was a standard practice in the SS who wore their cuff titles on the left sleeve. The army intended to make Grossdeutschland into a premier division with better equipment and manning tables than the standard division, which it ultimately acheived. As such the Grossdeutschland was always well resourced and adequately reinforced, which was not the case with most other divisions. Because of this, much was always expected of it, and it was sent to all the hot spots, being used as a fire brigade to restore dire situations. This was reflected in the enormous casualties it suffered during the war and the number of decorations—particularly Knight's Crosses—awarded to its members. That said, many standard panzer divisions, with fewer resources and lower equipment tables, equalled or surpassed Grossdeutschland's clutch of high combat decorations. The division's order of battle eventually made it comparable to a reinforced panzer division.

Its next campaign was the invasion of Yugoslavia in 1941, where it received support from Graf von Strachwitz's panzer battalion on detachment from the 16th Panzer Division. Some of its troops took part in the occupation of Belgrade and were responsible for activating Belgrade Radio Station, which made famous the great wartime song "Lili Marlene."[4]

The invasion of Russia saw the regiment crossing the river Bug a week after hostilities had commenced. Its first major battle was at the Dnieper Line in July where it suffered heavy casualties. On 10 August Colonel Walther Hörnlein took over command of the regiment from Colonel von Stockhausen. It then went on to fight at the Yelnya River and the encirclement battles of Kiev where Graf von Strachwitz and 16th Panzer also fought. The regiment was then moved to Army Group Centre, fighting particularly intense battles in the forests around Karachev in October where again it suffered heavy casualties. It fought its winter battles around Tula alongside the Berlin-Brandenburg 3rd Panzer Division. Its infantry battalions were by then down to below half strength. From a starting strength of 4,000 in 1941 to January 1942 it had lost 4,070 men.[5] In early December the 17th Company Motorcycle Reconnaissance Unit was infiltrated by Russian troops while they were sleeping. Almost the entire company was wiped out. As a punishment, Hörnlein ordered that the company would not be entitled to wear the prestigious cuff title until it had made amends. This it did a short time later when it mounted an attack which threw a superior Russian force back across the Oka river.[6]

The regiment then underwent a major reorganisation, and on 1 April 1942 was officially converted to a motorised division which became its official designation. This involved adding a tank battalion commanded by Captain Pössl with two companies to its establishment. Also added was another infantry regiment commanded by Colonel Garski. Like the original grenadier regiment commanded by Colonel Kohler, it had three battalions.

Unusually for the German Army, the new regiment was named "Fusilier" unlike the 1st regiment and other regiments of armoured units which were called grenadier. The term fusilier, although not common, was used by a few divisions as an honorific or to designate a separate battalion outside the infantry regimental structure, often being a converted reconnaissance battalion. These fusilier battalions were generally under the direct control of the divisional commander, to be used as a fire brigade or divisional reserve. Panzer and panzergrenadier divisions invariably named their infantry regiments as panzergrenadier. This had unfortunate consequences, as this second regiment—already considered an outsider by the first grenadier regiment—now had even greater difficulty finding acceptance, as members of the units considered themselves first and foremost as either grenadiers or fusiliers. In fact the fusiliers never did gain full acceptance, as a great rivalry developed between the two units. The mutual jealousy and rivalry was epitomised by the last Grossdeutschland divisional commander, General Lorenz. He had been the regimental commander of the Grenadier Regiment and blatantly favoured it when giving out awards, assignments and promotions. When the Fusilier Regiment commander protested about the negative treatment of his regiment, Lorenz dismissed him and his adjutant on the spot.

Alfred Novotny, a member of the Fusilier Regiment, recalled how "He always felt superior to other units and were even convinced that we were better than GD1 (the Grenadier Regiment) although this was not always true." He went on to admit that "in most instances GD1 had the better, more experienced fighting force."[7] However, as intended, it did make each regiment fight and try all the harder in order to outshine its rival, even though this was often taken to the extremes.

Also added to the new establishment were an anti-tank battalion under Major Haeke, a reconnaissance battalion under Major von Usedom, a full artillery regiment of three battalions under Colonel Jauer, an anti-aircraft battalion and extra signals and service units.

Hörnlein was a competent and caring officer, so much so that his men christened him Papa Hörnlein. His concern for his men often landed him in trouble with his superiors, as he complained about the excessive combat and casualties to which his division was subjected due to the high expectations associated with it, and the tough spots it was frequently thrown into. He was famously said to have sent a telex to the Führer's headquarters asking whether Grossdeutschland was the only German unit available on the Eastern Front, as it had been in continuous action from one crisis to another. Despite his caring reputation, Hörnlein could also be quite ruthless when required. He was also pro-Nazi, urging his company commanders in 1942 to carry out ideological training, and reiterating the call in 1943.[8] It should be noted that not all company commanders, battalion and regimental commanders carried out these instructions. Given Graf von Strachwitz's disgust at the Nazi regime due to Hitler's hold fast order and subsequent defeat at Stalingrad, it would hardly have applied to the Panzer Regiment. Otto Ernst Remer, a Grossdeutschland officer who helped crush von Stauffenberg's putsch, would have certainly been one officer who carried out Hörnlein's instructions. His speech to his troops at the time of the attempted coup gives a clear indication of his and other German officers' beliefs. "It is our duty to secure Lebensraum, defend the Fatherland and uphold our National Socialist ideals." The division certainly held many other officers like him as indeed it also had others like Graf von Strachwitz. In all German units, some fought for the Führer, some for a strong belief in Germany, while others fought simply because they had to.

Hörnlein's nickname would not have impressed Graf von Strachwitz overly much, coming as he did from a panzer division whose commander was called "Der Mensch." He would not have deemed "Papa" a suitable name for a panzer leader of a hard-hitting armoured formation. In fact as solidly competent Hörnlein was at commanding infantry, he lacked the cavalryman's flair and élan which epitomised the great panzer leaders like Balck, von Strachwitz, Raus, Meyer, Rommel and indeed his successor, von Manteuffel. All these men, as regimental and divisional commanders, did far better with units far worse equipped and manned.

Nevertheless he was a brave and capable leader, having earned a Knight's Cross on 30 July 1941 while commanding Infantry Regiment 80 and subsequently received the German Cross in Gold in February 1943, and he was the 213th recipient of the Oak Leaves to the Knight's Cross on 15 March 1943. It would be accurate to say that his Oak Leaves were earned on the back of Graf von Strachwitz's success in commanding Grossdeutschland's Panzer Regiment, along with the efforts of Pössl, Captain Frantz, Otto Remer and others. However this wasn't unusual as many German divisional corps and army commanders earned their awards directly through the courage and efforts of one or two extremely brave and competent subordinate commanders (see appendix 1 for further discussion). Hörnlein survived the war leading the XXVII Army Corps, settled in Cologne after the war, and died in 1961.

Unusually, no chaplains were allowed to the division. Most army, but not Waffen SS divisions,[9] had a Catholic and Protestant chaplain as a respected part of their establishment. Grossdeutschland, however, was forbidden to have a chaplain as a punishment for a prior one saying mass in Notre Dame Cathedral, attended by many of its troops. This no doubt disappointed the devoutly Catholic von Strachwitz.

The 1st Panzer Battalion was equipped with a mixture of Panzers IIIs and Panzer IVs, with both the long- and short-barrelled 75mm gun, which was normal for this time of transition, as the Germans sought to phase out the Panzer IIIs and replace the IVs with the long-barrelled gun. The changeover was taking unduly long as there were not enough long-barrelled tanks to go around and they couldn't afford to take the outdated and outclassed Panzer IIIs away from the already under-strength panzer battalions. The varying range and penetrating power of the guns, made their tactical use in combat difficult, and Panzer IIIs often had to be rescued by Panzer IVs.

Each company had 14 tanks, and the battalion headquarters had three. The battalion also had some Panzer III flame-throwing tanks, together with some Panzer IIs for reconnaissance, but these were later phased out. Its formation took place in Erfurt and it joined the division in May 1942. In addition, the division received a battalion of 21 assault guns (Sturmgeschütz IIIs) equipped with the 75mm long-barrelled gun.[10] They had been originally designed as infantry-support vehicles, but their efficiency as tank killers and the chronic shortage of tanks ensured that they were invariably used in the anti-tank role. Furthermore they were part of the artillery branch and not the panzer arm.[11]

The division was part of General Kempf's XLVIII Panzer Corps along with the 9th and 24th Panzer Divisions for the 1942 summer offensive. It launched its attack on 28 April capturing the railway bridge over the river Tim. The division then struck out towards Nikolayevka. Meeting little resistance at first, Captain Pössl's tank battalion had its first major tank engagement near Cologulovka when it repulsed an attack by T-34s without loss. This was followed by another engagement which saw 16 T-34s destroyed. Captain Pössl's tankers were making their presence felt.

The major objectives were the Don crossings. First Lieutenant Blumenthal from the 7th Company 1st Regiment captured the road bridge at Semiluk with a *coup de main* for which he was awarded the Knight's Cross. The Russians swiftly counterattacked and it was only the timely intervention of Stuka dive-bombers, bombing within a few hundred metres of their positions, that saved the German platoon and the bridge from being overrun.[12] The entire attack to the Don crossing covered 300 kilometres and saw the destruction of 200 enemy tanks.[13]

Voronezh was captured on 7 July, and the division was tasked with taking the lower course of the Don east of Rostov. It still retained 42 operational tanks, which for a panzergrenadier division was a substantial number. It also had most of its vehicles intact. Supplies ran short, with the division having to rely on airdrops which were barely sufficient to keep the forward momentum going. Frequent halts were necessary to allow for replenishment, and the strictly rationed fuel was mostly given to Pössl's tanks, with fuel sometimes being drained from other vehicles. Karpovka was taken with only relatively light resistance on 26 July. Fighting was fragmentary with the Russians resisting furiously in some instances while in others giving up without a struggle. One grenadier company captured an entire regiment without a fight. Savage clashes flared up along the lower Don, but despite the fierce resistance the Germans pushed on, crossing the river Muntysch on 1 August.

The division then had a brief respite, allowing for a quick refit before its next deployment. This proved necessary as the Russians launched a major offensive to retake Rzhev. The division was entrained to Army Group Centre to help counter this threat. This fighting in the Rzhev salient and the Luchessa valley was to be some of the bloodiest the division was to experience. Of the 12,000 men lost during 1942, the majority fell in the Rzhev battles.[14]

On 10 September the division struck the Soviet flank but suffered horrendous casualties from prepared Russian artillery batteries of some 240 guns, as well as aircraft and tank attacks. The panzer battalion went into action with 38 tanks and lost 28 destroyed or disabled by mines, artillery or tank fire. The division attack had to be called off. By the next day only four tanks were still in running order. Losses among the infantry were equally alarming with some platoons down from 42 men to 16 or fewer.[15] By 13 September the two infantry regiments were down to a few hundred men from the 6,000 they had started with, having been mostly slaughtered by massed artillery fire as they attacked over open ground without artillery or tank support.

The Germans resumed their attack on 30 September, this time with the division's tanks in support. They broke through the Russian lines led by the 2nd Regiment's commander Colonel Eugen Garski who directed the attack personally riding on the lead tank until he was killed, shot through the head. The tank battalion also clashed with the Soviets at Urdom and Sayzevo, where it blew up seven T-34s and one KV-2 heavy tank. On 30 November Pössl's men destroyed 22 T-34s and two T-26 light tanks with little loss. During December it accounted for eight Russian tanks near Vierfistar,[16] but was eventually reduced to a platoon of six tanks by 6 January.

On 9 January the division went into reserve to undertake a major replenishment and refit. This was badly needed as its serious losses made it unfit for any offensive combat. Even for defence it was considered marginal.

In the interim a second tank battalion was being formed at the Neuhammer training grounds in Germany. Along with this battalion a regimental headquarters was also established to oversee the new panzer regiment, which was now to become a part of the division. This addition technically made it a panzer division, but it retained its designation as a panzergrenadier division throughout the war. This was anomalous because among panzer divisions, only the elite Waffen SS panzer divisions—Leibstandarte, Das Reich, Totenkopf, Hitlerjugend and perhaps Viking—equalled or exceeded it in strength. An unusual addition for the panzer regiment was the inclusion of a company of nine Tiger tanks and 10 Panzer IIIs for scouting and security purposes. The Panzer IIIs were later removed from establishment due to their poor performance. Some Tiger commanders—Graf von Strachwitz probably one of them—bemoaned their loss, as they were useful for recce missions and could reach places that the Tigers couldn't as they were able cross lighter bridges and could be concealed more easily. They were also used to lure Russian tanks into traps as the Russians were quick to attack and pursue Panzer IIIs, but would avoid combat with the heavy Tigers. They also performed nighttime perimeter and daytime flank security, courier missions, the evacuation of wounded and a myriad of other tasks which would be considered wasteful for the Tigers to do.

Tigers were normally deployed in separate heavy battalions attached directly to corps or army headquarters. The Waffen SS divisions, LSSAH, Das Reich and Totenkopf also had Tiger companies, which were converted to separate battalions on semi-permanent attachment later, although Totenkopf retained its battalion on establishment strength. No army divisions were so favoured except for Grossdeutschland, whose company was later expanded to a battalion of 45 Tigers. These behemoths, with their 100mm thick frontal armour and powerful 88mm guns, added greatly to the division's striking power. Its Tiger battalion was one of the highest-scoring tank-killing units in the German Army. As a company it destroyed 100 enemy tanks for a loss of six Tigers, an astonishing kill ratio of 16.67:1. As a battalion this figure dropped to 5.10:1, albeit against a larger number of tanks, including the super-heavy Josef Stalin types.[17] In all, during the course of the war, Grossdeutschland's Tiger unit destroyed 1,036 Russian tanks and fighting vehicles, and over 300 anti-tank guns and artillery pieces. A large part of this tally was inflicted during Graf von Strachwitz's period as regimental commander. The comparatively low number of anti-tank guns destroyed was due to the fact that they were engaged less frequently, and were much harder to hit, owing to their low profile and ease of concealment.

Hyazinth von Strachwitz was the regiment's first commander, and was well received by his troops, his reputation having preceded him. The junior officers were especially pleased to have an experienced Oak Leaves wearer as their unit commander. Even the other ranks were proud of him, including members of other units, as Fusilier Alfred Novotny recalls in his memoir:

> The commander of our panzer regiment Graf von Strachwitz was simply a hero's hero. Wherever there was trouble Strachwitz and his men were there. I saw him a few times in 1943 when he and elements of his regiment were supporting our operations, or at least passing through our area of operations. Although dignified, he appeared to be down to earth.
>
> There was none of the haughtiness that was often displayed by other nobles. He also was often to be seen at the forefront of battle when things were hottest. We all thought highly of this especially courageous officer and were proud to be in the same division.[18]

This description sums up von Strachwitz reasonably well. He endeared himself to his men not just for his success and courage, but by being one of them, the front swine, old hares, without losing any of his dignity as an officer or as an aristocrat. He was immensely proud of his lineage and title, but was well aware that this did not make him better than others he was serving with.

His 2nd Battalion commander was Major Thiede, whom he got to know fairly well, as Major Pössl was serving at the front. However he soon got to know and like Pössl both as a man and superb panzer leader. The Tiger company was led by Captain Walleroth and came equipped with its own maintenance platoon, as its spare parts and maintenance requirements were different from those of the rest of the regiment.

The regiment's company and platoon leaders were officers, although this would change during combat, with senior NCOs often taking command of a platoon. The individual tank commanders were all veteran NCOs. The regiment, and indeed the division, at full strength was the strongest and best-equipped in the German Army. With its members being mostly volunteers it was a highly motivated, elite fighting unit, to which Graf von Strachwitz was proud to belong. It was his chance to put his mark on the new regiment, and with its excellent raw material in manpower and equipment, he had a good opportunity to make it an unqualified success. The fighting in the third battle of Kharkov would soon give him the chance.

NOTES

1. James Lucas, *Germany's Elite Panzer Force Grossdeutschland* (McDonald and James, London, 1979).
2. Ibid.
3. Ibid.
4. Paul Carrell, *Hitler's War on Russia. Vol 1. Hitler Moves East* (Ballantine Books, 1963).
5. Thomas McGuirl and Remy Spezzano. *God, Honor Fatherland. A Photo History of Panzergrenadier Division Grossdeutschland on the Eastern Front 1942–1944* (RZM Publishing, Fl 2007).
6. Alfred Novotny, *The Good Soldier* (The Aberjona Press, Bedford Penn, 2003).
7. Ibid.
8. Ibid.
9. Some Waffen SS divisions such as the Ukrainian "Galicia" Division had chaplains but called them liaison officers, while other non-German SS units had unofficial chaplains in their ranks.
10. Hans-Joachim Jung (trans. David Johnston), *The History of Panzerregiment Grossdeutschland: Panzer Soldiers for "God, Honor, Fatherland"* (J. J. Fedorwicz, Canada, 2000).

11. This anomaly came about despite General Guderian's strenuous efforts to make them part of his panzer arm. The artillery branch wanted the assault guns to add to its strength and to provide greater opportunity for its members to earn decorations such as the coveted Knight's Cross. The assault gun crews wore grey uniforms in the style of the panzer uniform while the panzer crews wore black. Graf von Strachwitz rarely wore field gray, preferring his panzer black.
12. Lucas, *Germany's Elite Panzer Force Grossdeutschland,* p.50; Jung, *The History of Panzerregiment Grossdeutschland,* p.20.
13. Jung, *The History of Panzerregiment Grossdeutschland.*
14. "Loss ratios", Tiger 1 Information Centre, www.alanhamby.com/losses.shtml/ (accessed 29 August 2013).
15. Novotny, *The Good Soldier*, p.75.
16. "Loss ratios", Tiger 1 Information Centre, www.alanhamby.com/losses.shtml/ (accessed 29 August 2013).
17. Ibid.
18. Novotny, *The Good Soldier*, p.75.

SIXTEEN

THE THIRD BATTLE OF KHARKOV

STALIN AND HIS GENERALS WERE NOT CONTENT WITH just the destruction of the German Sixth Army and its Axis allies around Stalingrad. With its armies having ripped a gaping hole through the sector, Stavka (the Soviet High Command) had grand plans to envelop and destroy the entire German Southern Front. Even while the agony of Stalingrad was still being played out, the Soviets launched major attacks in the Don bend, but lacked the resources necessary for a quick victory as a large proportion of their troops, aircraft, armour and equipment were still employed besieging the city. In this way German Sixth Army played a vital role even in its death throes by tying down half the Soviet forces in the counteroffensive and buying time, albeit with a heavy price in blood and pain, to allow other German forces to either withdraw or restabilise their front.

To restore this crumbling situation, Hitler turned to Field Marshal Erich von Manstein, probably the ablest strategist of the German Army,[1] appointing him commander of the newly formed Army Group Don on 27 November 1942 (the name was changed later to Army Group South). Moreover, by February Hitler had been chastened by the obliteration of Sixth Army under his own strategic direction, and was inclined to cede operational control, if only temporarily, to Manstein. He flew to the latter's headquarters at Zaphoroze on 17 February where he listened to Manstein's plan to continue German withdrawals, so as to overextend the Soviet attackers and render them vulnerable to a counteroffensive. As part of this plan he would pull First Panzer Army from the Caucasus and place it on his left, followed by a withdrawal of Fourth Panzer Army, which had been holding open its escape route. Finally, with these units plus a newly arriving SS Panzer Corps, as well as Grossdeutschland, he would again drive east, severing the Soviet spearheads with surprise counterthrusts to restabilize the front. But time had become urgent, and his plan needed to be enacted immediately. As to emphasis his point, Russian tanks approached within kilometres of the headquarters. Hitler quickly flew back to Germany after giving Manstein his assent to carry out operations as he saw fit.

Throughout January von Manstein had been seriously concerned with getting General von Mackensen's First Panzer Army safely withdrawn through the narrow gap at Rostov which was just barely being held open by General Hoth's troops. Finally the Germans squeezed through, and withdrew some 150 kilometres west of the Mius, with the Russian 3rd Guards Mechanized Corps chasing them the whole way. Hoth kept going until he reached Dnepropetrovsk and Zaporzhe. It was some of these pursuing Russian spearheads that posed the threat to the relatively unprotected headquarters that Hitler had been visiting; there was precious little to stop them as the Germans only had very few operational tanks along the front.

On 29 January, the burly Russian General Vatutin—one of Stalin's favourites, and the destroyer of the Italian Army outside Stalingrad—launched Operation *Gallop* with the Soviet Sixth Army and 1st Guards Army. They smashed into the Germans, breaking them up into uncoordinated groups. Along with this operation, the Russians launched Operation *Star* under Colonel General Golikov and spearheaded by four tank corps led by General Markian Popov, whose objectives were the capture of Kursk and Kharkov, the Ukraine's second largest city after Kiev.

Moving to defend Kharkov was the newly established II SS Panzer Corps under the one-eyed SS General Paul Hausser, an extremely capable ex-army general. He had under his command the Leibstandarte SS Adolf Hitler (Hitler's Bodyguard) and the SS Das Reich Panzergrenadier Divisions. They would be joined later by the SS Totenkopf (Death's Head) Panzergrenadier Division. All were seasoned veterans of the French and Russian campaigns, although Totenkopf had recently been replenished with a large number of Reich Labour Service draftees.[2]

Along with the SS Panzer Corps, two army divisions were deployed around the Belgorod area: the Grossdeutschland and the 168th Infantry Divisions. This force was designated Army Detachment Lanz after its commander, General of Mountain Troops Hubert Lanz.

The Waffen SS divisions were reasonably strong, if well below establishment, with the Leibstandarte having 52 Panzers IIIs, but only 21 Panzer IVs and 10 Tigers.[3] Graf Hyazinth's von Strachwitz's Grossdeutschland Panzer Regiment was not as strong. During March for instance, at its strongest on 11 March, it had 39 running Panzer IVs, 9 Panzer IIIs, six flame tanks and six Tigers. At its weakest on 23 March it only had operational six Panzer IVs, seven Panzer IIIs, nine flame tanks and no Tigers.[4] It was fortunate that von Strachwitz was accustomed to achieving a great deal with very little.

Grossdeutschland's front line consisted of battalion-strong battle groups, deployed along the major roads, with large gaps in between, with no major formations alongside guarding the flanks. These gaps had to be patrolled extensively. However the 168th Infantry Division lacked mobility and couldn't cover its open areas adequately. Lanz therefore ordered Grossdeutschland to assist, placing a greater strain on its resources. By late January it only had 13 operational tanks with another 14 undergoing short-term repair. This was clearly insufficient to carry out operations, as well as cover the open areas of both divisions.

At the beginning of February, the Soviet 69th Army attacked both Grossdeutschland and SS Leibstandarte. Lanz had to send Das Reich in as reinforcement and it deployed on Grossdeutschland's southern flank. Even so there was still a 15-kilometre gap between the two divisions which Grossdeutschland had to patrol.

The 168th Infantry Division came under strong Soviet pressure and was in danger of being overwhelmed. Grossdeutschland's commander, General Hörnlein, sent in his reconnaissance battalion to shore it up and clean out any Russian penetrations, which temporarily stabilised the situation. He then sent in his Grenadiers' 2nd Battalion and the Fusiliers' 3rd Battalion into the attack between Belgorod and Voltschansk. However during the next few days, 5–6 February, the Russians riposted with an attack of their own, using four divisions to push Grossdeutschland back westwards.

On 7 February the Red Army threw the 168th Infantry Division back into Belgorod which it held, along with Grossdeutschland's Reconnaissance Battalion and the Führer Begleit (Escort) Battalion which had just arrived at the front as part of its normal rotation between guard and front-line duties.[5]

The Russian 69th Army, under General Kazakov, carried out human wave attacks against both Grossdeutschland and Das Reich west of Belgorod. Both divisions were hard pressed to contain the hordes. Copious amounts of vodka gave the Russians the courage to face almost certain death and many

Grossdeutschland units gave way before the relentless attacks. Some grenadiers simply ran away with the maddened, howling Russians charging after them. The Russians overwhelmed the hapless 168th Infantry Division which simply broke up, with some units fleeing in panic-stricken flight as far as 25 kilometres west of Belgorod.[6] This made Grossdeutschland's position untenable, forcing it to pull back.

On 9 February the SS Panzer Crops took over the defence of Kharkov, with parts of Grossdeutschland, together with the Führer Begleit Battalion withdrawing to Dolbino. The Soviet 40th Army reached the northern and western approaches of Kharkov, threatening to outflank both the Grossdeutschland and Leibstandarte. Grossdeutschland was unable to launch a counterattack as it was too stretched, having to cover the area abandoned by the fleeing 168th Infantry Division. It was gradually forced back, fighting all the way to Zolochev, leaving Das Reich's northern flank exposed.[7]

On 10 February, at Dergatski north of Kharkov, Major von Usedom's Grossdeutschland's Reconnaissance Battalion was forced out by strong Russian units, despite General Lanz's orders to hold out to the last man. Reinforced by the Führer Begleit Battalion, which had now been reduced to the strength of a mere company of 150 men, and an SS anti-tank platoon, von Usedom mounted a counter-attack, retaking Dergatshi after savage fighting. The Reds suffered heavily, losing five T-34s on roads leading to Kharkov while the Führer Begleit Battalion was reduced even further.[8] On 12 and 13 February, the Russians mounted several attacks on Libzy, which was staunchly defended by the division's Fusilier Regiment. The attacks failed, so the Russians decided to bypass the town. This move outflanked Grossdeutschland, forcing it into a retreat pursued by the Russians.

The Russians now prepared to capture Kharkov. They massed three armies, the 40th, 69th and 3rd Tank. All were severely degraded by continuous combat, but they were still able to muster a combined strength of just under 200,000 men and 300 tanks. To oppose them Army Detachment Lanz had barely 50,000 men holding a sector of some 270 kilometres.[9] The German line was thus seriously overstretched and undermanned, making it relatively easy for the Soviets to make penetrations. These required a German counterattack or else a hasty withdrawal, if no mobile forces were available to mount an attack, as was often the case.

In Kharkov, SS General Paul Hausser was worried that the city would suffer the same fate as Stalingrad. He was determined to save his precious Panzer Corps at all costs. He asked Lanz's headquarters for permission to withdraw. Fully realizing that Hitler had strictly forbidden abandoning the city, Hausser went on to say that if permission was not forthcoming he would take the responsibility on himself and order the withdrawal. He added that there was shooting in the streets with civilians firing on German troops. The situation was fast becoming untenable and the city could not be held. In reply Lanz reminded him of Field Marshal von Manstein's order reaffirming the Führer's directive that the city be held at all costs. Hausser noted the reply and told his 1A that he couldn't leave his men there to be killed or taken prisoner, and so ordered the withdrawal.

An hour and a half later, Lanz personally called Hausser and repeated Hitler's order. Kharkov was to be held to the last man and Hausser's order to withdraw was to be rescinded. Hausser replied drily that rescinding the order would be difficult as the withdrawal was already well under way. Historian George M. Nipe contends that Lanz was in full agreement with the correctness of Hausser's decision and may have deliberately delayed before making his call, knowing full well that in doing so it would be difficult, if not impossible to cancel the withdrawal.[10] Lanz was also in the process of covering his tracks since he knew full well that ultimate command responsibility would rest with him, and not being a Führer favourite he could expect repercussions.

Throughout 15 February, the Russian 69th Army continued its assault on Das Reich and Grossdeutschland, making several penetrations in the army division's sector. Von Usedom's battalion, along with the Führer Begleit, fought desperately to hold Ljubotin where Grossdeutschland's medical clearing centre was located.

The Waffen SS completed their withdrawal from the burning city from Kharkov, pursued by the Russians entering from all directions. Alongside the SS, Major Remer's 1st Grossdeutschland Grenadier Battalion was fighting an increasingly desperate rearguard action. A very concerned Hörnlein sent in Captain Frantz's Assault Gun Battalion, numbering 30 guns due to the arrival of 20 new Sturmgeschütz IIIs, to help extricate him. Frantz took up positions in the almost abandoned city but Remer failed to appear. Frantz waited anxiously, knowing that at any moment he could be enveloped by the Russians, and without infantry support his guns were vulnerable in the narrow city confines. Here even Russian infantry was a real threat. He sent a Stug III forward to scout, but there was still no sign of Remer. Wait or withdraw, Frantz agonized. If he left, Remer was doomed, if he hadn't already been wiped out. If he stayed too long, his own battalion could be destroyed. Eventually, to

Frantz's immense relief, Remer appeared. Battle-weary, hunched over, exhausted, many showing wounds, the grenadiers came slowly into view. Their pace quickened when they saw the German self-propelled assault guns waiting to take them to safety. Spaeter described Captain Frantz's withdrawal:

> The long-awaited order was now given to the assault guns. They formed up and likewise drove out of the city toward the west. At the end of the column was the commander's vehicle. This in turn was eagerly awaited by the division's pioneer commander Hauptman. Chrapowski, at the bridge, for the pioneers also felt that it was time to withdraw from the city. They too had been fired at from all sides while they waited. With a huge roar the large road bridge in the centre of Kharkov flew into the air.
>
> The crews of the assault guns fired rifles and sub-machine guns at windows from which muzzle flashes were seen. We had no way of telling whether it was partisans or regular Russian troops doing the shooting. After a good two-hour drive the battalion drove into a small village just behind the new main line of resistance.[11]

If the Germans were suffering, the Russians also had their problems. Their casualties, particularly in the infantry, were enormous, with some regiments down to 600 men, or battalion strength. Their supply lines were stretched and not really coping with demand, while their vehicles were badly in need of maintenance. They simply lacked the strength to pursue and destroy the retreating Germans. Their tanks did, however, manage to ambush Grossdeutschland's Fusilier Regiment which was spearheading the division's withdrawal, and pin it down, halting the division in its tracks. Only the timely intervention of Peter Frantz's assault guns hitting the Russians on their flanks saved the situation.

In late February Grossdeutschland was attached to Korps Raus, under the beak-nosed Austrian panzer general and superb tactician, who would eventually command an army. Alongside, it had the 320th Infantry Division and SS Grenadier Regiment Thule on detachment from SS Totenkopf. Thule was commanded by Heinz Lammerding, a former aide to Heinrich Himmler. An engineer by profession, Lammerding was tall, blonde and good-looking, everything Himmler expected the perfect Aryan to be (and everything Himmler himself wasn't). Lammerding was reasonably competent and rose to command the Das Reich Panzer Division. He was commanding it when its troops committed the atrocities at Aradour-sur-Glane in France in 1944.[12]

On 18 February, 20 Russian tanks, supported by infantry, attacked Grossdeutschland Grenadiers from the 3rd Battalion on some high ground, near a collective farm on the outskirts of Korotisch. Bereft of any anti-tank weapons the grenadiers were easy prey for the rampaging Russian tanks. Nevertheless they steadfastly held their ground pouring fire down onto the T-34s, clearing the decks of many of the infantry mounted on them. Here and there a high-explosive shell blew to pieces a German machine-gun post as the Soviets drew nearer. The Grenadiers hung grimly on, firing resolutely at the brown-uniformed Russian infantry behind the tanks, but only a few shell-shocked and shattered survivors managed to reach the German lines to the rear. A German counterattack was quickly launched but was easily repulsed with the loss of two panzers. Hoping to escape the massacre of their comrades, the Germans fell back toward Ljubotin.[13]

Lammerding's Thule battalion was defending a line of strongpoints west of Olshanny while Grossdeutschland held positions around Ljubotin with Thule's right wing tied in with Grossdeutschland's Fusilier Regiment's left flank. However on Thule's left or western flank there was an undefended gap. Reconnaissance patrols reported Russians in this gap near Bairak but there were no troops available to drive them out.

On the night of 19/20 February the Russians struck the right flank of the Grenadier Regiment but were driven back with one T-34 destroyed. The grenadiers swiftly counterattacked, taking by surprise and destroying several Russian anti-tank guns and a supply column of 60 horse-drawn sleds.[14]

Meanwhile the Reds, milling around in the undefended gap, took Bairok in a surprise attack. Lanz promptly ordered a counterattack to recapture the town. Thule, along with a Grossdeutschland battle group of Major von Usedom's Reconnaissance Battalion, the Assault Pioneer Battalion, a battery of assault guns and some self-propelled artillery, assaulted the town. The gap left by the Reconnaissance Battalion's departure had to be filled by a mixture of cooks, clerks, butchers, bakers, supply and security troops, there being no fighting troops left to plug the hole. Russian attacks elsewhere meant that the Reconnaissance Battalion had to return to clear up the other penetrations. The most serious was an attack by Soviet General Rybalko's Third Army on Ljubotin. Von Usedom's men struck the Russian flank, smashing their infantry and destroying two T-34s and a KV-1.[15]

Undeterred, the Russians continued their attack on Ljubotin throughout 20 February, breaking through the Fusiliers' lines on the northern perimeter.

The Russians lost six T-34s in the fighting but managed to establish a strong position on the town's outskirts.

General Lanz meanwhile, was finally made the scapegoat for Hausser's withdrawal. He was dismissed by Field Marshal von Manstein, who gave the excuse that Lanz was a general of mountain troops and he wanted a general of panzer troops. Lanz's replacement was the dark-haired, moustachioed General Werner Kempf, who had led panzer troops in Poland and commanded the 6th Panzer Division and XLVIII Panzer Corps. The unit was renamed Army Detachment Kempf. Kharkov eventually also took Kempf's scalp when he was sacked for the city's final loss in August 1943.

On the same day that Lanz was being dismissed, the Soviets converged on Kovjagi with its vital railhead, and the Grossdeutschland's medical clearing station. There ensued a mad race to evacuate the wounded as all knew leaving them to the Russians was tantamount to a death sentence. A motley mixture of vehicles was scraped together, and with the help of various non-combat troops the evacuation was successfully completed.

On 22–23 February Grossdeutschland's Fusilier Regiment faced Russian human wave attacks once again. Yelling their hoarse battle cry of "Urra! Urra!" the Russian masses surged towards the fusiliers' lines. Sustained bursts from the machine guns scythed them down in long writhing rows. When the Russian assault finally withered away there were over 100 dead piled around the fusiliers' positions. Elsewhere, Grossdeutschland's Reconnaissance Battalion was fighting alongside SS Thule at the Sholestrovo and Iskrovkia areas, with Shelestrovo being taken in a joint assault.

On 22 February Grossdeutschland abandoned Ljubotin as the Russian 3rd Tank Army was threatening its escape routes. The division's casualties had been extremely high due to its involvement in almost continuous fighting, so that its combat value was considerably degraded. Von Manstein decided to pull it out for a refit, sending it to Poltava on 23 February. Here Graf von Stachwitz was already waiting with a second tank battalion, the Tiger company, and his regimental headquarters. It was while he was here, organising his newly arrived units, that he became involved in a plot to arrest and or kill Hitler (see chapter 17). The division also received an extra artillery battalion, its fourth, which was a considerable addition to the three battalions that most panzer and panzergrenadier divisions were allocated. The additional tank battalion was more than welcome as in mid-February the original battalion had only seven Panzer IVs and three Panzer IIIs operational, barely enough to equip a company. The division's Reconnaissance Battalion provided a security screen to allow the division to undergo its refit and reorganisation undisturbed.

The few days during the refit were hectic ones for von Strachwitz as he integrated the battalions as well as his regimental headquarters. It was also an opportunity for 1st Battalion officers and men to acquaint themselves with their new regimental commander. He had too little time to acquaint himself with them, or to accomplish everything he needed to, as the demands of the front drew the division back into battle.

On 24 February as part of von Manstein's masterful counteroffensive, General Mackensen's troops surrounded Popov's mechanized force, which was overextended, short of supplies, and severely short of supporting infantry. The Germans also surrounded large parts of the Soviet Sixth Army. On 1 March Hausser's SS Panzer Corps smashed into the Russian 3rd Tank Army of General Rybacko and defeated him soundly by 3 March.

A few days earlier, on 26 February, Theodor Eicke, the brutally tough, abrasive commander of the SS Totenkopf division, was killed when his Fieseler Storch command aircraft was shot down by Russian ground fire from a village supposedly unoccupied or held by units of his division. His men mourned him, for he was a soldier's general, sharing his men's privations, rations and dangers. Almost everyone else, including many in the Nazi hierarchy, were glad to see the coarse, former Nazi concentration camp commander go. His men mounted several attacks to retrieve his body, which they then buried with full military honours.

On 4 March Grossdeutschland had completed its refit, and entered the fray a much stronger division, with its full panzer regiment, replenished infantry, and extra artillery and support units. It was now stronger than most panzer divisions and would remain so throughout its existence, casualties notwithstanding. General Hörnlein organised the division into several battle groups on 6 March. These were Battle Group Beurmann, Battle Group Wätjen and Battle Group Strachwitz. The Panzer Graf's battle group was the strongest and comprised the Panzer Regiment—less one battalion which was with Beurmann's battle group. The Grenadier Regiment consisted of four infantry battalions instead of the usual three for a panzergrenadier division, and only two for a panzer division, which again highlights the army's determination to make Grossdeutschland its premier division. Three gun batteries from the artillery regiment together with headquarters and supply units, equivalent to a normal battalion in strength, plus the 3rd Company Assault Pioneer Battalion and the 3rd Company Anti-tank Battalion completed the organization. This represented the strongest force the Graf had commanded to date, and he would make good use of it. His battle group assembled in the Sidorenkovo–Chiabonovka area and it was tasked with taking Kontokusovo and Perekop.[16]

Enemy resistance was weak and Perekop was taken with very little fighting. The temperature was beginning to rise, but it was still cold, just above freezing, so the ground remained firm, providing good mobility for von Strachwitz's tanks. Leading from the tip of the spearhead, the Graf spotted an advancing Russian tank column in open ground. As he had seen the enemy first, and having his Tiger company with him, he decided to try them out taking the enemy on at long range. He watched carefully as they drew closer, wanting to keep them at a distance where his panzers were out of their range but not the Russians from the long-range 88mm guns of his Tigers. His Tiger commanders grew fidgety as the Graf coolly observed the enemy, giving his firing instructions. His order to fire finally came and the powerful 88s roared in unison. Immediately hits were registered, with Russian tanks suddenly flaring in flames and smoke with several turrets being blown cleanly away, the tell-tale smoke rings rising slowly into the sky. The Russians didn't stand a chance, their shorter-ranged 76mm guns totally ineffective. Even had they closed the range the Tigers armour would have withstood any hits. One after another the Russian tanks were blown away. A few, mainly damaged tanks escaped, and a few of their crews who had survived the initial hits made it back alive, though most were wounded or horribly burnt. The more seriously injured were picked up by the grenadiers who mopped up the scene of carnage. Nine T-34s and a KV-1 blackened the snow with their burnt-out carcasses.

On 7 March, von Strachwitz met up with Kurt Meyer's Leibstandarte Reconnaissance Battalion west of Babiska where Untersturmführer Iseke advised him where Meyer was and the Graf agreed to adjust his attack further to the north of Valki in order to avoid casualties from friendly fire. Meyer went on with his attack and was extremely lucky to come out of it alive as he related in his memoir:

> Anti-tank fire strikes our spearhead as we approach within range of the second village but the Tigers dispose of the enemy anti-tank weapons. The right hand tank company under Jürgensen moves forward swiftly exploiting the cover of some orchards and is about to outflank the village.

> Our car receives a hit from a 47mm anti-tank gun, which however does not cause serious damage. Unfortunately we cannot see where it is dug in. We are now within 200 meters of the village and are looking for a point to breach, machine-gun fire hammers armour plating. The leading Tiger hit a mined obstacle and lies to our rear with a shattered track. T-34s emerged and pitched into the fight. We must get into the village! Suddenly there's a tremendous explosion in the car and I find myself lying in a rut looking at my driver sitting headless at the wheel. A direct hit has torn a massive hole in the armour plating.
>
> Unterscharführer Albert Andres staggers dazedly into cover. With horror I notice that he only has one arm. I can't even see a stump among the remains of cloth and shattered bone.
>
> Bremer's company breaks into the village and fights its way down the street. Unexpectedly we run past a Russian tank and finish it off with a limpet charge. . . . The village is ours within the hour and we immediately occupy it and defend it with a "hedgehog" perimeter. The shortness of the days make it advisable to spend the night in the village. We lay my driver, Ernst Webelung, to rest in the twilight.
>
> Liaison officers from the Grossdeutschland Division report the entry of their division into the attack on our left hand neighbouring sector. I am glad to know that there is a tried and trustworthy unit to our north.[17]

Sometime afterwards Meyer and his men reached the Mischa river. There was still a bridge across it, but Meyer didn't want to use it as it was probably mined. He urged his men to rush across the frozen river, but no one moved. Then Meyer came up with an idea, and his men stormed across the ice in a rush. His secret? Three weeks' leave for the first man to reach the other side. It worked like a charm.[18]

Grossdeutschland's combat groups continued their assaults with the objective of cutting the road and railway lines from Bogodukhov to Oshanny, cutting off the Russians in Bogodukhov and preventing them from reinforcing Kharkov, which was being attacked by the SS Panzer Corps.

Von Strachwitz's panzers found it hard going because of strong winds and heavy snow which caused deep drifts on the roads. He thrust east from Kovjagi along the Poltava–Kovjagi–Kharkov railway line and road. At midday his tanks came across Russian infantry dug in with anti-tank guns. A short duel ensued, resulting in all the anti-tank guns being destroyed and the infantry driven off or killed. He arrived at Stary Merchik an hour later but without his supporting infantry, the majority of whom were about three hours behind as their wheeled vehicles found it extremely hard going in the icy conditions and poor roads. Nevertheless the Panzer Graf pushed on towards Bogodukhov. He was stopped by strong Russian defensive positions at a village on the route. He quickly deployed his tanks and grenadiers. His tank guns blazed in a hail of deadly fire at the Russian defences, silencing the anti-tank guns with high-explosive rounds and sustained machine-gun fire. The grenadiers stormed across to take the houses with machine pistols and hand grenades. The surviving Russians fled in disarray.

On 8 March, while Das Reich re-captured Ljubotin, von Strachwitz with his 2nd Tank Battalion crossed the Merchik River near Alexandrovka, intending to reach Maximovka the following day. The Russians mounted several weak counterattacks by a few tanks and supporting infantry, which were crushed with ease. Just before dawn von Strachwitz moved off, but his progress was slowed by severe snow squalls, which blocked the road with deep drifts. Visibility was poor, so he had to keep most of his torso outside the cupola, peering through the icy sleet. His tanks skidded and slid along the icy roads, testing the drivers' skill to the utmost. The wheeled vehicles could make no headway at all and had to be towed. His column gradually became strung out, as each vehicle grappled with the icy conditions. The wheeled vehicles had to be left behind, while he pushed on with his tanks and half-tracked APCs carrying the grenadiers of the 1st Battalion Grenadier Regiment.[19]

At 10:25 a.m. he reached a train station south of the town of Maximouka, five kilometres northwest of Bogdukhov. He sent a company of tanks towards Maximovka, which was attacked by T-34s just near the town. A firefight quickly developed which left several Russian tanks burning while the remainder fled. Then von Strachwitz's panzers seized the town. He quickly regrouped his tanks, sending the Tiger company with some grenadiers on board towards Popovpa ten kilometres east of Bogodukhov.[20]

The Russians then mounted a counterattack with 30 T-34s against his main strike force. The Graf quickly surveyed the ground, noting the enemy's location, and made his dispositions. He sent one company into some cover to engage the Soviets from the front. While they were thus engaged he led the remainder of his force to strike the Russians from the flank and rear. They did not fire until all the tanks were in position, which meant an agonizing wait for those to be deployed first. When everyone was ready and had sighted on an opponent, the Panzer Graf gave the order to fire. Almost instantly flames belched from stricken Russian tanks while others halted in confusion or because their tracks had been hit or damaged. Another salvo brewed up more T-34s, with the Soviets now realising that they were being attacked from the rear. Most turned to face the new, more immediate threat, at which point the Graf ordered his company which had been engaging frontally, to attack what was now the enemy rear. It proved too much for the Russians, who milled about in confusion firing randomly or seeking to escape. Explosion followed explosion as one after another the T-34s succumbed to the German fire. Only two T-34s managed to escape, leaving 28 shattered or burning hulks. Almost an entire Soviet tank battalion had been wiped out. The infantry who had been riding on their decks were nearly all killed, having had no chance in the crescendo of explosions and hail of machine-gun fire. The grenadiers swept through the battleground gunning down the dazed and shocked survivors. Von Strachwitz estimated that his battle group had killed around 2,000 Soviet soldiers throughout the action on 9 March.[21]

The Russians were determined to have their revenge. On 10 March units of the Russian 69th Army attacked von Strachwitz's battle group with infantry supported by a dozen T-34s. Von Strachwitz quickly and deftly outmanoeuvred the Russians, destroying several of them and putting the rest to flight towards Bogodukhov. The infantry who couldn't flee promptly surrendered.

The Graf's combat group was now low on fuel and ammunition and had to wait until nightfall for resupply. He did however send his grenadiers forward, and they captured two villages on the southern outskirts of Bagodukhov. Von Strachwitz then planned to attack the town from the east while the grenadiers struck from the south. Another unit, Battle Group Wätjen, was to attack from the west alongside SS Regiment Thule on its left flank, which went on to capture Shelostrova and Visokolye.

The attack was launched on 11 March, preceded by a heavy artillery bombardment. Stukas swarmed over the city making their long plunging dives, sirens howling. Long columns of Russians leaving the town were easy targets for both artillery and bombers. Sizing up the situation Graf von Strachwitz ordered his Tiger Company to some high ground where the long range of their guns could blast the retreating Russians columns. The Germans entered Bogodukhov from one end while the Russians were exiting from the other, harried all along by the Stukas and von Strachwitz's Tigers. The town was secured that evening.

While Grossdeutschland was fighting its battle for Bogodukhov, the SS Panzer Corps was fighting its way into Kharkov. Hausser's plan used the hammer and anvil principle: he lured the Soviets forward to strike them hard with Das Reich and Totenkopf, while the Leibstandarte circled around northwest to block the Soviets from the rear. He then closed the pincers around the Russians slamming them back against the Leibstandarte's panzers. This cleared the way for his attack into Kharkov where his grenadiers came up against fanatical resistance. Stukas and assault guns had to be called in for close support to blast the Russians from their positions. Belov, the Soviet commander of Kharkov, pulled his troops out from the west of the city which allowed Das Reich to break in there.

Around this time, Lammerding and his Regiment Thule finally returned to its parent unit, the Totenkopf Division. It had proved to be a valuable support unit for Grossdeutschland, especially for the Reconnaissance Battalion with whom it had fought closely.

On 12 March Graf von Strachwitz launched Major Pössl's 1st Battalion towards Graivoron which lay in the centre of the Vorskla river valley. His regiment followed on. It was now operating at 50% of its strength, although most of his disabled tanks were only in short-term repair and were dribbling back into the regiment on a daily basis. Close behind the panzers came the assault gun battalion, and a battery of 88mm guns, with close infantry support provided by the Grenadier Regiment. The Fusilier Regiment and Reconnaissance Battalion made up the rearguard.

The attack on Graivoron was spearheaded by Pössl's 1st Battalion, together with the Tiger Company. The Grenadiers rode on the tanks, ready to leap off as soon as contact was made. A small force of T-34s sallied out to challenge them but were swiftly battered into submission leaving several of their number shattered or burning, while the remainder fled back into the town. Pössl with his Panzer IVs and Tigers, along with some flamethrowing Panzer IIIs, stormed into the town. The flame tanks did fearful execution to the Soviets, burning up anti-tank gun positions and machine-gun nests, frying their crews from a range of 60 metres. Close behind the panzers the grenadiers swarmed in, engaging the Russians in close combat.

Meanwhile the Reconnaissance Battalion of the division had been ambushed by some cleverly concealed anti-tank guns eight kilometres south of Bogodukhov, and its lead assault gun destroyed. Uncertain of the enemy strength, the battalion halted in a village. Hörnlein, flying above in his Fieseler Storch, saw the immobilised battalion and landed on the road nearby. He called the officers together and, leaning on his carved campaign walking stick, stressed the importance of keeping the momentum going, ordering them forward once again. The battalion moved out and kept going until it reached Pissarovka when it came under heavy shellfire from dug-in Soviet artillery. The assault guns moved to flank the guns. The 2nd Battalion Panzer Regiment and the Fusilier Regiment were brought in to support the attack. The fusiliers mounted on the tanks stormed the town while the assault guns smashed the artillery in a slashing flank attack. The Russians abandoned their guns and fled north. The battle group reassembled and moved off to join the attack on Graivoron.

The grenadiers joined the savage street fighting which went on into the night. Flares and fires illuminated the scene as ghostly shadows flitted among the buildings, men seeking each other out to kill or maim in a frenzy of hand-to-hand combat. It wasn't until 9.00 p.m. that the last of the Russians were cleared out of the town.

On 13 March von Strachwitz attacked Golovttschino with the Panzer IVs of his regiment. Using fire and movement, his tanks cleared the anti-tank guns and fortified positions in front of the town. Excellent gunnery and observation ensured that the anti-tank guns barely got one shot away before being blown up. Soviet machine-gun posts were blown to pieces while the panzers' machine guns mowed down the Soviet infantry. Under cover of artillery fire some T-34s put in an attack on the panzers' flanks. Von Strachwitz took his rear company of Panzer IVs in a slashing attack on the flank and rear of the T-34s which left several of them burning while the remainder hastily fled the scene. General Hörnlein was so impressed that the divisional war diary recorded that the Panzer IVs had distinguished themselves in the action.[22] The next objective was Borisovka, which the division captured in a combined infantry-tank attack.

Also on 13 March the SS Panzer Corps had driven the Soviets out of Kharkov. Every house and building had to be cleared in savage close-quarter combat, as the defenders preferred to die rather than surrender. The Russians used the Stalingrad tactic of reinfiltrating buildings that had previously been cleared by the Germans. Howitzers, assault guns, mortars and self-propelled anti-tank guns blasted buildings at point-blank range, collapsing walls and buildings, burying the defenders alive. Soviet NKVD security troops withdrew to the tractor factory for a desperate last stand. They had to be methodically blasted out, not a single soldier surrendering. The defenders there held out until 16 March, and with their demise the last organised resistance collapsed.

On 14 March German reconnaissance planes reported 100 Russian T-34s from the 2nd Guards Tank Corps marching on Boriskovha. Von Strachwitz quickly sent his tanks to screen the town, and sent in the assault guns under Captain Magold, the 1st Battery commander, to set up an ambush. As the Soviets moved into a valley, Captain Magold fired into their flanks from concealed positions, the low profile of the assault guns making them hard to spot.

Rapid, well-armed fire at almost point-blank range saw 25 T-34s destroyed in short order. Another column of tanks veered north straight into the Panzer Graf's waiting panzers. Reacting quickly he divided his force to catch the Russians in pincer movement, hitting them on both flanks while a smaller force engaged them from the front. The battle raged all day in a crescendo of exploding fuel tanks, ammunition and barking guns. Flame and smoke marked the funeral pyres of 100 Russian tanks. Superior German tactics and gunnery had won the day once again.

On 15 March Grossdeutchland was involved in a major battle with elements of the Russian V Tank Corps and II Guard Tank Corps, which had 720 operational tanks, and III Tank Corps, which only had 50 tanks. The Russians converged around Borisovka some 60 kilometres north of Kharkov. Leading a reconnaissance group east of Boriskovha, von Strachwitz spotted a Russian tank column, showing as dark spots against the snow in the distance. A quick count revealed at least 45 to 50 Russian tanks. Russian aircraft flew overhead providing cover for the advance. The Red Air Force had been fairly quiescent up to this point, allowing the Luftwaffe a relatively free hand, to the extent that the Stukas had been flying without fighter escorts.[23] A force of 10 T-34s detached themselves to attack the bridge embankment at the northern edge of the town while the remainder continued on. The Graf quickly decided to ambush the main force. He moved his tanks, which included his three operational Tigers, to a small village, hiding them among the houses. The Russians halted, uncertain as to whether the Germans had occupied the village. They fired a few rounds to draw the Germans out, but the Graf was wise to that old trick. With the Russians uncertain but suspicious it became a waiting game, with neither side making a move as night approached.

At dawn, the Russian detached force approached Boriskovha, coming under fire from German anti-tank guns, which destroyed several of them.

The majority skidded away to the side making their escape, while two entered the side streets. Here the defending grenadiers took care of them with satchel charges.[24]

The noise of this action prompted the main force to move towards the village on a broad front, where Graf von Strachwitz was patiently waiting. He let them close in to around 100 metres then ordered his panzers to open fire. Flames and smoke billowed from several stricken tanks, another had its turret blown away, others stopped dead, then exploded with a flash and a roar as their fuel and ammunition ignited. At such close range every shot was a hit. The survivors fled and von Strachwitz ordered an immediate pursuit. A fast-moving, wide-ranging battle took place with the retreating Russians at a grievous disadvantage. In their eagerness to escape the Russians' return fire was erratic, nor did they help each other, making them easy prey. Seventeen Russian tanks were left burning on the field, not a single tank escaped.[25]

However the Panzer Graf didn't always have things go all his way. On 18 March his combat group, with the assault-gun battalion sent forward to clear his route of advance, was attacked by a small force of T-34s. They were easily driven off with the loss of one tank. Von Strachwitz continued his advance until he came across a Soviet armoured force of 25 tanks. Both sides manoeuvred for tactical advantage with the Russians being quicker, aggressively attacking von Strachwitz's flanks before he was ready. He promptly counterattacked. After a brisk exchange of fire the Russians withdrew with von Strachwitz in hot pursuit. Too late he realized he had fallen into a trap as concealed Russian anti-tank guns began firing at his tanks. Four Panzer IVs were burning before he could make a hasty withdrawal. It was the Russians' turn to pursue, their fire inaccurate as they fired on the move. The Graf ordered two platoons to swing out and counterattack from the sides while he regrouped his main force to attack from the centre. Being suddenly attacked and fired on from three sides surprised the Russians, who were thrown into confused disarray. In short order six T-34s were destroyed while the rest fled with von Strachwitz in pursuit. By the time the fighting was over the combat group had claimed 15 Russian tanks destroyed.

The planned attack on Tomarovka took place on 19 March. Its approaches were defended by units of the Russian III and V Tank Corps, as well as by the 305th, 309th and 340th Infantry Divisions. However the infantry divisions were badly understrength, and they could barely muster a regiment apiece.[26] The two tank corps were also badly depleted, as was von Strachwitz's Panzer Regiment.

During a reconnaissance to check out the ground he expected to be operating on, Graf von Strachwitz spotted a large force of some 100 Russian tanks in the distance. He quickly resolved to ambush them. Not having any Tigers operational at this time he knew he would have to engage at close range utilising the element of surprise. Using his keen tactical sense to judge the ground he deployed his tanks into their ambush positions. To lure the Soviets into his killing ground he used a few Panzer IIIs and APC-mounted grenadiers as bait. The Russians quickly spotted this small German unit and moved in for the kill. The Germans promptly fled with the Russians giving chase, into the prepared ambush site. The Graf calmly watched the Soviets approaching, letting the Russians close in to where his guns could do maximum execution. At almost point-blank range the Graf gave the order to fire. The barrage left the hapless T-34s and T-17s as molten, twisted metal wrecks encasing the blackened corpses of their crews. The shocked Russians could barely co-ordinate a response and their return fire had little or no impact.

With the battlefield obscured by smoke and flames, the Graf ordered independent fire. The Germans began picking off the panic-stricken Russian tanks one by one. The tanks at the tail of the column broke off and fled. The Graf had anticipated this and pursued them, firing at their flank and rear. A fast-moving fluid battle developed, but the Russians were handicapped by their panic, returning a desultory fire while on the move. The Germans halted and took careful aimed fire, leaving a trail of burning and brewed-up Soviet tanks along their line of pursuit. As the Germans had to halt repeatedly the distance between them and the Russians increased, but it was not enough as one by one the Russians were destroyed or disabled. Behind von Strachwitz's tanks, the grenadiers in their APCs mopped up the surviving Russian tank crews, many of whom were burnt or wounded and surrendered willingly in the hope of treatment. When it was all over 65 destroyed or disabled Russian tanks littered the ambush site and its approaches, spirals of black smoke marking the funeral pyres of their crews. It was a triumph of German tactical superiority and excellence in gunnery which, together with von Strachwitz's victories around Boriskovha, prompted a grateful Hörnlein to recommend his Panzer Regiment commander for the award of Swords to his Knight's Cross and Oak Leaves.

General Hörnlein had planned to push on to capture Belgorod but the delays caused by the continuous actions around Boriskovha and Tomarovka gave this opportunity to the Waffen SS. They too had dashing commanders with the cavalry flair in their ranks. One was the boyish, good-looking Stürmbannführer Jochen Peiper, commander of the Leibstandarte's armoured grenadier battalion. Seizing his chance, he made a dash for the city. He was reinforced by his friend, the Leibstandarte 7th Panzer Company commander, Joachim von Ribbontrop—son of the foreign minister—and some Tiger tanks from the Panzer Regiment.

Outside the city Peiper's battle group was attacked by a group of T-34s. The Tigers quickly deployed to engage the Reds. In a masterful display of fire and movement they swiftly hit or destroyed 17 Soviet tanks, and the Red attack petered out. Peiper's mobile group kept moving, crashing through several Soviet-occupied villages before the Russians could recover from their surprise, although they did provide some resistance to the SS following behind. Stuka dive-bombers provided Peiper with close support blasting Russian blocking positions. When Peiper's men entered the city's southern outskirts they were bombed by German aircraft who had not been informed that Peiper had reached Belgorod, with the grenadiers suffering heavy casualties from the friendly fire. The Russians defending the city were exhausted and badly demoralised, offering little resistance to Peiper's storm troops, who took the town. It was a feat typical of the brave and dashing Waffen SS commander, and one which earned him the Oak Leaves to his Knight's Cross.

This successfully completed Field Marshal von Manstein's superb counteroffensive, which had saved the German Southern Front from being overwhelmed. The spring mud set in, immobilising both armies and giving their weary troops a much-needed break.

Casualties had been heavy for both sides. In the fighting around and for Kharkov, the Leibstandarte reported 167 officers and 4,373 other ranks dead, wounded or missing. Das Reich lost 102 officers and 4,396 men, while Totenkopf—which had arrived later on the scene—lost 94 officers and 2,170 men. Including corps troops lost, this totalled 365 officers and 11,154 men killed, wounded or missing. Tank losses were also great with the strongest division having only 35 operational tanks at the end of the operation.[27] The Russians lost 40,130 dead, with probably double that number wounded, and 12,340 captured around Kharkov. Overall their losses for the Kharkov battles were 153,500 men with 1,020 tanks and 2,100 guns.

Kharkov itself suffered grievously with 20,000 civilians killed, 4,000 of whom were killed after the Russians took the city when they executed collaborators and women who had been with, or who had worked for the Germans. Three witnesses were enough for a summary execution. Some 15,000 men and boys were sent straight to the front without training and only a rifle—which they didn't know how to use. The lucky among them would only be wounded in the fighting. One Russian lieutenant sent his contingent of boys home as he couldn't be party to their slaughter. He then shot himself.[28]

Despite the defeat and massive losses Stalin nevertheless promoted Vatutin, one of his personal favourites, for his supposed efforts. Poetic justice overtook the Ukrainian-born Vatutin when he was ambushed and killed by anti-communist Ukrainian nationalist partisans on 28 February 1944.

Hitler was generous after the German triumph. General Hörnlein was awarded the Oak Leaves to his Knight's Cross on 18 March 1943. Major Pössl of the tank regiment and Captains Frantz and Magold of the Assault Gun Battalion were both awarded a well-deserved Knight's Cross. Otto Remer of the 1st Battalion Grenadier Regiment also received the Knight's Cross for his bravery and leadership. Colonel Hyazinth Graf von Strachwitz was awarded Swords to add to his Knight's Cross with Oak Leaves on 28 March 1943, becoming the 27th recipient of this extremely rare and prestigious award. Waffen SS General Paul Hausser had to wait to get his Oak Leaves as Hitler was tardy about awarding it because of Hausser's disobedience in holding Kharkov. He finally got his award on 28 July. General Erhard Raus also received the Oak Leaves for his efforts. It was the last major German victory in the east and the participants richly deserved the awards.[29]

Grossdeutschland went into reserve for rest and refitting on 23 March, enjoying a well-deserved break until 29 June. The division would need all its strength for the upcoming Operation *Citadel*, the Battle of Kursk.

NOTES

1. Certainly Field Marshals von Kluge and Rommel thought Manstein was the ablest strategist; at a meeting between the three field marshals, von Kluge said, "Manstein, the end will be bad, and I repeat what I told you earlier; I am prepared to serve under you." A short while later as Rommel was preparing to leave he also said to von Manstein "I too am prepared to serve under you." Alexander Stahlberg (trans. Patricia Crompton), *Bounden Duty* (Brassey's, UK, 1990), pp.309–310.
2. Charles W. Sydnor, Jr., *Soldiers of Destruction: The SS Death's Head Division 1933–1945* (Guild Publishing, 1989). Most of the Waffen SS divisions had to increasingly rely on draftees to fill their depleted ranks as the war dragged on, the third battle of Kharkov perhaps being the high-water mark of their superbly trained and motivated volunteers.
3. Tim Ripley, *The Waffen SS at War: Hitler's Praetorians 1925–1945* (Zenith Press, 2004).

4. Hans-Joachim Jung (trans. David Johnston), *The History of Panzerregiment Grossdeutschland* (J. J. Fedorwicz, Canada, 2000), p.44.
5. George M. Nipe, *Last Victory in Russia* (Schiffer Military History Books PA, 2000).
6. Ibid. After having their retreat covered by Grossdeutschland, units of this division refused to assist Grossdeutchland's Reconnaissance Battalion in its defence of Belgorod. Helmuth Spaeter, *History of the Panzerkorps Grossdeutschland Vol 2* (J. J. Fedorwicz Publishing Canada).
7. *Last Victory in Russia.*
8. Ibid.
9. Dana V. Sadaranda, *Beyond Stalingrad: Manstein and the Operations of Army Group Don* (Stackpole Books, 2009).
10. Nipe, *Last Victory in Russia.*
11. Helmuth Spaeter, *History of Panzer Korps Gross Deutschland Vol 2* (J. J. Fedorowicz Publishing), pp.44–45.
12. Sadaranda, *Beyond Stalingrad.*
13. Nipe, *Last Victory in Russia.*
14. Ibid.
15. Ibid.
16. Spaeter, *The History of the Panzerkorps Grossdeutschland Vol 2.*
17. Kurt Meyer (trans. Michael Mende), *Grenadiers* (J. J. Fedorowicz Publishing, Canada, 1994), p.108.
18. Ibid.
19. Nipe, *Last Victory in Russia.*
20. Ibid.
21. Ibid.
22. Jung, *The History of Panzerregiment Grossdeutschland.*
23. Nipe, *Last Victory in Russia.*
24. Günther Fraschka (trans. David Johnston), *Knights of the Reich* (Schiffer Military History, PA, 1989).
25. Fraschka, *Knights of the Reich.*
26. Nipe, *Last Victory in Russia.*
27. Karl Ullrich (trans. Jeffrey McMullen), *Like a Cliff in the Ocean: The History of the 3 SS Panzer Division Totenkopf* (J. J. Fedorowicz Publishing Canada, 2002). Added to the casualties were those killed in the earlier battles of Kharkov and the Jews taken from the city and murdered by the German Einsatzgruppen.
28. Nipe, *Last Victory in Russia.*
29. As generous as Hitler was with his rewards he was not as lavish as Stalin. After Stalingrad the Soviet dictator created 112 Heroes of the Soviet Union, the Soviet Union's highest honour; gave 48 generals the Order of Suvorov or Kutuzov along with 10,000 other decorations for officers and men; while 700,000 participants were given campaign medals for Stalingrad's defence.

SEVENTEEN

TO KILL HITLER

HYAZINTH VON STRACHWITZ'S DISILLUSIONMENT WITH Hitler was a gradual process. No doubt the Commissar order shocked him as much as it did many other officers. With the harshness of the war in the east still not yet apparent, the German leader was ordering the execution of serving Russian officers. This was against all the rules of warfare. Equally, allowing German troops to commit crimes against Russian civilians without mandatory punishment not only went against the maintenance of good order and discipline among the troops, but was a criminal act in itself. He had in all probability heard rumours or reports of the mistreatment of Jews and civilians during the invasion of Poland but would have put these down as isolated incidents committed by an undisciplined SS. This opinion was reinforced by the correct behaviour shown by the army in the French campaign.

The next step in his path to enlightenment was the callous incompetence that left soldiers without winter clothing during the disastrous winter campaign of 1941/42. Surely Hitler and the High Command should have foreseen the need for warm clothing, thus preventing the catastrophic casualties caused by exposure and frostbite.

What von Strachwitz knew of the treatment of Soviet prisoners of war and civilians further to the rear of the occupied area can only be guessed; he was probably too far forward and busy fighting to give it much attention. Similarly the murder of Jews by the Einsatzgruppen (German for "task forces," in this situation simply a euphemism for murder squads) would probably have been unknown to him, occurring as they did well in the rear where they were only seen by rear-echelon troops. Front-line troops would only have been aware of them from rumours or if they happened to be passing through or temporarily stationed in areas where they occurred.

Certainly the troops of 16th Panzer Division followed the rules of war. General Hube, a decent man to the very core, and all his divisional officers would have insisted and strictly enforced this, although no doubt lapses did occur. There would have been simply no question of mistreating Russian civilians or prisoners of war. Even had Hube been a different commander, von Strachwitz would have behaved correctly, no matter what the circumstances or who was in charge.

The next blow to his Nazi convictions came when, on Hitler's orders, General Paulus sacked General von Wietersheim, the commander of the XIV Panzer Corps, outside Stalingrad in 1942. The Graf knew von Wietersheim to be a very capable corps commander, a man of great decency, ability and integrity. The sacking was not only unjustified, but wrong on so many levels that an angry von Strachwitz complained to Hube about it, who sympathised but could do nothing.

Then there came Hitler's callous disregard for the agony and suffering of the men of Sixth Army when they were locked in a murderous battle of primitive attrition in the ruins of Stalingrad. Without food, proper shelter or clothing, and short of basic necessities and medical attention they were expected to do the impossible with minimal assistance from the overstretched Luftwaffe. Hitler was clearly writing off an entire army, denying it a chance for survival with his "hold at all costs" order. For the Führer, Sixth Army was a flag on the map, while for Graf von Strachwitz it was men he had fought with and alongside, many of whom he knew personally. So it came as a bitter blow when, much against his will, he was evacuated because of his wound on Hube's express orders. After he was flown out he noted with some despair, "The day I left my comrades in a hopeless situation . . . I took a firm resolve to seek a way of freeing our military leaders from the thralldom of Hitler, and restoring freedom of action to German politics."[1]

Von Strachwitz clearly blamed Hitler rather than the generals for leaving the men of Sixth Army to a miserable fate of starvation, misery, death or imprisonment, and clearly resolved to do something about it. This left him ripe for the overtures of the anti-Hitler conspirators. He just needed a push to finalise his resolve and, just as importantly, the opportunity to take action.

No doubt this resolve was nurtured throughout the long agony and final death throes of Sixth Army as he recuperated in the hospital at Bleslau. When Sixth Army finally capitulated, all of Germany went into mourning, as there was no disguising the scale of the defeat. Not only was it Germany's greatest defeat to date, but the large number of casualties meant that hundreds of thousands of Germans were personally affected, their friends or loved ones killed, wounded or captured.

During his long recuperation he met up with Colonel Wessel Freiherr von Freytag-Loringhoven, a descendant of a Baltic German family which had settled in Latvia. Freytag-Loringhoven had joined the Latvian Army after World War I, leaving for Germany in 1922 where he served in the 4th Prussian Cavalry Regiment. He and von Strachwitz were kindred spirits. A posting on General Staff duties with XI Army Corps followed, then with Army Group Centre's High Command. He was fully aware of the atrocities the Germans were perpetrating in the rear and within the occupied nations, and informed Graf von Strachwitz of some of the details. This information affected the Panzer Graf profoundly, ensuring his resolve to do what he could to end the loathsome regime he was forced to serve. No doubt he was offered the possibility of a staff posting by one of the conspirators, such as Henning von Treskow, a position where he could play an effective part in the conspiracy. As tempting as this involvement would have been, the Graf was a front-line soldier first and foremost. He resolved to stay at the front with the fighting troops, but no doubt told Freytag-Loringhoven that he could be counted upon when the appropriate time came about.

Having the resolve to act, and being able to translate that resolve into action, were two very different things. He needed an opportunity, and this came from a very unexpected quarter, none other than the headquarters of Army Detachment Lanz, to which the Grossdeutschland Division was attached during the battle of Kharkov.

The Chief-of-Staff of the army was the Württemberg-born General Major Dr. Hans Speidel. At first glance he seemed a most unlikely person to be involved in the dangerous game to overthrow Hitler. He had a studious, most unmilitary air, his rimless spectacles made him look like the academic he was, having studied at Stuttgart and Tübingen universities, and finally getting a doctorate for a historic graphical thesis in 1925. He had served as a company commander in the Württemberg Guard Grenadier Regiment King Charles during World War I. He became a staff officer in the post-war Reichswehr in 1930, reaching the rank of lieutenant colonel in 1936. After the invasion of France Speidel was employed in the headquarters of the military governor of Paris. Here he formed a small circle of anti-Nazis who met at the Hotel George V in Paris. He was strongly opposed to the wholesale looting of French art and treasures and later to the shooting of hostages, which was implemented by the military government. Speidel tried whenever possible to alleviate these excesses. In 1942 he was transferred to the Eastern Front, taking up chief-of-staff positions for which he was ideally suited. After the catastrophic defeat at Stalingrad he became convinced that the war could not be won and that Hitler would be the ruination of Germany. In talks with colleagues such as General Edward Wagner, the army quartermaster-general, and General Adolf Heusinger, chief of operations, he came to the conclusion that fundamental changes needed to take place and that Hitler had to be removed.[2]

Speidel found a receptive ear in General of Mountain Troops Hubert Lanz. Lanz was a troubled soul. A devout Catholic and officer of the old school, he strenuously disagreed with Hitler's anti-Semitic and racial views, feeling a great deal of disquiet with the whole Nazi regime. Yet he was also weak-willed, finding it difficult to deal with the young fanatical Nazi officers he often found himself commanding. Like Speidel, he had also served in a Württemberg regiment during World War I as a lieutenant, going on to join the Reichswehr after the war. He was awarded the Knight's Cross while serving as Chief-of-Staff of the XVIII Army Corps during the Battle of France in 1940. On 26 October he took command of the 1st Mountain Division of mixed Germans and Austrians, leading it in the invasion of Yugoslavia, and then Russia. On 30 June his division captured Lvov. There, following the discovery of several thousand bodies of prisoners executed by the NKVD, there took place a large-scale massacre of 4,000 Jews by Ukrainians and SS and German troops, which Lanz couldn't, or wouldn't, stop. This vexed him even more, so that he was ready to listen to Speidel's seditious talk when the pair finally met.

Hitler dismissed him from his command on 17 December 1942. Six days later, almost as a consolation prize, he was awarded the Oak Leaves for his division's excellent performance in the Caucasus. He was later reinstated and promoted to general with command of the army detachment that bore his name, which he led into the third Battle of Kharkov.

When Speidel received advance warning of Hitler's intended visit to the army's headquarters at Poltava, he quickly began to consider assassinating Hitler there. He couldn't do it alone and needed Lanz's active, or at least tacit, support. It was a major and defining step for both of them, amounting as it did to high treason. Most, if not all, German officers regarded acting against Hitler as treason, rather than as just a regime change, and Graf von Stauffenberg unambiguously said, "Let us get down to brass tacks; I am carrying on high treason with all the resources at my disposal."[3] However some distinction must be drawn between treason which gave direct aid or comfort to the enemy—as was committed by Admiral Canaris and some of his subordinates in Military Intelligence—and acts merely seeking a regime change without endangering the lives of friendly forces, as carried out by von Strachwitz, von Stauffenberg and others. The German officers who conspired against Hitler nevertheless regarded their actions as treasonable, going against their oaths of allegiance, but they all chose the call of their conscience over their loyalty to the regime.

Lanz and Speidel still needed troops specifically loyal to them, or their cause, to carry out the deed. Hitler not only travelled with an entourage but had a personal bodyguard of picked SS men under Standartenführer Rattenhuber whose sole duty was to ensure Hitler's safety, and who would be likely to resist with their lives any attempt to kill or abduct their Führer. Hitler also had special army and SS guard battalions stationed at his headquarters, while for travel his special close escort of SS men attached to the Reich Security Service (SD) always travelled with him. They also checked his travel routes, his quarters and the army headquarters itself, before Hitler's arrival. They also drove his escort vehicles and guarded his temporary quarters at all times. They were, however, singularly inept, as Hitler only survived the various planned assassination attempts against him through sheer luck, and his own erratic and unpredictable behaviour, although for several attempts they did act as a deterrent. These troops would have to be overcome and for this Lanz and Speidel needed loyal and determined men.

How they arrived at von Strachwitz's name is unknown. Von Strachwitz did have many attributes in common with a great many of the anti-Nazi conspirators. An aristocrat of the old school, from a distinguished military family with a long tradition of service and conservative values, he was also a devout Christian with a strong moral sense. He was also a man of great courage, as his high decorations clearly attested. Still all this didn't necessarily make him an anti-Nazi, as of course he was also a member of the Nazi Party and SS, as indeed were many aristocratic and decorated army officers. Doubtless Speidel and Lanz did their homework, checking von Strachwitz out with officers they knew to be soundly anti-Nazi and who knew von Strachwitz well, a likely candidate being Freiherr Rudolf-Christoph von Gersdörft, von Strachwitz's cousin, the intelligence general staff officer with Field Marshal von Kluge's headquarters at Army Group Centre, and an active anti-Hitler conspirator.

Once a background check was carried out it just remained to approach von Strachwitz. On 8 February 1943 General Speidel held discussions with von Strachwitz regarding the use of his Panzer Regiment, which was then acting as a mobile reserve. It seems certain that Speidel sounded out the Graf's views on Hitler at this time. Trusting Speidel, and outspoken as always, von Strachwitz would have made no secret of his feelings, and Speidel passed this on to General Lanz. That evening Lanz invited von Strachwitz to his headquarters in the village of Valki between Kharkov and Poltova. After some preliminary tactical discussions Lanz sounded out von Strachwitz himself, finding that their viewpoints converged. Lanz now had a combat commander who could provide the troops necessary for the plot to succeed.

What arguments Speidel or Lanz used to get a final commitment from the Graf are not known beyond the theme that most anti-Hitler plotters used, which was that Hitler was ruining Germany as well as the sheer criminality of the regime. In this way the crimes and atrocities being committed against the Jews, Poles and Russians would surely have come up. After all the generals needed some strong arguments to overcome the oath of personal allegiance von Strachwitz had made to Hitler. For men of von Strachwitz's generation, especially military officers steeped in tradition of service and the concept of allegiance and obedience, the oath meant everything. It could not, and indeed would not, be broken lightly. The German military oath was unambiguous:

> I swear by God this Sacred oath that I shall render unconditional obedience to the Führer of the German Reich and People; Supreme Commander of the German Armed Forces, Adolf Hitler, and that as a brave soldier I shall be at all times prepared to give my life for this oath.[4]

Even for those for whom the oath didn't mean anything it was still a good excuse to do nothing but continue to serve a reprehensible regime, even with full knowledge of its criminal actions. Nevertheless, it held many a German officer fast to his allegiance, when common sense and conscience dictated otherwise. With what von Strachwitz had already been told about the atrocities being committed he would not have needed much further persuasion. It is not clear how much senior generals like Speidel and Lanz knew about these crimes. Lanz of course had direct experience, but could have easily blamed it all on the outraged Ukrainians, but it is fairly certain other more organised mass murders would have come to his and Speidel's attention. The German murder squads had been in full operation behind the lines for some considerable time and could not be completely hidden from view, in the manner that the horrendous crimes being committed in the concentration camps generally were. Rear-echelon troops in the areas where the atrocities were committed not only saw what happened, with many taking ghoulish photographs, but some actually participating of their own volition. Others of course were appalled, and not a few officers complained to higher authorities. In this way the generals were made aware as to what was occurring in their rear areas. Some, like von Manstein, somewhat disingenuously refused to believe it. His aide Alexander Stahlberg informed him that the army group's senior quartermaster, Colonel Finckh, had been advised by some officers that the SS and SD had recently murdered over 100,000 Jews in the area of the army group's responsibility. Von Manstein's retort was that it was simply unbelievable, that if 100,000 Jews had really been killed in one area of woodland, then would someone kindly tell him how one could make 100,000 corpses disappear.[5] He clearly didn't want to believe it, or even make any further enquiries, as a genuinely concerned commander would have done.

Von Kluge, as has already been mentioned, made some protests early in the war and then gave up when he saw that it got him nowhere. His response was to allow—with his full knowledge and support—Henning von Treskow to operate freely in his attempts to kill Hitler. Von Kleist, on the other hand, firmly forbade any actions that were unjustly cruel or harmful to the local populations, while von Rundstedt was too tired to care, or be bothered by anything outside his immediate area of responsibility. He certainly wasn't prepared to complain or bother Hitler about it. Why add to his overall angst in what was to him a futile cause. So the mass murders were an open secret, at least to the senior officers and rear-echelon troops, if not to the front-line fighting troops, especially if they were not involved in anti-partisan actions. Until he was informed otherwise, this ignorance certainly applied to von Strachwitz, who had spent virtually his entire career serving at the front.

Once he was brought in, the conspirators had a regimental commander of combat troops on their side, but he still had to provide the troops. Grossdeutschland was not a homogeneous unit of troops from one locality with the bonding and loyalty this fostered. Nor did it have old traditions or values that would have quickly fused the men together; rather they came from all over Germany and Austria with their overriding loyalty to Germany and the Third Reich, personified by Adolf Hitler. Certainly the division included many anti-Nazis as Alfred Novotny, a Grossdeutschland fusilier, related in his memoirs, in the aftermath of the 20 July bomb attempt on Hitler's life:

> All of a sudden rumours flew around. "Hitler is dead, the war will be over quickly!" Then came the word that he had been assassinated! No one seemed to know anything more.
>
> However very shortly officers from other GD units came around telling us that they had finally gotten rid of Hitler, that we will all go home soon, that this was not Germany's war but rather Hitler's war! We had no idea what to make of it or how to behave. From youth we had been conditioned to show respect to our elders and for those in authority, especially our leaders; thinking on our own had never been encouraged. We were told to stay put as a new regime would be giving orders . . .

Equally however, the division contained many pro-Nazis like Otto Remer who went on to put the *putsch* down, as Novotny continues:

> It was not long before contrary rumours flew. Hitler is not dead; wait for orders from Oberst Remer . . . We ourselves were to witness the hanging of GD officers by Remer loyalists. In the morning these officers had been going around telling us things would be different, and different they were; later that day they were hanging from quickly erected gallows.[6]

Given the mixture of loyalties, selecting the right officers was clearly crucial, as von Stauffenberg discovered to his cost when he relied on someone like Otto Remer. Graf von Strachwitz obviously knew which of his officers he could trust and who would follow his orders in arresting Hitler. His officers in turn had to know that their men would obey them unquestioningly. Being hardened combat troops, they would have developed strong bonds with the officers who had shared their dangers, privations and above all cared for their well-being. The junior officers and men all had a deep respect for the Panzer Graf, who was one of them, sharing in their deadly daily life of struggle and pain. So the Graf had the men available although it is not known what explanation, if any, he provided to justify their actions. Certainly, he hand-picked them all, but only told a few officers, leaving explanations for the men if any, to be made at the last minute.

The next question was how to execute the plot and what to do with Hitler. This involved a great deal of planning and discussion. Assassination was rejected by von Strachwitz as being beneath the dignity of a German officer—they were soldiers, not murderers. That this distinction was lost on a large part of the German armed forces was a fact he perhaps did not even consider, as he had his own morals, by which he and most of the men around him lived. The alternative was to arrest Hitler, and the Graf volunteered to lead the arresting force in person. Weapons would only be used if his bodyguard resisted, it being preferred that they would surrender. Hitler was only to be executed if there was no other choice, due to resistance from him or his bodyguard. The next step was to put Hitler on trial, with either a hastily convened drumhead court martial or a public, properly constituted, trial by the hopefully newly installed regime. For this to happen other outside forces would have to become involved, so for this reason other senior generals had to be informed of the plot. Field Marshal Erwin Rommel was aware of it through Dr. Strolin, the mayor of Stuttgart, who was informed no doubt by Speidel. Von Kluge would also have been informed as Hitler would have been handed over to him for the properly convened trial. If von Kluge knew, then so did Henning von Treskow and all the conspirators around him, braced to form a new government after Hitler's arrest. Whether Rommel had any influence as to the decision not to assassinate is unclear, however this was certainly Rommel's view in 1944 when he adamantly opposed assassination in favour of putting Hitler on trial.[7]

Being the older and wiser head in the conspiracy, General Speidel probably opted for the straight-out assassination option. He no doubt realised that the longer they held Hitler the greater the chance of troops loyal to their Führer mounting a rescue attempt and the greater the risk of their own troops wavering. Whether the conspirators knew it or not, at this stage in the war, the vast majority of people, including the army, still loyally supported their Führer. In fact this loyalty would only waver in the very final dying days of the Reich, upheld as it was by unremitting propaganda, a natural support for the leadership when the nation was being assailed from all sides, and finally by a desperate belief in the new miracle weapons that the Propaganda Minister Josef Goebbels continually boasted about. Besides, occupation by the rapacious Russians was not even to be contemplated. The anti-Hitler conspiracy only involved the tiniest fraction of the population. Many tens of thousands despised Hitler, including many in the armed forces, but most had no opportunity or inclination to actively oppose the regime. A large number of those who did oppose the regime ended up in the hands of the Gestapo, betrayed by neighbours and friends who remained loyal to the regime.

Killing Hitler quickly, either immediately on contact during an ambush or afterwards on the completion of a very hasty trial offered the best solution. Even the drumhead court martial, however, presented problems, such as finding a willing firing squad. So assassination would have been the best option. In this event, who would have carried out the deed? Graf von Strachwitz refused on moral grounds; as a good Catholic he could not countenance cold-blooded murder, no matter how evil the target. It would have made him judge, jury and executioner, and in his eyes no better than Hitler himself, especially as he felt that other options existed. Killing an unarmed man in cold blood was not an act that all could countenance, as clearly illustrated in Alexander Stahlberg's memoirs when he recounted how he met with Henning von Treskow after Hitler's visit to von Manstein's headquarters at Zaporozye. Upon questioning, Stahlberg admitted he had had several opportunities over the preceding days when he could have shot Hitler, but that he hadn't because he didn't know what was going to happen when Hitler was dead, and also because he hadn't the strength to do it: "I have taken part in plenty of attacks with my division. I also have the assault badge. But I have had the great good fortune never to have had to shoot a man face to face."[8]

This then would have been the situation Graf von Strachwitz did not want to face. Nevertheless, the Graf was prepared to kill Hitler if it came to a firefight with his escort. So the basic plan was to arrest Hitler and put him on trial. As such it would in all probability have failed with dire consequences for von Strachwitz, unless he was prepared to shoot Hitler before his small force of panzer troops was overpowered by Nazi loyalists. But it never came to that. At the last minute Hitler changed his plans and flew to Zaporozye and von Manstein's headquarters instead of Poltava.

Von Strachwitz went on to fight in the third Battle of Kharkov, Kursk, the Baltic States and Germany. Lanz, after his dismissal for the loss of Kharkov, went on to lead his mountain troops in the Balkans where they committed numerous atrocities, killing innocent villagers as reprisals for partisan attacks. Some of these atrocities were sanctioned by Lanz, for which he was sentenced to imprisonment after the war. These killings were committed by ordinary German and Austrians in a standard army mountain division. It seemed that Lanz was often unable to assert control over his young pro-Nazi subordinate officers. One crime he was found not guilty of was the murder of Italian prisoners of war. As for General Speidel, after two years' service on the Eastern Front, he was promoted to lieutenant general and went on to serve as chief-of-staff of Army Group B in France under Field Marshal Rommel. He continued his conspiratorial activities until the failure of the 20 July plot.

The Poltava plot was only one in a long line of attempts or plans to kill Hitler. There were over thirty planned or actual attempts from July 1921 to 1945. Hitler feared that some nonentity might assassinate him before he could achieve his worldview. He particularly feared a sniper on a roof or building so that his cap was fitted with armour plating. The army made or planned most of the attempts; some civilians were also involved, while air force and navy officers were, apart from Admiral Canaris, unrepresented. Some attempts came very close to succeeding, such as the bomb painstakingly built into a pillar in the Burgerbrau Beer Cellar by Johann Georg Elser on 8 November 1939. It was set to detonate while Hitler was making a speech, but Hitler ended his speech 12 minutes early, hurriedly leaving the building so the bomb exploded after he had left, killing eight and wounding 65, including Eva Braun's father. While 1943 was a bumper year for planned assassination attempts, with several efforts being made including von Strachwitz's at Poltava, the most famous attempt, and the one which came closest to success, was the bomb plot enacted by Colonel Graf Claus Schenk von Stauffenberg on 20 July 1944.

Von Stauffenberg left a bomb in a briefcase under a map table a few metres from Hitler at Hitler's his headquarters at Rastenburg. He then made his excuses and left, returning to Berlin to initiate Operation *Valkyrie*, a plan to mobilise troops and prevent any revolt by the millions of slave labourers working in the Reich. The plotters were to use the plan for their own purposes to take over the government. Hitler survived the bomb blast with only minor injuries, so the plot failed. Loyal officers at the Home Army Headquarters where the plotters were based, along with the Nazi Otto Remer commanding a Grossdeutschland guard battalion, seized control of the Bendlerstrasse headquarters.[9] Von Stauffenberg, his aide von Haeften and General Olbricht were taken out to the courtyard and shot on the orders of Home Army Commander General Fromm. This particular general had supported the planned coup but hastily switched sides on learning that Hitler was alive. The round-up of plotters and suspects then began. These included Admiral Canaris, head of military intelligence, whose history of chicanery went back to the Freikorps days, and his chief subordinate, General Oster.

Canaris and Oster were clearly traitors who betrayed their country, passing on information and aiding the enemy. Oster himself calculated that by warning the Dutch of the German invasion he would cost 40,000 German lives, although the Dutch ignored the advanced warnings. The other conspirators may have been technically guilty of treason but they did not betray their country. Von Stauffenberg's wife was imprisoned, and released by the Allies at war's end. Admiral Canaris and others were less fortunate however, tortured and then hung from meat hooks by piano wire for a long painful death by strangulation which was filmed for Hitler's private viewing.

Field Marshal Erwin Rommel was also caught in the aftermath. He had been willing to arrange a separate peace with the Western Allies and serve the new anti-Nazi regime. Interestingly, SS General Sepp Dietrich, former commander of the SS Leibstandarte Division and now an army commander, was also prepared to serve an anti-Nazi regime. Knowing something was in the wind and in response to Rommel's query as to his support he stoutly replied, "You're my superior officer, so I'd carry out every single one of your orders." It was unequivocal and clearly indicated his support for the army should it rebel against the Nazi regime.[10] Waffen SS General Hausser was also not a Nazi fanatic, as von Gersdorff attests in his memoirs:

> He [Hausser] also appeared to have a notion of my attitude towards the regime. He asked me about it one day, point blank. "You're not one of the Führer's supporters?" I answered just as openly.
>
> "No Herr General Oberst. I regard him as the ruination of Germany." Hausser remained very calm and said only that he understood me; but I would be so good to understand in turn that as an SS commander he still had a sense of loyalty toward Hitler.[11]

It was hardly a ringing endorsement of the Führer, nor did he arrest, or report von Gersdorff as he was obliged to do. Clearly by this time the Waffen SS was aligned more with the army than with the regime. Certainly very few of their commanders, if any, had any love or respect for Himmler or the rest of Hitler's coterie.

Field Marshal Günther von Kluge was another victim of the purge of officers. He had actively supported and sheltered anti-Nazi conspirators including von Treskow, von Boeselager and von Gersdorff, and if not the stuff that great rebels are made of, he nevertheless deserves more credit than he is usually given for his anti-Hitler stance. On 12 July he and Rommel agreed that the war could not be won and Hitler had to be eliminated. This was far more than Field Marshal von Manstein was ever prepared to do. He maintained in his self-serving memoirs that when approached by Stauffenberg he was not asked to join the conspiracy to eliminate Hitler but to become chief of the army, which he was prepared to do. Von Manstein maintained that his chief concern was to preserve the integrity of the army, which indeed it was, but it was also to preserve and advance his own position by supporting Hitler.

When the bomb plot failed, Rommel was already out of action from wounds caused by an Allied strafing attack on his car, leaving von Kluge undecided what to do. Urged by von Gersdorff and others to make a separate peace with the Allies, he vacillated, telling von Gersdorff that he was not the "great man" to make such a momentous decision.[12] However he went missing from his headquarters for a whole day on 15 August, saying on his return that he had been caught in a traffic jam. However Allied intelligence was waiting to receive von Kluge or an emissary to discuss possible surrender terms, but no one showed up or made it through to the Allied lines. The whole truth will never be known. However, Hitler became suspicious when advised of an Allied signals intercept inquiring as to von Kluge's whereabouts. Hitler relieved him of his command and summoned him to appear at the Führer-Haupt Quartier. Knowing what this meant, von Kluge killed himself with a cyanide capsule on the road between Verdun and Metz.

Speidel was arrested by the Gestapo but only revealed that he knew of the conspiracy, which was of course sufficient to have him executed. However, he escaped this fate by saying that he reported this knowledge to his superior Field Marshal Rommel as he was obliged to do. This got him off the hook but implicated Rommel. A military court of honour exonerated Speidel, but at a separate hearing found Rommel guilty, who was subsequently forced to commit suicide to save Hitler the embarrassment of a trial of a popular war hero.[13] Von Treskow blew himself up with a hand grenade rather than submit to arrest and torture. Wessel von Freytag-Loringhoven also committed suicide on 23 July 1944 for the same reason.

For his part Hitler felt that destiny had saved him once again to continue his mission. He also felt a deep sense of betrayal as he confided to his Luftwaffe Adjutant Nicolaus von Below in December 1944: "After 20 July everything came out, things I had considered impossible. It was precisely those circles against me who had profited most from National Socialism. I pampered and decorated them. And that was all the thanks I got."[14] The fact that most of his officers remained loyal to him, despite the horrendous evil of his regime, and that he was leading them all to destruction, was lost on him.

In the hunt for the plotters Graf von Strachwitz's name came up, either in a document or during an interrogation. It was either connected to his Poltava plot, or because of some disparaging remarks he may have made about Hitler or the regime. It could also have been simply conspirators considering him as a useful friend or ally in their own conversations or correspondence. Either way he came to the attention of the dreaded Gestapo. In the heightened circumstances of the time a mention would have certainly involved further investigation and a summons for interrogation, but he wasn't called. In all likelihood this was because he had joined the Nazi Party before the massive 1933 influx, which made him a true believer, not just an opportunist. He was also by this time a high-ranking officer in the SS, and a highly decorated one, who clearly enjoyed Heinrich Himmler's support. To start implicating high-ranking and decorated SS officers on such flimsy grounds was just too big a step to take without further and stronger evidence. So Graf von Strachwitz was spared arrest and possible imprisonment. His Party and SS membership had ironically saved him.

The final words of this chapter should perhaps cite the memorandum that General Ludwig Beck, then Chief of the General Staff, read to senior generals in August 1938:

> History will indict those commanders [who blindly follow Hitler's orders] of blood guilt if, in the light of their professional and political knowledge, they do not obey the dictates of their conscience. A soldier's duty to obey ends when his knowledge, his conscience and his sense of responsibility forbid him to carry out a certain order.[15]

NOTES

1. Günter Fraschka, *Der Panzergraf: Ein leben für Deutschland* (Rastatt, 1962).
2. Klaus-Jurgen Muller (ed. Corell Bryant), *Hitler's Generals* (Phoenix Gian, 1995). Speidel himself stated that he decided to oust Hitler at the end of 1943, yet clearly he was prepared to do so at the beginning of the year with the Poltava plot.
3. Joachim Kramarz, *Stauffenberg: The Man who nearly killed Hitler* (Mayflower 1970), p.132.
4. Constantine Fitzgibbon, *The Shirt of Nessus* (Cassell & Co, London, 1956).
5. Alexander Stahlberg (trans. Patricia Crompton), *Bounden Duty* (Brassey's UK, 1990), pp.81–82.
6. Alfred Novotny, *The Good Soldier* (The Aberjona Press, PA, 2003).
7. Fitzgibbon, *The Shirt of Nessus.*

8. Stahlberg, *Bounden Duty.*
9. Remer's reward for thwarting the coup was rapid promotion to major general. He was also made a commander of the Führer Begleit Division (Hitler's Escort unit, which expanded throughout the war from battalion-size to division), but that was above his ability. He remained an unrepentant Nazi for long after the war.
10. Rudolf-Christoph von Gersdorff, *Soldier in the Downfall* (The Aberjona Press, PA, 2012) p.125. Dietrich's biographer Charles Messenger disputes this, maintaining Dietrich would not have rebelled against Hitler. Perhaps not, although von Gersdorff also wrote how Dietrich frequently fulminated against Hitler, and Dietrich was clearly an army supporter, although his friendship for Hitler was still strong. What is certain, however, is that had Hitler been killed, Dietrich would have unequivocally sided with the army against the Nazi regime.
11. Von Gersdorff, *Soldier in the Downfall.*
12. Ibid.
13. Speidel always strenuously denied betraying Rommel. He certainly didn't implicate Rommel any further, which he could easily have done. He went on to achieve high command with NATO after the war.
14. Von Below, *At Hitler's Side*, p.223.
15. James P. Duffy and Vincent L. Ricci, *Target Hitler: The Plots to Kill Adolf Hitler* (Praeger, Westport, CT, 1992), p.50. The memorandum was dated 16 July 1938.

EIGHTEEN

OPERATION CITADEL

At Poltava, the Grossdeutschland Division undertook training and repairs and received new equipment such as new self-propelled guns. Particularly noteworthy were 83 half-tracked armoured personnel carriers for the Grenadier Regiment's 1st Battalion, and the upgrading of Graf von Strachwitz's Panzer Regiment's Tiger Company to a battalion. Under its commander, Major Gomille, it was in formation at the Sennelager training grounds from the middle of May. Its personnel were all experienced tankers drawn from the 30th, 31st and 18th Panzer Regiments. It comprised a battalion headquarters, with signals, pioneer, and anti-aircraft units, along with a heavy workshop company. Its principal combat units were three tank companies, of 14 Tigers each.[1] Grossdeutschland was the only army division to have an organic Tiger battalion on its strength.

The Panzer Graf was kept busy supervising the training, the refurbishment of equipment, and the integration of the new Tiger battalion into the regiment. He also commanded the division as its most senior officer for a period while General Hörnlein went on leave. During his time as divisional commander, on 30–31 March, Colonel General Guderian visited the division, as part of his role as inspector-general of panzer troops. He was particularly interested to hear about the role the Tigers played in the Kharkov battles, and the Panzer Graf was the ideal man to fill him in. Von Strachwitz, however, could not have impressed him very much as Guderian mentions him only once, and very briefly, in his memoir *Panzer Leader*, regarding his actions in 1944. Of vital importance to the Graf were the company, battalion and regimental exercises he conducted to weld his troops into a smoothly running,

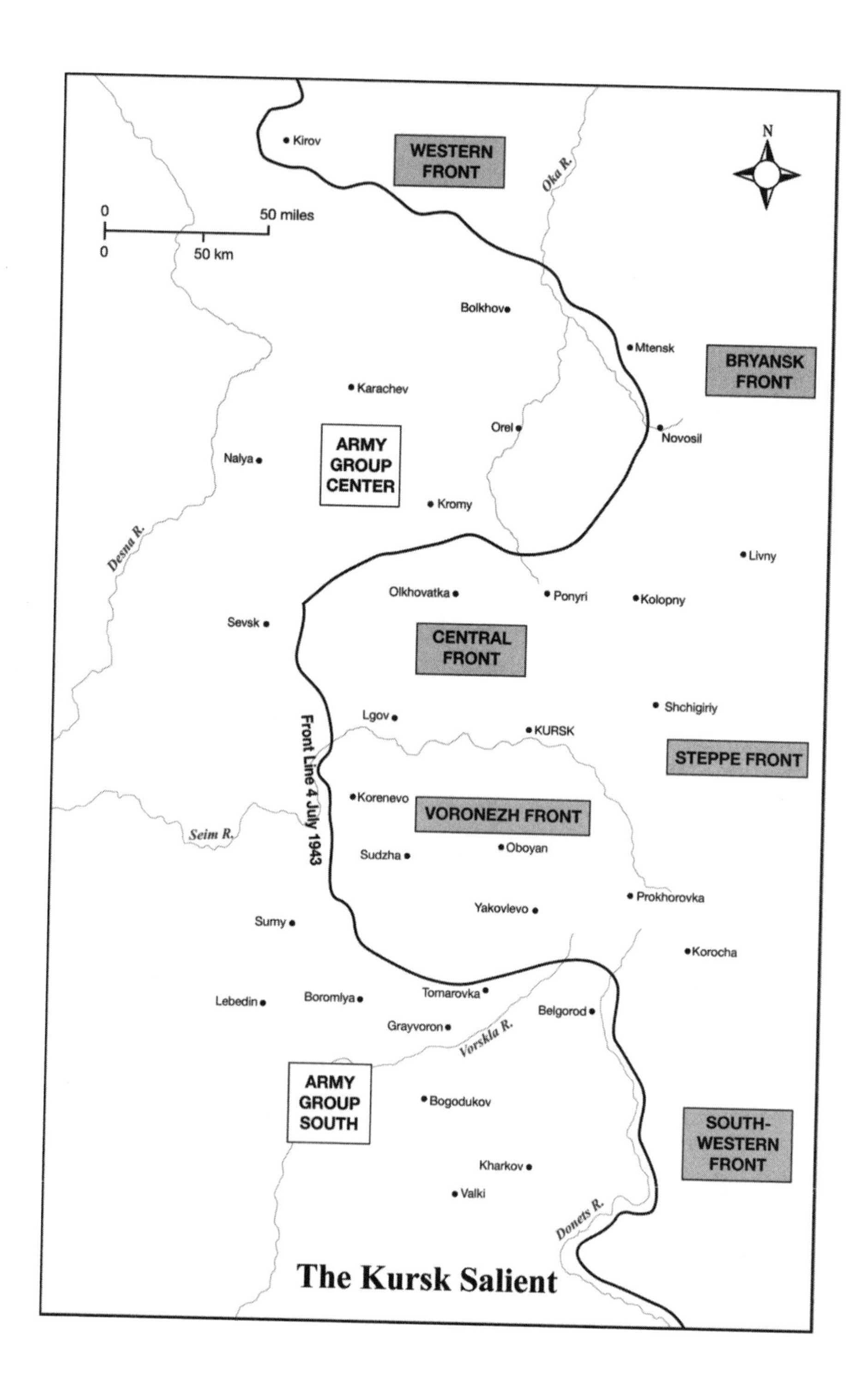

WESTERN FRONT
BRYANSK FRONT
ARMY GROUP CENTER
CENTRAL FRONT
STEPPE FRONT
VORONEZH FRONT
ARMY GROUP SOUTH
SOUTH-WESTERN FRONT
0
50 miles
0
50 km
N
Kirov
Oka R.
Bolkhov
Mtensk
Karachev
Orel
Novosil
Nalya
Kromy
Desna R.
Livny
Olkhovatka
Ponyri
Kolopny
Sevsk
Shchigiriy
Lgov
KURSK
Front Line 4 July 1943
Korenevo
Seim R.
Sudzha
Oboyan
Prokhorovka
Yakovlevo
Sumy
Korocha
Tomarovka
Lebedin
Boromlya
Belgorod
Grayvoron
Vorskla R.
Bogodukov
Kharkov
Valki
Donets R.
The Kursk Salient

well coordinated unit, especially the integration of the Tigers with the medium tanks. His tanks also took part in divisional exercises, honing their skills to work with the armoured infantry.

However it was not all work and training. Relaxation was vital for the combat-weary, exhausted troops. Sports events were organised, with races, football matches, tugs-of-war, relays, swimming and even races between the amphibious volkswagons of the Reconnaissance battalion. There were plays, concerts and for the officers, dining and card evenings. There was also a theatre in Poltava playing the *Gypsy Baron* as well as German films.

The Graf also had time to mix with his junior officers, who absolutely doted on him not just for his decorations and his success as a panzer commander, which ensured their own success as well as their survival, but at the human level. He was generally pleasant, never aloof, approachable at any level—personal or military—and quite relaxed without the intensity, focus and drive that he showed during combat operations. The same could not always be said for his superiors, not all of whom liked him, finding him at times a willful, opinionated and difficult subordinate. The performance of his panzers during the Kharkov battles also cemented his reputation with the ordinary troops, who were always grateful for the life-saving presence of his tanks. They were also aware that he was always in the thick of the action, leading from the front, ensuring the success of his units by his tactical skill and personal example.

From 23 June, the division's title was officially changed to Panzergrenadier Division Grossdeutschland, which was a misnomer as its armoured strength exceeded that of nearly every army panzer division, and was equal to the premier Waffen SS panzergrenadier divisions which shortly became officially designated panzer divisions.

While Grossdeutschland was refitting, Hitler and his High Command were planning a new offensive, which had been proposed by General Zeitzler, the army Chief-of-Staff. The Eastern Front had a large bulge—257 kilometres long and 160 kilometres deep—jutting out westwards into the German line with the industrial city of Kursk at its centre. This helped create a corresponding bulge into the east at Orel. Zeitzler proposed a two-pronged attack with pincers from the north and south cutting off the bulge and destroying the Russian forces trapped within. This would eliminate several Soviet armies and considerably shorten the German line, freeing the troops deployed around the edges of the salient.

That the bulge was an attractive target was of course not lost on the Russians, who began pouring in reinforcements and preparing their defences for the inevitable attack. Their activities depressed the observant General Model. Sitting on the salient's northern edge, he took countless pictures which he showed to Hitler at a meeting on 4 March, and made several well-reasoned arguments why any planned attack should be abandoned. He told his Führer the Soviets were ready and waiting for any rash move to pinch the bulge off. Hitler agreed with Model, but was under pressure from his command staff to go ahead with the plan. He called a conference on 3 May, which was attended by Zeitzler; von Manstein, commanding Army Group South; von Kluge, commanding Army Group Centre; Model commanding Ninth Army; Guderian, inspector general of armoured forces; as well as Keitel, Jodl, Albert Speer, the armaments and production minister, and sundry others.

After much discussion Hitler remained undecided.[2] Eventually Zeitzler, along with Keitel, won him over; the temptation of a great victory was just too much to resist. Following the conference, Guderian—who was keen to preserve his carefully built-up panzer reserve—tried to persuade Hitler not to proceed with Operation *Citadel* as it was now named. But the bulge was still there so, clutching at straws, Hitler became convinced that sufficient numbers of the new Panther tanks would make a difference. So he kept delaying the assault to allow time for them to reach the front. The Panther was a magnificent beast, with sloping armour copied from the T-34, wide mud-riding tracks, a 600–700hp Maybach engine and a high-velocity 75mm gun with beautiful optics. Once its teething difficulties were overcome, it would arguably be the best tank of the war.[3]

The Russians in the meantime were still ahead of the game. Their Swiss-based Lucy spy ring was keeping them informed of all the German moves and delays. Not that the Russians needed their spy ring for this information; their own reconnaissance told them of the large-scale movements of entire armies for the build-up. The Soviets strengthened their defences accordingly. By the time they had finished they had strung over 800 kilometres of barbed wire and laid 1,500,000 anti-tank and 1,700,000 anti-personnel mines. Their forward defence stretched 80 kilometres to the rear with two more defence lines manned by their Steppe Front beyond that. In the main defence zone there were five trench lines, each 150–250 metres apart, totalling 5,000 kilometres of trenches. They would have made even the obsessive World War I trench-builders proud. The trenches all had interconnected strongpoints, anti-tank guns, machine-gun and mortar posts, along with dug-in T-34s with barbed wire and mines laid in front. The Russians then packed 1.3 million men inside the salient supported by 19,000 guns of various calibres and 3,500 tanks. They were supported by close to 3,000 aircraft. The genial General Rokossovsky commanded the northern sector. He had been purged by Stalin in the early 1930s, suffering torture in the process, and though since rehabilitated, he was still not altogether trusted, especially by Zhukov, who serially disliked anyone with personal charisma, a quality he himself singularly lacked. General Vatutin, now recovered from his bloody defeat at Kharkov, commanded the South, while Marshal Koniev led the reserve army, ready to mount a massive counterattack when appropriate.

To help motivate their loyal communist soldiery, the Russians applied a good old capitalist incentive programme. For every German tank they destroyed, Russian tank commanders, gunners and drivers were paid a bonus of 500 rubles while the other crewmen got 200 rubles. An anti-tank rifleman also got 500 rubles while his assistant received 200. They could only hope they didn't run into a Tiger which was impervious to their weapons, and the medium tanks were hard enough to take out in any event. Artillery gun commanders and crew received the same bonuses. Any soldier knocking out a tank using an individual anti-tank weapon received 1,000 rubles.[4] On that basis Hitler was getting his tank kills on the cheap—no cash for tank or gun crews, while an infantryman got a tank destruction badge to wear on his sleeve. It was a justifiably well-respected badge and many individuals sported several.

By stripping other fronts, the Germans came close to matching the massive Russian force. They had between 770,000 and 1,000,000 men, 10,000 guns, 2,700 tanks and close to 3,000 planes. Of course the estimated numbers for both armies vary between the different sources, bearing in mind that wartime—and for the Soviets postwar—propaganda had a major bearing.

The German forces were divided into two attack groups. Coming from the south from around Belgorod there were 10 panzer, one panzer grenadier and seven infantry divisions, under the overall command of Field Marshal von Manstein. The northern pincer coming from around Orel was commanded by General Walter Model who had seven panzer, two panzer grenadier and nine infantry divisions.

Graf von Strachwitz and Grossdeutschland were in the XLVIII Panzer Corps—along with the 3rd and 11th Panzer Divisions under General von Knobelsdorff—which formed part of von Manstein's southern wing. It in turn belonged to the 4th Panzer Army under General Hoth, which was the mainstay of the southern attack, and indeed the strongest force in the entire offensive. It had 1,176 armoured fighting vehicles and 1,100 aircraft, facing off against 1,699 AFVs of the Soviet Voronezh Front.[5]

While the various high commanders were finalising their respective attack plans, Grossdeutschland was kept busy with its refit and training programme. As the date of the attack drew closer actual rehearsals for the assault began. Tactical attack exercises at all levels were carried out with an emphasis on assaults against enemy defensive positions. Mock attacks were carried out against bunkers and trench systems with engineers clearing mines and barbed-wire obstacles. Combined armour-infantry assaults were a special feature, training the tanks and infantry how to work in very close cooperation with each other.

War games—tactical exercises using mud maps, aerial photos and drawings of actual Soviet defensive positions—were conducted by the division's officers. Working with these aerial photos was difficult as there was no way of knowing which defences were real and which were dummies. The Russians were masters of deceit and camouflage, effectively using every trick available to good effect at Kursk. They built dummy gun positions, trench lines, tanks, even airfields and supply dumps, and managed to fool the Germans, particularly the Luftwaffe, which carried out frequent bombing raids against them.

It wasn't long before von Strachwitz began to develop his own misgivings about the assault. Like Guderian he could see the potential for heavy tank losses in battering through the strong multi-layered Soviet defence systems, covered as they were with minefields and anti-tank weapons. This was not going to be the battle of manoeuvre that he was accustomed to and excelled at, but a grinding battle of attrition against a well-prepared determined enemy. His experience, training and finely honed cavalryman's instincts all protested against using his precious panzers as battering rams. There were also no alternative flanking moves he could use, or gaps he could exploit, just a foolish frontal assault in a restricted attack area. For all outward appearances he radiated confidence, telling his junior officers like 1st Lieutenant Hans-Joachim Jung that he was confident of success, it being counterproductive to sow seeds of doubt in the young officers undertaking the frontal assaults. Faith in ultimate victory would make them fight all the harder, a forlorn hope being a poor prescription for success.

Given his outspoken forthright nature the Panzer Graf undoubtedly expressed his doubts to his commanding officer General Hörnlein, who perhaps may have shared them, but being fundamentally an infantryman in outlook was probably more optimistic. This dichotomy of infantry/cavalry outlook, along with their personalities, set these two officers apart. Hörnlein, sympathetic by nature, did not have Hube's gift for understanding basic human nature nor his strength in tank tactics. Nor was Hörnlein as intense a person as von Strachwitz and he certainly didn't appreciate the latter's outspokenness and frank opinions, being himself far more circumspect in his personal dealings. He probably considered von Strachwitz a flamboyant panzer prima donna. He may have also been a little envious of the panzer commander's popularity among the men, especially the junior officers. Whatever the reason, the two men did not get along, and their feelings had time to fester, and were likely exacerbated, during the relative calm away from combat in the spring of 1943.

During this time in May the Graf received one piece of good news. On 29 May his eldest son Hyazinth, who was serving in the 11th Panzer Division, was awarded the German Cross in Gold for his bravery and leadership in battle. This breast star, emblazoned with the swastika, ranked between the Iron Cross (1st Class) and the Knight's Cross. The year also saw his eldest son marry Countess Constance (Huschi) von Franken Sierstorff who lived in a castle literally next door to the von Strachwitz family at Gross-Stein, so it was a very important year for the young officer.

After its refit Grossdeutschland had a strength of 20,468 men, which made it much stronger than nearly every panzer or panzergrenadier division, which rarely had more than 15,000 men, and more usually a strength of 10,000 to 12,000. Sustained combat often reduced these numbers down to an average of 3,000 to 6,000 men with some divisions almost ceasing to exist. With its heavily reinforced panzer and artillery regiments, a full assault-gun battalion of 34 Sturmgeschütz IIIs, two infantry regiments of three battalions each, together with various sub-units, it was an unwieldy division to handle. General Balck—who was an infantry regimental commander in the Battle of France, and who went on to become a hugely successful panzer leader—commanded Grossdeutschand for a brief period, and actually recommended it be broken up into two average strength panzer divisions. OKH refused, as it still wanted an army formation that could surpass the privileged Waffen SS panzer divisions.

As a one-off temporary reinforcement, two battalions of the long-awaited Panthers, designated the 51st and 52nd Battalions, were attached to the division. They had 200 Panthers between them, 188 battle tanks, ten command tanks, and two Bergepanther recovery tanks. They were placed under the regimental command of Colonel Meinrad von Lauchert, a veteran officer. He had served with the highly efficient 4th Panzer Division in France and Russia, where he received the Knight's Cross on 8 September 1941, eventually going on to earn the Oak Leaves on 2 December 1944. He later fought alongside Graf von Strachwitz, serving under his command in the Baltics. Guderian had personally selected him to command and train the two Panther battalions.

The Panthers were deployed alongside Graf von Strachwitz's Panzer Regiment with its 163 Panzer IVs[6] to form Panzer Brigade 10 which became part of the Grossdeutschland Division. However, at Guderian's behest, the brigade was to be commanded by Colonel Karl Decker, who was senior to von Strachwitz, having been promoted to Colonel on 1 February 1942, earlier than the Graf's promotion in May 1942. Decker's appointment was most likely due to his having served on the staff of Guderian's newly formed Inspectorate of Panzer Troops from April 1942 to January 1943. But his appointment was not due solely to favouritism: he had previously served with the 3rd and 35th Panzer Regiments, and received the Knight's Cross on 13 June 1941. He was a highly experienced and capable panzer commander.[7]

Graf von Strachwitz's pride was deeply hurt at being passed over, ostensibly because of a slender margin in seniority. He doubtless blamed General Hörnlein for not fighting the appointment. To make matters worse, Decker was late in taking up his post, arriving after the battle had started on 5 July and then with only some of his headquarters staff. To all intents and purposes the Brigade was almost leaderless for the crucial preparation and early phases of the offensive.[8] If that wasn't enough, many of the Panther crewmen were insufficiently trained on the specifics of their new tanks and lacked practical combat experience. Their equipment was also not fully tested, while their engines had serious faults which quickly became apparent as they commenced their deployment.[9]

On 29 June the departure orders for the division were issued, with assembly areas assigned on the Vorska northwest of Tomarovka. The division moved out the next day. Traffic jams quickly developed as the vehicles crammed onto the few available roads, being further delayed by the dusty, poor conditions, which caused numerous vehicle breakdowns.

On 2 July all units had reached their respective assembly areas, with the combat officers wasting no time in moving forward to get acquainted with the terrain. This they did visually, together with studying abundant maps and aerial photos. It had been all too usual in the past, for von Strachwitz and his officers to operate with, at best, poor, often inaccurate maps, or with no maps at all. What the Graf saw now was only marginal tank country, consisting of an open plain cut with numerous gullies, creeks, shallow valleys and some rivers, the largest being the fast-moving Pena. The tracks and roads were just dirt, which could become impassable during the sudden heavy summer showers common to the area. Large areas were covered with cornfields, which obscured visibility and could hide significant tank and infantry units. All this, coupled with the well-camouflaged enemy defences, filled von Strachwitz with some disquiet. A narrow attack frontage of two kilometres didn't give him the room for the wide-ranging manoeuvre that was his forté, especially as it would be filled with not only his tanks, but engineers and infantry as well.

The 11th Panzer Division was deployed on Grossdeutschland's right flank with II SS Panzer Corps—consisting of the Leibstandarte, Das Reich and Totenkopf Divisions—further along. On the left was the 3rd Panzer Division, the second weakest panzer division in Army Group South, with only 56 tanks.[10] All the Graf could hope for was an early breakthrough of the Soviet defences, so that he could range behind their lines in open country and attack their rear and flanks.

The next few days were spent finalising attack plans, studying the terrain, attending orders groups and dealing with the last-minute details of logistics, supply and future troop movements. Lights, noise and movement was kept to an absolute minimum. Plans were constantly reviewed and memorised as officers fussed over details. The sultry days were filled with a tense calm. The troops were imbued with the importance of the coming offensive and all, given the massive force on display, were quietly confident. Their superiority over "Ivan" was never in doubt and most felt that this could be the knockout blow that had eluded them hitherto, the one that would bring an end to the war in the east. If they had any doubts, Hitler's message to the troops would have dispelled it:

> Soldiers! Today you set out to a great onslaught, the outcome of which could well decide the war.
>
> Your victory must serve to convince the world more than ever that any resistance to the German Wehrmacht is fruitless. In addition, new defeat for the Russians can only serve to shake further the already wavering belief among the men in army units of the Red Army that a Bolshevik victory is possible, Just as in the last war, they will one day be defeated.[11]

The Panthers arrived late on 4 July, giving their officers and crews no time to study the terrain or make all the necessary final preparations and adjustments. As radio silence was already in force, their radio operators were not even able to tune their radios.[12] Even more seriously, their numbers had already been reduced due to mechanical failures. Six Panthers had spontaneously caught on fire due to leaking fuel lines and were completely burnt out. A further 20 tanks had broken down due to mechanical defects ranging from faulty fuel pumps and defective side clutches of the power transmission unit, to the driving wheels lacking the strength to perform, or failures in the control systems of the inlet shutters causing engines to overheat and burst into flames. Most of these defects had been identified much earlier during testing, but Hitler wouldn't wait for these to be rectified and ordered the tanks into battle. This made for a devastating debut for the luckless Panther regiment. It also didn't help that Lauchert's hapless crews lacked the experience to react quickly enough to either fix or avoid some of the problems. What von Strachwitz must have thought when he heard of all these problems can only be imagined. If one believed in omens, it didn't make for a very good start for the supposedly decisive offensive.

It would only get worse, as on the actual day of attack even more Panthers broke down, although many problems were minor and could be fixed by short-term repair. In all 45 Panthers did not take part in the opening attack. In fact both von Knobelsdorff, the Panther's corps commander, and Hoth, their army commander, both thought all along that Hitler's absolute trust in them was misplaced, and that their much-awaited contribution to the outcome would be negligible. As for Guderian, his grim forebodings had been proven correct. Hitler's delays in starting the offensive would bear bitter fruit.

NOTES

1. Helmuth Spaeter (trans. David Johnston), *The History of the Panzerkorps Grossdeutschland Vol 2* (J.J. Fedorowicz Publishing, Canada, 1995).
2. General Heinz Guderian, *Panzer Leader* (Futura Publications 1977), pp.306–307.
3. Some would argue that the Tiger was the best, certainly with justification. In a kill ratio of enemy tanks the Tiger was unsurpassed. At Kursk, Heavy (Tiger) Battalion 503 destroyed 72 Russian tanks for a loss of four Tigers, a kill ratio of 18:1 (see Christopher W. Wilbeck, *Sledgehammer* (The Aberjona Press). It also had a strong presence on the battlefield way out of proportion to its numbers employed. Enemy tanks would often withdraw rather than face them, it being regarded as suicidal to

take them on. Its survivability was superb. Nevertheless it had its drawbacks. Being an extremely high-maintenance vehicle it was never deployed in optimum numbers. Its weight made for problems with deployment, as most bridges couldn't bear their weight. They were also expensive and difficult to build.

4. Valery Zamalin (trans. Stuart Britt), *Demolishing the Myth: The Tank Battle at Prokhorovka, Kursk July 1943* (Helion & Co, UK, 2011).
5. Robert Kirchubel, *Hitler's Panzer Armies on the Eastern Front* (Pen & Sword, UK, 2009).
6. The Panzer Graf's tank figures vary according to the sources. E.W. von Mellenthin who was on von Knobelsdorff's Corps staff listed 180 tanks in his memoirs *Panzer Battles*. Another source cited 300, including 180 Panthers.
7. The Panther debacle and disagreement with Graf von Strachwitz didn't affect Decker's career adversely in any way. He went on to command the 5th Panzer Division and the XXXIX Panzer Corps, as a Lieutenant General. He was awarded the Oak Leaves on 4 February 1944, and the Swords posthumously on 26 April 1945. He committed suicide on 1 April 1945.
8. Hans-Joachim Jung (trans. David Johnston), *The History of Panzerregiment Grossdeutschland* (J.J. Fedorowicz Publishing, Canada, 2000).
9. Ibid.
10. Werner Haupt (trans. Dr Edward Force), *A History of the Panzer Troops 1916–1945* (Schiffer Publishing, USA, 1990). The average number of tanks per panzer division in Army Group South, excluding Grossdeutschland and the Waffen SS divisions, was 68, which amounted to one battalion when each division should have had two battalions.
11. Rudolf Lehman, *The Leibstandarte, Vol III* (J.J. Fedorowicz Publishing Canada, 1990).
12. Jung, *The History of Panzerregiment Grossdeutschland.*

NINETEEN

THE BATTLE OF KURSK

Looking across the silent steppe, with only a lone German reconnaissance aircraft circling lazily like a bird over the Soviet lines, the Panzer Graf prepared his battalion commanders for what was to come before releasing them to address their men, some of whom would be involved in the preliminary attack scheduled for 4 July. Its aim was to secure better observation and start positions against the Belgorod–Gotnya railway line and village of Gertsovka.

The attack was launched at 3:00 p.m., taking the Russians completely by surprise. The grenadiers stormed into the forward trenches clearing the Russians out in a frenzy of sub-machine gun fire, grenades and close-quarter fighting. Prompt Russian artillery fire and minefields halted further progress. A sudden thunderstorm soaked the ground, which, together with the minefields, prevented any of the Graf's tanks taking an effective part. Father Ruzek, a Catholic chaplain, went into the minefield to succour some wounded who were mangled and bleeding from multiple injuries. He calmly walked across to the wounded and, placing one over his shoulders, slowly walked back through the minefield unscathed. He repeated this five times, carrying a badly injured man each time without triggering a mine.[1]

Russian aircraft joined the fray, making repeated strafing runs. German Ju-87 Stukas were also out in force and managed to silence the Soviet artillery with repeated dive-bombing attacks. Their screaming, plummeting dives had a demoralizing psychological effect almost as devastating as their bombs.

Captain Bolk, a battalion commander in the Fusilier Regiment, stepped on a mine and had his leg blown off in a fiery blast. His fusiliers, however, never let up and by nightfall had taken their objectives, although at heavy cost.[2]

The next day, 5 July, dawned with the promise of another hot and sultry day. Von Strachwitz's Panzer Regiment had moved up during the night, moving carefully to avoid any unnecessary noise or show any light, to take up attack positions behind the Fusilier Regiment. The stealthy preparations were unnecessary, however, as the Russians knew the exact time of the attack—a German pioneer, Private Fermello of the 6th Infantry Division, had been captured in a firefight with a Russian patrol in no man's land and had revealed the date and start time of the main attack—3:00 a.m., 5 July.

Grossdeutschland's pioneers went forward to clear the minefields, with the 2nd Pioneer Company clearing some 2,700 mines.[3] However before the start of the attack and the Germans preliminary artillery barrage, the Russians commenced a spoiling bombardment of their own which disrupted the preparations. However, as Soviet Marshal Zhukov admitted later, their bombardment was premature, catching the Germans while still in their trenches and fixed positions, rather than in the open forming up or commencing their attack. The result was only a minor disruption, with far less casualties than would otherwise have been the case.

The Germans commenced their artillery barrage along the entire Kursk front. As Grossdeutschland was the spearhead of the attack, its artillery was reinforced by the guns of the 3rd and 11th Panzer Divisions, making for 120 guns blasting ahead of the division's line of advance. Irrespective of the number of guns involved, a shortage of ammunition meant that the division's regimental artillery commander, Lieutenant Colonel Albrecht, could only provide a barrage of short duration. He had the same aerial photos as von Strachwitz, and like the Panzer Graf could not distinguish the real from the dummy positions, so consequently he had to spread his salvoes rather than concentrate his fire, in order to hit enough of the genuine positions to make a difference.

The rockets fired by the Nebelwerfers arched across the sky and shredded the Soviet trenches, killing the Red infantry by the sheer concussive effects of their blasts. Smoke from the barrage rose into the air, mingling with the smoke of grass fires and burning villages. The noise, as always, was horrendous, with the crashing and howling of guns and the grind of tracked vehicles, along with the roar of low-flying aircraft streaking across the ground in search of targets. Soon the crackling of small-arms fire was added to, then lost in, the infernal din.

The Soviets' first outpost lines vanished in a hail of metal and fire with a few brave survivors continuing to snipe at the German pioneers trying to clear the minefields. The Russians' second line however, was much stronger than the first, consisting of dug-in T-34s, machine-gun nests, and numerous anti-tank guns just waiting to claim their victims.

All too soon the German guns fell silent, with the grenadiers and fusiliers moving out in long files into the open. Von Strachwitz was surprised by the brevity of the barrage and wondered what Hörnlein was doing. Surely the divisional commander had ensured an adequate stock of ammunition? He knew that the limited number of shells expended would have left the Russian defences largely unscathed, with the infantry sure to sustain heavy casualties. Russian artillery fire however, never let up, clearly experiencing no shortage of guns or ammunition. A thunderstorm broke, soaking the hapless grenadiers stoically advancing in the heat of heavy enemy fire.

"Panzers march!" von Strachwitz commanded, and led his tanks forward. His regiment was spearheaded by Captain Wallroth's 1st Tiger Company. They moved carefully through the minefields with the engineers showing the way. Almost instantly they engaged the enemy tanks, guns and infantry who swarmed towards them with foolish courage.

Following behind von Strachwitz's Panzer Regiment were the Panther battalions, which ran into an undetected minefield. Explosions rent the air as vulnerable tank tracks were damaged, bringing the steel monsters to a shuddering halt. Fourteen Panthers were rapidly put out of action, standing stationary in the minefield, perfect targets for Soviet artillery and anti-tank guns. Engineers hastily rushed in to the clear the mines, taking fire from the Russian snipers and artillery as they carried out their painstaking work.

The Graf pushed on towards Cherkasskove, defended by the elite Russian 67th Guards Rifle Division. He was supported by infantry, who stormed through the first Russian line and managed to penetrate deeper into the Russian defences. In his command tank the Graf would have later heard the chilling message: "Panzer 11-01 hit. Battalion Commander seriously wounded."[4] He knew the battalion commander well; he was his wife's brother, Graf Saurma. Captain von Gottberg took over command of the battalion. Graf Saurma was evacuated to the main hospital in Breslau where he later died of his wounds.

The Panther battalions in the meantime had been extricated from the minefield only to get bogged down in some marshy ground, bringing their attack to a standstill once again. When von Strachwitz was informed of this he was furious. Not to have reconnoitred the ground was an act of gross incompetence. The Panther regiment had been badly led from the very beginning, and instead of being the great hope of the offensive was rapidly becoming a liability.

Major Remer's armoured personnel carrier battalion attacked Cherkasskoye after the Graf's panzers and the Fusilier Regiment were halted by minefields—the Panthers were not the only ones to run into those fiery traps. One of von Strachwitz's most experienced officers, Lieutenant Hausherr, was killed along with his gunner when his tank was destroyed by a direct hit. Even with a direct hit some, or even most of the crew of a tank could survive, although often with wounds. A great many were killed or wounded only after they had exited their stricken tank.

The Graf's stationary panzers were subjected to continuous artillery fire while the long-suffering pioneers cleared the minefields. These men performed heroic feats, clearing dangerous, sometimes booby-trapped, mines in the open under artillery and small-arms fire with little in the way of recognition or reward. On this occasion their task took ten long agonizing hours. In the meantime the neighbouring 11th Panzer Division, where von Strachwitz's son was fighting, was making better progress. It would have frustrated von Strachwitz that the elite Grossdeutschland, reinforced as it was with the long-awaited Panthers, was going nowhere, being surpassed by an average panzer division which had started Operation *Citadel* with only 74 tanks. He unfairly blamed both Hörnlein and Lauchert for the failure.

The Grossdeutschland's grenadiers however, were making reasonable headway despite a Russian bomb hitting their regimental headquarters and killing the regimental adjutant, Captain Beckendorff, and two other officers. So congested was this sector of the battlefield that their 2nd Battalion was delayed by a battalion from 11th Panzer which blocked its way.

The Graf's Panzer Regiment resumed its momentum that afternoon, assisting the Grenadiers' 1st Battalion in destroying a Russian artillery battery at Cherkasskoye. Flame tanks were brought forward attacking the Russian defences with streams of fire, destroying gun positions and trench lines. The Graf's tanks were also tasked with supporting Major Remer's 1st Grenadier Battalion in attacking Points 237.7 and 247.1. By nightfall Cherkasskoye was taken after heavy fighting and frightful losses. Russian Boston bombers attacked the division's positions during the night without doing much damage.

That evening the Panzer Graf was still fuming over the day's events, with the mishandling of the Panther regiment uppermost in his mind. He couldn't contain his anger and, going over his commanding officer Hörnlein's head, he went straight to the corps commander, General Knobelsdorff, to complain. Knobelsdorff was surprised to see him, but listened patiently, as he respected the Graf's tactical ability and command experience.[5] Still exasperated, von Strachwitz pointed out that the duality of command—with Decker commanding the Brigade and himself the Grossdeutschland Panzer Regiment—was unworkable, added to which there was Lauchert's command of the Panther Regiment, making the whole command structure unwieldy and cumbersome. He went on to point out the command deficiencies regarding the minefield and swampy terrain, which had all but removed the Panthers from the crucial early stages of the battle.

Von Knobelsdorff could see for himself that drastic change was needed, and being in the middle of operations couldn't prevaricate or worry about niceties of military protocol. He gave the overall panzer command to von Strachwitz, sidelining Decker in the process. Needless to say Decker was singularly unimpressed by this turn of events and justifiably livid over the Panzer Graf's actions. He wrote a letter of complaint to Guderian on 17 July after the offensive was over. In it he said that working with the "Panzer Lion"—another commonly used nickname for von Strachwitz—was unpleasant. He went on to say that von Strachwitz refused to answer radio calls and had acted "independently," which was probably true. Because of von Strachwitz he had been called before von Knobelsdorff to defend his actions while von Strachwitz after taking command had employed "the Panthers outright crazily," which was certainly not true, resulting in "mine damage." Not mincing his words he went on, saying that his 200 Panthers had shrunk to a mere 12 due to "idiotic tactical employment." He continued by saying that "Grossdeutschland was very reasonable" but not its commanding general, which suggests that Hörnlein, unknown to Hyazinth, must have been favouring von Strachwitz over Decker,[6] and very probably did try to have von Strachwitz take command of the Brigade. What Decker didn't say in his letter, however, was that two Panther battalion commanders had been replaced within two days of each other for incompetence, one of whom froze in action due to his inexperience, having to be replaced on the spot by a Captain Gabriel.

Needless to say von Strachwitz's actions did not go over well with General Hörnlein who, despite the soundness of the decision, was justifiably angry that von Strachwitz had ignored the chain of command. It was an inexcusable breach of protocol and discipline, but it was in keeping with Graf von Strachwitz's character, who could not tolerate fools or foolish decisions no matter from whom they came. This grated with Hörnlein, who disliked hot-headed officers.

Hyazinth von Strachwitz's regiment lost 30 tanks in the day's fighting, the greatest loss he had sustained in a single day to that point. Mercifully, most were disabled due to track and other minor damage from mines and could be brought back into action relatively quickly. Most of the serious losses and damage had been caused by the anti-tank guns, which generally applied to all the panzer divisions fighting at Kursk. The III Panzer Corps for instance—which had the 6th, 7th and 19th Panzer Divisions—lost 60% of its tanks to anti-tank guns between 9 and 12 July. Only 5% were lost to mines.[7] Most tankers hated these stealthy killers and feared them more than the enemy tanks. They could often spot a T-34 first, but the anti-tank gun usually only announced its presence with the first shot, and if it was a hit, it would often prove fatal to the tank and some of the crew. The Panther Regiment lost 18 of its tanks for the destruction of six Soviet tanks, three heavy anti-tank guns and one close-support aircraft shot down. The Graf's order of battle showed four Panzer IIs, 12 Panzer IIIs, 51 Panzer IVs, 12 flame tanks and only three Tigers available for action after a hard day's fighting.[8]

The exhausted, hard-working engineers were again sent out during the night to continue clearing the minefields. The next morning dawned warm and sultry. A smoky haze shrouded the battlefield from grass fires and burnt-out tanks. Now in sole command of the Brigade, including what remained of the Panthers, von Strachwitz was resolved to show just how much better he could do.

The attack on the Soviet second defence line resumed at first light after a 90-minute artillery barrage. The Graf's panzers spearheaded the attack, supported by Remer's battalion. The second line was even stronger than the first, with deep bunkers, 50 dug-in T-34s, more minefields, heavy machine guns, flamethrowers and 30–40 anti-tank guns, all of which were well camouflaged.[9] The infantry stormed forward to clear the way for the Graf's tanks and suffered appalling losses from the heavy Russian defensive fire. It took an entire day's intensive fighting by the Graf's tanks and Remer's armoured infantry to take Hill 247.2 near Dubrova. Too many good men of both sides died on this small hill. Having seized the hill, the tanks and grenadiers set up an all-round defence for the night.

The Grenadiers' 2nd Battalion closed up during the night. Von Strachwitz planned to push his panzers through the following day to an open battlefield where he would be free to manoeuvre. He called up the repair unit to fix the numerous tanks suffering track damage, rendering them fit to fight the following day. Russian bombers harassed his men during the evening, having made several appearances during the day whenever German fighters were absent.

Elsewhere, in contrast to von Strachwitz's and the army's stalled attack, the Leibstandarte SS Adolf Hitler Division had made good progress, spearing 32 kilometres through the Soviet defences and tearing a deep gap in the Soviet 6th Guards Army. A Leibstandarte tank crewman described the action:

> On separate slopes some 1,000 metres apart the forces faced each other like figures on a chess board.... All the Tigers fired. The combat escalated into an ecstasy of roaring engines.... They rolled ahead a few metres, pulled left, pulled right, manoeuvred to escape the enemy crosshairs and bring the enemy into their own fire. We counted the torches of the enemy tanks which would never again fire on German soldiers. After one hour 12 T-34s were in flames. The other 30 curved wildly back and forth firing as rapidly as their barrels would deliver. They aimed well but our armour was very strong. We no longer twitched when a steely finger knocked on our walls. We wiped the flakes of interior paint from our faces, loaded again, aimed, fired.[10]

The Tiger's armour, even if not sloped, was so thick that at Kursk two Grossdeutschland Tigers each sustained 10 hits from 7.62mm anti-tank guns without being knocked out.[11]

The next day, 7 July, was another of unremitting attack. However the Graf was now finding the Soviet armour more numerous and aggressive. The reason, although unknown to him, was that the Luftwaffe had withdrawn a significant number of ground attack units to support General Model's Ninth Army on the northern pincer. Model's attack had ground to a halt after penetrating barely nine kilometres. Model's armoured fighting vehicle of great expectation had been the super-heavy Ferdinand, or Elefant, a large turretless, but enclosed self-propelled gun on a Porsche Tiger tank prototype body mounting an 88mm gun. These 73-ton behemoths were slow, unwieldy and cumbersome, making them easy targets for T-34s and anti-tank guns, and as they were without machine guns, they were even vulnerable to Russian infantry. They failed to have any impact on the fighting.

As a result of the switch to the north, the Luftwaffe lost air supremacy over Kursk and only achieved air superiority over critical local sectors where the support was provided. For instance on day one, the Luftwaffe flew 1,958 sorties while on day two only 899 sorties. The Reds on the other hand flew 1,632 sorties on the second day. The Germans lost 100 aircraft during those first two days, but the Russian losses were much higher. On 5 July, before the German assault commenced, the Russians launched a pre-emptive bomber strike against the packed German airfields. It was a bold move but the German Freya radars spotted them well beforehand and the German Jagdfleigers (flying hunters) scrambled to meet them. Messerschmidts and Focke-Wulf 190s tore into the bomber streams, tearing them to pieces. The Russians stoically droned on holding formation as best they could while the Germans blasted them out of the sky one by one. Over 120 Russian aircraft were destroyed for only 26 German fighters shot down. Being over their own lines, the Germans who baled out or crashlanded returned to fly again, while any surviving Russians went into captivity. Very little damage was sustained by the targeted airfields. Elsewhere on the Kursk front the German fighters shot down 200 Russian aircraft on the first day, knocking out any aggression from the survivors. The Russians then took on a largely defensive stance against the German fighters, making their presence felt only when the Germans were absent.[12] Nevertheless vicious dog-fights still took place all over the sky as the German Jagdfleigers sought out their Soviet counterparts. This of course gave the German ground-attack planes, Stukas and Focke-Wulfs, plenty of opportunities, and they flew continuous sorties, as Herman Buchner, a Focke-Wulf ground-attack pilot who fought at Kursk and Orel, pointed out in his memoir:

> The battle for Orel and Kursk raged to a ferocious climax. . . . Our Russian opponents were now not only greater in number, but were also using much better equipment and were tactically more aware. As always I was on the go from early morning until late evening when with daylight almost gone, I would grab a late night meal and collapse onto my bed, totally exhausted. The weather was glorious almost every day so there was no respite to the intensity of operations, which in addition to taking its toll on the exhausted pilots, put enormous pressure on the mechanics and armourers. . . . As the daily grind of mission after mission continued . . . it was only the exceptional trips that we remembered. One such mission was when we

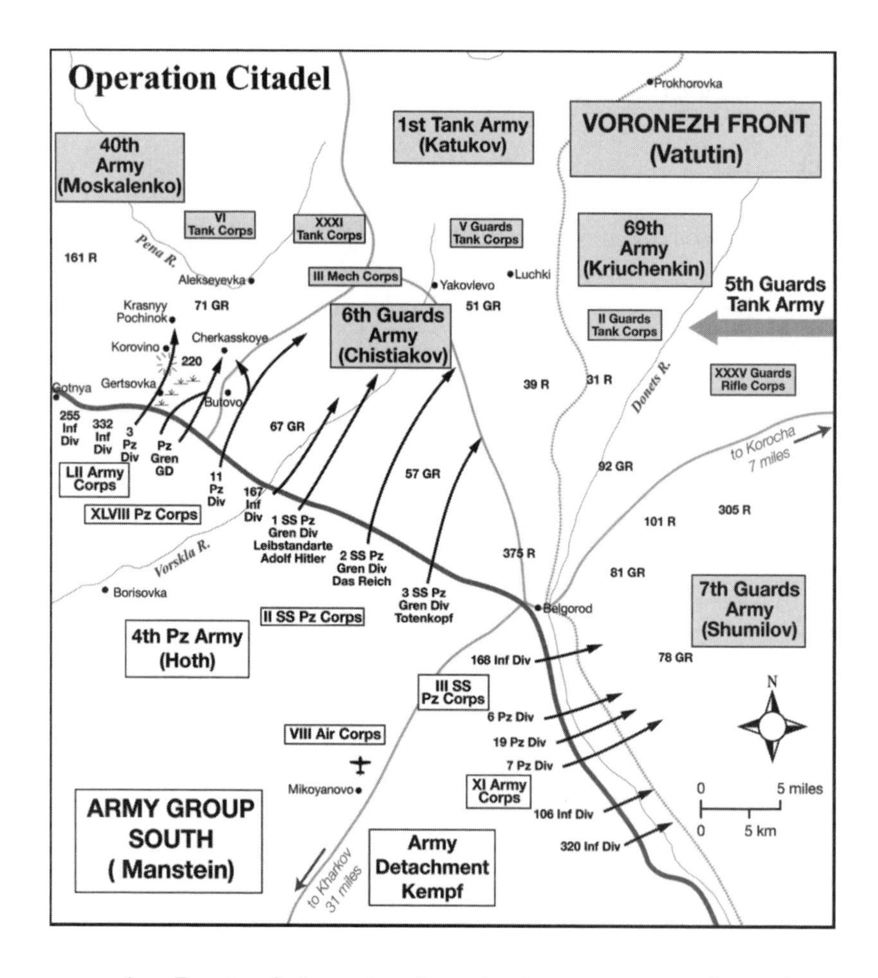

caught a Russian fuel supply column in the open as it tried to make its way to re-supply the tank units in the south. There were between ten and fourteen vehicles in the convoy, and electing to attack my Rotte leader took the lead vehicle and I set about the rearmost vehicle immediately setting it afire with my guns. The column was brought to an immediate stand still . . . The target shooting began in earnest with us attacking entirely at will. . . . The game lasted a quarter of an hour until all the vehicles were burning brightly with the dense smoke climbing to some 500 or 600 metres into the air.[13]

As 7 July dawned, the Grenadiers' 2nd Battalion with Panther support attacked the village of Dubrova, with the Panthers getting caught in another minefield. By this time the Panther crews should have been reading mine-clearing manuals and becoming experts in this field. The Panzer Graf sent in his 2nd Panzer Battalion to save the situation, which they proceeded to do by helping the grenadiers take Dubrova.[14] The Russians poured concentrated artillery fire on the Germans, causing considerable casualties. A force of T-34s appeared, quickly launching an attack on Von Strachwitz's 1st Battalion, but were easily repulsed with the Graf destroying several Russian tanks. Unfortunately his adjutant, Captain von Seydlitz, suffered a serious stomach wound and had to be evacuated immediately. Russian tanks with supporting infantry were crowding around and cutting off the evacuation route. Graf von Strachwitz didn't hesitate. He launched his tank amongst them, firing rapidly left and right, scattering the Russian infantry with his machine-gun fire and swiftly moving tracks. He cleared a path for the panzer carrying his wounded aide, then swung around to block the Soviet pursuit. His gunner destroyed two T-34s in quick succession but a third slammed a shell into his tank disabling it. Another Panzer IV despatched the Russian tank as von Strachwitz abandoned his stricken tank to take over one nearby to resume his command. This meant running across open ground swept by fire with Red infantry still scattered around firing at anything that remotely looked German. Map case and pistol in hand he dashed across. A machine gun chattered behind him but it was his former crew providing him with covering fire from their machine pistols. Bullets and shrapnel whizzed over his head as he clambered into his replacement tank where eager hands helped him inside. Unfortunately the rescue effort was all in vain as von Seydlitz died before he could reach medical assistance.

Heavy fighting took place around the small but heavily fortified town of Sirtsevo. In a combined tank and infantry assault the defences near the town were taken but only after heavy fighting, often at close quarters, the Germans having to clear the Russians out with bayonets, knives, hand grenades and entrenching tools as well as with rifles and machine-guns. No quarter was asked or given. Von Strachwitz lost his only operational Tiger in the fighting. At the same time Hill 230.1 was captured, again after savage fighting, with the Russians desperately resisting the Fusilier and Reconnaissance Battalions, who only captured it with assault-gun support.

The air war had a life of its own and continued to rage overhead. Flying in his Me-109 with its bleeding heart personal insignia, was Erich "Bubi" Hartmann who downed seven Soviet aircraft during the day. His score during the war eventually reached 352, making him the world's leading air ace with a total never likely to be surpassed. He also joined Graf von Strachwitz in the small elite band of recipients of the Knight's Cross with Diamonds.[15]

Stukas provided close air support, swooping down to dive-bomb Russian positions immediately in front of the Panzer Graf's tanks. They came in waves, hurtling down to take out artillery batteries and where known, forward observer positions. Their howling sirens and near-vertical dives, with bombs being released very close to the ground, often broke the Russians' morale so that they offered little or no resistance to the attacking Germans.

On the left of von Knobelsdorff's XLVIII Panzer Corps, Hausser's Waffen SS Panzer Corps continued to make good progress, surpassing their army neighbours' penetrations. Unlike the army units, who advanced on a broad front, the SS made narrower penetrations on a separate divisional basis; still, outpacing the army was a source of satisfaction for the SS troops, who with the exception of Grossdeutschland considered themselves superior to the army panzer divisions. As well they might with double the tank strength of the army panzer divisions, three battalions of infantry to the army's two in the panzergrenadier regiment, and greater allocations of artillery and other equipment.

A tank driver of the 7th Company of Leibstandarte's Panzer Regiment describes his platoon's mission to bail out Jochen Peiper from a hot spot at Kursk:

> "Driver, march!" was his order to me. In moments the smoke was closing in around us. I had to drive slowly so as not to run into things. The image before my window were like pictures from a silent movie: wrecks, flames, ghostly figures with Russian helmets. Shell after shell. Suddenly a heavy hit somewhere. . . . Weiser radioed several times asking for more covering fire and ordered other vehicles to stay back. He reported shells were hitting and that he would go on alone with his panzer. . . . We were riding right toward the enemy, in the middle of the enemy. . . . Suddenly the alarmed cry: T-34 at two o'clock. Load a tank shell! Fire! The gunner reports the turret was stuck. It was really becoming serious. "Driver, aim with the panzer, turn right!" came the order. I moved up, drove in their rear, really needing to shift gear but knowing I didn't have time. Turned the panzer around. Suddenly an explosion, then silence! One look at the tachometer told me the motor wasn't running. Was it just stalled or was it hit? . . . I asked "What should I do?" The radio operator pulled

> down my earphones and shouted "The gunner is dead. On board communications are dead" I yelled back, "Tell the loader to ask what I should do?" The answer came. "The commander is dead" . . . In the seconds which had passed since the shell hit our gunner's side I had seen Russians storming towards us. I drove on, and suddenly saw our opponent, the T-34, at most one hundred metres away. . . . I turned around ninety degrees and there was an explosion. I was probably only a fraction of a second faster than he. My sixth sense steered me behind a wreck which served as a shield from him. . . . The glass of my window was too shattered to see out of. I drove with my head out of the hatch. Hauptsturmführer Tiemann motioned me to drive on; Stein was covering me with his gun at six o'clock. . . . Someone later counted the hits on my panzer. . . . They counted seventeen infantry hits and three from the tanks.[16]

At nightfall, von Strachwitz's panzers, along with the panzer grenadiers, set up all-round defensive positions. He remained dissatisfied with the day's fighting, as the major breakthrough had still not occurred and remained as elusive as ever. His regiment had knocked out 62 Soviet tanks, destroyed 55 guns and an Illyushin Il-2 ground-attack plane. But by now he only had 23 Panzer IVs, 20 Panthers, six Panzer IIIs, and four flame tanks. It was a huge diminution of strength from the more than 360 tanks Grossdeutschland had started with, a clear result of the battle of attrition being waged, the type of battle which von Strachwitz had so desperately wished to avoid. The neighbouring divisions had not done any better. The 3rd Panzer had made little headway while 11th Panzer had reached a line equal to Grossdeutchland's advanced outposts. These forward elements were halted by Soviet flanking fire because of 3rd Panzer's inability to keep up, which, given its initial tank strength, was not surprising.

After routine maintenance and restocking of fuel and ammunition, the tank crews collapsed into a coma-like sleep from sheer exhaustion, so that officers and NCOs had to be particularly vigilant to ensure sentries were actually sent out and remained awake. Many tank crews were taking methamphetamine (Pervitin) to stop from collapsing into a sleep of utter exhaustion during the fighting.

Thursday 8 July dawned with a promise of more of the same—heat, death, relentless attacks, and determined defence with no end in sight. Von Strachwitz was feeling bitter and frustrated. No matter how many T-34s remained brewed up on the battlefield, trench lines taken, guns destroyed, ever more seemed to spring from the ground in a seemingly endless procession. He went over his plans for the assault on Sirtsevo. Welcome reinforcements had arrived in the shape of some of his Tigers returning from the repair company, along with some more Panzer IVs. He despatched a screening force under Lieutenant Hausherr, which had no sooner taken up blocking positions when it was attacked by a large force of 40 T-34s. Not content to wait for von Strachwitz to attack, they launched a spoiling attack of their own. Very quickly Hausherr's panzers were overwhelmed with his four tanks destroyed and the young lieutenant killed.

The Soviets swept on to Point 230.1, where von Strachwitz quickly deployed his force to meet them. His Tigers went forward, their powerful guns smashing the Reds before they could get within range to retaliate. A brief but intense firefight quickly developed where the superior German gunnery and formidable Tiger won the fray. Ten T-34s were left burning in almost as many minutes. The remainder withdrew in some disorder. Stukas, which had been hovering over the battlefield like birds of prey, now seized their chance, swooping down onto the fleeing Russian tanks and blowing many of them up. Not all the Stukas escaped unscathed. Above Sirtsevo, Stuka *experten* Captain Karl Fitzer—a Knight's Cross wearer with 600 missions to his credit—was killed when his plane was blown apart in the air.

Von Strachwitz supported Remer's 1st Grenadier Battalion in the attack on Sirtsevo. German fighters, Focke-Wulf 190 ground-attack planes and Stukas provided air support. They came in waves of up to 50 aircraft in a show of aerial strength the Panzer Graf was personally never to see again. German fighter ace Günter Rall shot down four Russian aircraft in the swirling combat above the town, adding to a score that would eventually reach 275 in over 700 missions, earning him the Knight's Cross with Oak Leaves and Swords. Also in the sky was Erich Hartmann who shot down two more Russians—including the 22-victory Russian ace Major Tokarev—which brought his kills to 275.[17]

Just after midday Remer's grenadiers succeeded in seizing the town, a feat which would not have been possible without von Strachwitz's panzers and reinforcements from the 11th Panzer Division, together with the much-needed Luftwaffe support. The Panzer Graf then moved on towards Verkhnopenye, coming under heavy fire from dug-in T-34s which had to be taken out one by one. This was a difficult task as only their turrets were above ground and these were well camouflaged. Eventually 11 were destroyed.

At the same time, Grossdeutschland's Reconnaissance Battalion under Major Wätjen, supported by Peter Frantz's Assault Gun Battalion came under attack just north of Gremuchiy—40 T-34s of the Soviet VI Tank Corps attacked them in successive waves. The infantry took up defensive positions while Frantz sallied out to meet the Russians. He placed his guns in flanking ambush positions along a reverse slope and waited for the Russians to close in. Each platoon began blasting the Russians as they moved past in turn. Sergeant Senkhiel's guns took out the first four. More and more T-34s perished as their advance continued. Finally, having had enough, they withdrew to regroup, then attacked again in the same manner, with exactly the same formation. This was a result of their operating procedure, which stressed that they should follow the same orders precisely until they were successful or the orders were changed. Personal initiative was not only discouraged but forbidden without approval from a higher authority. Basically the officer issuing the orders was held personally responsible and was the only one allowed to alter them without permission. Fear of failure and the dreaded penal battalion kept everyone obedient to the original orders. After several hours 35 Russian tanks remained burning or disabled in the killing ground. The assault guns also destroyed 18 anti-tank guns that had followed in support. This now cleared the road to the town of Verkhnopenye, which straggled along both sides of the River Pena, and was heavily fortified, as was every town and village in the area.

Von Strachwitz took his 1st Battalion, along with his surviving Panthers and the 2nd Grenadier Battalion, to Point 230.1. There they clashed with the Russian 200th Tank Brigade, near Verkhnopenye. As he was grossly outnumbered, von Strachwitz called for his 2nd Battalion at Sirtsevo to reinforce him. He planned to use the hammer and anvil tactic, pinning down the Soviets frontally while his 2nd Battalion took them in the rear. The Panzer Graf had to hold out until his 2nd Battalion arrived. The Panthers finally showed what they could do, their sloped armour and 75mm high-velocity guns coming into their own against the massed T-34s, and he was once again helped by Stukas who continuously dived onto the Russian tanks, blowing them to pieces with well-placed bombs. His 2nd Battalion finally arrived, destroying five T-34s from the rear, forcing the remainder to withdraw in surprise from the attack. Two German tanks were knocked out, with a third damaged but capable of returning to the maintenance facility on its own. Soviet Sturmovik ground-attack planes made several strafing runs against Remer's Battalion with three shot down by the self-propelled light anti-aircraft guns he had attached to his unit, for the price of one gun damaged. It was an excellent result given that the Sturmoviks were armoured and difficult to bring down.

Elsewhere the SS Panzer Corps continued to advance steadily. In three days of heavy fighting it claimed 290 Russian tanks destroyed, which was a testimony to their panzers' and grenadiers' fighting ability. The Russians, however, remained undeterred, despite their massive casualties. They were stoically determined to fight to the end regardless of the cost, as Vasily Grossman, the Soviet writer present at Kursk records:

> A gun-layer fired point-blank at a Tiger with a 45mm gun. The shells bounced off it. The gun layer lost his head and threw himself at the Tiger.
>
> A lieutenant wounded in the leg, with a hand torn off, was commanding a battery attacked by tanks. After the enemy attack had been halted he shot himself because he didn't want to live as a cripple.[18]

The young lieutenant clearly understood the nature of the regime he served as after the war crippled veterans were treated abominably. Grossman continues:

> At dawn German tanks started to attack. . . . Battery commander Ketselman was wounded. He was dying in a puddle of black blood; the first artillery piece was broken. A direct hit had torn off an arm and the head of a gun layer. Senior Corporal Melekhin, the gun commander . . . was lying on the ground with heavy shell shock, looking at the cannon, his stare heavy and murky . . .
>
> Only the ammunition bearer, Dawydov, was still on his feet. And the Germans had already come very close. They were seizing the barrels as the artillerists say. Then the commander of the neighbouring gun, Mikhail Vasiliey, took control. And he ordered them to open fire at the German infantry with canister. Then having run out of anti-personnel rounds, they began to fire at the German submachine gunners at point-blank range with armour-piercing shells. That was a terrible sight.[19]

Graf von Strachwitz's regiment had now been whittled down to a mere nine operational tanks and was desperately short of ammunition. Although he was accustomed to operating with just a few tanks, he had always operated from a much larger base, and had never before been reduced to such low numbers. It was very worrying, given that the Soviet defences were still immensely strong. However, that evening saw more tanks return from the workshops, which gave his numbers a much-needed boost.

At the tip of Grossdeutschland's spearhead, von Strachwitz was now only 11 kilometres from the division's major objective of Oboyan. To seize this objective the Graf now had 24 Panzer IVs, 11 Panthers, and eight Tigers, an improvement on the previous day but by no means a strong force.[20]

The following day, 9 July, was another clear day, giving plenty of scope for the opposing air forces to intervene in the grinding battles below. Von Strachwitz's first objective was Point 240.4. A Nebelwerfer regiment launched a continuous stream of rockets onto the Russian positions, creating a huge cloud of smoke and dust in the distance beneath which untold Russians were maimed or killed in the maelstrom of explosions. Flanking fire continued to rake Grossdeutschland as the badly depleted 3rd Panzer Division continued to lag behind, leaving Grossdeutschland's flank exposed.

Behind the Graf, the Fusilier Regiment advanced past Verkhnopenye but was halted by Soviet tanks and anti-tank guns. Watjen's Reconnaissance Battalion with Frantz's assault guns moved along the road to Oboyan. Ahead of them Stukas pounded Russian tank assembly areas.

Von Strachwitz, along with the 1st and 2nd Battalions of the Grenadier Regiment, stormed into the attack on Verkhnopenye. Entire squadrons of Stukas swooped into the attack in waves of screaming destruction on the Russian lines. Russian tanks streamed out to meet Grossdeutschland's panzers and battle commenced at the 3,000-metre range, with the Stukas streaking down to support the panzers. Smoke, dust and flames obscured the battlefield while the action turned into a grinding slugging match between the tanks. Russian anti-tank guns also made their presence felt, with one hitting the turret of 6th Company's Lieutenant Authenried, killing him instantly. Once again the Stukas had an impact, among them that flown by the famous *experten* Hans Ulrich Rudel. He had been experimenting with a cannon-mounted tank-busting Stuka in the Crimea and had it flown over to take part in Operation *Citadel* where it made its destructive debut. He described it in his memoir:

> In the first attack four tanks explode under the hammer blows of my cannons; by the evening the total rises to twelve. We are all seized with a kind of passion for the chase, from the glorious feeling of hav-

> ing saved much German bloodshed with every tank destroyed. . . .
> Sometimes we dive onto the steel monsters from behind sometimes from the side. . . . We always to try to hit the tank in one of its most vulnerable places.[21]

The satisfaction that came from saving German lives was a theme frequently repeated by the ground-attack pilots and was a strong motivating factor. Rudel's aggressive attitude also epitomises that of the Jagdfleigers, the fighter pilots. They went into combat avid for kills, keen to add to their scores, knowing they would be amply rewarded. Survival wasn't sufficient for them. To make kills was everything. They were ambitious, many actively seeking the Knight's Cross, which required a set number of kills, eventually 100 for the Eastern Front. A pilot seeking combat and kills was said to have a "throat ache," which could only be assuaged by the Knight's Cross. German tankers had a similar attitude, wanting to kill Russian tanks and paint kill rings on their barrels and maybe get the Knight's Cross. This hunting/kill attitude had a similar result, with the emergence of notable tank aces, many having 100 kills or more. For Hyazinth von Strachwitz, his personal kills were a by-product of his battle success and leadership and not a motivating factor per se. Nevertheless he was one of the few tankers to wear the Gold Panzer Assault Badge for 100 engagements, so he easily accumulated over 100 Soviet tanks destroyed.

The German fighter ace Günther Rall continued his run of success, shooting down eight Russian aircraft before being shot down himself and having to be rescued by a German panzerjäger (self-propelled tank hunter) in no man's land. Rudel, seeing the success of his Stuka cannon, arranged for his squadron to be similarly equipped and so his specialized tank-attack unit was born. One of his air crew, Sergeant Hans Krohn, was involved in the fighting at Kursk and later Orel and describes the methods they used:

> Our cannon planes took a terrible toll on the Russian armour. We attacked at very low altitude—I often feared that we were going to hit a ground obstacle with our landing gear—and my pilot [the Stuka had a two man crew, and he was the rear gunner] opened fire at the tanks at a distance of fifty metres. That gave us very little margin to pull up and get away before the tank exploded. . . . Most of our attacks were made against the side of the tanks, in that way they offered the largest targets. I know that some pilots attacked from

behind because that was where the armour was weakest but that also meant that the target was so small that it was difficult to hit.[22]

The continual attacks proved too much for the Soviets, who withdrew, but not before destroying three of the Graf's panzers. Captain von Wietersheim led his tank company to the village of Novosiovka, taking the high ground and opening the way for the Fusilier Regiment to continue the advance to a road fork at Point 244.8 on the way to Oboyan. The Panzer Graf then received new orders to make a 90-degree turn, leaving the Oboyan road to assist the 3rd Panzer Division which was equipped with mainly obsolete Panzer IIIs and was making little headway against strong Russian resistance. His tanks encountered a screening force of T-34s along the way near Point 1.3 near Verkhnopenye and were forced to halt for the night in order to refuel and rearm. The Reconnaissance Battalion which had been following him halted at Point 251.4. This movement to rescue 3rd Panzer Division, which reached Point 244.8, was the furthest the Grossdeutschland Division would penetrate the Soviet lines during Operation *Citadel*—a disappointing result for all concerned.

Early in the morning of 10 July von Strachwitz was conducting an armed reconnaissance when he spotted Russian tanks in a small valley. Although heavily outnumbered, his first instinct was to attack, which he did at 4:00 a.m. taking the enemy by surprise. In a matter of minutes rapid accurate German gunfire began brewing up the T-34s. Explosions rent the air as tank after tank went up in flames. However their numbers were so large that the Russians were undeterred, merely shrugging the losses off and hitting back, destroying several Panzer IVs including two command tanks. Going to the assistance of one of the command tanks von Strachwitz interposed himself between the Panzer IV and the Russians, destroying a T-34 in short order. The Russians were everywhere, providing a plethora of targets, with the Graf concentrating hard to ensure that his gunner took out the ones who posed the greatest threat. In the heat of the battle his awareness of the internal machinations of his tank failed him and he was hit hard in the shoulder by the recoil of his gun. The blow was so serious that his crew sent out a distress call and promptly withdrew to seek medical attention for their regimental commander. Von Strachwitz promptly radioed for von Wietersheim to take over command while his tank sped back to safety and the medical clearing station where his wound received immediate attention. Its severity meant that he was evacuated, eventually reaching the hospital in Breslau. He was bitterly disappointed at leaving the battle unfinished. Kursk was a personal failure for him. It was not the type of battle where he could excel; his talents lay in the fast-ranging battles of manoeuvre where surprise, speed, tactical skill, imagination and the clever use of ground made all the difference. All the more galling was that the honour of fighting in the greatest tank battle of the war at Prokhorovka was to go to the Waffen SS.

Soon after the Graf's removal, the Russians withdrew to regroup, while von Weitershem resumed the advance towards Hill 243.0, but heavy flanking fire forced him to halt. He was then ordered to take the crossroads near Point 258.5 with assistance provided by the fusiliers, but once again he was brought to a halt from glancing fire as the neighbouring division was still lagging behind. Russian tanks mounted several counterattacks but didn't pursue them too aggressively. A greater problem came from the concealed anti-tank guns, which were difficult to detect even after they had fired. Von Wietersheim had to call on a Nebelwerfer battery to destroy a nest of these guns which were proving difficult to eliminate.[23]

On the Oboyan road the Fusilier Regiment captured Hill 244.8, while east of the road 11th Panzer took a point nearby with Stuka support. For its part 3rd Panzer took the commanding heights of Berezovka, capturing some 2,000 Russians in the process.[24] As good as these advances were, they were not spectacular and the major breakthrough remained as elusive as ever.

To the north, General Model's Ninth Army was going nowhere. His Army was well below the strength of Hoth's, and the major success was always expected to come from the south, but he did not perform as well as had been expected.

On von Wietersheim's right flank Watzen's Reconnaissance Battalion with Frantz's assault guns were attacked by 15 T-34s emerging from a cornfield. In a brisk firefight the assault guns drove them off destroying several in the process.[25] The strong Soviet defences forced Hörnlein to halt the attack and form a defensive line, which the Russians quickly tested with several battalion-sized attacks supported by tanks against the Grenadier Regiment.

The massive casualties the Reds had suffered forced them to release seven tank corps from their strategic reserve. That they had these to utilize while leaving strong forces still available for a major counterstroke boded ill for the Germans' chances of success.

That same day, 11 July, the Soviet Bryansk Front[26] northeast of Kursk launched a major offensive against Model's Ninth Army which ended his participation in Operation *Citadel* forcing him as it did on to the defensive.

The Grossdeutschland Panzer Regiment was meantime in such a perilous state that its two battalions had to be disbanded and combined into a combat group comprising two companies.[27] Nevertheless it resumed its advance, smashing Russian defensive positions despite ferocious resistance and causing the survivors to run, abandoning artillery pieces and anti-tank guns. The division's Panthers retook Hill 258.5, which had been lost earlier, and were involved in heavy fighting in the Tolstoi area before being forced to withdraw due to lack of infantry support. The division noticed the large quantities of American equipment, especially trucks, and captured a supply dump of American rations. No doubt they enjoyed the corned meat as a welcome change from army bread, soup and sausage.

12 July saw the epic tank battle between the German IInd SS Panzer Corps and the Russian 5th Guards Tank Army at Prokhorovka. A major battle of its own within the broader battle for Kursk, it was a localised tactical victory for the Germans, with between 300 and 400 wrecked Russian tanks littering the battlefield. Prokhorovka gets caught up in the general German defeat that Kursk clearly was, but it must be remembered that Operation *Citadel* was a wide-ranging offensive, with various battles contained in its ambit. Prokhorovka was just one of these battles, albeit the most important one, and given the scale of tank forces employed it is the most written about. The Germans won at Prokhorovka but failed in their offensive. It is noteworthy because afterwards the Germans, having squandered their tank reserves, lacked the resources to mount another major offensive, and apart from local counterattacks and minor offensives such as in Hungary in 1944, would remain on the defensive in the east. If the Russians had had too many "victories" like that which they claimed at Prokhorovka, they would have lost the war, for the losses they sustained were massive. SS General Paul Hausser was so incredulous at his division's tank-kill claims that he actually walked over the battlefield numbering the wrecked Russian tanks with a piece of chalk. Despite Russian propaganda claiming Prokhorovka as a victory, Stalin was so alarmed by the losses that he wanted General Rotmistrov court-martialled, hardly the reward for a victorious general. Clearly Stalin regarded Prokhorovka a defeat.

On 13 July Hitler called von Manstein and von Kluge to his headquarters, telling them that because of the Allied invasion of Sicily he was cancelling Operation *Citadel*. Von Manstein objected, telling his Führer he wished to continue. Von Kluge for his part told Hitler that the Russians had launched an attack against the German Orel salient, which had Model fighting for his life and screaming for reinforcements. The Soviets had been waiting all along to take out the bulge in their line and were simply waiting for the Germans to burn themselves out at Kursk. It was a testimony to the huge resources they still had that they were able to attack there, as well as mount a counteroffensive on the Kursk front, which eventually took back all the Germans' gains in five days on 23 July.

Despite Hitler calling the offensive off, fighting still continued. Grossdeutschland mounted an attack on 14 July along with the 332nd Infantry Division in the Dogij forest, wiping out a female anti-tank brigade stationed there. The attack continued on to take Hill 240.2 with solid Stuka support. The attack had to be abandoned for lack of ammunition, a problem which would increasingly affect the Germans as the war continued. The following day the 7th Company of the 2nd Panzer Battalion under Captain Lex destroyed 16 T-34s among a far superior Russian force. His bravery and leadership earned him the Knight's Cross. The Panzer Regiment now had 44 Panzer IVs and three Panzer IIIs as total write-offs since the attack began on 5 July. This shows the importance of the repair companies to the division and the vital importance of holding possession of the battlefield so that damaged tanks could be recovered, as happened at Prokhorovka.

On 18 July von Lauchert's Panther Regiment was removed from Grossdeutschland's order of battle and directly subordinated to the XLVIII Panzer Corps. Between 5 and 14 July, the Regiment had destroyed 263 Russian tanks, 144 anti-tank guns, 22 artillery pieces, 60 trucks and various other pieces of equipment, and despite its poor start had more than redeemed itself. Some but by no means all of their achievement could be attributable to the leadership of Graf von Strachwitz. On that same day the Grossdeutschland received orders for deployment elsewhere and it returned to Tomarovka. Operation *Citadel* was over, not as a massive defeat, but as a costly failure.

The Russians could, and did, claim a victory. It wasn't, however, the decisive triumph they claimed it to be. The Russians called it decisive to magnify a victory which barely exceeded a stalemate, while Guderian called it decisive because it was for him—he had lost his panzer reserve. The fact remains that no matter what the Germans did from this point, the war was lost due to the lack of manpower, fuel, transport, ammunition and resources. Blitzkrieg—the short lightning war they had planned—had been their only hope.

If they had not undertaken Operation *Citadel*, then what? The accumulated resources would have been used for a counteroffensive as Manstein wanted and had achieved at Kharkov. It would have meant fewer German casualties, heavier Russian ones, and perhaps checked the Russians for a time. However the Russians would have attacked again, elsewhere or simultaneously in several places, and the Germans would have been back in the same situation, and on the long bitter road of retreat. The truth was that the Germans only had sufficient resources for one big and one medium-size offensive, and whether used at Kursk, the Ardennes or elsewhere, the result would have been the same. It is also probable that Hitler wouldn't have allowed Manstein his counter-blow, and the armour resources would have been merely frittered away fighting numerous breakthroughs in attempting to carry out Hitler's "no retreat" orders. The likelihood of the tanks being kept to counter the Allied invasion as Guderian wanted would have remained slim, as too many crises would have developed in the east not to use up the armour.

Did the constant delays in launching *Citadel* make a difference? Certainly, as von Manstein maintains, had the attack been launched in April it would have stood a greater chance of success with fewer German losses. However, given the Russians' overpowering resources they would still have halted the Germans, though they might have needed a little longer, or they would have launched the attack against Model at Orel earlier, creating a crisis which would have halted *Citadel* in any event.

As usual, casualty figures vary depending on the sources or calculations used. Steven Newton in his book *Kursk, the German View* holds an interesting discussion on this topic, as do Glantz and House in *The Battle of Kursk*. German dead, wounded and missing were probably 49,822 while Russian dead, wounded and missing possibly exceeded 177,847. The Germans lost 323 armoured fighting vehicles, with 1,612 damaged, most of them repairable; the Soviets lost 1,614 tanks with over 1,000 damaged.[28] Aircraft losses on the southern flank were 97 German aircraft to the Russians' 707. Between 5 and 11 July on the northern flank, the Germans lost 57 aircraft and the Soviets 430. The huge imbalance was largely due to the greater experience and aggression of the German pilots. The Germans also used self-propelled light anti-aircraft guns to accompany their tanks and infantry in the front lines, something that the Russians did not do. The German Stuka squadrons lost eight of their best pilots—all Knight's Cross holders—in the fighting, sounding the death knell for the Stukas as a major combatant for the remainder of the war, steadily but quickly replaced by the Focke Wulf 190 in the ground-attack role.[29]

Overall for the Soviets, Kursk was a defensive, pyrrhic victory at best, and Prokhorovka a localised tactical defeat. Both sides fought with raw, stubborn courage, and the Soviet soldier would never again be underestimated, despite the fact that the Germans left the battlefield still convinced of their superiority on a personal level. Their advance against massive and impossible odds was, as Colonel T.N. Dupuy observed in his book *A Genius For War*, an "incredible accomplishment" and one which should not be overlooked in the euphoria of the Soviet victory.[30]

NOTES

1. Will Fowler, *Kursk: The Vital 24 Hours* (Amber Books, UK, 2005).
2. Helmuth Spaeter (Trans David Johnston), *The History of the Panzerkorps Grossdeutschland, Vol 2* (J.J. Fedorowicz Publishing, Canada, 1995).
3. Ibid.
4. Paul Carrell, *Hitler's War on Russia: Scorched Earth* (Corgi Books, UK, 1971).
5. Hans-Joachim Jung (trans. David Johnston), *The History of Panzerregiment Grossdeutschland* (J.J. Fedorowicz Publishing, Canada, 2000).
6. Thomas Jentz, *Panzertruppen 2*. See also The Dupuy Institute www.dupuyinstitute.org/wbb/forum
7. Didier Lodieu, *III Panzer Korps at Kursk* (Histoire and Collections, Paris, 2007).
8. Jung, *The History of Panzerregiment Grossdeutschland.*
9. Ibid.
10. Fowler, *Kursk*, pp.83–84.
11. Thomas L. Jentz, *Germany's Tiger Tanks: Tiger I and II Combat Tracks.*
12. Steven H. Newton, *Kursk, the German View: Eyewitness Reports by the German Commanders* (Da Capo Press, USA, 2002).
13. Hermann Buchner, *Stormbird* (Crecy, 2009), p. 132.
14. Carrell, *Hitler's War on Russia, Vol 2.*
15. Some dispute the German aces' high kill rates, maintaining that they were inflated. In fact, the Germans were most meticulous in confirming kills. Unconfirmed kills were not counted, and as most pilots had some unconfirmed kills, an argument could be made that scores were in fact higher. Ivan Kozhedub, a 62-kill Soviet ace, claimed after the war that his actual score was over 100. The same could be said of the German aces, and they didn't count shared or disputed kills, which were credited to the squadron. German 78-kill ace Georg-Peter Eder, for instance, had 40 probable kills, which were not counted. Writers trying to explain the high German scores put it down to the fact that, being outnumbered, they had more targets to shoot at, though that also meant there were more enemies to shoot them down. Source R. F. Toliver and T. J. Constable, *Horrido!* (Arthur Baker, UK, 1968).
16. Rudolf Lehmann (trans. Nick Olcott), *The Leibstandarte, Vol III* (J.J. Fedorowicz Publishing, Canada, 1990), pp.219–220.
17. Christer Bergström, *Kursk: The Air Battle, July 1943* (Allan Publishing, UK, 2007).

18. Vasily Grossman (ed. & trans. Antony Beevor and Luba Vinogradova), *A Writer at War With the Red Army 1941–1945* (The Harvill Press, UK, 2005), p. 233.
19. Ibid., p.235.
20. Bergström, *Kursk: The Air Battle, July 1943*; Jung, *The History of Panzerregiment Grossdeutschland.*
21. Hans Ulrich Rudel (trans. Lynton Hudson), *Stuka Pilot* (Euphorion Books, Dublin, 1952), p. 107.
22. Bergström, *Kursk.*
23. Bergström, *Kursk.*
24. Jung, *The History of Panzerregiment Grossdeutschland.*
25. A Soviet Front was their equivalent to a German Army Group.
26. Carrell, *Hitler's War.*
27. Jung, *The History of Panzerregiment Grossdeutschland.*
28. See David Glantz and Jonathan House, *Battle of Kursk* (University of Kansas Press, 1999) and Steven H. Newton (trans. and ed.), *Kursk: The German View* (Da Capo Press, USA, 2002) for detailed analysis of German and Soviet casualties.
29. Bergström, *Kursk.*
30. Colonel T. N. Dupuy, *A Genius for War The German Army and General Staff 1807–1945* (McDonald & Jones, London, 1977).

TWENTY

OPERATIONS STRACHWITZ

After the battle of Kursk, it took the Graf several months to recover from his wound, including weeks of convalescent leave. The question then arose as to his deployment. It seems clear that he did not wish to return to the Grossdeutschland Division, and General Hörnlein equally did not want him back. The two did not got on, and the Graf had not covered himself with glory at Kursk as he had done in previous battles. Nevertheless the Panzer Graf's undoubted talents could not be wasted. A divisional command was the next step for him, which meant that he was under consideration to take over the Panzer Lehr Division. This superbly equipped formation had been established from demonstration and training units trialing and demonstrating new weapons and tactics. All its infantry regiments were mechanized with armoured personnel carriers while its equipment tables were far more lavish than that for a standard panzer division, which for instance only had one battalion equipped with APCs with the remainder being truck borne, and here also both APCs and trucks were often in short supply.

He didn't get this command, which instead went initially to Fritz Bayerlein.[1] This may have been for several reasons. The least favourable was that the Graf's personality, outlook and tactical approach did not make him suitable for a standard divisional command, which required a great deal of preoccupation with logistical and administrative matters as well as controlling a diverse range of formations not necessarily connected with direct combat, such as signals, transport, supply, medical, engineering and administration. Perhaps von Strachwitz was considered too much a hands-on front-line combat commander to have his abilities diverted by the numerous non-combat tasks often required of a divisional commander. Equally, tying down such an independent-minded commander to the chains of divisional and corps structures would not be the best use of his talents. Being independent with a regiment was a far cry to acting independently with a whole division. Perhaps the deciding factor was that the Graf could be better used for special missions or in a fire brigade role. His skill clearly lay in achieving a great deal with very little. He was one of the few commanders who could make a very real difference through his sheer presence and ability. Putting it bluntly, any reasonably competent general could achieve fair results with a well-equipped panzer division. However, very few commanders could manage a superlative result with little or few resources.

In any event, he was passed over for Panzer Lehr. The division was later deployed in Normandy, and had von Strachwitz been in command it might well have caused the Allies more difficulties than it did under its actual commander, General Fritz Bayerlein, a dilettante who had established his reputation as Erwin Rommel's Chief-of-Staff in North Africa. His handling of Panzer Lehr during the Allied invasion of France was average, bordering on the lacklustre. He displayed none of the flair and imagination of von Strachwitz or other commanders such as Bäke, von Manteuffel or Raus, so that the superb division underachieved under his control. Later, during the Ardennes Offensive, Hasso von Manteuffel, Bayerlein's army commander, went to great lengths, to avoid promoting him to command the XLVII Panzer Corps after its commander, General von Luttwitz, had mishandled it, being held up unduly at Bastogne. Bayerlein, as the senior divisional commander, was next in line to command a corps but, unwilling to make the promotion, von Manteuffel left well enough alone, a scathing indictment of Bayerlein.[2]

So in April after being awarded the Swords to his Knight's Cross as the twenty-seventh recipient, Graf von Strachwitz was sent to Army Group North, which had been grossly under-resourced almost since its inception. Of all the army groups, its performance in achieved objectives could be considered the most successful, despite getting little in the way of resources or reinforcements, especially in armoured fighting vehicles. The Russians themselves admitted after the war that Army Group North had fought the hardest, especially when compared to Army Group Centre in the later years.

In January 1944 the Soviets launched their Leningrad-Novgorod offensive, pushing the Germans back to the River Nava. They hoped to annihilate Army Detachment Narva and sweep through Estonia, utilising it as a base for a quick thrust into East Prussia. This army detachment, a euphemism for an understrength army, comprised seven infantry divisions, one panzergrenadier division and three Waffen SS divisions of European volunteers—11th SS Panzergrenadier Division Nordland, 4th SS Panzergrenadier Division Nederland and the 20th SS Estonian Division—along with sundry smaller units including Estonian border guards and the wholly German 502nd Heavy Panzer Battalion under Major Jahde. The foreign volunteer SS divisions performed heroically at Narva, accumulating no fewer than 29 Knight's Crosses. The 502nd Heavy Panzer Battalion, with 70 Tigers, was a highly effective unit with several tank aces, including Lieutenant Otto Carius (150 tanks destroyed), Lieutenant Johannes Bölter (139 tank kills), Albert Kerscher (106 kills), Johann Muller and Alfredo Carpaneto (50 kills each). Its total kills for the war were 1,400 Russian tanks of all types, for a loss of only 107 Tigers, a kill/loss ratio of 13.08:1, the second best kill/loss ratio of any Tiger battalion after Grossdeutschland's battalion which achieved 16.676:1.[3] Bölter and Carius were originally NCOs who had climbed through the ranks. This was one of the factors of the German Army's success, promoting a great number of officers from the ranks of distinguished NCOs, with officer candidates having to serve in the ranks to prove themselves.

The Soviets' winter offensive was successful in breaking the 900-day siege of Leningrad on 27 January, with the Germans making such a hasty withdrawal that they left behind 85 guns which had been shelling the city. Two German divisions were destroyed with the Russians capturing 1,000 prisoners and 30 tanks.[4] After a period to regroup the Soviets resumed their offensive in February, forcing the Germans back to the Panther Line, which was more illusion than a fortified defensive line. The Germans now stood on the River Narva in Estonia to await the next Soviet onslaught. Here, the III SS Panzer Corps, led by the redoubtable SS General Felix Steiner, set up defensive positions across 11 kilometres east of the town of Narva. It would be the scene of intensely savage fighting.

The Russian Eighth Army did, however, manage to establish two bridgeheads across the river on 23 February, which became known as Eastsack and Westsack. These threatened to unhinge the German line. The Germans had very little in the way of armour to eliminate them, with the 502nd Heavy Tank Battalion deploying four Tigers against Westsack and two against the Eastsack. On that day the battalion destroyed its 500th Russian tank. The battalion's 2nd Company alone destroyed 38 tanks, four assault guns and 17 other guns between 17 and 22 March.[5]

Although the Germans lacked a large armoured force they did have the Panzer Graf, who could achieve more with a handful of tanks than any other commander in the German Army. Hitler also sent General Model to take over Army Group North without any reinforcements. When asked what he had brought with him he confidently replied "Why, only me gentlemen." So the Panzer Graf was not the only one expected to perform miracles. Perform miracles they both did. The Graf was initially promised three divisions, which would have made him feel confidant about his task, but they never arrived. Along with the promise of panzers the Graf was given the grandiose title of armour commander of Army Group North which would have been more impressive had he any sizeable armoured formations to command. As it was he had to make do with what was available: the 502nd Heavy Tank Battalion with just 12 Tigers still operational, Battle Group Böhrendt with a few assault guns and Panzer IIIs, units of the Feldernhalle Division with a few Panthers, and some Panzer IVs from the SS Nordland Division. His infantry was supplied by Grossdeutschland's Fusilier Regiment mounted in APCs. Grossdeutschland also provided some tanks and Nebelwerfer rocket launchers. As a last-minute reinforcement Hitler sent over a battalion from his escort brigade, which was literally the last reserve he had available. The Russians had entire armoured and infantry corps sitting idly in reserve while the Germans could only scrape up a battalion that wasn't urgently needed, so parlous had the German manpower and weapons situation become.

The Graf's mission was to eliminate the Soviet Narva bridgeheads. His actions have been generally categorized as operations *Strachwitz I, II* and *III*. He chose the Westsack for *Strachwitz I* and spent a great deal of time preparing for it. As always, good reconnaissance was paramount along with intelligence from radio intercepts and prisoner interrogations. Most prisoners, including officers, were willing to talk, as were German captives, the very real fear of being executed proving a strong motivating factor. Leaving nothing to chance he also had his troops rehearse the attack. The training exercises were conducted with live ammunition with several casualties incurred as a result. Careful reconnaissance led him to give the Tigers a secondary supporting role due to the marshy nature of the terrain. He had to rely on his lighter Panthers, Panzer IVs and assault guns for the spearhead. After careful consideration von Strachwitz decided to attack Westsack from the west. He reasoned, correctly, that the Russians would be expecting an attack from the east as this had a good road and the German artillery had good observation points from the nearby Blue Hills. As well, a regiment of the German

61st Infantry Division was entrenched in a salient there, called the boot.

At 5:55 a.m. on 26 March, von Strachwitz launched his attack on the Westsack. It was preceded by, for what was for this period of the war, a heavy artillery and Nebelwerfer barrage. The panzers followed, supported by the infantry of Grenadier Regiments 2, 44 and 23 from the East Prussian 11th Infantry Division, a hard-fighting unit commanded by General Lieutenant Helmuth Reymann. Eight Tigers had been ordered to support the infantry but they were forced to withdraw due to the softness of the ground. The Graf's decision not to use the Tigers at the forefront had proven correct.

Ferocious fighting took place in the trackless swamps and forests with heavy casualties on both sides. The German officer losses were especially severe with all platoons and most companies being led by surviving NCOs. The Graf led from the front as usual, a familiar figure in his bulky sheepskin coat, bringing chocolates and cognac to comfort and encourage his troops. He also brought with him several Iron Crosses Second Class, which he awarded on the spot to the best fighters. When not accompanying him, his adjutant Lieutenant Famula was close behind ensuring that ammunition, food and fuel arrived on time wherever they were needed.

So vital was this operation that the Graf received Stuka support, a fairly rare event given the stretched resources of the Luftwaffe. This proved a mixed blessing however, with one bomb landing on the narrow track on which the German tanks were advancing. One minute later and it would have wiped out von Strachwitz himself. The Stuka pilots had great difficulty in finding their targets amongst the trees, and the bombs were less than effective in the forested terrain.

Early progress was good with a large number of prisoners taken, but the Russians were not prepared to give ground easily. On 27 March they counterattacked, pushing the Germans back with their first onslaught. They continued their attack into the night. This led to some very frightening close-quarter combat in the pitch-black woods. The next morning the Russians commenced a sustained artillery bombardment causing heavy casualties, many caused by the wood splinters from the fractured trees, so that companies of normally over 100 men were reduced to platoons of fewer than 30. Von Strachwitz summoned reinforcements, but they too suffered heavily from the Soviet artillery fire, arriving already badly depleted.

Immediately after the artillery barrage the Russians sent in their infantry in massed attacks which penetrated the thinly manned German defences at several points. The Luftwaffe sent in ground-attack aircraft but failed to dislodge the Russians. Several batteries of Nebelwerfers added their weight to the fire, blasting the Russian positions in a crescendo of shattering explosions. The Graf then ordered a counterattack, which threw the demoralised Russians back with cold steel. He pushed forward with everything he had to maintain the momentum. The Russians fought back tenaciously, but were steadily forced to give ground. When driven out of their trenches their resistance turned into a precipitous retreat with many surrendering. The retreat turned into a rout. They left behind some 6,000 dead and 50 guns, along with the large quantities of equipment on the battlefield.[6] In addition, the Germans took some 300 prisoners. Against those Soviet losses the Germans suffered 2,200 dead or missing. It was a superb if costly victory at a time when the Germans were in retreat, or barely holding on along the rest of the front.

On 1 April Hyazinth von Strachwitz was promoted to the rank of major general. For a colonel of the reserve this was a very unusual promotion, and may have been unique. His monthly salary increased by around 50%. He wasn't as fortunate as some generals, General Guderian for instance, who received a large amount each month on top of his ordinary salary as a personal gift from Adolf Hitler. Other generals and field marshals, such as von Kluge, also received monetary gifts, as well as landed estates.

The Panzer Graf's next operation was *Strachwitz II*, the elimination of the Eastsack bridgehead. He knew the Russians were expecting him to attack as he had attacked the Westsack. So he did the opposite, attacking at Eastsack's northern tip to surprise them. This attack also took meticulous preparation, which was becoming his trademark. As Otto Carius stated in his memoir, *Tigers in the Mud*, regarding the planning for *Strachwitz III*, "his careful, methodical planning amazed us once again" and that "the Graf was a master of organisation." This would seem at odds with his devil-may-care cavalrymen's approach, but it shows that, despite his reputation for dashing raids and slashing cavalry-style attacks, he was a calm calculating man, and it was this, together with his boldness, that made him such a formidable commander and adversary.

Once again the attack was rehearsed, this time twice. The road for the attack was narrow but could support a Tiger so they were to lead the assault. However they had to move in single file and would not be allowed to stop unless the whole column had to halt. As it was also the only passable road, the Russian had packed the culverts with explosives so the Graf had arranged for artillery to take out the explosives control bunker where the detonators were left. Failing this, his engineers were to cut the wires. For this operation, as with *Strachwitz I*, the infantry went into action without their bulky winter clothing to allow them freedom of movement. The winter clothing was bundled up and sent on to the troops in the evening. However fighting without their white camouflage clothing made them easier targets for the Soviets.

For this attack the Tigers were placed at the forefront with Otto Carius' platoon of four Tigers at the tip of the spearhead. It was launched on 6 April, after a heavy barrage from Nebelwerfers, heavy artillery and 88mm anti-aircraft guns. Von Strachwitz observed proceedings at the very front, calmly leaning on his carved Volkhov stick as he waited for the breakthrough. The low-hanging trees made the barrage twice as effective as they prevented the blast effects escaping upwards causing severe casualties to the Russians cowering in their bunkers, particularly from the sheer effects of concussion, which was a feature of the Nebelwerfer rockets.

Some of the artillery fire landed near Carius' Tigers, forcing them to move back and forth in the mine-infested terrain in order to avoid being hit. When the shots kept on coming despite his radio calls to cease, he was forced to fire a few rounds close to the artillery observers' positions, obliging them to move and so give him some respite. A Russian anti-tank gun not observed in the confusion damaged one of his Tigers before being put out of action.[7]

Heavy Russian return fire caused casualties among the infantry who were clumped together around the Tigers. The Tigers' protection was illusory, as they attracted fire more than they provided shelter, but the infantry felt safer so they kept close, despite being actively discouraged from doing so. These were veteran hand-picked troops selected by the tankers themselves, as Otto Carius pointed out in his memoirs:

> "The responsibility for the success of the operation lies squarely on the tank commander regardless of rank. Is everything clear?"
>
> "Jawohl, Herr Graf"
>
> The Oberst [Von Strachwitz] twisted his mouth into a sarcastic smile. It wasn't unbeknownst to him, that we had allowed ourselves a few remarks about his desired form of address [Graf not Herr Oberst as regulation demanded]. None of them to be found in a handbook of good manners.
>
> "Very well. So far it's also been quite simple. But now a different question for the 'Tiger' people. What battalion do you want to fight with?"

> We looked at each other, astonished by the generosity of this offer. We immediately agreed upon a light infantry battalion we had already worked with.
>
> "Very well, that's what you'll have."[8]

With nightfall, Lieutenant Famula and his APCs brought up much-needed fuel, ammunition, and food, despite Russian attempts to stop him with interdictory fire and snipers who had infiltrated behind the lines.[9]

The Russians vigorously counterattacked throughout the night, causing serious casualties. The seriously wounded were taken back for treatment in Famula's APCs with the lightly wounded staying to help hold back the Soviets. Stukas, long since relegated to a primary night-attack role unless scarce fighter escort could be provided, tried to bring the battered infantry and tanks some relief, but their bombs had to be dropped well back to avoid friendly casualties. They also made little impression due to the softness of the ground, which absorbed the blasts. The heavy Tigers gradually sank ever deeper into the marshy soil, only extricating themselves with difficulty at daylight. One Tiger was damaged by the artillery fire and required towing. Von Schiller, the Tiger Company commander, was nowhere to be found so Otto Carius had to step in and continue with the mission. Another artillery barrage swept over them with one tank commander wounded after foolishly exposing himself from the turret. The column then moved towards Auware. Near the railroad station two assault guns from the Führer Begleit Brigade were attacked by a force of 20 Russian tanks. Corporal Rudolf Salvermoser, a gunner in one of the assault guns, described the action. They were in an ambush position and opened fire as the Russians approached:

> Our first shot hit it, but didn't do any damage. As soon as you shoot the loader puts in a shell right away and its ready. I knew the distance, just had to turn a few degrees or two and shoot again. Then we knocked it out. One after another they came out (from behind the trees). They had ten tanks. They shot but they missed. Its like they didn't know what to do. It was a common saying in the German Army, "Don't worry about the Russians, they always miss the first shot." The guy next to us, he was about 100 yards away, he knocked out two. The third one started to back away when I shot it. The fourth one was further back already and I still hit it. One took off and my buddy chased him and knocked him out. The others all

> disappeared. We shot six tanks. They didn't hit one of us. They were too slow. We were just faster and better. I told my commander Unter-offizier Hoffmann that I was just lucky that I hit them all. He said, "You were not lucky, you were trained to hit them all at the first time with the first shot."[10]

Salvermoser destroyed three T-34s and one KV-2, while the other assault gun under Unter-offizier Rahn destroyed three T-34s. It highlights how small numbers of German tanks and assault guns, could still defeat far larger Soviet forces. Elsewhere, Lieutenant Bölter and Sergeant Goring from the 502nd Tank Battalion engaged 35 Russian tanks and assault guns while giving support to the 8th Jäger Division. Bölter destroyed 15 enemy tanks and Goring seven. This brought Bölter's total kills to 89, earning him the Knight's Cross.[11]

Overall the German surprise was so complete that in another battle group tanks from the Grossdeutschland Division overran a Soviet divisional headquarters. The divisional commander just barely escaped but his operations officer was caught, still partially undressed. Some of their anti-tank guns still had their barrel caps on, and many Red Army men were caught carrying out peaceful rear-area activities, having no idea that the Germans had gotten so close.

Skilfully combining armour, infantry, artillery and the Luftwaffe, von Strachwitz had eliminated the Eastsack with the well-crafted operation *Strachwitz II*. Both operations were well-planned and coordinated, gave Army Detachment Narva extra time for its defence, and prevented the Soviets from breaking out of their bridgeheads to cut off the German force and thence to sweep through Estonia. This now left *Strachwitz III* to address the Krivasso bridgehead on the German side of the River Narva, along with the capture of Krivasso. The Graf carried out his meticulous planning as usual, but was under no illusion as to the difficulty of the task. As he explained to his officers at a briefing:

> Looked at superficially, this operation is very similar to both our previous ones. Only this time there are going to be considerably more difficulties. . . . We have already surprised the Russians twice in their bridgehead. They know this bridgehead is a pain for us. A third surprise will therefore probably not be possible. Especially as they know a new attack can only be carried out on this road. This

> naturally diminishes our chances of success compared to the previous operations where we were successful using the element of surprise.[12]

He went on to tell them the advance road was narrow but could support a Tiger, so his intructions for the Tigers were similar to those in previous operations. As the Graf was addressing the officers his adjutant rushed in. Visibly annoyed, the Graf turned around. "What's going on?" he snapped. The officer straightened up "Herr Graf. I would like to report that the announcement has been made in the news that the Führer has awarded you the Diamonds to the Knights Cross! If I may take the liberty I would like to be the first to congratulate you!"[13] The other officers wanted to congratulate the Graf and celebrate but, as Otto Carius remembered,

> Before we could say a word however the Graf made an abrupt sign of disapproval.
>
> "First, the news is not an official source of information. Second, I don't have any time for that now and don't wish to be disturbed again." That was meant for the adjutant, who turned beet red. He raised his hand to his cap and disappeared rapidly.[14]

The Graf's reaction did not imply that he was unimpressed by the award of Germany's highest honour, but rather reflected his attitude to planning and combat. However he could still allow some levity when he rounded on Carius after the young officer told him that a ditch was impassable due to the surrounding marshy terrain.

> "Take note of this Carius," he said in a friendly manner. "If I say that the ditch doesn't exist as an anti-tank ditch to me, then it doesn't exist, do we understand each other?"
>
> In my entire military career, I had never experienced such an elegant, and at the same time, unmistakable rebuff. Graf Strachwitz did not want to see an anti-tank ditch. So there was none there. Period—end of discussion. I was so nonplussed that I could only choke out a short "Yes sir!" Still smiling in his slightly caustic manner the Oberst nodded and continued his briefing.[15]

Near the end of the briefing von Strachwitz turning towards Carius again:

"I've thought about the matter one more time Carius. Do you still foresee difficulties with the ditch?"

"Yes Herr Graf!"

"Well I don't want to spoil your fun. Especially not when there really could be something to the matter. Do you have a suggestion?"[16]

Otto Carius then suggested that wooden beams be taken on the APCs and used to ford the ditch, a solution that von Strachwitz quickly approved. He went on to note that he thought that deep down the Panzer Graf didn't believe the operation would be a success and would much rather have called the whole thing off.[17]

The attack commenced on 19 April, with eight Tigers leading, followed by Panzer IVs and APCs with an engineer APC behind the second lead Tiger. A squad of infantry rode on each of the tanks. Just prior to moving off, Carius' loader had an accidental discharge from the hull machine gun wounding two infantrymen from the Fusilier Battalion. It was an inauspicious start to the operation. With the only hope of surprise now lost, the attack went in. Russian artillery quickly joined the fray while Illuyshin ground-attack planes made a quick appearance, only to be chased away by Focke Wulf 190s of JG54—the only fighter unit in the north—which shot down two. Stukas, under Lieutenant Colonel Klumey based at Tallinn, then swarmed in, but heavy Russian anti-aircraft fire kept them to a height which made their attacks ineffective, bringing down two of them.[18]

The lead Tiger ran onto a mine, which immobilised it, bringing the entire attack column to a halt. Despite von Strachwitz enquiring several times why the attack was still stalled, the Tiger Company's commander, von Schiller, did nothing, remaining bottled up in his tank. Finally von Strachwitz called von Schiller and Carius to his command post. Von Strachwitz was angrily swinging his Volkhov stick back and forth, then he let fly at von Schiller before placing Carius in command, ordering him to get the attack moving. This Carius did by simply moving the column around the obstructing Tiger, something von Schiller could and should have done himself.[19]

The Germans quickly broke through the Russian lines, only to be halted by an anti-tank ditch. Von Strachwitz called a halt to allow the engineers to demolish the ditch so that the attack could resume the following morning. Russian artillery and mortars crewed by women fired a few salvoes to keep the Germans unsettled but no further action was taken.

During the night Russian bombers flew overhead on their way to bomb

Narva, which was now nothing more than a pile of rubble, but still stubbornly resisting the Soviets' best efforts to take it. Lieutenant Famula continued indefatigably with his nightly resupply efforts, earning high praise from an extremely appreciative Otto Carius.[20]

The ditch was blown apart on the morning of 20 April. The Graf, sleeping in his pyjamas as was his usual practice, was not even disturbed by it. Like many senior commanders involved in a very long war the Graf allowed himself a few luxuries whenever circumstances permitted, not least of which were a good cigar and French cognac. For his part Carius was hoping the whole thing would be called off, but the attack went ahead, supported by Nebelwerfers whose rockets dropped short, landing on the Tigers and fusiliers waiting to move forward. For a full five minutes they endured the massive blasts, which tore the Fusilier Battalion apart, killing or wounding many. Only the heavily armoured Tigers escaped unscathed. Three Tigers were sent forward to cover the evacuation of the dead and wounded by Lieutenant Famula and his APCs. Now Otto Carius felt sure that the attack would be abandoned, but Graf von Strachwitz arranged for another battalion to be sent forward. The attack was to go ahead as planned.[21]

A Russian assault gun opened up on Carius' Tiger, and he survived a hit to his turret cupola solely because he had ducked down to light a cigarette. A little later, however, his tank was knocked out by another hit.

The attack had by now completely stalled. The Russians were simply too strong while the marshy ground, made worse by the spring thaw, curtailed movement so much that it was becoming impossible to move the attack forward. Elsewhere another battle group was equally stalled. The Tigers slowly pulled back, harried by Russian artillery fire as they towed their disabled tanks. A Russian bi-plane used for nuisance bombing flew over, dropping its bomb. Lieutenant Famula, standing alongside the road lighting a cigarette, was mortally wounded by shrapnel and died a short while later. The infantry was forced to give way and couldn't hold the line. Reluctantly von Strachwitz gave the order to withdraw. *Strachwitz III* was over.

NOTES

1. Some sources, such as Warren Odegard, *Uniforms and Organisation and History of the Panzertruppe* (RJ Bender Publishing, USA, 1980) show Graf von Strachwitz commanding Panzer Lehr from 8 June to December 1944. However this was not the case.
2. Bayerlein was a master of publicity and public relations and the darling of Western

historians, whom he went to great lengths to assist, assuring him of their high regard. He was also a technical adviser to film sets and a contributor to various articles, ensuring him a comfortable place in history. Also because he fought mainly against the Western Allies he is well known to Anglo-Americans while more deserving generals like von Strachwitz and Hans Hube remain more obscure. See also Samuel W. Mitchum Jr., *Panzer Legions* (Stackpole Books, USA, 2000), p. 205.

3. "Loss ratios," Tiger 1 Information Centre, www.alanhamby.com/losses.shtml/ (accessed 29 August 2013).
4. Robert Jackson, *Battle of the Baltic: The Wars 1914–1945* (Pen & Sword Books, UK, 2007).
5. Wolfgang Schneider, *Tigers in Combat* (Stackpole Books, 2004) and Wilhelm Tieke (trans. F. Steinhardt), *Tragedy of the Faithful* (J.J. Fedorowicz, Canada, 2001).
6. Mansel Denton, *Battle For Narva 1944* (History Facts Documentation, 2010).
7. Otto Carius (trans. Robert J. Edwards), *Tigers in the Mud* (Stackpole Books, 2003).
8. Carius, *Tigers in the Mud*, p. 102.
9. Ibid.
10. Interview with Rudolf Salvermoser, *Greatest Tank Battles: Battle for the Baltics* (History Channel, series 2, episode 5, first aired 14 February 2011).
11. Carius, *Tigers in the Mud.*
12. Ibid.
13. Ibid. p.122.
14. Ibid.
15. Ibid. p.123.
16. Ibid. p.124.
17. Ibid.
18. Wilhelm Tiecke, *Tragedy of the Faithful.*
19. Carius, *Tigers in the Mud.*
20. Ibid.
21. Ibid.

TWENTY-ONE

THE BATTLE OF TUKUM

IN JUNE THE SOVIETS LAUNCHED THEIR GREATEST OFFENsive of the war to date. Named Operation *Bagration* after the Russian marshal who was mortally wounded at the battle of Borodino against Napoleon in 1812, its objective was nothing less than the destruction of Army Group Centre, which it accomplished in a masterly manner. This army group, under the sycophantic and largely incompetent Field Marshal Busch, had been fighting a fairly static battle of attrition while the major events were playing out in the south. Busch had been warned of the massive Soviet build-up opposite his lines, which formed a tempting bulge or salient. He requested permission for a withdrawal to shorten his line but this was refused and, reassured by Hitler, he elected to wait for developments.

The storm broke on 22 June, the third anniversary of *Barbarossa*, when four Soviet fronts—comprising some 200 divisions and 6,000 tanks and assault guns supported by 7,000 aircraft—smashed through the central front. Four German armies—consisting of 38 infantry divisions, one panzer division, two panzergrenadier divisions, two Luftwaffe field divisions and seven security divisions—were almost obliterated. German casualties numbered some 350,000 men, of whom 150,000 were taken prisoner, many of whom would perish in the gulags. The 4th Panzer Army alone lost 130,000 of its 165,000 men while 3rd Panzer Army lost ten divisions. A huge gaping hole appeared in the German front. It was Germany's greatest defeat of the war.[1] The Russians admitted to losing 178,000 dead and missing and 590,000 wounded. Busch, at OKW headquarters when the blow struck, threw himself on the map table showing his army group's massive defeat, sobbing uncontrollably. That was about all he could do, for Hitler summarily dismissed him on 28 June, despite the fact that he had done no more than follow orders.[2] The Führer replaced him with Walter Model who had been promoted to field marshal on 18 March 1944, the youngest in the German Army.

Along with Operation *Bagration*, the Russians launched a major offensive against Army Group North on 22 June. The attack forces consisted of four fronts—the Leningrad Front under General Govorov, 3rd Baltic Front under General Maslennikov, 2nd Baltic Front under General Eremenko and 1st Baltic under General Bagramyan. These fronts totalled 1,200,000 men with 2,500 tanks against the German 16th and 18th Armies and Army Detachment Narva, which together had only 540,000 men and some 300 tanks.

The 1st Baltic Front launched the initial attack to drive a wedge between Army Groups Centre and North. The gap created was some 97 kilometres, which needed to be bridged or closed. With Army Group Centre rapidly collapsing, Hitler ordered the 12th Panzer and 212th Infantry Divisions from Army Group North to try and shore up Army Group Centre, leaving Army Group North in a very vulnerable position without any complete armoured division of its own. On 11 July the Russian 2nd Baltic Front attacked Six-

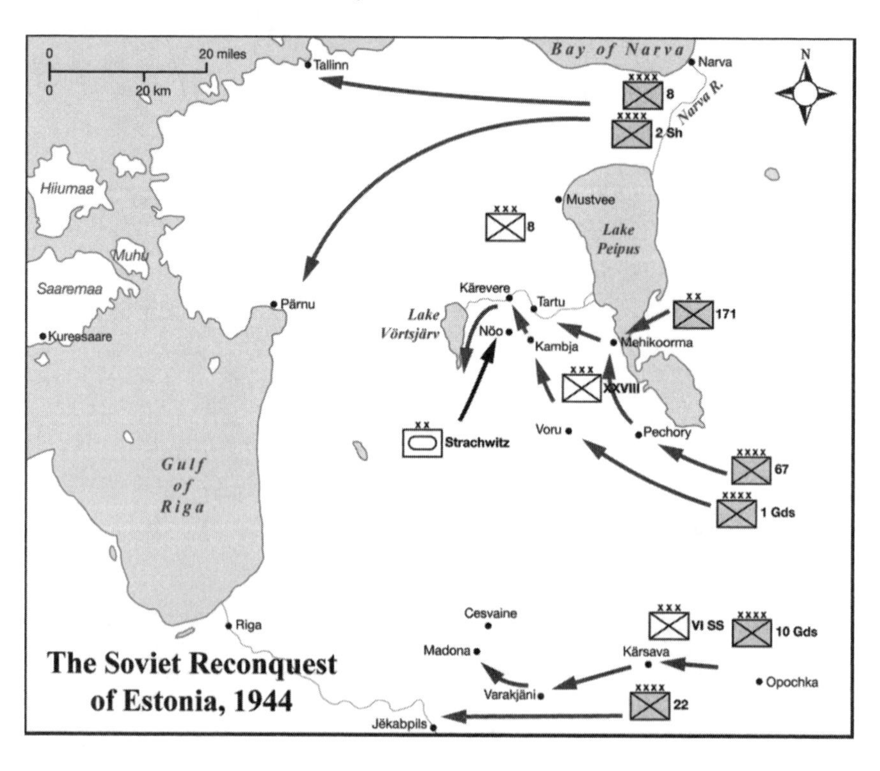

The Soviet Reconquest of Estonia, 1944

teenth Army's left flank where Rudolf Sieckenius was commanding the 263rd Infantry Division. On 14 July the 3rd Baltic Front struck the right flank of Eighteenth Army and by 20 July both German armies were in full retreat, with only Army Detachment Narva still grimly holding on.

At Daugavpils the indomitable 502nd Heavy Tank Battalion encountered the super-heavy Stalin tanks with their massive 122mm guns for the first time, knocking out 17 of them in a single day's fighting. The defence of Narva was so stoutly maintained that the Russians halted their attacks there on 29 July. However this did not prevent them from advancing elsewhere, thrusting into central Lithuania, to be checked at Siauliai by a small battle group for three days before resuming their advance for some 160 kilometres north to take Jelgava, so cutting the last rail link between Army Groups North and Centre.[3] A Russian mechanized force then lunged ahead to take Tukum on 30 July. On 1 August the Reds reached the Gulf of Riga just west of the city, thereby cutting off 30 German divisions in Latvia and Estonia. Meanwhile, Narva had fallen after a heroic resistance, the defenders withdrawing to the so-called Tannenberg Line. Immediate steps were taken to close the gap between the German army groups with pincer attacks to cut through the neck of the Soviet salient. The main thrust was to come from the Third Army led by the Austrian Colonel General Raus, spearheaded by the XL Panzer Corps. This corps had the 4th, 5th and 14th Panzer Divisions as well as the Grossdeutschland Panzergrenadier Division, having some 400 tanks in total.[4] Grossdeutschland, 14th and 4th Panzer were particularly hard-fighting units, with the latter two fighting bitterly in the Baltics until the end of the war.

On 5 August, the Soviet 2nd and 3rd Baltic Fronts resumed their offensive but were considerably weaker, having lost 1,325 tanks since 22 June. General Schorner, who had taken command of Army Group North on 24 July, resorted to draconian methods in order to hold the line. A formidable and personally brave officer who had been awarded the Pour le Mérite in World War I, and achieved renown for his command of the Nikopol pocket in January/February 1944, he was nevertheless an ardent Nazi, and a thug to rival Georgy Zhukov. He resorted to demoting soundly efficient officers on the spot for minor infractions, real or imagined, and summarily shooting front-line soldiers found in the rear without documented reasons. He even stripped officers and men of hard-earned combat decorations, all to instill discipline through fear. Hitler liked him, his men hated him, and in the end he deserted them, escaping in a light aircraft wearing civilian clothes.

Graf von Strachwitz, after his third operation had been abandoned, continued to carry out some of his characteristic actions against the Soviets. He conducted a raid deep behind enemy lines with a small column of tanks. He shot up and destroyed supply columns, headquarters and rear-echelon units that sat smugly in the rear, oblivious to any threat from the overstretched and retreating Germans. He also came across a tank laager that the Russians hadn't even bothered to camouflage or provide security for. The tanks were not placed defensively so were easy prey for the rampaging Germans. It was gunnery practice, pure and simple. Nor were the crews spared, being machine-gunned without mercy. Tanks could be mass-produced but it took months and years to create experienced, combat-wise and efficient tank crews.

He was invariably mistaken for a Russian tank column, allowing him to move with impunity alongside and around the Russians. The few times he was challenged it was always too late for the Russians to put up effective resistance or cause him any casualties. He simply shot up the units who challenged him. So angry did the Soviets become at his depredations that they put a price on his head that would have made anyone who killed him wealthy for the rest of their life.

He took part in various actions, most often with ad-hoc units, including an attempt to relieve Vilnius, the surrounded Lithuanian capital holding out against merciless Soviet assaults. His actions enabled Major Theodor Tolsdorff who was defending Vilnius to evacuate thousands of German wounded from the city, an action which earned him the Swords to the Knight's Cross and a promotion to colonel. Tolsdorff would later join von Strachwitz in the elite group of Diamonds wearers.

On one occasion von Strachwitz let the Russians know—via a radio message he knew they would intercept—where and when he was going to attack them. They promptly set up an ambush for him at that location, enabling the Graf to infiltrate the Soviet lines some distance away, then curve around to catch his would-be ambushers in their flanks and rear. But instead of simply attacking, he carefully reconnoitred the ground, noting the positions of each Russian tank and anti-tank gun pointing towards the expected direction of his approach. Each target was allocated to one of his tanks, with ranges carefully calculated. At first light he gave the order to fire, and every shot fired was an instant hit. The Russian tanks, including some Shermans still being used this late in the war, were blown away, turrets shot off, burning and destroyed, as most hits were to their weak points at the sides and rear. Five tanks went up in flames, then another five were brewed up, followed by a further four, all in rapid succession. Concealed anti-tank guns were taken out with high-explosive rounds.

Confusion, fear and panic broke out among the Soviets. Their first thought was of an aerial attack as Rudel's Stukas had been active over the northern front. Eventually the Soviet infantry spotted their antagonists and warned their tankers, who broke cover to counterattack. This left them in the open and vulnerable as they sought to acquire targets. More and more of them were blown away without getting in an effective shot in reply, with most firing in panic in the general direction of the German attack. The surviving anti-tank guns had to be turned around by hand, a difficult task at best and almost impossible while under machine-gun and high-explosive fire. The infantry, at the frantic urgings of their officers and commissars, made an attempt at assault, but were smashed by machine-gun and cannon rounds. The survivors fled or dived for cover. Von Strachwitz ordered his panzers forward to provide a more difficult target and acquire better firing positions through manoeuvre. His gunner needed little direction as there was a plethora of targets, so he calmly directed the other tanks as well as his own for the best advantage. In a short while it was all over, with the Graf quickly returning to his own lines before retribution, especially from the air, could overtake him. It was about this time that signal intercepts were picked up with the Russians warning that the "Devil's general" von Strachwitz was in the area and was to be avoided until reinforcements could arrive. This and the price on his head—as much as his decorations and promotions—were testimony to his tactical genius and effectiveness.

In late July his ad-hoc panzer division was disbanded, having distinguished itself on the Narva front and southern flank of Army Group North. The continuous Soviet offensives necessitated its reactivation but this time with different forces. His promised three divisions were still not forthcoming, despite several requests, as they were simply not available, unsurprising given the desperate situation on both the Eastern and Western Front at this time. Any reserves were scrapings from the bottom of the barrel, or stripped from other formations that also desperately needed them. One man on a bicycle was considered a reinforcement, and if he was a veteran it was considered a miracle. By way of compensation General Guderian eventually managed to scrape together 10 tanks and 15 APCs to add to Panzerverband *Strachwitz II*. It wasn't three divisions, but it was the best he could do. These tanks were not from reserves, as there weren't any, but came from other units, which disliked parting with them.

Von Strachwitz's Panzerverband II had at its core two brigades. These were Panzer Brigade 101 under Colonel Meinrad von Lauchert—with whom he had fought at the battle of Kursk and who had served as his son's commanding officer in Panzer Regiment 15 of the 11th Panzer Division—and SS Panzer Brigade Gross, named after its commanding officer, SS Sturmbannführer Martin Gross, an experienced panzer commander who had also fought at Kursk with the SS Leibstandarte Division, earning his Knight's Cross at the epic German victory of Prokhorovka where his division destroyed several hundred Soviet tanks.

Von Lauchert's Panzer Brigade 101 consisted of Panzer Battalion 2101 with its tanks being provided by Battalion 102 at Neuruppin and from the 18th Panzer Division, consisting of three companies. It also had a Panzergrenadier Battalion designated 2101, which was insufficient, as a panzer brigade normally had two or three infantry battalions. In addition it fielded a light anti-aircraft platoon barely adequate for the task, an engineer company and various support and supply units. Its headquarters staff came from Armoured Brigade 108 and Panzerjäger Regiment 656. This cobbled-together unit was sent into combat three weeks after its formation with training incomplete. Nevertheless the brigade had some very experienced and competent officers in its ranks. These included its panzer battalion commander, Knight's Cross holder Frederich-Wilhelm Breidenbach, and Guido von Wartenburg who had been awarded the Knight's Cross in 1943. He was killed at Riga on 16 September 1944. The Brigade's engineering maintenance officer, Lieutenant (Eng.) Römer, was a holder of the Knight's War Service Cross, a high non-combat efficiency decoration.

SS Panzer Brigade Gross initially had 30 tanks, mainly obsolescent Panzer IIIs with some old Panzer IVs and a solitary Panther. A Tiger company detached from the 103rd SS Heavy Panzer Battalion was also added, although at one point the brigade had only one operational Tiger. Eventually its tank strength reached that of a battalion with four companies. To those 30 tanks were added two panzergrenadier battalions, an armoured reconnaissance battalion under Hauptstürmführer Runge, together with support units. So by 16 August it numbered some 2,500 men, who were a mixed bunch of veterans, ex-Luftwaffe personnel, and even an officer from neutral Sweden, Unterstürmführer Wolfgangeldhalbiez, who was subsequently wounded outside of Riga. He survived, returning to Sweden in 1945, and died in 1984. Another Swede was SS Obersharführer Johan Westrin who had served in both the Finnish and Swedish armies before joining the Waffen SS. He was killed along with five men of his squad when they ran over a land mine near Saukenai, Lithuania, in September 1944. On 18 August it was attached to the Graf's Panzerverband Strachwitz, which in turn was attached to the XXXIX Panzer Corps of General Raus' Third Panzer Army. Support units belonging to this essentially ad-hoc panzer division included the 337th Signal Battalion, 3rd Battalion of the 19th SS Artillery Regiment, and the divisional staff of the 337th Infantry Division. Welding together this eclectic mixture required excellent command skills and a strong personality.

The attack to close the yawning gap between the army groups and reconnect them was codenamed Operation *Doppelkopf*. It was set to commence on 20 August but was launched on 16 August in perfect weather, with the morale of the troops, who were on the attack at last, high. Unfortunately there was no central focus of attack, as there were four separate spearheads dispersed along a front of 100 kilometres. General Knobelsdorff's XL Panzer Corps, with the Grossdeutschland Panzergrenadier Division and the 7th and 14th Panzer Divisions, attacked the southern flank of the Soviet salient. General Dietrich von Sauken's XXXIX Panzer Corps assaulted the centre with the 5th Panzer Division, and the northern flank with the 4th and 12th Panzer Divisions. Graf von Strachwitz's Panzerverband was to strike the northern flank, near Saldus, break through there to take Tukum, then move on to Riga. General Erhard Raus thought that without a central point of attack, and given the strong Russian reserves, the attack had little chance of success. This, apart from Graf von Strachwitz's battle group's success, proved to be the case. The 7th Panzer Division under General Major Karl Maus took Kelmi after some savage fighting with heavy casualties on both sides.

Grossdeutschland, now under Hasso von Manteuffel, advanced as far as Siauliai where its panzers bogged down in the swampy ground. General Martin Unrein's 14th Panzer got itself caught up in ferocious forest fighting, so overall von Knobelsdorff's XL Panzer Corps only gained some 40 kilometres. General Karl Decker's 5th Panzer Division gained 20 kilometres to advance into a forest where its advance guard was surrounded and was only extricated with some difficulty by the main body. It was then pushed back to its start line by a Russian counterattack. General Sauken's XXXIV Panzer Corps fared even worse. Its two panzer divisions, the 4th and 12th, encountered such heavy Russian resistance that they could only manage some 10 kilometres before being halted.[5]

Graf von Strachwitz's divisional attack plan called for Panzer Brigade 101, with an attached SS panzer grenadier battalion from SS Panzer Brigade

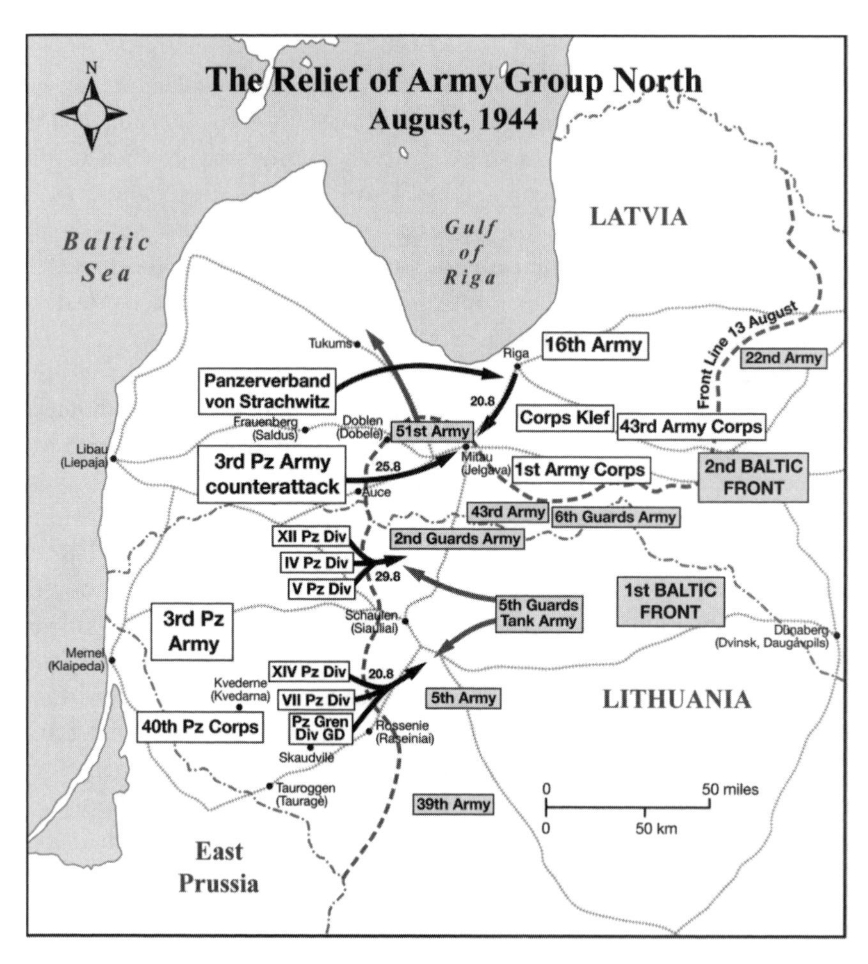

Gross, to clear the area around the railway station at Berzupe, being followed by Panzer Brigade Gross. They would then divide into two axes of advance, with Panzer Brigade 101 on the right and Panzer Brigade Gross on the left. Panzer Brigade 101 would then attack the Russians at Biksti towards Berze. Panzer Brigade Gross would leave some security units in Dzukste and to guard the Velkroai–Silisi road, then attack the western part of Tukum, advancing from the south. Both brigades would then advance through Kummern or along the coast to meet up with Battle Group Kieffel holding the Riga sector.[6]

Graf von Strachwitz commenced his attack on 4:00 a.m. on 20 August. He was in the lead tank ready to intervene or alter the plan on the spot. Despite strong Russian resistance everything proceeded roughly to plan. Steaming along the coast nearby was the veteran German heavy cruiser *Prinz*

Eugen, with the destroyers Z-25, Z-28, Z-35 and Z-36. Also with the small fleet were the torpedo boats T-23 and T-28.[7] The battle cruiser was returning to combat duty, having been a training ship for cadets since April 1943. Commanding her was Captain Hans Jurgen Reinicke, who had taken command on 5 January 1944. The ship itself had been lucky, surviving many encounters with the enemy. It had sallied out with the *Bismarck* and helped in the destruction of HMS *Hood*, but had already left the *Bismarck* when that ship was caught by the British fleet and sunk. It took part in the dangerous dash along the English Channel in 1942, survived a bomb hit in Brest 1941, a torpedo hit from the British submarine *Trident*, a collision with the light cruiser *Leipzig* and various aerial attacks from British and Soviet aircraft. It was the only major German warship to survive the war, only to be destroyed during atom bomb tests at Kwajalein Atoll in 1946.

Thinking laterally, Graf von Strachwitz made contact with *Prinz Eugen* requesting gunfire support from the fleet against the enemy tank force he knew was occupying his target, Tukum. Reinicke readily agreed, although this was the first time the *Prinz Eugen* had engaged enemy ground forces.

The Graf pushed on with his force to get close to his target before the bombardment began. A gunner from Panzer Brigade Gross describes his part in the action. He was in his unit's only operational Tiger, which was itself marked as not ready for combat, nor was it watertight:

> During our trip to the staging area we encountered our first problem. As we reached a small river, one of us got out to direct the driver over a narrow wooden bridge. The wooden planks were quite thick, but would the bridge hold? The bridge was checked out and slowly the Tiger tank was directed on to the span ... Right in the middle of the bridge it happened! With a very loud crack and an equally loud knock, we fell into the stream! Besides a few scrapes and bruises, plus the shock of the fall, we were all right. Members from Grossdeutschland were able to pull our tank from the stream so that we could continue our trip to the staging area near Tuckum ...
>
> The first day at the staging area was a particularly hard one for us. We had already lost our tank commander from a shot to the head earlier in the day when our second tank commander died in the afternoon in the same manner. Our third tank commander was an SS Unterscharführer who had recently joined our group from the Luftwaffe.

We were not even together for fifteen minutes when the order came to move out. We had been ordered to advance in the direction of Tukum, without infantry support, in order to observe the effects of the heavy shelling on that town by the German heavy cruiser *Prinz Eugen*. To this day I cannot understand that order. After crossing slightly fallen ground we had to rise again among some huge shell holes, before reaching the city. In the process, we were able to knock out a few anti-tank positions.

Suddenly, we found ourselves in the middle of a huge lumberyard. Cut wooden planks were stacked up high for as far as the eye could see. We just as quickly began to receive small arms and anti-tank rifle fire from all directions. We could only see directly in front of us through the gun sights and machine gun slits. Just vaguely, covered up by smoke and piled wooden planks, we recognized the turret of a T-34 tank!

Our reaction time was faster than the enemy's (much to our relief!). One round was all it took and the enemy tank smouldered where it stood, lying in wait, damaged. We then proceeded to clear a path through the enemy infantry by firing high-explosive shells and bearing machine-gun fire on the enemy infantry hiding all around us. Moving forward a few hundred metres, we moved through a narrow winding alley. At that moment another T-34 came into our gun sights. The T-34 was so close that its 76mm gun was now within effective range and capable of knocking out our own tank.

Sweat was pouring from all of us the situation reached its zenith. We quickly loaded the first round and just as quickly fired the armour-piercing shell. "A miss! Shit! Load again before they burn us." The first shot had knocked out a telephone pole next to the T-34. Luckily for us the sun was directly in their eyes. Our next shot blew off the turret of the T-34 with a loud bang, sending it skyward about twenty feet.

Our mission was practically over by then, as most of the town had been cleared of the enemy.[8]

At 8:02 a.m. the *Prinz Eugen*'s guns fired their first exploratory shots, having launched its three Arados seaplanes to observe the fall of shot. Gunnery Officer Schmalenbach's task of directing fire was made more difficult as the ship had to constantly change course to avoid becoming an easy target for submarines or aircraft. A thick mist covered the ground so he had to rely on a map and his own calculations as the Arados could not report the fall of shot. The first salvo from the ship's eight 203mm guns—which took nearly 90 seconds to reach its target—crashed right onto the centre of the town. Eleven more followed, hitting the railway yard and station and destroying the town square, where an entire Soviet armoured brigade had parked its tanks. The entire brigade was blown away; 48 T-34s were utterly destroyed, their tank crews perishing in the inferno. The Russians targeted the circling seaplanes, but did not bring any down, although Lieutenant Stoll's aircraft was holed by machine-gun fire.[9] The destroyers then added to the bombardment. Each carried five 127mm guns, in all firing 150 shells at the Soviets.[10] After the seaplanes were relaunched at 10:00 a.m., the bombardment shifted to the south-east of the town, and later to destroy a gun emplacement north of the town. Russian fighters finally appeared and attacked the seaplanes. Despite their slower speed, their manoeuvrability enabled them to escape back to the *Prinz Eugen* virtually unscathed.

The *Prinz Eugen* was not the only supporter the Panzer Graf had. His old aerial comrade-in-arms, Hans Ulrich Rudel, was also flying support missions around the northern front and the Tukum area with his tank busters. On one tank-hunting mission his Stuka was hit:

> Now I see straight in my line of flight a black moving mass: the road, tanks, vehicles, Russians. I at once yell: "attack!" Already at almost point-blank range the defence looses off a concentrated fire from in front of me, twin and quadruple flak . . . I am flying at 90 feet and have bumped right into the middle of the hornet's nest . . . I twist and turn in the craziest manoeuvres to avoid being hit, I shoot without taking aim . . . Now I climb a little as I reach the vehicles and tanks and soar over them. I feel I am sitting on eggs and waiting for the smash. This is bound to end badly; my head is as hot as the metal screaming past me. A few seconds later a tell-tale hammering. Gadermann yells: "Engine on fire!" A hit in the engine . . . Flames lick the cockpit.[11]

Rudel tried to climb so they could bail out, but the aircraft was too badly damaged and they crashed. The tree canopy slowed the aircraft, which then broke up on impact. Rudel was badly injured, but the actions of Gadermann and nearby soldiers meant that he went on to fly again, supporting von Strachwitz again in the battles for Upper Silesia.

When von Strachwitz finally entered Tukum with 10 of his tanks he was confronted by a scene of complete devastation: wrecked tanks everywhere, some burning, some upside down, others just scattered lumps of twisted metal. Blackened bodies lay around the tanks and buildings, while here and there staggered a dazed and disoriented survivor. A few Russian tanks had survived, but these were swiftly put out of action, their shaken crews incapable of meaningful resistance. Von Strachwitz left a few APCs from the SS Panzer Grenadier Battalion to secure the town. He then moved off to engage a force of 60 Russian tanks and lorry-borne infantry that had been sighted. He took them completely by surprise. The infantry, along with a number of T-34s, surrendered in the mistaken belief that they were surrounded, which was just as well as they totalled several thousand men.[12] The Russians were convinced that they had been facing a superior force, and to excuse their failures, the 51st Army reported that von Strachwitz had used over 300 tanks for his attack on Tukum and that the Germans had launched amphibious landings from the *Prinz Eugen* fleet.[13]

Due to mechanical breakdowns and having left some panzers to guard his prisoners and secure his booty, the Graf moved east to Sloka, encountering only light resistance on the way. With a much-diminished force—only nine Panthers—the Panzer Graf moved towards Eighteenth Army, which he reached on 21 August, making contact with the men of the SS Nordland Division. Contact had now been established between Army Groups North and Centre. The 52nd Security Division was sent to provide a security screen around the narrow breakthrough corridor Graf von Strachwitz's forces had forged. Unfortunately the situation would not last, with Army Group North being cut off in the Kurland peninsula, fighting on there in three epic battles to the end of the war.

Battle Group Kieffel attacked from Riga with the 81st and 93rd Infantry Divisions, along with some guns from Sturmgeschütz Brigades 202, 909 and 912. The German attacks took them to Dobele, which they assaulted on 23 August. By this time Panzer Brigade Gross was down to 720 men, three Panthers, five Panzer IIIs and IVs, 20 APCs and three captured T-34s.[14]

When an exhausted Graf von Strachwitz finally entered Riga he emerged from his panzer dishevelled and sweat-stained, his face black from the cordite. Some generals nearby chorused: "Bravo Lieutenant! Well done!" Von Strachwitz walked stiffly over: "Not Lieutenant, I'm a General like you gentlemen. Just a little dirtier that's all." He finished with a grin, taking some delight at the look of astonishment on their faces.[15]

Von Strachwitz was subsequently involved in a fire-brigade role, moving his ever-dwindling force to wherever it was needed. He was also involved in reorganising panzer and panzer grenadier units, taking into account their losses, reinforcements required, and the needs of the front. While necessary, it wasn't a task he particularly enjoyed, preferring active combat duties. In fact he couldn't keep away from attacking the enemy. At one point he played his old trick again: warning the Russians of an impending attack, then striking his would-be ambushers from the flank and rear. He used T-34s captured at Tukum to lead his panzer column, enabling him to move relatively easily behind enemy lines. He took part in actions west of Siauliai in Lithuania, and along the Latvian–Lithuanian border.

Panzer Brigade 101—under its new commander, Lieutenant Colonel Erhard Zahn, a Knight's Cross with Oak Leaves winner, who had taken over in late September—fought southwest of Riga. In October it fought defensively in Lithuania before retreating to East Prussia. It then fought at Wirballen and Goldap. It was disbanded in mid-November.

In November 1944, von Strachwitz left his ad-hoc division near Lake Vortsjarv—after attacking the Russian 1st Guards Army in the flank—and travelled towards Elva to visit a divisional headquarters for a briefing. Near Sangaste Manor, his Kubelwagon[16] skidded at high speed, then rolled over several times. His driver and aide were killed instantly, while he suffered horrific injuries. He had a fractured skull, broken ribs, legs and hands. The doctors at the aid post gave him up for dead, but his indomitable will kept him alive despite all expectations to the contrary. He was sent to a hospital in Riga until he was fit enough to be repatriated to Germany in a Ju-52 transport plane for rest and rehabilitation.

His injuries, though grievous, had one fortunate side effect: taking him away from Army Group North before it became trapped in the Latvia's Courland Peninsula, where it fought until the end of the war with the remnants going into Soviet captivity. Had he remained with the army group he might well have shared the fate of his cousin, General Lieutenant Mauritz von Strachwitz, a Knight's Cross winner and commander of the 89th Infantry Division, who became one of the 1,350,000 Germans who died in Russian slave labour camps from hunger, disease, exhaustion and neglect.

The same month as Von Strachwitz's accident, his panzerverband was disbanded. An understrength division, combining both army and SS units, the panzerverband had achieved some significant, albeit temporary victories under von Strachwitz. General Eduard Raus maintained in his book *Panzer Operations* that the attacks by his panzer corps had drawn forces away from von Strachwitz's front, making his victories possible. That may have been the case, yet the fact remains that von Strachwitz achieved the most with the smallest force available. It was the hallmark of his tactical ability and genius.

Following its disbandment, units of Panzer Brigade 101 were sent to reinforce the badly depleted 20th Panzer Division. Panzer Brigade Gross, after fighting in Tartu, around Lake Peipus and at Memel (Lithuanian Klaipeda), returned to Westphalia in Germany. Its remnants were used to reinforce other Waffen SS units preparing for the Ardennes offensive at the end of 1944.

NOTES

1. Paul Adair, *Hitler's Greatest Defeat—The Collapse of Army Group Centre, June 1944* (Arms and Armour Press, 1994). See also Richard Brett-Smith, *Hitler's Generals* (Osprey Publishing, 1976).
2. Busch managed to get himself reactivated, however, to continue his inglorious career, fighting the Allies as Commander-in-Chief North West in April 1945.
3. Samuel W. Mitcham Jr., *German Defeat in the East.*
4. Bryan Perrett, *Knights of the Black Cross* (Wordsworth Editions Ltd, 1997).
5. General Erhard Raus, *Panzer Operations* (trans. Steven H Newton).
6. Antonio Munoz, *Forgotten Legions—Obscure Combat Formations of the Waffen-SS* (Paladin Press Col. USA, 1991).
7. German torpedo boats were in reality small destroyers, while their equivalent to the British and American torpedo boats were called Schnell Boots commonly referred to as E-boats.
8. *Forgotten Legions*, p.137.
9. Fritz-Otto Busch (trans. Eleanor Brockett), *The Story of the* Prinz Eugen (Robert Hale, London, 1960).
10. Abwehr Kämpf am nord Flügel de Ostfront.
11. Hans Ulrich Rudel (trans. Lynton Hudson), *Stuka Pilot* (Euphorion, Dublin, 1952).
12. Peter McCarthy and Mike Syron, *Panzerkreig* (Constable and Robinson Lou, 2002).
13. Prit Buttar, *Between Giants*, p. 226.
14. Antonio Munoz, *Forgotten Legions.*
15. www.leikon-der-wehrmacht.de and Helmut Schiebel (trans. Klaus Scharvey), *A Better Comrade You Will Never Find* (J.J. Fedorowicz, 2010).
16. The Kubelwagon was the German equivalent to the American jeep.

TWENTY-TWO

THE BATTLE FOR GERMANY

FOLLOWING HIS REPATRIATION TO GERMANY, VON Strachwitz underwent a painful period of recovery and rehabilitation in Breslau. His limbs were slow to improve, and horrendous headaches would plague him for years. However, he was not a man to meekly accept his fate. He undertook his rehabilitation with the single-minded focus that was his hallmark. He pushed himself to his limit to get his body functioning again, in order to get out of hospital and return to active duty. Finally he discharged himself while still considered by the doctors to be unfit.

Still on crutches, the Panzer Graf reported to Field Marshal Schorner at his army group headquarters, eager to undertake a combat assignment. The field marshal couldn't accept him for duty, but von Strachwitz persisted until Schorner relented and offered him a position on his staff. But the Graf would not accept that, insisting on a combat assignment and actually requesting he be given command of a panzer or tank-destroyer unit. Finally Schorner agreed; after all, he had to admire the Graf's persistence and courage. So von Strachwitz was given a unit called Panzerjäger Brigade Oberschleisen[1] (Tank-hunter Brigade Upper Silesia). It was a brand-new formation, as the time necessary to assemble, equip and train the brigade would give the Panzer Graf time to recover from his wounds. He was clearly unfit to walk into an existing formation and go straight into battle.

The brigade consisted of an infantry regiment of three battalions, with some 650 men each, an artillery battalion, with whatever guns could be scraped together, an armour battalion, and signals, engineer, transport and support units. Armour was a problem as tanks were scarce, with full panzer divisions having only 20–30 operational tanks, being often down to four or five. As a result the Graf received turret-less tank hunters, initially 10 Jagdpanzer IVs, with a promise of more armour to come, although he knew would have to scrounge or steal whatever he could. The Jagdpanzers, however, were highly effective tank killers. Their low silhouette made them hard to hit and easy to conceal while their high-velocity 75mm gun was sufficient to destroy a T-34 and even a Josef Stalin heavy tank if they could get in close enough.

His three infantry battalions were a motley crew of eager volunteers, grizzled veterans, callow youths and returning convalescents taken from replacement battalions. The fit, well-trained young men of the 1939 Blitzkrieg were long gone; what now remained were old men, World War I veterans, fanatical Hitler youth or hastily trained and malnourished levies, with a leavening of combat veterans to stiffen the inexperienced majority. A clear example is Günter Kosemorrek, a veteran sent to the Führer Begleit Brigade, part of the Grossdeutschland Panzer Corps, as a replacement:

> Back in the days when I was a recruit I would probably have been very proud to wear the narrow black sleeve insignia with the silver inscription "Führer Begleit Brigade Grossdeutschland." Now the designation Grossdeutschland struck us as more of a joke, not least because this supposedly elite unit is now nothing but a bunch of half-trained Hitler Youth members, re-trained Kriegsmarine [Navy] and Luftwaffe personnel and elderly ethnic Germans from Eastern Europe who can only speak broken German—a dreadful bunch the like of which I have never seen even in 1942 after the flight from Stalingrad.[2]

Yet for all that, they fought extremely well. Not just for their primary group, as these had been subject to continual change through casualties and transfers. Combat formations underwent 200% to 300% personnel turnover so that the primary group was no longer represented by individuals. It was the division, and regiment, the original combat unit, which nourished, nurtured and guided them throughout the war that held them together as their wartime family. At this point in the war they were basically fighting for the survival of their homeland, but above all it was their disciplined character that kept them fighting, their obedience to their superiors and the regime. Germany had been a militarised society since before World War I. Taught to obey from a young age, they continued to do so to the very end. Severe discipline and draconian punishments for disobedience also played a part. The German Army prided itself on its discipline, and spent a great deal of effort to keep it at a high standard. Also, even at this late stage in the war, sufficient numbers still believed in Hitler and final victory to maintain a fierce resistance. Ultimately the sheer professionalism and obedience of the army kept it fighting to a high standard.

Most, if not all, of von Strachwitz's men felt privileged to be commanded by the legendary Panzer Graf, a Diamonds wearer, with a reputation for brilliant success. Although not all felt so sanguine, as one grizzled veteran was overheard to remark: "With the Panzer Graf leading us we'll be for it. They'll be sending us to all the hot spots." He wasn't wrong.

Signals, equipment and transport were equally hard to obtain, along with the fuel to drive the vehicles, so that the brigade was deficient in all three. What they did have in abundance, however, was the panzerfaust [armour fist], a hand-held single-shot anti-tank rocket projectile that could pierce 200mm armour at a range of 60 metres. The close range required for an effective hit was a problem, requiring cool nerves and courage, but at least it gave the infantry an effective weapon, and many soldiers earned multiple tank destruction ribbons using it.

Throughout January, while von Strachwitz was busy establishing his formation at its headquarters at Bod Kudova, the front was crumbling around him. The German Army was in retreat everywhere, despite a brief fling against the Americans in the Ardennes in December. Everywhere the hard-pressed infantry relied on small numbers of tanks from the battered panzer divisions to give them some respite or prevent them from being overrun. These panzer units lurched from one crisis to another, never staying long enough to consolidate a gain before being called elsewhere by urgent appeals for help from another infantry unit. Then they in turn would have to withdraw, as one or both units on their flank collapsed, threatening them with encirclement. This was the role the Panzer Graf's brigade would play, responding to alarm calls to stop Soviet spearheads, and mounting counterattacks to restore a local situation or front-line position.

The Germans were increasingly using Stalin's tactics of executing their soldiers for retreating or not pressing an attack vigorously enough. Even a comparatively mild field marshal, the Luftwaffe's Albert Kesselring, "Smiling Albert" to his men, chided Graf von Strachwitz's cousin Rudolf-Christoph von Gersdorff for not hanging any cowards or deserters, as he did not see any swinging from the lamp posts on his way to the latter's headquarters.[3]

On 12 January the Allies announced the results of their conference at Yalta in the Ukraine. It had serious implications for Graf von Strachwitz: large tracts of German territory were to be given to Poland including Upper Silesia, his home, the area he had fought the Poles for in 1921. The German inhabitants were to be resettled. On the same date, the Russians launched their final major offensive, heralded by a massive drum-fire artillery bombardment calculated to drive the strongest surviving soldier insane. It shattered the German front, with the Russians breaking through over the Vistula.

This led to the hurried completion of Panzerjäger Brigade Oberschleisen's formation. Every man and gun was needed to contain the Russian onslaught. On 15 January Stuka expert Hans Ulrich Rudel, himself a Silesian, requested the transfer of his unit to Upper Silesia, taking all but one of his squadrons to Udetfeld. On their first day there, they destroyed 11 Soviet tanks, three among buildings, and eight in a convoy along the road, plus several trucks and other vehicles.[4]

The Russians crossed the old Silesian/Polish border on 19 January so Strachwitz was now defending the sacred soil of Germany. Refugees were streaming along the roads carrying their possessions in carts or carriages or simply trudging disconsolately following those in front. The Wehrmacht estimated that some 3,500,000 German civilians were on the move in the east at this time.[5] Tens of thousands were killed by Russian artillery fire or strafing attacks by fighters or bombers, callous attacks which only served to harden German resistance. Refugees were often assisted by French or Allied prisoners of war who had worked for them as farm labourers, and who were equally unwilling to fall into Russian hands. A small detachment of British prisoners actually attached themselves to a Waffen SS Unit of the 33rd SS Volunteer Division just to get away from the Russians. Even more pitiful were the starving, emaciated concentration camp inmates being forced on death marches to prevent their liberation by the Russians.

The Germans fighting desperately to stave off the Soviet and Allied invasions probably did not stop to think that only recently they had been the invaders. In fact many may not have considered such a description appropriate, reasoning that the British and French had declared war on them and the invasion of Russia had been a crusade against communism. Von Strachwitz probably also held this view, quite common as it was among all Germans, especially the officer class, and Strachwitz certainly felt the invasion of Poland was necessary, to end Polish claims to his beloved Silesia.

German hopes were meantime kept alive by promises of miracle weapons that would alter—and win—the war. The Panzer Graf held no such illusions. He fought hard to give his fellow Silesians time to escape. This overriding motivation totally absorbed him, enabling him to tolerate the pain of his wounds. Nonetheless, his adjutant often found him slumped in his vehicle almost prostrate by the severity of his headaches. At the end of January, he found out that his Schloss at Gross-Stein had fallen into Russian hands on the 24th. It was a not an unexpected blow, but still difficult to accept when it happened. Fortunately his family had managed to fly out. His home was plundered and its chapel was destroyed. After the war, the Red Army used it for a time before it was destroyed by fire in 1955.

He did get some good news in January, a promotion to lieutenant general on the 30th. This was the rank for a corps or divisional commander, so commanding a brigade was technically a downgrading, although given his state of health he was lucky to have a command at all. Also, the promotion wasn't a reflection of his formation command status but of his overall tactical genius in armoured warfare and to his courage. The question of status didn't overly concern him because he was well aware that a command at divisional level would not allow him any latitude to act independently, as Hitler was micromanaging down to divisional level and sometimes even below. As a lieutenant general he was of equal rank to army corps commanders, and out-ranked most divisional commanders, so would not encounter too many problems from the generals in his area of operation. His reputation and tactical ability also gave him a great deal of latitude, which was helped by the confusion and fast-changing situation, which allowed him greater freedom of movement. He basically slipped through the net in the chain of command for extended periods of time, which suited him perfectly.[6]

He did however work in close co-operation with Rudel who had moved his squadrons to Klein-Eig, near the Panzer Graf's home. The Russians rapidly became aware of his presence, and at the first sign of his Stukas the Russian tanks would try to hide, usually in and around buildings. Rudel, reluctant to bomb houses where civilians might be hiding, would call on the Panzer Graf to flush the Soviets out so he could pounce. Equally the Graf would stealthily move up to where the Russians were hiding and his men would blast them, usually with the panzerfaust. Most had become adept at using this weapon, with some earning 10 or more tank destruction badges (although owing to the chaos of those days, many kills were not recorded or badges awarded). Rudel would often decimate a tank convoy enabling von Strachwitz's small force to move in and mop up the survivors. The two Silesians worked well together as a team, causing the Russians heavy tank losses and providing the battered German infantry with much-needed respites. Rudel, however, was soon called away by Himmler to fight in his command area of operations in Marisch Friedland, East Pomerania.

Von Strachwitz's brigade continued to strike hard counterblows against the Russians. When checked the Russians would often outflank any stubborn holdouts, forcing them into a retreat. The Panzer Graf was thus often forced to retreat, but not before thrusting into the exposed Soviet flanks, causing at least a momentary halt to their advance. Despite being wracked with pain, and no doubt affected by the devastation of his beloved Silesian homeland, the Graf fought on with focused fury as he continued to move among his troops, urging them on with his seemingly fearless example. His doubts and misgivings he kept to himself.

By the end of January the greater part of Upper Silesia, the industrial heartland of mines, steel mills and armaments factories, had fallen into Soviet hands. With the Ruhr bombed out—and soon to be captured by US forces—Germany had little industrial capacity left to maintain meaningful resistance. The end was only months away. Breslau was surrounded by the Red Army on 13 February and Sagan was taken on the 15th. The Soviet 1st Ukrainian Front commenced its major offensive in Ratibor on 15 March. German territory was constricting at an alarming rate, but its defiant resistance in the east never slackened.

The Graf's tactics of ambush and rapid surprise attacks were easily carried out on an over-confident and often careless enemy. In the Russians' immediate rear there was little security because German artillery was chronically short of ammunition and the Luftwaffe was almost non-existent so the endless stream of Russian tanks and vehicles pushing towards the front was virtually unmolested. The Graf's armoured vehicles and tank-hunting grenadiers gave the Soviets several salutary lessons, but his attacks had very little impact on the flood of armour, men, and vehicles, pouring in. No matter how many Russian tanks or vehicles his men destroyed, the advance only paused briefly before continuing. The enemy was too strong and thick on the ground for the Panzer Graf to remain in his rear for long as he had done in the past, and so he was always beating a quick retreat. Even when retreating, however, he took out Russian troops and gun positions who were feeling secure, even close to or at the front line.

At this time the German Eastern Front contained 103 infantry divisions and 32 panzer or panzergrenadier divisions plus various ad-hoc formations or independent brigades like the Graf's Oberschleisen. On the Western Front, now sitting on Germany's border, there were 65 infantry and twelve panzer divisions, though four of these were to be sent east. None of the German forces were strong enough to do anything beyond delay the enemy advances. All the divisions were seriously under-strength, mere shadows of the formations that invaded France in 1940 or Russia in 1941. Acknowledging its acute shortage, the German Army reduced its panzer divisions from two to one panzer battalion, and even this had to often be made up to strength with assault guns rather than tanks. The diminished strength of the German forces did not matter to Hitler, who still expected the divisions marked on his maps to perform as fully equipped and supplied divisions, with a full complement of trained troops. He did, in one of his rare frank and honest moments, admit to his Luftwaffe Adjutant von Below, in late December 1944: "I know the war is lost. The enemy superiority is too great."[7] However capitulation was never an option.

Although not as severe as the Germans' issues, the Russians also had manpower problems. Their enormous losses in the war to date meant that the Russians were pressing into service any male they could get their hands on in the areas formerly occupied by the Germans. In this way countries with no love for Russia, such as Lithuania, which had to provide a whole division for the Red Army and reinforcements for existing units, were pressed into service without any training at all.

Around mid-March von Strachwitz received a visit from Colonel Freiherr von Jugenfeld, on behalf of Army Group Weichsel, which was looking to form more brigades like the Panzer Graf's. The Colonel sent an extremely favourable report as to Oberschleisen's organisation and effectiveness. However by this time the brigade was sorely depleted in heavy weaponry, but thanks to von Strachwitz's inspired leadership its morale was still high. It was not a beaten force seeking only to escape, but one that struck back hard and fast at the enemy. He was then given overall command of several tank-hunting units consisting mainly of men who were armed only with the ubiquitous panzerfaust and who often rode to battle on bicycles in a parody of the former fast-moving armoured battalions. Nevertheless they proved effective, with the Russians learning to have a healthy respect for their deadly ambushes and at least one Knight's Cross was earned by a young tank-hunter lieutenant.

Von Strachwitz managed to find reinforcements for his units by incorporating stragglers from the retreating flotsam, who were only too glad to find a home and with it a greater chance for survival. Despite this, by 10 April the three battalions of his original brigade were badly depleted and they only had some 60 vehicles of all types remaining. Infantry weapons were still adequate, and they still had several hundred panzerfausts, which allowed them to continue some semblance of an anti-tank role. The panzerfaust and its larger cousin, the panzerschrek, should not be discounted as literally hundreds of Russian and Allied tanks were destroyed by them, especially towards the end of the war. They were particularly effective in urban warfare, where the user could conceal himself in a building or rubble, and fire from very close range. Some 70% of Russian tanks were destroyed in this way in the towns and cities of the east.

At the beginning of April von Strachwitz received the awful news that his youngest son, Hubertus Arthur, Harti for short, a lieutenant in a panzer regiment, had been killed while fighting in Holstein on 25 March. Harti, a gentle, good-looking, slim young man, had previously been seriously wounded, and had had his leg amputated.[8] His conscience would not allow him to stay back while Germany was under attack, and when he volunteered to return to active service the army accepted him back. Given his previous wound his father would have had reason to be confident that Harti would survive the war, and he only had his eldest to worry about. So the blow when it came had double the effect.

His eldest son, Hyazinth, a successful panzer commander in the 11th Panzer Division, who favoured his father in looks, had also been severely wounded and was still recovering. His convalescence no doubt ensured that he survived the war, but it left him so deeply traumatised that he never fully recovered. The Graf's daughter, Lisalotte, was safe in Bavaria, much to the Graf's relief. She had arrived there after a sojourn in Italy where she and 36 other German girls armed with rifles had travelled from Brindisi to Rome through Communist partisan-infested territory, to report for duty. The commander wisely sent them home, much to their disappointment.[9]

Hitler ultimately took the coward's way out, and shot himself on 30 April. Göring and Himmler had already betrayed Hitler so Admiral Dönitz was appointed as führer. The Panzer Graf's reaction to the news of Hitler's death was not recorded, but would no doubt have been "not before time and it should have happened much earlier," an opinion shared by many. Hajo Herrmann, an expert bomber pilot with the Knight's Cross, Oak Leaves and Swords recounted, "Doenitz announced 'Fuehrer had fallen in Berlin' The women [Eva Braun's mother and sister with whom he was staying] wept. I did not weep. The conclusion seemed to me to be inevitable, necessary."[10] On the other hand, Hans Ulrich Rudel noted, "The shock of the news that the Head of State and Supreme Commander of the Reich is dead has a stunning effect on the troops."[11] Helmut Altner, a young conscript defending Berlin, on hearing an order of the day that Hitler had fallen but the fight against Bolshevism would go on, said "I am astonished. No word of peace. Only 'holding on."[12] Claus Sellier, a newly minted lieutenant, on hearing Hitler's last testament on the radio: "We were on the threshold of victory, however the German people betrayed me, the German Army refused to fight—officers and soldiers alike betrayed me . . ." said "I was raging mad. He dared to say that. When twelve million Germans have died. That's his testament? Did you hear that arrogant lunatic bastard?"[13] Georg Grossjohann, who was attending a regimental officers' course recorded, "The news announced on 30 April that Hitler had been killed during the defence of Berlin was received in different ways by the participants in the course. Astonishingly the numerous SS officers working in this area reacted especially coolly."[14] Perhaps equally astonishing, and perhaps a testament to German confidence in victory, they were still conducting training courses in the final desperate days of the regime. The veterans of the Waffen SS too had become disillusioned with Hitler and the Nazis, as they saw that their many sacrifices had been unappreciated and in vain. Their motives for fighting on were now similar to the army's, with the extra psychological burden of having been ultimately betrayed by their Führer, for whom they had given their all.

The Panzer Graf was not prepared to go down to Valhalla after a Götterdämmerung-style struggle against the Soviet forces, so with his usual meticulous planning he organised his retreat away from the Russians, towards the Americans. Allocating one battalion as a rearguard, he led the remains of his brigade through to the Sudetenland. It was fortunate that he didn't stop and surrender in the Sudetenland, as many Germans who surrendered to Americans there were handed over to the Russians. Perhaps the Graf suspected this, as he continued into Bavaria. Here he encountered the Americans where an astonished young lieutenant sitting nonchalantly in his jeep was only too glad to accept the surrender of a highly decorated general. Von Strachwitz was so haggard and drawn that the officer thought he was wounded and inquired whether he needed medical attention. The Graf merely replied "No." With that he went into American captivity. His war was finally over.

NOTES

1. Some publications show it as a Panzerjagd Brigade. I have adopted the terminology used in Georg Tessin's work listing all of the Wehrmacht's formations, which lists a Panzer Jäger Brigade Oberschleisen. There were numerous ad-hoc units, with various, often similar names operating at the end of the war with little or nothing known of them in official records. There was a Knight's Cross recipient in a Tank Destruction Brigade "Oberschleisen," but whether this was the Panzer Graf's brigade or another with the same title is unclear.
2. Günter K. Koschorrek, *Blood Red Snow: The Memoirs of a German Soldier on the Eastern Front* (Greenhill Books, UK, 2002), p. 299.
3. Baron Rudolf-Christoph von Gersdorff (trans. Anthony Pearsall), *Soldier in the Downfall: A Wehrmacht Cavalryman in Russia; Normandy and the Plot to Kill Hitler* (Aberjona Press, USA, 2012).
4. Hans Ulrich Rudel (trans. Lynton Hudson), *Stuka Pilot* (Euphorion, Dublin, 1952).
5. Christopher Duffy, *Red Storm on the Reich* (Atheneum, NY, 1991).
6. For all these reasons not a great deal is known or recorded as to his activities during the last months of the war. Similarly commanding ad-hoc formations, as he did in Estonia, Latvia and Lithuania as well as in Upper Silesia also meant little in the way of records and documentation such as war diaries etc which were kept by larger and more established formations. The 16th Panzer Division also lost much of its documentation with the surrender at Stalingrad.
7. Von Below, *At Hitler's Side*, p. 223.
8. Günter Fraschka. *Knights of the Reich.*
9. Ibid.
10. Hajo Herrmann, *Eagle's Wings* (Airlife Publishing, UK, 1991).
11. Rudel, *Stuka Pilot.*
12. Helmut Altner, *Berlin Dance of Death* (Casemate, PA, 2002).
13. Claus Sellier, *Walking Away from the Third Reich—A Teenager in Hitler's Army* (Hellgate Press, USA, 2006).
14. Georg Grossjohann, *Five Years, Four Fronts* (Aegis Consulting Group, PA, USA).

TWENTY-THREE

CAPTIVITY AND POST-WAR YEARS

THE PANZER GRAF'S FIRST EXPERIENCE OF CAPTIVITY was benign. As a general he was quickly separated from his men and treated with a great deal of respect, the more so because of his high decorations. The US front-line soldiers could respect a highly decorated combat officer, and identify with one who was also a front-line soldier. It would have been different had his captors recently liberated a concentration camp; after seeing the horrors within the camps, liberators often shot the SS guards out of hand and were none too merciful to any subsequent prisoners they took.

Soon after his capture, von Strachwitz was interrogated by his captors, who wanted to find out whether he was a political general or a fighting soldier, and whether he had committed any war crimes. If he had committed war crimes, he would have been handed over to the Russians for justice. It is probably correct to assume that during these interrogations he didn't mention his party or SS membership. US interrogators were a very mixed bag, with quite a few inflicting what would by any standard be regarded as torture. For instance SS General Kurt "Panzer" Meyer was subjected to several mock executions, threats and sleep deprivation, and his was not an isolated case. Beatings and other forms of harassment were frequent, calculated to wear a prisoner down.

Being an anti-Nazi certainly didn't provide any extra privileges, as Baron Rudolf-Christoph von Gersdorff found out, recounting an encounter with the prison commandment after the release of Hitler's former adjutant and now general, Gerhard Engel. When asked his thoughts on Engel's release, von Gersdorff replied, "I was happy for his freedom . . . however I was amazed that such proven resistance fighters as Colonel-General Baron von Falkenhausen or myself, for example, had not at least been released at the same time."

The commandant explained that Engel had always only carried out the orders he had been given, would likely put up no resistance in civilian life, and therefore posed no danger. By contrast, von Gersdorff's behaviour showed that he would, if necessary, follow his own conscience, "Therefore people like you, or General von Falkenhausen, are dangerous to us. That's why we need to keep you in custody for a while longer."[1]

So the Graf's anti-Nazism might have kept him from being labelled a true Nazi, but might possibly kept him incarcerated for a lot longer. It is of interest to note that when it became known that von Gersdorff had been an active anti-Hitler conspirator he was ostracised by most of the other prisoners. The senior German prisoner, General Hollidt, told von Gersdorff that a group of generals had approached him to have von Gersdorff removed from the camp, and failing that they wanted him killed.[2]

Von Strachwitz's conditions deteriorated, as they did for all captive soldiers, when US General Eisenhower declared them to be disarmed enemy persons and not POWs, therefore putting them outside the protections of the Geneva Convention. Almost at once food rations were drastically cut and treatment became distinctly harsher. The least fortunate were the 400,000 POWs in the Rheinwiesenlager (Rhine meadows camps), with no shelter, little or no food, non-existent medical attention and arbitrary brutality. Totals for deaths through sickness, hunger and neglect are not known and have been quoted to be as high as 40,000, but were probably closer to half that figure. The Americans did eventually improve conditions, assisted by large-scale releases, while the French on the other hand continued to starve and abuse their prisoners for years afterwards.[3]

Eventually von Strachwitz was sent to the prison camp at Allendorff, which housed a great many generals who were incarcerated for longer terms. Many were tasked with recording their experiences and comments on the war and to provide other useful information for the Western Allies. Graf von Strachwitz was required to provide information on tank tactics and his impressions of the Red Army, now rapidly becoming the USA's new enemy. Von Gersdorff thought that the Americans also had a penchant for collecting war heroes, particularly Diamonds winners, which is why fighter ace General Adolf Galland was also sent there.

The barracks in which the prisoners were housed were basic and primitive, having been used at one time for Soviet POWs, then later for disarmed Italian soldiers taken after Italy's capitulation. Jewish workers had been housed there when it had been a sub-camp of the Buchenwald concentration camp. As time went by conditions improved and the prisoners were housed in more solid accommodations in the nearby city of Neustadt.

On 8 May 1946 Hyazinth von Strachwitz received some shattering news. Alda, Countess Saurma-Jeltsch, his wife of over 28 years had been run over and killed by an American truck in a tragic accident. He had now lost his wife and youngest son. His mother had died on 26 January 1940, and his father on 28 April 1942. He had some family left: his eldest son was still alive, though traumatised; his brother Manfred had come through unscathed having earned the Iron Cross First and Second Class; and his three sisters, Aloysia, Elizabeth, and Margarethe, had survived the war, but it was little consolation. He was denied permission to attend his wife's funeral.

His captivity finally came to an end in June 1947. On 30 July he married Nora von Stumm in Holzhausen near Marburg. She was descended from the minor nobility, not that ancestry mattered much in the new Germany. She loved the Graf dearly, and they had two sons and two daughters.

For the second time Hyazinth von Strachwitz emerged from captivity to a much-altered Germany. He faced a bleak future without a home, job, and very few prospects, so for Nora it had been a true love match. Conditions in Germany were still grim; food was scarce, and the 1946 official ration was 1,275 calories per person per day, barely sufficient to maintain reasonable health. Women were still selling themselves for food or cigarettes to trade on the black market, while men stole, operated the black market, or did whatever they could to feed themselves and their families. Most were having to rebuild their homes and lives. It was particularly hard for the Graf to adjust. He had been transformed from a wealthy, respected count, decorated general and war hero to a jobless, homeless ex-prisoner. His war record and high decorations now meant less than nothing. In fact they labelled him as a warmonger, his exploits and heroism putting him at a disadvantage in the new Germany. The inherited title of which he was so proud—which had been already been devalued after the fall of the Kaiser but still had some cachet in the Third Reich—was now totally meaningless.

He was eventually given a small pension and left to adjust to post-war life as best he could. However, an opportunity presented itself in 1949. The president of Syria, Jhukri-al-Quwatli, needed someone to put the Syrian Army, and particularly its armoured corps, into shape, after its ignominious defeat by the Israelis in the Arab–Israeli war of 1948. A good salary and accommodations were offered, along with the opportunity to be involved with what he did best—train and organise an armoured formation. It was also an opportunity to leave drab, depressing Germany for a new and brighter beginning. As a cover he was listed as an adviser on agricultural affairs.

He arrived in Syria with his wife on January 1949 and quickly went to work. His ideas and plans were well received by the Defence Ministry, but their enthusiasm quickly died when they saw the costs involved. The Syrian government was a shambolic mess, with systemic corruption and nepotism rampant. Government ministers, generals and officials were only concerned with enriching themselves, as much and as quickly as possible. No one knew how long the money supply would last and any cash for new equipment and armaments quickly vanished into private bank accounts. The CIA-sponsored coup of June 1949 put von Strachwitz out of a job, and possibly in some danger as an official of the previous regime.

Graf von Strachwitz and Nora hurriedly fled to Lebanon, then quickly moved on to Italy. They settled in the Tuscan wine-growing area near Livorno where the Graf started a business as a wine merchant. He wasn't very successful in this new and strange line of work, so in 1951, travelling on Red Cross passports, his family returned to Germany.

Life settled down to a leisurely pace and they bought an estate from his wife's inheritance in Winkl near Grabenstatt in the district of Chiemsee in Catholic Bavaria, a very pleasant place to live. His focus—apart from his family—became the Upper Silesian refugees for whom he founded the Upper Silesian Refugee Foundation.

It had been agreed at the Teheran conference that Russia would keep the Polish territory conquered in the stab-in-the-back invasion of 1939 that everyone had conveniently forgotten about. Poland would be compensated with German territory, namely Danzig, Pomerania and Silesia. As a result some 7,000,000 Germans were, or would be, displaced. Those who did not flee on the earlier refugee treks in the winter of 1944/45 were later forcibly evicted. The Russians later annexed East Prussia, calling it Kaliningrad, bringing the total of displaced Germans to some 10,000,000. His work helping the refugees gave von Strachwitz some real purpose.

His son Hyazinth had taken control of his life after his divorce, becoming a businessman working for a machinery company owned by his brother-in-law. He remarried and adopted a boy, while his daughter from his first marriage stayed with her mother, who had married an American involved in the

Dachau concentration camp trials. The younger Hyazinth died in 2003 in Germany.

The Graf's new family was healthy and flourishing, so his later years were calmer and fulfilled. He became a Knight of Devotion of the Catholic branch of the Order of St John[4] and no doubt tied this in with his work for refugees. His Catholic faith also sustained him over the years.

Like most soldiers he had been a heavy smoker, and he died of lung cancer in the hospital of Trostbergin, Upper Bavaria, on 25 April 1968. His funeral was attended by an honour guard of the Bundeswehr, and he was laid to rest next to his first wife in the family plot in Grabenstatt.

His life had been a full, and indeed an honourable one, carried out under extremely difficult circumstances. He had done nothing that brought shame, and indeed a great deal that brought honour to his name, and to his country. Obliged to serve an evil cause, he answered the higher call of his conscience when he agreed to arrest Hitler, but at no time did he betray the duty he owed to the men with whom he fought, or to his country. However, he remains best known for being the most dashing and successful panzer regiment commander of the war, the last great cavalryman and true cavalier. He was indeed the Panzer Lion.

NOTES

1. Rudolf-Christoph von Gersdorff (trans. Anthony Pearsall), *Soldier in the Downfall*, (Aberjona Press, USA, 2012), p. 156.
2. Von Gersdorff tried to join the post-war German Army, but was blocked by Chancellor Konrad Adenauer's chief bureaucrat, a pro-Nazi who had been responsible for drafting many of the anti-Semitic laws. His actions were purely for revenge, because of Gersdorff's attempts to kill Hitler. *Soldier in the Downfall.*
3. Joining the French Foreign Legion offered a way out, which is why so many Germans went on to fight and die in Indo-China.
4. The second military order of monks to be founded during the Crusades, the Hospitallers of St. John were named for the hospital they had established in Jerusalem. The Hospitallers went on to take Rhodes, then Malta after the fall of the Holy Land, from where Napoleon ousted them in 1798. Tsar Paul of Russia, took them over briefly, ending their existence as a Catholic knightly order. They were revived in the 19th century as a gentlemen's club for Europe's Catholic nobility.

APPENDIX 1

THE AWARDS OF HYAZINTH GRAF VON STRACHWITZ

GRAF VON STRACHWITZ WAS ONE OF THE MOST DECOrated soldiers in the German armed forces. His decorations were centred around the Order of the Iron Cross, which was instituted in 1813 by the Prussian Emperor Frederick Wilhelm III to reward officers and men in the wars of liberation against the French under Napoleon Bonaparte. Designed by the architect Kalfred Schinkel, it was based on the black cross worn by the German Order, more often called the Teutonic Knights, who conquered medieval Prussia.

Schinckel's design was a silver cross pattée with an iron centre painted or enamelled black, edged in silver or white. It came in three grades, the Grand Cross, Iron Cross (1st Class) and (2nd Class). Some 16,000 Iron Crosses (2nd Class), 670 Iron Crosses (1st Class) and seven Grand Crosses were awarded of the 1813 institution.

The Order was re-instituted on 19 July 1870 at the time of the Franco-Prussian War. The 2nd Class was given out 41,770 times, including 3,500 to non-combatants, among whom were four British officers, including Surgeon-General W.G.N. Manley, a Victoria Cross recipient who had been in charge of an ambulance unit. The Iron Cross (1st Class) was awarded on 1,300 occasions and the Grand Cross eight times, including one to General Field Marshall von Manteuffel a relative of the Grossdeutschland Division commander in World War II, Hasso von Manteuffel.

With the advent of World War I, Kaiser Wilhelm II reinstituted the Iron Cross on 5 August 1914. As with the previous 1870 Order it was open to all Germans, although the individual German states continued to award their own bravery awards and medals. Hyazinth Graf von Strachwitz was awarded both the 1st and 2nd Class of the 1914 Iron Cross. At that early stage of the war it was still a relatively scarce award and considered quite a feat to receive both grades so quickly. By the time the war was over on 11 November 1918, 163,000–250,000 Iron Crosses (1st Class) had been awarded and a staggering 4,000,000–5,000,000 of the 2nd Class.[1] Only five Grand Crosses were presented, including one to the Kaiser, which was given to him at the "request" of his generals.

The premier bravery award during World War I was the Pour le Mérite, nicknamed the Blue Max, which, unlike its World War II replacement, the Knight's Cross, was reserved exclusively for officers. A total of 687 Pour le Mérites were awarded during World War I, a very small number compared to the Knight's Cross, but it must be remembered that each German state issued its own awards, so the Kaiser could afford to be parsimonious with the Pour le Mérite.

Von Strachwitz's reckless courage might well have earned him a Pour le Mérite had he not been captured so early in the war. Hermann Goering, Manfred von Richthofen, the Graf's classmate from Lichterfelde, Erwin Rommel, Ferdinand Schörner and Robert Ritter von Greim, last chief of the Luftwaffe, were all prominent wearers of the Pour le Mérite. Hans Hube just missed out as the war ended before his recommendation could be approved.[2]

Adolf Hitler renewed the Iron Cross on 1 September 1939. His decree began as follows: "After arriving at the conclusion that the German people must be called to arms in defence of an imminent attack I will renew for the sons of Germany, as in the past great wars in the defence of the home and Fatherland, the Order of the Knight Cross."[3]

He decreed five classes:

Iron Cross (2nd Class), worn in full on the day of the award and thereafter as a ribbon in the buttonhole or ribbon bar, unless in full on formal occasions.

Iron Cross (1st Class), worn as a breast badge.

Knight's Cross, worn as a neck decoration.

Knight's Cross with Oak Leaves, both worn as a neck decoration.

Grand Cross, a much larger version of the Knight's Cross, also worn around the neck. The Pour le Mérite was abolished with the Knight's Cross with Oak Leaves effectively replacing it, although World War I recipients were entitled to wear the decoration in full during World War II, and all in fact did so.

In addition Hitler instituted in 1939 a clasp for those who had received the Iron Cross 1st or 2nd Class in World War I, and who were awarded one or both decorations again in World War II. It consisted of a silver eagle with wings outstretched, clasping a Swastika in its talons, with the year 1939 inscribed in a plaque below the swastika. Both clasps were awarded to Graf von Strachwitz who was awarded both classes of the Iron Cross in World War II. This meant he wore the black and white 1914 ribbon of Iron Cross (2nd Class) in his buttonhole with the 1939 clasp appended to it and his 1914 Iron Cross (1st Class) on his breast with the 1939 clasp pinned above it. It was a far more sensible solution than wearing two Iron Crosses of the same grade. Any World War I Iron Cross recipient not awarded a World War II Iron Cross simply wore the original 1914 ribbon or cross.

As the war progressed, the need arose for higher grades of the Knight's Cross to reward further acts of courage and/or leadership. On 21 June 1941 Hitler instituted the Swords to be attached to the Knight's Cross with Oak Leaves, with fighter ace Adolf Galland the first recipient, being awarded the Swords on the very day of its institution.[4] Soon after, on 15 July 1941, Hitler proclaimed the award of the Diamonds to the Knight's Cross with Oak Leaves and Swords. This was until 1945 the highest gallantry and military leadership award of the Third Reich.

A new Knight's Cross was not presented with each grade after the original Knight's Cross award. Instead the Oak Leaves, Oak Leaves with Swords, and Oak Leaves with Swords and Diamonds were all presented as a separate piece on each occasion in its own case, and having then to be attached to the original Knight's Cross. The Diamonds were studded in the Oak Leaves and sword hilts, weighing in total 2.7 carats.[5] Unlike the others, the Diamonds were not machine made, but individually handcrafted by a jeweller. Virtually all the Diamonds winners wore copies with paste diamonds, in order to preserve their original awards.

From the Iron Cross (1st Class) upwards, the actual decoration was worn on the uniform even during combat, rather than just a ribbon as was common in most other armies. This had several significant benefits. Firstly, the wearer's courage, experience and/or leadership was clearly on display, a personal source of pride for the wearer and, in its higher grades, for his unit. The medals and decorations also informed any observer that they were in the presence of a man of proven bravery and combat experience. This was a confidence boost to others before going into battle, as Gunter Koschorrek recounts:

> The three men from the ATG (anti-tank gun) crew are still being thanked by another group of soldiers. The Geschützführer (gun commander) is an unter-offizier. On his breast he is wearing the Iron Cross (1st Class) and the Silver Wound Badge proving that he has some experience behind him. In our eyes he is a hero, and had he not got the Iron Cross he would certainly be awarded one now.[6]

This also illustrates a gap in the German awards system. The Iron Cross (1st Class) and Iron Cross (2nd Class) could only be awarded once, so subsequent acts of bravery often went unrecognised. If a soldier, like the paratrooper Martin Pöppel, received his awards early in the war, then there was little left to reward him, as the German Cross in Gold and Knight's Cross required higher standards than that for an Iron Cross (1st Class). Pöppel got his Iron Cross in 1940 during the invasion of Holland. He took part in the paratroop assault on Crete and while his comrades were awarded the Iron Cross, "I received as consolation one of the relatively few Crete Commemorative badges from General Student."[7] This unofficial badge highlights the problem of subsequent rewards. Pöppel was fortunate, most soldiers simply got a handshake and a bottle of wine or schnapps if they were lucky. By comparison, if he had been in the US Army he could have received an additional Bronze or Silver Star.

A similar situation existed with the Knight's Cross, where a large gap existed between the Swords and the Diamonds. Someone given the Swords early in the war cold go unrewarded for further acts of gallantry or numerous tank or aircraft kills, as the Diamonds were the highest decoration generally given, and were extremely rare. The case of Lieutenant Colonel Heinz Baer (Bär) is a classic example. He fought in the Battles of France and Britain scoring 17 victories, and being shot down over the Channel once. He went to Russia in 1941, rapidly building his score to 60, earning the Knight's Cross on 2 July 1941 and the Oak Leaves on 14 August 1941. By February 1942 he had 90 victories, including seven in one day, and was awarded the Swords. After this he went on to shoot down six more Russian aircraft and 107 British and American planes, including 24 heavy bombers. In all he flew over 1,000 missions, shot down 244 aircraft, was shot down 18 times, commanded the elite JG77, and was the highest scorer flying the Me-262 jet, with 16 kills. Despite this impressive record, the Diamonds eluded him, and he received no recognition after the Swords.

Not all troops were proud of their officers' decorations, especially the

Knight's Cross and its higher grades, as Günter Koschorrek bitterly pointed out:

> We soldiers know how it is with the handing out of decorations. One for all, they say—and the "one" is always the chief and the superior. When the chiefs are taken care of, then, something can also be dished out to the Indians. For example if a regular soldier is written up for an IC1, [Iron Cross 1st Class] then he really must have risked his neck. As a result, we the *frontschwein*, do not rate the decorations awarded to our superiors as highly as those at home do. Officers' decorations are usually awarded on the basis of what their soldiers contribute, when, en masse, they manage to save their officers' necks. In general, no one quarrels with this system as long as the superior has demonstrated his ability to lead. Unfortunately, I have also met those who never remotely deserved their decorations based on their own performance.[8]

The above comments highlight the fact that the Iron Cross Order was not only bestowed for courage in the field, but for leadership and the performance of a fighting unit as well. So the award of a Knight's Cross could reward a single act of courage or a superlative display of leadership. An example of the former is Flemish SS volunteer Remy Schrijnen, who while wounded manned an anti-tank gun on his own and destroyed seven Russian T-34s. An example of the latter is Leon Degrelle, who by his own initiative and courageous leadership prevented a Russian breakthrough. For a general such as Rommel, von Manstein and Guderian, it was for winning a major battle or leading a formation that achieved significant results, as von Strachwitz did in eliminating the Eastsack and Westsack salients in the Baltics. Overall the Graf's awards were for a combination of personal courage as in *Barbarossa* and the Stalingrad and Kharkov battles, along with his higher command results with Army Group North.

A junior officer or enlisted man invariably gained their Knight's Cross for outstanding valour, although quite often a junior officer could and did, halt a Soviet advance by mounting a rapid counter-attack or cobbling together an ad-hoc blocking unit. Many higher commanders admitted that their Knight's Crosses were due to the courage and fighting ability of their troops, and their men often felt proud of the award for this very reason. Nevertheless it was the commander who wore the decoration and not the men.

Some commanders, such as SS General Sepp Dietrich who won the Diamonds, achieved little themselves, owing their award almost exclusively to their troops, in his case principally the SS Leibstandarte division. One only has to look at the commanders and Knight's Cross winners in his division—Kurt Meyer, Joachim Peiper, Fritz Witt, Theodor Wisch, Max Hansen to name a few—to see where the grades of his Knight's Cross really came from.

It would therefore be inaccurate to say that the roll of Diamonds winners is a pantheon of heroes. It was in fact a combined roll of superlative leaders and heroes, notable also for its omissions, such as Gerd Barkihorn, the 301-kill Luftwaffe ace, Kurt Buhligen (112 kills), Wilhelm Batz (237 kills), Heinrich Baer (220 kills), Joachim Brendel (189 kills), and others.

In other nations a distinction between valour and leadership was made, e.g. the American Medal of Honour and British Victoria Cross, given for outstanding courage only. Nevertheless the leadership requirement for the Knight's Cross had to be extraordinary, and very often meant great personal risk and courage to the recipient. Graf von Strachwitz clearly demonstrated examples of both outstanding courage and leadership. Where his achievements were for the leadership role they were carried out with heavily outnumbered, understrength and often ad-hoc forces and involved inspired leadership from the front, undertaken at great personal risk. He always managed to achieve a great deal with very little in the way of resources, but a great deal in the way of initiative, courage, tactical knowledge and imagination. In all of the actions for which he received his awards, he personally made the difference, and it was not just a case of being rewarded for the fighting qualities and abilities of his soldiers.

Fighter and bomber pilots earned their decorations on a points system: for planes shot down in the case of fighters, and missions flown for bomber and ground-attack pilots, although a single act of great skill or courage could short-circuit the system. Hajo Herrmann, a bomber expert, is a case in point. His attack on allied shipping in Piraeus harbour destroyed the ammunition-carrying ship *Clan Fraser*. The subsequent cataclysmic explosion destroyed 10 other ships, totalling 41,000 tons, and demolished the harbour, rendering it out of commission for months. It was a major blow for the Allied cause.[9] Another example is Hans Ulrich Rudel, who sank the Russian battleship *Murat* in Kronstadt harbour, in a brilliant piece of dive-bombing while under intense anti-aircraft fire. Erich Hartmann got his Diamonds for 352 aerial victories, Hans-Joachim Marseille for 158 kills (all British, the majority in North Africa). The amassing of aerial kills involved maintaining one's flying skills, superb marksmanship and nerve over a sustained period. The fighter pilots earned their awards through personal effort, and not through the efforts of others.

Soldiers, pilots, and submariners all coveted the Iron Cross, although this didn't apply to the Iron Cross (2nd Class) which was a relatively easy award to obtain. An idea of the relative values of the Iron Cross 1st and 2nd Class can be gauged by General Scherer's request for these decorations to be dropped into his besieged fortress of Cholm in 1942. The Luftwaffe sent him 400 Iron Crosses (2nd Class) and only 40 1st Class.[10] Certainly, however, the Iron Cross (1st Class) and the Knight's Cross were particularly admired and sought after. Fighter pilots deliberately set out to acquire the Knight's Cross and its higher grades, with Gerd Barkhorn, a 301-kill ace, lamenting after the war that he never received the Diamonds, as the points required always increased as soon as he drew close to the award.

Kurt Knispel, the highest-scoring tank ace of the war, with 169 kills as a gunner and then commander, never even received the Knight's Cross, although tank aces with lower scores did so. His omission was largely attributed to his not getting on with his battalion commander. The whims of a commander could make all the difference to an award. Some commanders deliberately didn't write up subordinates for awards, instead claiming all the credit for a particular action or result for themselves and ensuring their own promotion or award. So the awards system did not always operate as fairly or even-handedly as it should. Nevertheless it was a major motivating factor. Pilots vying for the Knight's Cross were said to be afflicted with a sore throat or neck ache, so it was generally accepted among the *experten* in the Luftwaffe to be a major incentive to go out and get kills.

The desirability of earning awards, especially the Iron Cross, certainly played a greater part in the German armed forces than it did in other armies, and should not be discounted as a reason for the Wehrmacht's outstanding performance. Even the Iron Cross (1st Class) inspired officers and men to excel, and keep fighting, as the young officer Armin Scheiderbauer pointed out:

> For the time being I had to go to the front line again. I had enough of the barracks, its many shirkers and its defeatists ...
>
> I had an additional determining factor. I had won the Iron Cross Second Class, the *Infanteriesturmabzeichen* i.e. the infantry assault badge, in silver, and the *Verwundetenabzeichen* i.e. the wound badge.

> But I did not have the coveted decoration of the Iron Cross First Class and a hoped for *Nahkampfspange*, i.e. the close combat clasp. Without those, it appeared to me you were not a "proper" infantry officer. I had therefore voluntarily signed myself "kv" i.e. fit again, which the medical officer would not have done.[11]

Total Awards of the Iron Cross during World War II

Iron Cross (2nd Class)	approximately 4,750,000[12]
Iron Cross (1st Class)	approximately 730,000[13]
Knight's Cross	7,361, including 43 to foreigners
Oak Leaves	882, including 8 to foreigners
Swords	160
Diamonds	27

Graf von Strachwitz was a relatively early recipient of the Knight's Cross. The first non-General award was to Günter Prien, on 18 October 1939, for the sinking of the British battleship *Royal Oak* at Scapa Flow.

There is contention over some recipients who received their award at the end of the war, being approved by army or army group commanders, such as Ferdinand Schörner or Sepp Dietrich, who made and approved several awards on the very last days of the war. The chaotic conditions at war's end, loss of documentation, and above all the singular lack of time remaining for an approval to go through official channels all played a part in the awards and their controversies afterwards. Poor record-keeping meant that some awards were not officially made until long after the war was over, with at least one recipient not even being aware that he had been recommended, let alone approved.

Graf von Strachwitz was an early recipient of the Oak Leaves, being presented with them by Hitler at the Führer Headquarters Wolfsschanze sometime shortly after 13 November 1942. Of those awarded the Oak Leaves, 234 were killed in action. Graf von Strachwitz was the 27th recipient of the Swords. He was awarded his Swords by Hitler, together with General Major Georg Postel, who was given the Oak Leaves (215th recipient). Thirty-eight Swords wearers were killed in action.

Graf von Strachwitz was the 11th recipient of the Diamonds. Hitler presented them to von Strachwitz at his Bavarian mountain retreat, the Berghof, on 15 April 1944. His former divisional commander Hans Valentin Hube received his Diamonds five days later, being the 13th recipient. It was while returning from this ceremony that Hube was killed when his plane crashed. Other notable recipients included Lieutenant Erich Hartmann, Luftwaffe Squadron Leader 12/JG52, with 352 aerial victories (awarded 25 August 1944); Korvette Kapitan Wolfgang Luth, commander of U-81, sinking 47 ships, 221,981 tons (awarded 9 August 1943), however he and the other naval recipient sank fewer ships with lower tonnage than U-boat ace Otto Kretschmer, who sank 56 ships totalling 313,611 tons, but only received the Swords for his efforts. Nine Diamonds wearers were killed during the war.

The majority of Knight's Cross winners, from Oak Leaves and above, also earned the German Cross in gold. This was an intermediate award to bridge the rather large gap of award criteria for an Iron Cross (1st Class) and the Knight's Cross. There was also a large gap between the 1st Class and German Cross, hence the problem of rewarding servicemen who had earned the first two grades of the Iron Cross still remained. There was a silver wreathed version of the German Cross but it was generally awarded for non-combat achievements. Many servicemen were submitted for a Knight's Cross, only to have the recommendation downgraded to a German Cross in Gold of which some 24,204 were awarded during World War II. Graf von Strachwitz was one of the few Swords wearers who did not receive the German Cross. This could be because all his actions which were written up as meriting an award were sufficient for a higher grade of the Knight's Cross rather than the lower-grade German Cross. In several books, articles and websites he is mentioned as being awarded the German Cross in Gold because it was common—almost expected of a Swords or Diamonds wearer—to have this award. There was also confusion because his eldest son, also called Hyazinth, did receive a German Cross in Gold.

The value and significance of the Knight's Cross becomes clear when it is considered that there were some 17,800,000 men in the German armed forces during World War II, of whom some 13,000,000 were in the army. Far less than 0.1% of those in the army, just 4,524, received the Knight's Cross.[14] It should be mentioned that a significant number of Knight's Crosses were awarded to NCOs and enlisted men, a total of 1,676. Junior officers—captain and below—received 3,413 awards, so the higher officers were a distinct minority.

The Diamonds were not the highest bravery or service award. This distinction went to the Knight's Cross with Golden Oak Leaves, Swords and Diamonds which was instituted in December 1944, which was to be awarded to a maximum of 12 combatants. In the event only one was given out, to

Hans Ulrich Rudel who received it on 1 January 1945. This *experten* flew over 2,500 combat missions, destroyed 519 tanks, sank one battleship, two cruisers, one destroyer, shot down 11 Soviet aircraft and destroyed more than 1,000 vehicles of all types. He was shot down 31 times and wounded five times. He also landed and rescued several of his comrades who were shot down. His record is unique, and surpasses that of any other flier in the world, past or present, and is unlikely ever to be surpassed. His last missions were flown against Hitler's express orders, after his right leg had been amputated below the knee. He destroyed 26 Soviet tanks on these last missions, and his kills were credited to his squadron so his superiors would not find out that he was still flying. One could call him a Nazi—he was a staunch but apolitical admirer of Hitler as his memoir *Stuka Pilot* shows—but in truth he was a fervent nationalist, who was supremely good at his job. Von Strachwitz was in a similar mould, a born fighting man. It is more than fitting that the two warriors fought together in some battles, at Kursk, and in the Baltics and Upper Silesia.

Von Strachwitz's other awards are worth mentioning. The Tank Assault Badge in Gold for 100 engagements was instituted in June 1943, and only around 14 were awarded, all in 1944 and 1945, to men of the panzer arm. The badge consisted of a Panzer III surrounded by a gold wreath with a plaque inscribed with the number 100. A similar badge was awarded with plaques for 75, 50, and 25 engagements, becoming more common as the number of tank actions dropped. The basic award with bronze wreath and no numerals was awarded after three separate combat days. Wearers of the 25 engagements badge were numerous, it was only with the 75 engagements did it become scarce, and rare for the 100. A total of 22,000 silver badges were issued during the war covering three to 50 engagements. There were only a few hundred in the 50 and 75 categories. The 14 wearers of the "100" were, like the Diamonds holders, a very small elite band indeed.

Of those who received the "100" badge, only Kurt Knispel, 503rd Heavy Panzer Battalion, may have achieved more kills than the Panzer Graf. Knispel's total was 168, while von Strachwitz's tally was somewhere between 150 and 200. Graf von Strachwitz is not usually found in lists of tank aces as he did not keep score, so that his tally is an estimate only. Based on the number of engagements he took part in, his tally may have been closer to the 200 mark. Sean McAteer credits von Strachwitz with 200 kills.[15] He was always in the thick of the action, usually ambushing a much larger Russian force with often only a handful of tanks. He also commanded a properly equipped tank rather than a command tank. He also added to his kill tally while serving with Army Group North. The Panzer Graf was responsible for destroying many hundreds of Russian vehicles, probably in excess of a thousand, as in one action alone his small force took out over 300 vehicles together with a large number of anti-tank guns and artillery pieces. The German tankers didn't often bother counting vehicles destroyed as a personal tally except for purposes of unit records. Many German aces also destroyed large numbers of anti-tank guns which were a dangerous adversary and often harder to "kill" than a tank. SS ace Michael Wittman is credited with destroying over 130 anti-tank guns.

Almost all of the recipients of the Tank Assault badge in Gold were from heavy panzer battalions. These were equipped with Tiger tanks; however, the aces from these battalions also acquired kills while serving in prior units using medium tanks or even assault guns. For instance Michael Wittman started out with Stug.III assault guns. Balthazar Woll and Kurt Knispel scored many of their kills as tank gunners as well as tank commanders. A gunner was vital in scoring kills, so tallies as a gunner count to an individual total. No matter how skilled the commander in placing his tank for the greatest effect, without a skilled gunner those command skills could often be wasted, or worse, result in his own tank being hit by a quicker, more accurate adversary. A tank commander and gunner were both indispensible for success. For this reason Michael Wittman insisted that his gunner Balthasar Woll also be awarded a Knight's Cross. Most ace tank commanders began their careers as gunners. Fritz Lang was Germany's top scoring assault gun ace with 112 kills. In addition, there were at least 11 tank aces with between 50 and 100 kills and numerous aces with a score below 50.

Von Strachwitz's other badge of note was the gold wound badge, awarded for five or more wounds. One to two wounds merited a black badge, two to four, in silver. Given the intensity of the fighting and the length of the war, the Gold Wound Badge was not uncommon, nevertheless it was highly valued by its recipients, including the Graf. However, not all ascribed any value to it. Some armchair generals who had never faced the enemy or suffered front-line hardships regarded it with derision, as General Guderian related in his memoir. He was defending a brave newly promoted lieutenant colonel, whom Hitler wished to demote to a mere lieutenant:

> Tried and trusted officers as the front were, in the heat of the moment and without any proper inquiry, being demoted one or more

> ranks. I saw this happen to the commander of an anti-tank battalion, a man who had been wounded seven times and had won the Golden Decoration for Wounds. . . . An important personage who during the course of the whole war had never once seen the front, thereupon remarked drily: "The Golden Decoration for Wounds means absolutely nothing!"[16]

Yet it did for every front-line soldier, and was the mark of a true veteran. Hitler himself had a high regard for it; he always wore his Wound Badge in Black for being gassed in World War I, one of only three decorations he ever wore, the other two being his World War I Iron Cross (1st Class), and Gold Party Badge.

Hitler personally awarded the Knight's Cross to his field marshals and senior generals, but only to lower ranks for propaganda purposes or to a particular favourite of his, or someone he wished to meet. The higher grades of Knight's Cross he awarded personally, although towards the end of the war some Oak Leaves were awarded by his subordinates; for instance, Otto Carius was presented with his Oak Leaves by Heinrich Himmler.

For his awards of Swords and Diamonds, von Strachwitz went to Berchtesgaden, being flown there in a Focke Wulf 200 Condor transport, accompanied by his wife Alda. The Panzer Graf would have found Hitler much changed from when he met him to receive his Diamonds.[17] Von Strachwitz would also have seen how much security had increased since the July bomb attempt. SS guards were ever present and when the Graf reached into his pocket, his wrist was quickly and firmly grasped. He slowly withdrew his hand to show the handkerchief he was reaching for.[18]

Each of von Strachwitz's Knight's Cross awards also meant publicity, particularly his Diamonds award, which was his last home leave period while still healthy. The local press did an article, and he had to pose for an official portrait which was used for a postcard. These cards were avidly collected by many Germans, the most popular being those of the dashing young fighter pilots and U-boat commanders. Naturally the Graf's hometown and surrounding areas were particularly impressed so that he had to meet delegations and review parades of Hitler Youth and the League of German Girls, as well as other groups. He also gave radio interviews. All this publicity attracted a great deal of fan mail, which he replied to, assisted by his eldest son who was also on leave, and his daughter-in-law. It also meant attending numerous functions, parties and presentations. Best of all however, was the period of leave he received, which he could spend with his wife who also accompanied him to the various social and public functions. The time spent with his eldest son, who as a serving officer rarely got home, was particularly welcome. It would have been a period of tranquillity, the last he would enjoy before injury and captivity claimed him.

THE GRAF'S AWARDS IN ORDER OF RECEIPT

	Award	Date
1.	Iron Cross (2nd Class)	1914
2.	Iron Cross (1st Class)	1914
3.	The Silesian Eagle 2nd Class	1921
4.	The Silesian Eagle 1st Class with Oak Leaves and Swords	1921
5.	Sudetenland Medal	1938
6.	Iron Cross (2nd Class) 1939 Clasp	1939
7.	Iron Cross (1st Class) 1939 Clasp	1940
8.	Sports Award in Gold	1941
9.	The Order of the Romanian Crown	1941
10.	Wound Badge in Black	1941
11.	Eastern Front Winter Campaign Medal	1941
12.	Panzer Assault Badge in Silver	1941
13.	Knight's Cross of the Iron Cross	25 August 1941
14.	Wound Badge in Silver	1942
15.	Knight's Cross with Oak Leaves	13 November 1942
16.	Wound Badge in Gold	1943
17.	Knight's Cross with Oak Leaves and Swords	28 March 1944
18.	Panzer Assault Badge in Gold for 100 Engagements	1944
19.	Knight's Cross with Oak Leaves, Swords and Diamonds	April 1944
20.	SS Honour Ring	
21.	Mention in the Wehrmacht Report	

The Panzer Graf also wore his Grossdeutschland cuff title as an honorific even after he had left the division.

The official recognition of the Silesian Eagle in 1933 did not include the Swords and Oak Leaves, and so were worn unofficially only.

NOTES

1. Numbers cited for awards in all periods are approximate only. Sources vary as to the actual numbers involved while the exact numbers are unknown. The major sources for Iron Cross data are: Gordon Williamson, *The Iron Cross: a History 1813–1957* (Blandford Press, UK, 1985); John R. Angolia, *For Führer and Fatherland: Military Awards of the Third Reich* (R.J. Bender Publishing, USA, 2nd ed, 1985); John R. Angolia, *On the Field of Honour: A History of the Knight's Cross Bearers Vols 1 & 2* (R. J. Bender Publishing, 1980).
2. John R. Angolia and Clint R. Hackney Jr, *The Pour le Merite and Germany's First Aces* (Hackney Publishing, USA, 1984).
3. Gordon Williamson, *The Iron Cross.*
4. J. R. Angolia, *For Führer and Fatherland.*
5. J. R. Angolia, *On the Field of Honour Vol 1.*
6. Günter Koschorrek, *Blood Red Snow*, p.97.
7. Martin Pöppel (trans. Dr L. Willmot), *Heaven & Hell: The War Diary of a German paratrooper* (Spellmount Publishing, 1996).
8. Koschorrek, *Blood Red Snow.*
9. Hajo Herrmann, *Eagle's Wings* (Airlife Publishing, 1991).
10. Jason D. Marks, *Besieged* (Leaping Horseman Press).-
11. *Adventures in My Youth*, p. 83.
12. Sources vary as to the exact number, Bender cites 3,000,000. The exact number is unknown. Despite the high number awarded, it is nevertheless a grade higher than a campaign medal or shield. It had to be earned by a specific action or a series of actions over a period.
13. Again figures vary, John R. Angolia cites 450,000 while Gordon Williamson lists 750,000.
14. Gordon Williamson.
15. *Panzer Leader*, p. 407.
16. Sean McAteer, *500 Days: The War in Eastern Europe, 1944–1945.*
17. *Panzer Leader*, p. 442.
18. Von Gersdörff, *Soldier in the Downfall.*

APPENDIX 2

RANK EQUIVALENTS

GERMAN ARMY	WAFFEN SS	US ARMY	BRITISH ARMY
Shutz	SS Shutz	Private	Private
Obershutz	SS Obershutz	Private 1st Class	
Gefreiter	SS Sturmann		Lance Corporal
Obergefrifter	Rottenführer	Sergeant	Corporal
Unterfeldwebel	SS Sharführer	Staff Sergeant	
Feldwebel	SS Obersharführer	Technical Sergeant	Sergeant
Oberfeldwebel	SS Hauptsharführer	Master Sergeant	Staff Sergeant
Hauptfeldwebel	SS Stabscharführer		Warrant Officer Cl.2
Stabsfeldwebel	SS Sturmscharführer	Sergeant Major	Warrant Officer Cl.1
Leutnant	SS Untersturmführer	2nd Lieutenant	2nd Lieutenant
Oberleutnant	SS Obersturmführer	1st Lieutenant	Lieutenant
Hauptmann	SS Hauptsturmführer	Captain	Captain
Major	SS Sturmbannführer	Major	Major
Oberstleutnant	SS Obersturmbannführer	Lieutenant Colonel	Lieutenant Colonel

Oberst	SS Standartenführer	Colonel	Colonel
General Major	SS Oberführer	Brigadier General	Brigadier
General Leutnant	SS Gruppen Führer	Major General	Major General
General	SS Oberstgruppenführer	Lieutenant General	Lieutenant General
General Oberst	SS Oberstgruppenführer	General	General
Generalfeld Marshall	Reichsführer SS	General of the Army	Field Marshal

The German Army also had the rank of Fahnrich, a Senior NCO equivalent for officer candidates awaiting their commission.

APPENDIX 3

CIVIL RANKS AND TITLES OF NOBILITY

GERMAN	BRITISH	FRENCH
Ritter	Knight	Chevalier
Freiherr	Baron-Viscount	Vicomte
Graf	Earl *(Count in other countries)*	Comte
Markgraf	Marquess	Marquis
Herzog	Duke	Duc
Gross Herzog	Grand Duke	Grand-Duc
Kurfurst	Elector	
Prinz	Prince	Prince
König	King	Roi
Kaiser	Emperor/Tsar (Russian)	Empereur

APPENDIX 4

HOLDERS OF THE PANZER ASSAULT BADGE IN GOLD

RANK AT AWARD	NAME	BRANCH OF SERVICE UNIT	DATE OF AWARD
Lieutenant Colonel	Franz Bake	11th Panzer Regiment	27 April 1944 Awarded along with Swords to the Knight's Cross
Sergeant	Hermann Bix	35th Panzer Regiment	22 March 1945
Major	Gerhard Fisher	23rd Panzer Regiment	18 Dec 1944
SS Major	Hans Flugel	5th SS Panzer Regiment	1944
Sergeant	Kurt Goering	502nd Heavy Panzer Battalion	
Major	Bernhard Gehrig	4th Panzer Regiment	
Major	Rudolf Haen	103rd Panzer Battalion	5 August 1944
Lieutenant	Karl Heinz Kallfelz	502nd Heavy Panzer Battalion	

SS Captain	Alois Kalss	502nd SS Heavy Panzer Battalion	
Lieutenant	Emil Rossmn	Brandenburg Panzer Regiment	27 March 1945
Lieutenant Colonel	Paul Schulz	21st Panzer Battalion	
General Lieutenant (Res.)	Hyazinth Graf Strachwitz von Gross-Zauche und Camminetz	16th Panzer Division, Grossdeutschland Panzergrenadier Division, Panzerverband von Strachwitz	
Senior Sergeant	Honnigan		16 Jan 1945
Sergeant	Schmidtke	Heavy Panzer Battalion 503	

The last two names listed are unconfirmed so are probable only. Several more could have made the list but the lack of proper records in the chaotic last months of the war would have prevented their due recognition.

APPENDIX 5

ACES OF THE PANZERWAFFE

NAME	KILLS	UNIT
Kurt Knispel	168	503rd Heavy Panzer Battalion
Hyazinth Graf Strachwitz von Gross-Zauche und Camminetz	150–200	16th Panzer Division, Grossdeutschland Panzergrenadier Division, Panzerverband Strachwitz
Martin Schroit	127–161	102nd Heavy Panzer Battalion
Otto Carius	120–150+	502nd Heavy Panzer Battalion
Johannes Bolter	139–144	502nd Heavy Panzer Battalion
Michael Wittman	138–144	101st Heavy SS Panzer Battalion
Karl Mobius	125	101st Heavy SS Panzer Battalion
Hans Sandrock	100–125	21st Panzer Division, Hermann Goering Panzer Division
Paul Egger	113	102nd Heavy SS Panzer Battalion

Arno Giesen	111	2nd SS Panzer Regiment—Das Reich Division
Heinz Rondorf	106	503rd Heavy Panzer Battalion
Heinz Gärtner	103	503rd Heavy Panzer Battalion
Wilhelm Knauth	101+	505th Heavy Panzer Battalion
Albert Kerscher	100+	502nd Heavy Panzer Battalion
Karl Korne	100+	503rd Heavy Panzer Battalion
Balthazar Woll	80–100	101st Heavy Panzer Battalion

The kills listed in some cases include a range, where sources vary as to the maximum total.

APPENDIX 6

GERMAN ARMY LISIT OF CIVIL COURAGE

This list honours those German Army officers who went against their oath of allegiance to conspire against Hitler, an action punishable by imprisonment or death. It is not meant to denigrate in any way all those who fought for their country and remained loyal to their oath, but to provide a particular honour to those who overrode their oath, risking their lives or careers for a greater cause—that of humanity. It also includes some names of soldiers who saved Jews at personal risk to themselves (indicated by an asterisk).

The list does not include police officers or the civilians who were also actively involved in plotting against Hitler. Nor does it include military personnel such as Admiral Canaris or General Oster who actively plotted but also committed treason in the real sense of the word, when their actions provided aid to the enemy and endangered the lives of their own people.

The list is partial only, the names of those listed being representative of all those who dared.

Colonel Otto Armster—imprisoned

Colonel General Ludwig Beck—committed suicide

Lt Colonel Robert Bernardis—executed

Lt Colonel Hasso von Boehmer—executed

Lt Colonel Baron Georg von Boeselager—killed in action

Lt Colonel Baron Philip von Boeslager

Major Baron Axel von dem Bussche-Strethorski

General Major Count Heinrich Dohna-Schlobitten—executed

Lt Hans Martin Dorsch
Captain Count Man-Ulrich von Drechsel
Lt Karl Heinz Engelhorn
Lt colonel Hans Otto Erdmann
General Baron Alexander von Falkenhausen
General Erich Fellgiebel—executed
Colonel Baron Wessel von Freytag-Loringhoven
Captain Ludwig Gehre—executed
General Major Baron Rudolf von Gersdorff
Colonel Helmuth Groscurth
Lt Werner von Haeften—executed
Colonel Kurt Hahn Colonel Georg Hansen Colonel Bodo von Harbon
General Lieutenant Paul von Haese—executed
Major Egbert Hayessen—executed
Lt Hans von Herwarth
Colonel General Erich Hoepner—executed
Captain Wilhelm Hosenfeld*
Major Roland von Hösslin—executed
Colonel Friedrich Gustanjaeger—executed
Lt Colonel Bernhard Klamroth—executed
Captain Frederich Karl Klausing
Lt Ewald-Heinrich von Kleist-Schmenzin
General Field Marshal Gunter von Kluge—committed suicide
Lt Commander (Navy) Alfred Kranzfelder—executed
Major Joachim Kuhn
General Hubert Lanz
Major Baron Ludwig von Leonrod—executed
General Fritz Lindemann—died in prison
Colonel count Rudolf von Marogna-Redwitz—executed
Colonel Joachim Meichssner—executed
Lt Colonel Karl Michel
Lt Colonel Ernst Munziger
Major Hans-Ullrich von Oertzen—committed suicide

General Frederich Olbricht—executed Major Karl Plaage*
Major Michael Pössinger*
Colonel Baron Albrecht Quirnheim—executed
General Frederich von Rabenau—executed
Lt Colonel Karl Rathgens
Colonel Baron Alexis von Roenne—executed
General Field marshal Erwin Rommel—forced to commit suicide
Lt Colonel Joachim Sdrozinski—executed
Major Count Hans Victor von Salviati
Lt Fabian Schalbrendorff Sergeant Anton Schmid* Colonel Hermann Schone
Lt Colonel Werner Schrader—committed suicide
Colonel Georg Scultz-Buttger
Lt Colonel Gunther Smend—executed
General Hans Speidel Colonel Wilhelm Staehle Lt Alexander Stahlberg
Colonel Count Claus Shenk von Stauffenberg—executed
Colonel Baron Hans-Joachim von Steinaecker
General Major Helmuth Stieff—executed
General Lieutenant Hyazinth Count Strachwitz von Gross-Zauche und Camminetz
Colonel General Carl-Heinrich von Stülpnagel—executed
Major Carl Szokoll
Lt Colonel Gustov Tellgmann
General Lieutenant Fritz Thiele—executed
Major Busso Thoma—executed
General Georg Thomas
General Baron Karl von Thüngen—executed General Major Henning von Tresckow –committed suicide
Lt Colonel Hans-Alexander von Voss Quartermaster General Edward Wagner
Colonel Siegfried Wagner—committed suicide
General Field Marshal von Witzleben—executed
General Gustov Heistermann von Ziehlberg—executed

BIBLIOGRAPHY

Adair, Paul. *Hitler's Greatest Defeat: The Collapse of Army Group Centre, June 1944* (Arms & Armour Press, UK, 1994).

Adamczyk, Werner. *Feuer! An Artilleryman's Life on the Eastern Front* (Broadfoot Publishing, USA, 1992).

Ailsby, Christopher. *SS Roll of Infamy* (Brown Books, 1997).

Anderson, Duncan, Clark, Lloyd and Walsh, Stephen. *The Eastern Front: Barbarossa, Stalingrad, Kursk and Berlin 1941–45* (David Charles, UK, 2001).

Angolia, LTC John R. *For Führer and Fatherland: Military Awards of the Third Reich* (R.J. Bender Publishing, USA, 1976).

John R. Angolia, *On the Field of Honour: A History of the Knight's Cross Bearers Vols 1 & 2* (R.J. Bender Publishing, 1980).

Angolia, LTC John R. and Hackney, Clint R. *The Pour Le Merite and Germany's First Aces* (Hackney Publishing, USA, 1984).

Bamm, Peter (trans. Frank Herrman). *The Invisible Flag* (Faber and Faber, UK, 1956).

Barnett, Correlli (ed.). *Hitler's Generals* (Phoenix Giants, UK, 1995).

Bartov, Omer. *Hitler's Army* (Oxford University Press, NY, 1992).

Baxter, Ian. *Battle in the Baltics: The Fighting for Latvia Lithuania and Estonia* (Helion & Co, UK, 2009).

Beevor, Antony. *Stalingrad* (Penguin Books, UK, 1999).

Below, Nicholas von. *At Hitler's Side: The Memoirs of Hitler's Luftwaffe Adjutant 1937–1945* (Greenhill Books, UK, 2001).

Bergström, Christer. *Bagration to Berlin: The Final Air Battles in the East 1944–1945* (Chevron Publishing, UK, 2008).

Bergström, Christer. *Kursk: The Air Battle 1943* (Ian Allan Publishing, UK, 2007).

Biderman, Gottlob Herbert. *In Deadly Combat: A German soldier's memoir of*

the Eastern Front (University Press of Kansas, USA, 2000).
Blosfelds, Mintauts (trans. Lisa Blosfelds). *Stormtrooper on the Eastern Front Fighting with Hitler's Latvian SS*-(Pen and Sword Books, UK, 2008).
Brandt, Allan. *The Last Knight of Flanders* (Schiffer Books, 1998).
Brett–Smith, Richard. *Hitler's Generals* (Osprey Publishing, UK, 1976).
Busch, Fritz–Otto (trans. Eleanor Brockett). *The Story of the* Prinz Eugen (Robert Hale, UK, 1960).
Buttar, Prit. *Between Giants: The Battle for the Baltics in WWII* (Osprey Publishing, UK, 2013).
Carius, Otto. *Tigers in the Mud* (Stackpole Books, USA, 2003).
Carrell, Paul. *Hitler's War on Russia Vol 1 Hitler Moves East 1941–1943* (Ballantine Books, 1963).
Carrell, Paul. *Hitler's War on Russia Vol 2 Scorched Earth 1943–1944* (Corgi Books, UK, 1966).
Cawthorne, Nigel. *Reaping the Whirlwind: The German and Japanese Experience of World War II* (David and Charles, UK, 2007).
Chant, Christopher Corey (ed.). *Warfare and the Third Reich: The Rise and Fall of Hitler's Armed Forces* (Salamander Books, WY, 1996).
Cooper, Matthew and Lucas, James. *Panzer: the Armoured Force of the Third Reich* (Book Club, 1976).
Cornish, Nik. *Armageddon Ost* (Ian Allan Publishing, UK, 2006).
Cornwell, John. *Hitler's Pope*. (Viking, UK, 1999).
Cross, Robin. *Citadel: the Battle of Kursk* (Michael O'Mara Books, 1993).
Davies, W. J. K. *The German Army Handbook 1939–1945* (Ian Allan, UK, 1973).
Degrelle, Leon. *Campaign in Russia: The Waffen SS on the Eastern Front* (Institute for Historical Review, 1985).
Denton, Mansel. *Battle for Narva 1944* (History Fact Documentation, 2010).
Diczbalis, Sigismund. *The Russian Patriot: A Red Army Soldier's Service for his Motherland and Against Bolshevism* (Spellmount Books, UK, 2008).
Dinardo, R. L. *Germany's Panzer Arm in WWII* (Stackpole Books, USA, 1997).
Dollinger, Hans (trans. Arnold Pomerans). *The Decline and Fail of Nazi Germany and Imperial Japan* (Bonanza Books, NY, 1965).
Duffy, Christopher. *Red Storm on the Reich* (Atheneum, NY, 1991).
Duffy, James P. and Ricci Vincent. *Target Hitler: The Plots to Kill Hitler* (Praeger, USA, 1992).
Dupuy, Col T. N. *A Genius for War: The German Army and General Staff 1807–*

1945 (McDonald and Davies, UK, 1977).
Edwards, Roger. *Panzer: a Revolution in Warfare 1939–1945* (Brockhampton Press, UK, 1998).
Fitzgibbon, Constantine. *The Shirt of Nessus* (Cassell & Co, UK, 1956).
Fowler, Will. *Kursk: the Vital 24 Hours* (Amber Books, UK, 2005).
Fowler, Will. *Barbarossa: The First 7 Days* (Greenhill Books, UK, 2005).
Fraschka, Günter. *Der Panzergraf: Ein leben für Deutschland* (Rastatt, 1962).
Fraschka, Günter (trans. David Johnston). *Knights of the Reich* (Schiffer Books, USA, 1989).
Friesen, Bruno. *Panzer Gunner* (Helion & Co, UK, 2008).
Fritz, Stephen G. *Frontsoldaten: The German Soldier in World War II* (University of Kentucky Press, USA, 1995).
Gaidis, Henry L. *A History of the Lithuanian Military Forces in World War II 1939–1945* (Lithuanian Research and Study Centre, USA, 1998).
Gersdorff, Rudolf–Christoph Baron von (trans. Anthony Pearsall). *Soldier in the Downfall, A Wehrmacht Cavalryman in Russia; Normandy and the Plot to Kill Hitler* (Aberjona Press, USA, 2012).
Gilbert, Felix (trans. & ed). *Hitler Directs His War* (OUP, Oxford, UK, 1951).
Glantz, David M. and House, Jonathan M. *The Battle of Kursk* (University of Kansas Press, 1999).
Goodspeed, Lt Col D. J. *The German Wars* (Bonanza Books, USA, 1976).
Grossjohann, Georg (trans. Ulrich Abele). *Five Years, Four Fronts: A German Officer's World War II Combat Memoir*-(Aegis Consulting Group, USA, 1999).
Grossman, Vasily (ed. & trans. Antony Beevor and Luba Vinogradova). *A Writer at War With the Red Army 1941–1945* (The Harvill Press, UK, 2005).
Guderian, General Heinz (trans. Constantine Fitzgibbon). *Panzer Leader* (Futura Publications, UK, 1974).
Gunther, Helmut (trans. Fred Steinhardt). *Hot Motors, Cold Feet: a memoir of service with the Motorcycle Battalion of SS–Division "Reich" 1940–1941* (J. J. Fedorowicz Pub, Canada, 2004).
Haape, Dr Heinrich with Henshaw, Dennis. *Moscow Tram Stop: A Doctor's Experience with the German Spearhead in Russia* (Collins, UK, 1957).
Hart, S. and Hart, R. *German Tanks of World War Two* (Spellmount, UK, 1998).
Hastings, Max. *Armageddon: The Battle for Germany* (Macmillan, UK, 2004).
Haupt, Werner (trans. J. G. Welsh). *Army Group North 1941–1945* (Schiffer Publishing, USA, 2000).

Haupt, Werner. *A History of the Panzer Troops 1916–1945* (Schiffer Publishing, USA, 1990).

Held, Werner, Trautloft, Hannes, and Bob, Ekkehard (trans. D. Cox). *JG 54: Photo history of the Grunherzjäger*-(Schiffer Books, USA, 1994).

Herold, Misoslav (trans. Matthias Noll). *Gefreiter Walter Thomaschek* (http://members.shaw.ca/grossdeutschland/thomas.htm), (accessed 24 August 2013).

Herrmann, Hajo. *Eagle's Wings: The Autobiography of a Luftwaffe Pilot* (Airlife Publishing, UK, 1991).

Herwarth Hans von with Starr Frederich. *Against Two Evils* (Rawson Wade Publishers, USA, 1981).

Hinze, Rolf (trans. Federick P Steinhardt). *To the Bitter End* (Casemate, USA, 2010).

Holl, Adalbert (trans. Jason D. Mark and Neil Page). *An Infantryman in Stalingrad* (Leaping Horseman Books, Sydney Australia, 2005).

Horn, Daniel. *The German Naval Mutinies of WWI* (Rutgers University Press, USA, 1969).

Jackman, Robert. *Battle of the Baltic The Wars 1914–1945* (Pen & Sword Books, UK, 2007).

Jentz, Thomas. *Panzertruppen: the complete guide to the creation and combat employment of German's Tank Force, vol 2, 1943–1945* (Schiffer Publishing, 1996).

Jentz, Thomas. *Germany's Tiger Tanks: Tiger I and Tiger II—Combat Tactics* (Schiffer Publishing, 1998).

Jones, Nigel. *Hitler's Heralds: The Story of the Freikorps 1918–1923* (John Murray Publishing, 1987).

Jung, Helmut (as told to Mike Nesbitt). *But not for the Fuehrer*-(AuthorHouse, USA, 2003).

Jung, Hans–Joachim (trans. David Johnston). *The History of Panzerregiment Grossdeutschland: Panzer Soldiers for "God, Honor, Fatherland"* (J.J. Fedorowicz, Canada, 2000).

Junge, Traudl (ed. Melissa Muller, trans. Anthea Bell). *Until the Final Hour: Hitler's Last Secretary* (Weidenfeld and Nicolson, UK, 2002).

Just, Günther. *Stuka–Pilot Han Ulrich Rudel* (Schiffer Publishing, USA, 1990).

Knappe, Siegfried and Bryson, Ted. *Soldat: Reflections of a German Soldier* (BCA, 1993).

Koschorrek, Günter K. *Blood Red Snow: The Memoirs of a German Soldier on the Eastern Front* (Greenhill Books, UK, 2002).

Kirchubel, Robert. *Hitler's Panzer Armies on the Eastern Front* (Pen & Sword Books, UK, 2009).

Kramarz, Joachim. *Stauffenberg: The Man Who Nearly Killed Hitler* (Mayflower, USA, 1970).

Kurowski, Franz. *Knight's Cross Holders of the U–Boat Service.* (Schiffer Publishing, USA, 1995).

Kurowski, Franz (trans. Joseph G. Welsh). *Hitler's Last Bastion 1945* (Schiffer Books, USA, 1998).

Kurowski, Franz. *Panzer Aces* (Stackpole Books, USA, 2004).

Laffin, John. *Jackboot: The Story of the German Soldier* (Cassell, UK, 1965).

Lehmann, Rudolf. *The Leibstandarte Vol III* (J. J. Fedorwicz Publishing, Canada, 1990).

Lodieu, Didier. *III Panzer Korps at Kursk* (Histoire and Collections, Paris, 2007).

Lubbeck, William with Hurt, David B. *At Leningrad's Gates* (Casemate, USA, 2006).

Lucas, James. *Germany's Elite Panzer Force Grossdeutschland* (Macdonald and Jane's Publishers, UK, 1978).

Lucas, James. *Last Days of the Reich* (Arms and Armour Press, 1986).

Lucas, James. *War on the Eastern Front 1941–1945* (Book Club Associates, UK, 1980).

McCarthy, Peter and Syron, Mike. *Panzerkrieg: A History of the German Panzer Divisions in WWII* (Constable and Robinson, UK, 2003).

McGuirl, Thomas and Spezzano Remy. *God Honour Fatherland: A Photo History of the Panzer Grenadier Division Grossdeutschland* (RZM Publishing, USA, 2007).

McNab, Chris. *German Luftwaffe in WWII* (Amber Books, UK, 2009).

Mark, Jason D. *Beseiged: The Epic Battle for Cholm* (Leaping Horseman Books, Sydney, Australia, 2011).

Mark, Jason D. *An Artilleryman in Stalingrad* (Leaping Horseman Books, Sydney, Australia, 2006).

Mark, Jason D. *Island of Fire: The Battle for the Barrikady Gun Factory in Stalingrad* (Leaping Horseman Books, Sydney, Australia, 2006).

Mark, Jason D. *Nine Months of Destruction The Story of Pioneer Battalion 305* (Leaping Horseman Books, Sydney, Australia).

Manstein, Erich von (trans. A. G. Powell), *Lost Victories: The War Memoirs of Hitler's Most Brilliant General* (London 1958).

Matthews, Rubert. *Hitler as Military Commander* (Capella, UK, 2003).
Meconis, Charlie. *The Panzer Count's Ostfront* (www.blowtorchscenarios.com).
Mellenthin, Major General F. W. (trans. H. Belzer). *Panzer Battles* (Futura Publications, UK, 1977).
Messenger, Charles. *Sepp Dietrich: Hitler's Gladiator* (Brassey's, UK, 1988).
Metelmann, Henry. *Through Hell for Hitler* (Guild Publishing, UK, 1990).
Meyer, Kurt (trans. Michael Mende). *Grenadiers* (J. J. Fedorwicz, Canada, 1994).
Mitcham, Samuel W. *Crumbling Empire: The German Defeat in the East 1944* (Praeger Publishing, USA, 2001).
Mitcham, Samuel W. *The Generals Who Served Under Rommel* (Stackpole Books, USA,).
Mitcham, Samuel W. *The Panzer Legions: A Guide to the German Army Tank Divisions of WWII and their Commanders* (Stackpole Books, USA, 2000).
Munoz, Antonio. *Forgotten Legions: Obscure Combat Formations of the Waffen SS* (Paladin Press, USA, 1991).
Nagorski, Andrew. *The Greatest Battle: The Fight for Moscow 1941–42* (Simon and Schuster, USA, 2007).
Newton, Steven H. *Kursk, the German View: Eyewitness Reports by the German Commanders* (DaCapo Press, USA 2002).
Novotny, Alfred. *The Good Soldier: A Soldier of Panzergrenadier Division Grossdeutschland* (Aberjona Press, USA, 2003).
Nipe, George M. *Last Victory in Russia* (Schiffer Books, USA, 2000).
Obhodas, Amir, and Mark, Jason D. *Croatian Legion* (Leaping Horseman Books, Sydney, Australia, 2010).
Odegard, Warren. *Uniforms, Organisation and History of the Panzertruppe* (R. J. Bender Publishing, USA, 1980).
Pencz, Rudolf (trans. C. F. Colton). *For the Homeland: The 31st Waffen SS Volunteer Grenadier Division in WWII* (Stackpole Books, USA, 2010).
Perret, Bryan. *Knights of the Black Cross* (Wordsworth Editions UK 1997).
Perret, Bryan. *Iron Fist* (Cassel & Co, UK, 1995).
Pöppel, Martin (trans. Dr L. Willmot). *Heaven and Hell: The War Diary of a German Paratrooper* (Spellmount, USA, 1996).
Quarrie, Bruce. *Encyclopedia of the German Army in the 20th Century* (Patrick Stephens Ltd, UK, 1989).
Raus, General Erhard (trans. Steven H. Newton). *Panzer Operations* (DaCapo Press, USA, 2003).

Rees, Laurence. *War of the Century: When Hitler Fought Stalin* (BBC, UK, 1999).
Reese, Willy Peter (trans. M Hofman). *A Stranger to Myself: The Inhumanity of War in Russia 1941–1944* (Farrar, Strauss and Giroux, USA, 2005).
Reitlinger, Gerald. *The SS: Alibi of a Nation 1922–1945* (Heinemann, London, 1956).
Riebenstahl, Horst. *The 1st Panzer Division 1935–1945: A Pictorial History* (Schiffer Books, USA, 1996).
Ripley, Tim. *Wehrmacht: The German Army in World War II* (Routledge, UK, 2003).
Ripley, Tim. *Steel Storm: Waffen SS Panzer Battles on the Eastern Front 1943–1945* (MBI Publishing, USA, 2000).
Ripley, Tim. *The Waffen SS at War: Hitler's Praetorians 1925–1945* (Zenith Press, 2004).
Roll, Hans Joachim. *Hyazinth Graf Strachwitz* (Fleschig, Germany, 2011).
Rossino, Alexander. *Hitler Strikes Poland: Blitzkrieg, ideology, and atrocity* (University Press of Kansas, 2003).
Rudel, Hans Ulrich (trans. Lynton Hudson). *Stuka Pilot* (Euphorion, Dublin, 1952).
Ryder, Rowland. *Ravenstein: Portrait of a German General* (Hamish Hamilton, UK, 1978).
Sadarananda, Dana V. *Beyond Stalingrad: Manstein and the Operations of Army Group Don* (Stackpole Books, USA, 1990).
Schaufler, Hans. *Panzer Warfare on the Eastern Front* (Stackpole Books, USA, 2012).
Scheiderbauer, Armin. *Adventures in My Youth: A German Soldier on the Eastern Front 1941–1945* (Helion, UK, 2010).
Schiebel, Helmut. *A Better Comrade You Will Never Find: A Panzerjäger on the Eastern Front 1941–1945* (J.J. Fedorowicz Canada 2010).
Scheibert, Horst. *Panzer in Russland* (Dörfler im Nebel–Verlag, 2000).
Schneider, Wolfgang. *Tigers in Combat* (Stackpole Books/J.J. Fedorowicz, Canada, 2000).
Schmitz, Günter. *Die 16 Panzer Division Bewaffnung–Einsatz–Manner–1938–1945* (Dörfler im Nebel Verlag Gmbh, 2004).
Sellier, Claus. *Walking Away from the Third Reich: A Teenager in Hitler's Army* (Hellgate Press, USA, 2006).
Showalter, Dennis. *Hitler's Panzers: The Lightning Attacks that Revolutionised Warfare* (The Berkley Publishing Group, USA, 2009).

Spaeter, Helmut (trans. David Johnston). *The History of the Panzer Corps Grossdeutschland, Vol 2* (J.J. Fedorowicz Publishing, Canada, 1995).

Stahel, David. *Kiev 1941: Hitler's Battle for Supremacy in the East* (Cambridge University Press, UK, 2012).

Stahlberg, Alexander (trans. Patricia Crompton). *Bounden Duty: The Memoirs of a German Officer 1935–1945* (Brassey's, UK, 1990).

Stein, George H. *The Waffen SS: Hitler's Elite Guard at War 1939–1945* (Cornell University Press, USA, 1966).

Syndor, Charles W. *Soldiers of Destruction: The SS Death's Head Division 1933–1945* (Guild Publishing, 1989).

Tarrant, V. E. *Stalingrad* (Leo Cooper, UK, 1992).

Taylor, Federich. *Exorcising Hitler: The Occupation and DeNazification of Germany* (Bloomsbury, UK, 2012).

Tieke, Wilhelm (trans. F Steinhardt). *Tragedy of the Faithful* (J.J. Fedorowicz Canada 2014).

Tissier, Le Tony. *Slaughter at Halbe* (Sutton Publishing, 2005).

Toliver, R. F. and Constable T. J. *Horrido!* (Arthur Baker, UK, 1968).

Trevor–Roper, H. R. *Hitler's War Directives 1939–1945* (Pan Books, UK, 1966).

Tsouras, Peter G. (ed.). *Fighting in Hell: The German Ordeal on the Eastern Front* (Presidio Press, NY, 1995).

Tsouras, Peter G. (ed.), *Panzers on the Eastern Front. General Erhard Raus and His Panzer Divisions in Russia 1941–1945* (Greenhill Books, 2002).

Tuchman, Barbara W. *The Guns of August* (Folio Society, UK, 1994).

Tuchman, Barbara W. *The Proud Tower* (Folio Society, UK, 1997).

Ullrich, Karl (trans. Jeffrey McMullen). *Like a Cliff in the Ocean: The History of 3 SS Panzer Division Totenkopf* (J.J. Fedorowicz, Canada, 2002).

Wilbeck, Christopher W. *Sledgehammers: Strength and Flaws of Tiger Tank Battalions in WWII* (The Aberjona Press, USA, 2004).

Williamson, Gordon. *The Iron Cross: A History 1813–1954* (Blandford Press, UK, 1985).

Young, Brig. Peter. *The Almanac of WWII* (AP Publishing, Sydney, Australia, 2009).

Zemalin, Valery (trans. Stuart Britt). *Demolishing the Myth: The Tank Battle of Prokhorovka, Kursk July 1943* (Helion, UK, 2011).

Zetterling, Niklas and Frankson, Anders. *The Korsun Pocket* (Casemate, USA, 2008).

INDEX